BREWED
in the
NORTH

BREWED
in the
NORTH

A History of Labatt's

Matthew J. Bellamy

McGill-Queen's University Press

Montreal & Kingston · London · Chicago

ISBN 978-0-7735-5915-8 (cloth)
ISBN 978-0-7735-5965-3 (ePDF)
ISBN 978-0-7735-5966-0 (ePUB)

Legal deposit third quarter 2019
Bibliothèque nationale du Québec

Printed in Canada on acid-free paper that is 100% ancient forest free
(100% post-consumer recycled), processed chlorine free

This book has been published with the help of a grant from the Canadian
Federation for the Humanities and Social Sciences, through the Awards
to Scholarly Publications Program, using funds provided by the Social
Sciences and Humanities Research Council of Canada.

We acknowledge the support of the Canada Council for the Arts.

Nous remercions le Conseil des arts du Canada de son soutien.

Library and Archives Canada Cataloguing in Publication

Title: Brewed in the north : a history of Labatt's / Matthew J. Bellamy.
Names: Bellamy, Matthew J., 1967– author.
Description: Includes bibliographical references and index.
Identifiers: Canadiana (print) 20190119330 | Canadiana (ebook) 20190119373 |
ISBN 9780773559158 (hardcover) | ISBN 9780773559653 (ePDF) | ISBN
9780773559660 (ePUB)
Subjects: LCSH: Labatt's Canada Limited—History. | LCSH: Beer industry—
Canada—History.
Classification: LCC HD9397.C24 L3 2019 | DDC 338.4/7663420971—dc23

Contents

Tables and Figures

Figures

Unless otherwise specified, all figures are from The Labatt Brewing Company Collection, University of Western Ontario Archives, and are provided courtesy of the Archives and Research Collections Centre.

Acknowledgments

This book was long in the making, so I have a number of people to thank. It is not an exaggeration to say that this book would have been impossible without the help of Amanda Oliver and Bev Brereton at the Archives and Research Collections Centre at Western University. Their talents as archivists allowed me to locate the "needles" of primary material in the "haystack" of the Labatt Collection. Many times, I was not exactly sure what I was looking for, or what might be in the collection. But Ms Oliver and Ms Brereton patiently listened to my ramblings and then went about finding the principal material that undergirds this book. Robin Keirstead, at the Western University archives, was also generous with his time and advice during the research phase of this project. Thank you to Jean Hung at the Archives Research and Collections Centre for putting up with my multiple requests for images, many of them coming toward the end of this project and thus with tight time restrictions. I also thank Sharon McKay, Labatt Breweries of Canada director of public affairs, for supporting this project and for taking an interest in my work and Labatt's history more generally. And to everyone else at the Western University archives: thank you for creating such a welcoming and friendly environment in which to conduct my research.

I am lucky to work in the history department at Carleton University. It has long been my home away from home. The current chair, Dominique Marshall, like all the chairs before her, has created an environment that is convivial, scholarly, and professional. I thank the former dean of the Faculty of Arts and Social Sciences at Carleton University, Wally Clement, for his encouragement and support. Many of my friends and colleagues have allowed me to bounce ideas off them in the course of writing this book. Thank you to Dimitry Anastakis, John

Bellamy, Rafael Castro, Craig Heron, Teresa da Silva Lopes, Dan Malleck, Brian McKillop, James Opp, Patricio Sáiz, and Andrew Smith. I particularly want to acknowledge the late Adam Day for his insights. I am sure that wherever he is perched, he is smiling and nodding. My thanks to the editors of *Brewery History*, the *Canadian Historical Review*, *Histoire Sociale/Social History*, and *Business History* for giving me permission to use some of my previously published material in this book. Once again, it has been a pleasure to work with everyone at McGill-Queen's University Press. I would particularly like to thank Jonathan Crago, Kathleen Fraser, Casey Gazzellone, and Eleanor Gasparik for helping me get this book ready for publication.

I also need to thank my mother, Annette Bellamy, for proofreading every chapter and offering a few suggestions. Finally, I extend my deepest thanks to Dr Duncan McDowall. He, too, read most of this book while it was being written. He constantly remarked on the substance and the tone of this work and made numerous suggestions on how it might be improved. I can never repay the debt that I owe him. His advice has made this book much better. That being said, where mistakes exist, they are solely my responsibility.

BREWED
in the
NORTH

Introduction

The past is littered with examples of firms that have risen from lowly beginnings to the pinnacle of their industries; remained there for a while, overshadowing the competition; and then, usually because of some combination of managerial folly and external shock, tumbled from their perch, either going bankrupt or, as was the case with Canada's John Labatt Limited, falling into the hands of another firm. In many ways, Labatt's story reads like a classic Greek tragedy in which the protagonist is brought down not by blind accident but by fatal flaws in judgment, by hubris, and by other self-inflicted wounds.

Just a few decades ago, the name Labatt was synonymous with beer in Canada. The company controlled roughly half of the national beer market, and its flagship brand Blue accounted for almost one in every five beers sold. Its huge breweries dotted the Canadian landscape. Not a single Canadian province was without a Labatt plant. The breweries stood as monuments to mass production and the great Canadian thirst for beer. Flush with cash in the 1970s and 1980s, Labatt bought a major league baseball team, the Blue Jays; a football team, the Toronto Argonauts; The Sports Network (TSN); Toronto's entertainment palace, Sky-Dome; Discovery Channel; and Canadian chocolatier and ice cream company Laura Secord. At the same time, through its subsidiary Concert Productions International, the company promoted rock spectacles featuring the likes of David Bowie, Pink Floyd, and The Rolling Stones. Red may have been the predominant colour of our national flag, but blue hued many of our national pastimes. And that was not all. Labatt's also owned all sorts of other food and beverage companies. John Labatt Limited was everywhere – a genuine Canadian conglomerate in an age of corporate bigness. It was one of Canada's largest corporations, up there in the rarefied air with such other late twentieth-century high flyers as Bell Canada Enterprises, Power Corporation, Manulife, and the Royal Bank of Canada. Labatt sat proudly in the pantheon of national enterprise.

But not anymore. The historic Canadian brewery now resides in the private globe-straddling stable of Belgium-based AB InBev (Anheuser-Busch InBev), the world's largest brewer. Labatt's subsidiaries have all been sold off. And many of its historic brands, including the iconic Blue, have been eclipsed by such AB InBev–owned brands as Stella Artois and Budweiser. How did this happen?

In her classic 1959 study *The Theory of the Growth of the Firm*, Edith Penrose argued that growth and survival are consequences of a complicated interaction between a company's resources, capabilities, and market opportunities. The pace and direction of growth is determined by a synergy of a firm's technical and managerial capabilities as well as by developments in the marketplace. According to Penrose, growth is strongly associated with the number of competitive advantages a firm capitalizes on in its environment. In the long run, the profitability, growth, and survival of an enterprise depend on its ability to establish "relatively impregnable bases" from which to adapt and extend their operations in an uncertain, changing, and competitive world.[1]

All firms can succumb to what we might call the "buggy whip phenomenon": change only occurs in response to some dramatic opportunity or threat. Of all the external disruptions that can send shockwaves through the boardrooms of fundamentally stable companies, those that strike at core competencies pose the greatest existential threat. These external shocks can take a variety of forms, from the arrival of a new competitor with an unbeatable cost advantage to a technological innovation that makes current modes of production or distribution obsolete, to a change in consumer tastes and behaviour, to new laws and regulations mandated by the state that shift the whole structure of an industry under a company's feet. Whatever form it takes, an external shock presents the biggest seismic challenge to corporate decision-makers. These disturbances provoke management to react and change the firm's strategy to cope with the new set of circumstances.[2] How well a company adapts to a changing landscape beyond its boardroom and the factory fence is the key determinant of survival and a central theme of this study.

This book is structured around the rise and fall of Labatt. From the 1840s, when John Kinder Labatt joined Samuel Eccles in the business of brewing in the Upper Canadian town of London, it moves to the 1850s and 1860s, when beer was still seen as a daily necessity of life and brewing an essential enterprise in a pioneer society. It then follows rhythms in the life cycle of the firm through the stormy waters of the late nineteenth and early twentieth centuries, when an anti-alcohol sentiment worked its way into the hearts and minds of a large number of morally exercised Canadian do-gooders, to prohibition in the 1910s and 1920s, when Labatt turned to bootlegging in an attempt to survive, to Labatt's efforts to escape its "sinful" past and to the kidnapping of its president in the 1930s. It then picks up the story after the Second World War, when Labatt became part of a national brewing oligopoly known as the "Big Three," and examines the company's efforts to create Canada's first national beer brands in the 1960s and the diversification drive of the 1970s and 1980s. Finally, it follows the firm through the Americanization and globalization of the brewing industry in the 1980s and 1990s, when Labatt ultimately fell into the hands of the 600-year-old Belgian brewery Interbrew.

Although this story proceeds chronologically, the book reflects the underlying premise that successful companies incessantly grow and change in response to opportunities and threats. Firms act like biological species, and only the fittest are able to adjust to changes in their external environments. Those that don't – or can't – die or get devoured by the fitter species. Think, for instance, of Canada's banks and railways: once there were many; now there are few. During Labatt's long life, the decision-makers formulated strategies and created structures to meet the shifting demands of the marketplace. Their formulations did not always result in success. From its pioneer beginning in the southwest corner of the British colony of Upper Canada, Labatt's grew, sometimes stumbled, and grew again to the point that by the 1980s, it dominated as one of Canada's most successful breweries and a player on the world's stage. But then it fell once more, this time for good and into foreign hands.

That Labatt trajectory is the subject of this study. What did the decision-makers at Labatt do right and what did they do wrong? The book looks at both the decisions made by those at Labatt – some who were family owners and others who were drawn from the managerial ranks – in response to opportunities and external shocks and the regional and national context in which those decision-makers operated. All of them were entrepreneurs in that they were tasked with making tough decisions when no perfect information or obviously correct answer was available in an often-foggy marketplace.[3] Thus, this book is squarely rooted in the tradition of business history, which seeks to understand why firms exist, grow, survive, expand across borders, and change in response to environmental challenges and opportunities.

When one reflects on Labatt's history of brewing beer as an autonomous Canadian enterprise between 1847 and 1995, a number of recurring themes suggest
themselves, some possibly the causes and others the consequences of the strategic
choices of Labatt's decision-makers. These themes invite us to consider Labatt's
rise and fall through a number of analytical portals: the ownership and control
structure of the firm, state regulation and public relations, brands and brand
management, and the consolidation and globalization of the industry.

Ownership and Control

During the period 1847 to 1921, a Labatt family member was at the helm of the
firm: first, John Kinder Labatt; then his third-eldest son, John Labatt II; and then
his grandson, John Sackville Labatt. According to much-cited English economic
historian David Landes, this made the Labatt family business a dynasty – "three
successive generations of family control."[4] Among historians and economists,
there has been a renewed interest of late in families like Labatt. Think, for instance, of the fascination with the Irving, Thomson, Stronach, Richardson, and,
perhaps most famously, the Eaton families. For years it was believed that family
firms were relatively inefficient forms of operation compared to the "managerial
enterprise," and thus those firms that remained family-owned and -controlled
operated at a competitive disadvantage. Following the lead of eminent Harvard
University business historian Alfred Chandler, scholars asserted that family firms
were useless and obsolete, dinosaurs on the verge of extinction. Their growth, to
the extent that it occurred at all, was based on the archaic use of networks, personal relationships, limited ownership and control, and personal trust. Chandler's
large managerial firms, on the other hand, were the embodiment of modern efficient enterprise. As companies grew and increased in scale and scope, problems
emerged that could be solved only by employees with functional specialization.[5]
The level of managerial ability and technical understanding required went far beyond that which any given family member, however proficient, could manage.
Family firms were simply incapable of meeting demands of large-scale production and distribution, Chandler maintained. As a result, ownership became di-
vorced from control. The rational decisions of top managers, who exerted their
"visible hands" over the unpredictable marketplace, allowed their firms to achieve
economies of scale, earn enormous profits, and, ultimately, dominate the national
economy, particularly in the United States.[6] The rise of "managerial capitalism"

along with technological innovation helped propel the United States to new economic heights in the years leading up to the First World War. Chandler even went so far as to attribute the relative decline of British industry in the twentieth century to the persistence of "personal capitalism," by which he meant family firms.[7] Thus, national economic competitiveness, in the Chandlerian view, was dependent on replacing family-run companies in key industries with professionally managed joint-stock companies.

Recently, a number of historians have begun to challenge the Chandlerian argument. For example, Bocconi University business historian Andrea Colli, in examining the history of family business between 1850 and 2000, has found that resilience and efficiency are often present in family businesses, contrary to the anecdotal image of family emotion over economic reason.[8] This was certainly the case at IKEA. Having started the business in 1943 at the age of seventeen, Ingvar Kamprad pragmatically put his vision of making a wide range of household furnishings of appropriate design at affordable prices into action. The firm's key innovation was a new distribution system. In 1956, Kamprad revolutionized the furniture market by introducing "flatpacking," the method now synonymous with IKEA that cuts costs by letting consumers purchase their furniture in pieces and assemble it themselves. Despite IKEA's phenomenal worldwide growth since the 1980s, Kamprad refused to delegate the decision-making process to paid managers. Instead, he brought in his three sons to help him run the business. The Kamprads, like the Wendels, Haniels, and Falcks – three European dynasties in the steel industry – and many other family businesses, have been better able to weather periods of instability and upheaval because they are often driven by non-economic motivations. They are able to look beyond short-term results and the daily stock value of their company and thereby think more strategically.[9] Longevity rather than short-term profit maximization is often the true objective of family firms.[10] Loyal stewards will continue to operate the family firm no matter how precarious the financial situation becomes and will only give up, states British economist Mark Casson, when all of the resources are gone because the identity of the family is intertwined with the fortunes of the firm.[11] This is particularly true when it comes to the business of brewing, which has long been a candidate for family ownership, according to business historian Teresa da Silva Lopes. Beer brands are "cool," and owning a brand or a firm involved in the industry generates private benefits that do not necessarily enrich the shareholders. This has led Lopes to challenge the assumption that in order to grow, firms need to abandon or increase distance between owners and managers.[12] She maintains that continued family ownership and control is a key determinant of survival. Was this the case at the Labatt brewery? How did its ownership and control structure help or hinder the growth and survival of the firm?

Assuming for the moment that there is nothing inherently dysfunctional about family firms, why do some succeed and others fail?

According to Andrea Colli, the success of a family firm is determined, at least initially, by the ability of the founder to continually seek new survival strategies and to bridge the aspirations of family members within the constraints imposed by market competition and the institutional environment. Firms without that kind of founder quickly fail. But beyond that, to be successful over time, a family firm has to be able to balance two things: first, the ability to create the competencies that can be transmitted from generation to generation and, second, the skill to build new competencies in addition to the old. The first generation of owner-operators usually establishes all of the values that normally guide the business over time.[13] For example, John D. Rockefeller learned an extraordinary sense of thrift when he was young and the trait never left him. He brought up his children in exactly the same manner, requiring them to account for every rare dime he gave them: his son and heir, John D. Jr, like his father before him, was required to wear his sisters' outgrown dresses as a form of parsimony.[14] Sometimes these values serve as a great asset because they help establish the "soul" of the firm. At other times they are very dangerous "path dependents" because the next generation of owners are not able to think outside of the box and to reinvent themselves as entrepreneurs because they are trapped in the "cage of tradition."

The mutually reinforcing phenomena of place and culture also matter in the success or failure of firms. With regard to the success of family firms, some countries, like the United States and Canada, have more favourable laws governing inheritance and tax arrangements, which allow more money to remain in the hands of the family members. While family-controlled companies exist in many places, they are a particular hallmark of Canadian capitalism. It has been suggested by Canadian journalist and writer Peter C. Newman that this is because Canadian owners of family firms have been more protective and indulgent of their offspring.[15] However, Newman's generalization overlooks the fact that many first-generation immigrants to Canada often broke the mould. For example, Frank Stronach, founder of international automotive parts company Magna International; Thomas J. Bata, "shoemaker to the world"; and Sam Bronfman, founder of Distillers Corporation Limited, were driven by a belief that they had control over the outcome of events in their lives – what scholars of entrepreneurship term an internal locus of control – and pragmatically demanded the same commitment to individual effort on the part of their children.[16] This was also evident at the other Canadian brewing dynasty that is not the subject of this book. After emigrating from England in 1782, John Molson built a thriving business in Montreal and laid the foundations for a commercial empire with interests in banking, distilling, steamships, and railroads as well as brewing.[17] He demanded discipline and individual effort from his three boys, John Jr, Thomas, and William, before bringing them into partnership with him before his death in 1836.

Molson was fortunate to have had a number of sons. This allowed him to pick the most capable of his offspring, John Jr, to run the business after his death. According to historian David Landes, the fortunes or misfortunes of family firms are often determined by the reproductive capabilities of those in charge. Firms that succeed have generally been led by entrepreneurs who have been philoprogenitive; that is to say, who have had a lot of children. This gives those in charge a deep pool of familial talent from which to draw. And if the "chosen one" proves to be incompetent, then he or she can be removed and replaced by another one of the founder's descendants.

But sometimes, no matter how many children are sired, a family-owned and -controlled firm has a difficult time surviving beyond three generations. Historians and economists refer to this phenomenon as the Buddenbrooks effect.[18] The term derives from Thomas Mann's 1901 novel *Buddenbrooks*, in which a bourgeois family loses its initial entrepreneurial vitality over succeeding generations. While the founder usually dedicates all of his or her energy to the business because, in the words of Casson, "it is the true object of his devotion … a living symbol of his own achievement,"[19] and while the next generation regularly consolidates the business, the third-generation owners often prefer to indulge in leisure and non-productive activities. As a consequence, they neglect management of the business, inducing its decline. Hence the saying: "from shirt sleeves to shirt sleeves in three generations."

This was certainly the case at the Canadian department store Eaton's. Its founder, Timothy Eaton, was an Irish emigrant with a solid work ethic who purchased a dry-goods store in 1869 and turned it into a national chain. Creative measures such as introducing one of Canada's first mail-order catalogues and sponsoring an annual Santa Claus parade helped him transform the way that people shopped and experienced society's commercial pleasures. Joseph Schumpeter,

the renowned Austrian economist who so famously dissected the rhythms of capitalism, once remarked that entrepreneurs like Eaton were the heroic agents of
economic innovation and subsequent development.[20] Along with Hudson's Bay
Company and Simpson's, Eaton's helped to create a "national community of consumer citizens" by the early twentieth century by promoting the idea that retail
consumerism was an essential feature of Canadian life.[21] When Timothy Eaton
died of pneumonia in 1907, he left $5 million and the family business to his
youngest son, John Craig Eaton. At age thirty, he was the first in a long and unin-
terrupted line of Eatons to ascend to the presidency. While his father had been
austere, reserved, and devoutly religious, John Craig Eaton was an extroverted
pleasure-seeker who bought fancy cars, racehorses, and yachts. He spent huge
sums of money on foreign trips and built a Georgian-style fifty-room mansion
called Ardwold on the Davenport Hill in Toronto. He was ruthless and uncaring
in business, particularly when it came to dealing with those who worked for him.
For example, when the company's predominantly Jewish garment workers
protested the deteriorating working conditions on Eaton's factory floor in the winter of 1912, John Craig Eaton cold-heartedly locked them out and refused to
negotiate with the union. As the strike dragged on, Eaton made the workers one
final offer: "apologize and I will reinstate you."[22] The strike collapsed three months
later. As self-indulgent, arrogant, and nasty as he was, John C. Eaton managed to
consolidate the business under his watch. At the time of his death in 1922, Eaton's
empire of department stores controlled over 60 per cent of the Canadian market.
The real decline in the family's fortunes set in over the next two generations. The
hidebound adherence to a rigid conceptualization of mass retail and a kind of *folie
de grandeur*, especially on the part of John David Eaton, who reluctantly took over
as head of the business in 1942, was accompanied by a complete lack of business
acumen and vision.[23] John David displayed all of the overconfidence and arrogance of his father but none of his vigour in business – a deadly combination
according to some scholars.[24] Stores that once served as landmarks in their communities fell into disrepair. When new suburban stores were finally built away
from the downtown core in the 1960s and 1970s, they were largely indistinguish-
able from other chain stores populating Canada's burgeoning mallscape. This
further reduced Eaton's status as a destination store.[25] The termination of the
Eaton's catalogue and of the Santa Claus parades ensured that the company lost
its special place in the hearts and minds of Canadians. At this point, the company
desperately pursued a policy of breaking its big-store business into boutique

retailing, but once again, its lack of managerial expertise undercut the exercise. By 1995, Eaton's had lost all but 10 per cent of the national market; two years later, it filed for bankruptcy protection. The decline was complete.

Canadian business history is full of stories similar to Eaton's. In his book, *In the Blood*, business journalist Gordon Pitts examines the operations of more than twenty family-run companies, including the Molsons, the Batas, and the Cuddys, and concludes that the best performers owe their success to "the ability of family to step aside and let professional managers run the business" – which is exactly what the Eatons did not do.[26] When firms are both owned and controlled by family members, there is often a dearth of new ideas and an inability to look outside of the national boundary for new opportunities and markets. As historian Harold James points out, business nationalism – an engrained Canadian mindset in business circles since the National Policy, and an attitude that would only be shattered by post-war tariff reductions and 1980s free trade accord – has proved especially tempting to many family-owned and -controlled firms regardless of location.[27]

To make a bad situation worse, family businesses are often plagued with infighting. Take for instance the Olands, who started brewing in Dartmouth, Nova Scotia, in 1867. Ever since they were young, the third generation of Oland boys, Sidney and George B., had been in competition with one another. While their father, George W.C. Oland (who had taken over control of the brewery in 1895), was alive, the intense rivalry was never allowed to descend into a family feud. But when George Sr died in 1933, the brothers went their separate ways in business. By the end of the Second World War, there were two distinct branches of the Oland family – the Nova Scotia Olands, who owned and operated the Alexander Keith's Brewery, and the New Brunswick Olands, who controlled Moosehead Breweries.[28] The infighting continued and intensified thereafter, leaving the brewery open to the classic Maritime business dilemma: finding sufficient scale of production in a small market. In 2011, Richard Oland, the former vice-president of Moosehead, was found bludgeoned to death in his office. His son was later charged with the brutal murder.[29]

So, what was the nature of family relationships at Labatt? Was there internal rivalry and animosity? And if so, did it hinder the growth of the firm? Did the family business experience a Buddenbrooks effect? How did the entrepreneurial skills of one generation of Labatt compare to those of another? What values did John Kinder Labatt establish to guide the business over time? Were these values dangerous path dependents that trapped his heirs in the cage of tradition?

State Regulation and Public Relations

Throughout history, numerous nations have wrestled with the moral economy of alcohol.[30] Indeed, few other goods for personal use have been subject to so much, so varied, and so persistent regulation as intoxicating beverages. Generally speaking, the means of regulation has fallen into two broad and not always mutually exclusive categories: moral suasion and legal coercion. The balance between the two has changed from time to time and place to place, and within each impulse new forms of regulation have appeared and disappeared. State regulation has targeted nearly every aspect of alcohol, from the raw materials that can be used in production to where the final product can be consumed and by whom. The fundamental issue has never been whether intoxicating beverages should be regulated, but rather *how* and to *what extent*. That being said, as social historian Craig Heron notes: "at some point in the nineteenth century in most parts of the Europeanized world, the state began to intervene more aggressively to enforce a moral code of sobriety."[31] There has been a persistent tension in Western civilization between the dialectic of capitalism and the attempt to control some of the social ills that alcohol promotes.

In a number of places, state intervention initially took the form of "local option," whereby municipal, county, state, or provincial governments were given the legal power to prohibit or limit the production and/or consumption of intoxicating beverages.[32] But local option often created more problems than it solved, and as a result, temperance groups pushed for national prohibition.[33] In Canada, there was a national plebiscite on the issue in 1898. At the dawn of the twentieth century, prohibition became part of a broader impetus in Northern American and Nordic countries to regulate the production and consumption of alcoholic beverages. The "noble experiment" lasted longer in some nations than in others. For instance, in the Russian Empire and the Soviet Union, prohibition existed from 1914 to 1925; in Iceland, it lasted from 1915 to 1922; in Norway, it remained a sobering fact of life for eleven years (1916 to 1927); in Finland, prohibition was enforced from 1919 to 1932 – thirteen long years, the same length of time it existed in the United States (1920 to 1933).[34]

In the wake of the industrial revolution in Canada in the late nineteenth century, the state grew in power, and moral entrepreneurs turned to it instead of other mechanisms to combat John Barleycorn.[35] Under the terms of the nation-forming British North America Act of 1867, the provinces had the constitutional power to prohibit the retail sale of alcohol, while the federal government had regulatory authority over the manufacture of intoxicating drinks. This vast power was first exercised by Canada's smallest province, Prince Edward Island; its prohibition period lasted the longest – from 1901 to 1948. But generally, it took the passion loosed by the First World War to tip the balance between the manufacture of drink and its regulation. Nova Scotia was the first Canadian province to jump aboard the wagon during the war (1916–30), then came Ontario (1916–27), Alberta (1916–24), Manitoba (1916–23), Saskatchewan, (1917–25), New Brunswick (1917–27), British Columbia (1917–21), and the Yukon Territory (1918–21). Newfoundland, which was not part of Canada at that time, imposed prohibition in 1917 and repealed it in 1924. Quebec's experiment with banning the sale of all alcoholic drinks, in 1919, lasted only a few months, principally because the Catholic Church never worked itself into the same moralistic fervour over drink as did its Protestant counterpart in English Canada. While the temperance acts in each of the Canadian provinces varied, they generally closed legal drinking establishments, prohibited the sale of alcohol for beverage purposes, and banned its possession and consumption except in a private dwelling. Prohibition had a devastating effect on the brewing industry.

The prohibitionists might have lost the war, but they continued to fight the fight long after prohibition ended. Many of their views were eventually woven into public policy. For example, post-prohibition provincial liquor control boards placed restrictions on liquor advertising, limited imports, and restricted where, when, to whom, and at what price beer could be sold.[36] In Ontario, the government's regulatory body, the Liquor Control Board of Ontario (LCBO), aimed to cut down on "the bootlegging evil" and to stimulate "temperance in all things." As historian Dan Malleck writes: "Whereas prohibition simply prohibited the consumption of alcohol, liquor control permitted consumption, although under certain conditions that were controlled by the state but negotiated with the citizen."[37] On top of this, the federal government set its own restrictions on liquor advertising and production and, during the Second World War, rationed consumption and even threatened to nationalize the brewing industry. The regulations contributed to Canada's reputation as a "coldly austere, culturally repressed country whose public cultural life matched its often-forbidding climate."[38] Thus, in Canada, prohibitionism was a force to be reckoned with between the 1870s and the 1940s – a force that was bound to intrude on any enterprise involved in brewing or distilling in Canada. When the prohibitionists won victories in the court of public opinion or in the legislatures across the nation, it caused an external shock that shook the breweries of the nation. Therefore, a major theme of this book is how Labatt's responded to the challenges of prohibitionism as a cultural and political force.

When operating in a hostile environment – i.e., when public perceptions and laws are unfavourable – innovative businesses often engage government and public relations, or what is today referred to as "public affairs." For example, when British brewer Scottish & Newcastle embarked on an aggressive merger strategy during the 1980s and 1990s to augment its corporate objective of creating national brands, it used its political connections to get government approval for the landmark acquisition of Courage Brewery in 1995, which prompted the subsequent exit from the domestic scene of leading competitors Bass Brewery and Whitbread Brewery.[39] Likewise, Canadian manufacturers in the 1870s adeptly equated their narrow sectoral interests with the broader political interests of politicians in order to get a "national policy tariff" to protect them from foreign competition.[40] Still, as various scholars have pointed out, lobbying the government has a better chance of working if coordinated with a campaign to align corporate need with the public good.[41] In the United States during the Great Depression, when many blamed business for the economic downturn, top managers and public relations hustlers adopted promotional tactics in an effort to have big business seen in a more positive light. For example, chemical giant DuPont de Nemours, Inc. launched a massive public relations venture in 1935 that included the network radio show, *The Cavalcade of America*. The radio show created prestige for DuPont through the broadcast of historical dramas. By teaching Americans about the past with uncomplicated, inspirational stories of heroism and public service, the show improved DuPont's public image, which had been compromised during the Nye Committee (formally, the Special Committee Investigating the Munitions Industry), when DuPont was portrayed as a warmonger.[42] Similarly in Canada, during the Second World War, Seagram Company Limited employed much-loved humorist Stephen Leacock to write upbeat national history emblazoned with the distiller's corporate logo.

Alliances across class and profession also matter when it comes to influencing the public and the government. In response to the rising temperance tide in Britain at the end of the nineteenth century, the brewers reached out to the workers and pub keepers of the nation to prevent the prohibitionist legislation.[43] In the United States in the 1970s, when American businessmen felt that their interests were threatened by inflation, labour unions, and increased regulations, they lobbied for policies that would increase their seemingly diminished economic and political influence within the nation. Their efforts coalesced around a growing conservative critique of liberalism, thus developing a natural symbiosis among pro-business groups against government regulation and in favour of free markets. Utilizing advertisements, editorials, and cartoons, they sought to weaken public support for "big government." Despite these successes, lobby groups often had a difficult time remaining united and speaking with a single voice. As historian Benjamin Waterhouse notes in his recent study *Lobbying America*: "In an anxious world of fractured interests, conflicting policy visions, and high political stakes, looking out for one's own proved a more appealing strategy than working collectively for a broader goal."[44]

How, therefore, did Labatt, a company situated at the crossroads of many economic and moral tensions in Canadian society, influence the culture around brewing and beer drinking? How, if at all, did it encourage the state to do its bidding? What role, if any, did the firm play in bringing an end to the prohibition? How did the state's regulations affect the growth and survival of Labatt after the noble experiment had come to an end?

Brands, Advertising, and the National Identity

Developing a pervasively recognized, top-of-the-mind brand awareness is essential for success in the alcoholic beverage industry.[45] Brands add value to a firm by sustaining a constant revenue stream resulting from the consumer's propensity for long-term brand loyalty.[46] For the consumer, brands clarify the decision-making process and "enable consumers to associate certain values and rewards with particular products."[47] Brands also provide security to consumers when it comes to the quality and consistency of the product.[48] Successful brands – i.e., those that have become leaders in their product categories[49] – have emotional characteristics that appeal to the self-image of the consumer and his/her aspirations and fantasies.[50] In regard to beer, such intangible elements are especially important in establishing the identity of a brand.[51] And while a brand's identity is developed over time, it is usually embedded in a particular culture and a specific set of values.[52] The identity of a brand is particularly important in the brewing industry where products tend to have long life cycles and have very strong associations with tradition, heritage, craftsmanship, naturalness, and the place of origin.[53]

These elements give a brand its authenticity, which according to a number of re-cent studies constitutes a cornerstone of modern marketing.[54]

In many countries, national beer brands existed by the turn of the last century. In the United States, for example, a handful of large firms, like Pabst and Schlitz in Milwaukee and Anheuser-Busch in St Louis, which had highly mechanized factories and merchandising chains extending beyond their hometowns, devel-oped a national market for their brands in the late nineteenth and early twentieth centuries.[55] The entrepreneurs who founded these firms or their descendants used their "sticky" knowledge - i.e., that type of marketing knowledge that is path dependent, "tacit," and accumulated within the firm over time.[56] Many of these "shipping brewers" - as they came to be called - appropriated the markers of the national identity to promote their brands. For example, in 1872, Anheuser-Busch began using an image of the American eagle on its beer labels. Five years later, the "A and eagle" became a registered trademark with the U.S. Patent Office. In a similar effort to tap into the national enthusiasm of the late nineteenth and early twentieth centuries, Pabst introduced "Red, White and Blue" beer in 1902.[57] In the United Kingdom, national beer brands had also emerged before 1900. Dur-ing the nineteenth century, enterprising brewers invested in capital-intensive brewing technologies in order to achieve scale economies and utilized the railroad to branch out into distant regions of the nation. The fact that the brewers' major markets were public houses that were limited in number by law inspired some brewers to buy or lease these retail outlets. [58] A small number of brewers, however, managed to develop a national market for their brands without investing heavily in "tied houses." For example, Bass did not invest substantially in pubs prior to 1914. Instead, Bass's success was based on having access to a good water supply, the growing national preference for lighter pale ale, a central location in the rail-way network that facilitated distribution, and an easily recognizable trademark – the famous red triangle with the name "Bass" stamped in gold.[59] Likewise, Guinness was heavily dependent on free trade and brand recognition.[60] In 1862, Guinness began using the harp – the national symbol of Ireland – to brand its beer. Because Guinness and Bass did not control the entire supply chain, the two brew-eries were prone to infractions of their trademarks. But they both proved inde-fatigable when it came to defending their brands, as Labatt would find out.[61] Unsurprisingly, therefore, they were among the first brewers to register their brands after the passing of the Trade Marks Registration Act of 1875. Thus, due to the institutional and cultural environment, national beer brands developed relatively early in the United States and the United Kingdom.

But in Canada, it has been difficult for firms to create successful national brands. Given the diversity of the nation and its flimsy distribution networks, some companies appealed to history and their role in "helping Canada grow" to build brand identities.[62] For instance, the Bank of Nova Scotia ran a series of advertisements during the 1950s celebrating the accomplishments of various prominent Canadians who were "responsible" for Canada's development. The ads then reminded the reader that such triumphs were only possible due to the financial backing of Canada's banks, specifically the Bank of Nova Scotia.[63] As public historian Ira Wagman has recently written, this approach to branding reveals a "certain conservatism about Canadian cultural life; one which appreciates various kinds of difference, but not without some need to reassert a past in which such differences were less prominent than they are today."[64] Other firms have appropriated the symbolic markers of the national identity to promote their brands.[65] As Paul Rutherford points out, a variety of companies, including Molson Breweries, Bank of Montreal, and Red Rose Tea, used Canadian patriotism to sell their products in the 1970s.[66] In 1901, Merchants Bank of Halifax rebranded itself as the Royal Bank of Canada, a name that smacked of Canada's British heritage and associated it with the "good old Queen."[67] Similarly, Canadian retailer Roots used Canadian symbols – beavers, canoes, and the maple leaf – in the 1980s and 1990s to allow Canadians "to purchase identity and proudly display their country's cool image to the rest of the world."[68]

Other companies, however, have taken a more nuanced approach to branding. Take, for example, the Hudson's Bay Company during the 1960s, when the firm found itself navigating the historical attachments of its western base, the nationalist aspirations of Quebec – Canada's French-speaking province – and the indifference of metropolitan Ontario. The rebranding of the Hudson's Bay Company as The Bay/la Baie was ultimately successful because the company managed to bridge multiple identities and align its "image worlds" to meet the demands of language and place.[69] Such was not always the case. For instance, when Dow Breweries, a subsidiary of Ontario-based Canadian Breweries Limited, launched Kebec ale in an effort to capitalize on the rising tide of French-Canadian nationalism that was fuelling the Quiet Revolution in Quebec during the 1960s, it met with resistance and a consumer backlash. What raised the ire of nationalists was the fact that the blue-and-white label looked suspiciously like the Quebec flag.[70] What made the nationalists in Quebec even angrier was that it appeared that English capitalists were exploiting Quebec's sacred symbols to market beer and line their pockets. Unlike such patriotically named brands as Molson's Laurentide

Ale and a cigarette called La Québecquoise, the Kebec brand failed because it "linked a symbol considered sacred with the profane aim of selling beer."[71] In the parlance of modern-day marketing experts, the brand was "inauthentic" because it lacked a concrete relationship to place and was seen by consumers as being tied to commercial motives.[72] Thus, creating national brands has been difficult due to the diversity of the nation.

How then, if at all, did Labatt overcome these obstacles when it came to creating its own brands? How did the marketing managers at Labatt's bridge Canada's many identities to meet the demands of race, place, and language? What do Labatt's advertisements, which are a highlight reel of Canadian marketing, tell us, if anything, about the nature of the Canadian identity? Why don't Canadian beer brands have a global presence today? What lessons do we learn about building and managing brands from Labatt's experience?

Consolidation and Globalization

The brewing industry has long served as a research paradigm for those interested in the causes of concentration and globalization. With its relatively simply production technology and its appeal to a mass consumer market there were plenty of opportunities to achieve economies of scale. [73] The concentration in Belgian brewing during the interwar years has been attributed to technological change, economies of scale, and escalating endogenous sunk costs in advertising.[74] The same factors are widely credited with transforming the U.S. brewing industry after the Second World War. An increase in minimum efficient scale due to technological innovation combined with competition in advertising outlays led to the emergence of a national brewing oligopoly.[75] After their triumph, the national brewers in the United States proved to be largely invulnerable to competition from new entrants because of their large sunk investments in television advertising. This was also the case in West Germany after 1990, where local brewers were dealt a fatal blow by national television advertisements promoting the brands of the nation's biggest brewers. As in the United States, large national brewers bought exclusive network rights to major sporting events, and local spots entailed significant cost disadvantages compared to national advertisements.[76]

For those who have studied the U.K. brewing industry from an "institutionalist" perspective, the practice of tying pubs to brewers, the legal restrictions on opening retail outlets, and the permissive policy to mergers were key drivers of post-war consolidation. Institutional factors also played a critical role in the emergence of a brewing oligopoly in New Zealand and Australia.[77] Finally, there are those who stress the role of entrepreneurship in determining the extent, nature, and speed of consolidation in the brewing industry.[78] For instance, in his study of the British brewing industry after 1945, historian Tony Millns argues that one of the key factors in the emergence of the national brewing oligopoly was "the strategic vision and the influence of personality, best seen in the example of Eddie Taylor."[79] Having built a brewing giant in Canada, E.P. Taylor set his sights on changing the way the British brewing industry operated. "His pioneering vision had a profound impact both on the structure of the brewing industry and, with the rise of lager, the nation's drinking habits."[80] Thus, there is a good deal of debate regarding the causes of concentration in the brewing industry.

Prior to the 1960s, the global brewing industry was fragmented, tastes were largely local, and competition took place within national boundaries rather than across international borders. The successful brewery was generally one that could produce a good, consistent product that appealed to consumer tastes, was manufactured at a competitive cost, and was readily available at retail outlets across the nation. With the exception of a few breweries like Holland's Heineken and Denmark's Carlsberg – which were driven to expand beyond their national borders because of relatively small domestic markets – few firms internationalized before the 1960s. Thereafter, however, a greater level of international activity occurred as an increasing number of large domestic breweries looked abroad for growth opportunities. The result was a further consolidation of the industry in global terms.

To succeed internationally, breweries had to have firm-specific advantages relative to their competitors. On the global stage, firms had to be agile and focused, take calculated risks, and then pursue their growth opportunities aggressively. Brewers also needed to be creative in terms of developing alliances and global brands and careful when it came to diversifying into other businesses. The most successful brewers were those that remained highly focused on their core competencies and expanded their geographic scope of activities, often through a complex process of mergers, acquisitions, and other cross-border network arrangements, like licensing agreements.[81]

What role did Labatt play in the consolidation of the Canadian brewing industry? How did the decision-makers at Labatt attempt to overcome the institutional barriers that stood in the way of becoming a truly national brewery? How, if at all, did the firm's senior managers meet the challenges of globalization? What did they do right and what did they do wrong?

Method

This book is both a case study and a microhistory. It is a case study in that it presents an in-depth and detailed examination of Labatt's growth, survival, and eventual exit as an autonomous agent from the business of brewing. It is a microhistory in that it aspires to "[ask] large questions in small places," to use the definition of the renowned historian of the American South, Charles Joyner.[82] That is to say, it examines the evolution of a single firm, and how it has been involved in important issues that have shaped not only business but also laws, culture, morality, and identity in Canada. Throughout the years, Labatt's used its huge pool of beer money to diversify into many businesses in a number of industries, from fast food to cable networks. However, first and foremost, the focus of this book is on the evolution of the brewery, which is used in turn to draw out broader conclusions. I leave it to others to explore in detail the history of Labatt's various subsidiaries.

Little has changed since Craig Heron lamented in 2002 that "very little systematic research has been done on the [brewing] industry in Canada."[83] We are without a published history of Canadian Breweries Limited, perhaps because the papers of its founder and president, E.P. Taylor, have not been located and might not even exist. Furthermore, the best history of the Molson Brewery, journalist Merrill Denison's romantic tale *The Barley and the Stream*, was published in 1955 and, therefore, is dated and incomplete. Labatt's history has been chronicled once before, by York University historian Albert Tucker, as a commissioned work to commemorate the company's 150th anniversary. But for reasons unknown to this author, the work was not published. Tucker's work, however, is groundbreaking and is relied upon in this work for insights into the dynamics of the Labatt family and the characteristics and temperament of a number of the personalities involved in the affairs of the firm. Tucker did extensive interviews with those who worked at Labatt, many of which can be found among his personal papers, which are located at York University in Toronto. While the transcripts of the interviews were used in researching and writing this book, my principal reliance has been on the printed material, some of it published, but most of it unpublished and housed at the Western University Archives and Research Collections Centre where The Labatt Brewing Company Collection has been kept since it first became accessible to the public in 2011. The Labatt Collection is one of the largest corporate archives in Canada and reflects an industry intimately related to London, Ontario. The archive is testament to the important role brewing – and Labatt – has played not just in London but also writ large in Canadian history. With documents dating from as early as the 1840s, the Labatt Collection provides insights into entrepreneurship and managerial styles, technology and innovation, public and government relations, brands and advertising, corporate strategies and structures, mergers and acquisitions, beer production, drinking cultures and consumer tastes, and the spirit of Canadian capitalism, by which I mean the ideas, assumptions, values, and what British historian Gareth Stedman Jones calls the "structure of feeling" that influenced business people to do what they did over the decades.[84] I chose to rely primarily on this archive, in part because of its scale and scope but also because the Molson Papers at Library and Archives Canada have been previously mined. Indeed, Molson has had elements of its story told at least five times in book form.[85] The sources do not always agree, nor will my interpretation thereof satisfy, much less please, some of the people involved. But as one historian has recently noted, such is "the nature of history and historiography."[86]

Structure of the Book

Labatt's history is as complex as it is long, and as a result this book is divided into three parts. Each chapter deals with Labatt's growth and change in response to historically specific challenges. As business historians Davis Dyer and David Sicilia have argued: "How well a company responds to the key business problems of a given period is the primary determinant of its survival and success."[87] The structure of this book reflects this fact.

Part I covers the period 1847 to 1921, when Labatt was family-owned and -controlled, and is comprised of five chapters. Chapter 1 examines the birth of the Labatt brewery and challenges the widely accepted image of the successful entrepreneur as a self-confident risk-taker. Chapter 2 examines how John Kinder Labatt and, following his death in 1866, his son John Labatt II confronted the challenges of the 1855–77 period. The departure of the military from London,

Ontario, the advent of the railroad, and changing consumer tastes made this a difficult period for John Labatt II to consolidate the business. Chapter 3 examines how John Labatt II met the challenges of the Canada Temperance Act period, 1878–89, when local option was in effect. Chapter 4 examines the reasons for Labatt's expansion into the United States at the end of the nineteenth century. It analyzes both the push and pull factors that caused John Labatt II to attempt to sell his ales, porters, and stouts in Chicago. The chapter examines both the entrepreneurial factors and structural factors that propelled him forward and pushed him back. Chapter 5 examines the effects that the chaos of war and the onset of the noble experiment of prohibition had on the business of brewing at Labatt's. It analyzes the leadership of John S. Labatt and the schemes that those at the old London Brewery devised in an attempt to survive the initial onset of the dry regime.

Part II analyzes the near-death experience, renascence, and domination of the national beer market by Labatt as a managerial enterprise during the period of state regulation and expansion, 1921–62. It comprises the four middle chapters of the book. Chapter 6 examines how Labatt struggled to survive the final years of prohibition, 1921–27. It concentrates largely on the actions of Labatt's general manager, Edmund Burke, when the brewery was effectively his unchallenged domain. Chapter 7 examines how Labatt attempted to move beyond its sinful past and still retain its status as a large and prosperous brewery during the Great Depression. Chapter 8 examines how Labatt and its allies dealt with the resurgence of the temperance movement in Canada during the Second World War. Chapter 9 examines the factors that led to the emergence of a national brewing oligopoly in Canada.

Part III explores how Labatt's managers handled the challenges and dealt with external shocks of the period from 1962 to 1995, when a small group of multinational enterprises embarked on a global quest to dominate the brewing industry. It covers chapters 10 to 13. Chapter 10 examines the attempted takeover of Labatt by American brewing company Schlitz – the maker of "the beer that made Milwaukee famous" – and how the executives at Labatt fought to keep American capitalism at bay. The chapter situates the corporate manoeuvrings in the broader context of the political economy on both sides of the border. Chapter 11 examines how the quest for popular brands ultimately led to the Americanization of Canadian beer. It analyzes the challenges faced by the marketing managers at John Labatt Limited in developing Canada's first truly national brand and the legacy of "solving the national lager problem." Chapter 12 examines the strategic decision-making process that led to Labatt's diversification drive in the 1970s and 1980s. The chapter analyzes the motivations and logic behind the firm's expansion into wine, food, candy, sports and entertainment, and a number of other industries. Chapter 13 examines the corporate strategic missteps of the 1990s and the ultimate takeover of Labatt by the Belgian brewing company Interbrew.

PART ONE

**Family Firm
to
Managerial
Enterprise**

Out of the Blue

The Birth of John Labatt's Brewery,
1847–55

With the letter clasped in his calloused hands, John Kinder Labatt took a seat in the Upper Canadian brewery that he now co-owned and continued reading. "With respect to the Brewery," the letter from his brother-in-law Robert Kell read, "we all think you are undertaking a great deal and if you were of a wild and speculative turn, instead of being cool-headed and far-seeing, we should tremble for you."[1] The letter was in response to a recent series of bold initiatives by Labatt. Having sold off virtually all that he owned, Labatt made the most momentous decision of his life. In 1847, at the age of forty-four, he decided to wager everything and enter the business of brewing.

There was good reason for Robert Kell's concern: being an entrepreneur in Upper Canada during the nineteenth century was risky business. The limited size of the marketplace, wide fluctuation in prices, lack of credit, high transportation costs, and low returns on investments impeded the growth of many firms.[2] Colonial manufacturers often found it difficult to get their products to market. Hot and dry summers created difficulties for power and navigation because of havoc wrought on the forested slopes by the settler's axe. Spring and fall rains led to muddy roads, and frigid-cold winters to ice-packed waterways. Added to that, businessmen of all sorts lacked concrete information upon which to make sound business decisions. Economic vulnerability to the vagaries of international markets was exacerbated by the chain of long-term credit – from British suppliers of manufactured goods to wholesale merchants to retail merchants, and on to their customers in rural areas and small towns.[3] As a result, those who owned businesses failed as often as they succeeded. Even among prominent entrepreneurs, incidents of failure were astonishingly high and their consequences dreadful.[4]

Within this environment, entrepreneurship mattered. As historian Douglas McCalla writes of the nineteenth-century business world, "entrepreneurship ... was the quality that led the independent, risk-taking profit-seeking agent, the entrepreneur, to innovate by combining economic resources in a new way."[5] Risk-taking and self-confidence were key. According to eminent economist Mark Casson, successful entrepreneurs had to be optimistic and self-confident in order to take resources away from rival entrepreneurs. "These optimistic self-confident and opinionated people not only look for new opportunities to found a firm," Casson writes, "they also look for opportunities to take over resources from ageing or failing entrepreneurs less able than themselves."[6] Conversely, a lack of self-confidence hinders entrepreneurs.[7] Michael Bliss's classic survey of five centuries of Canadian business, *Northern Enterprise*, is a celebration of self-confidence and risk-taking and a condemnation of the state's interventionist practices that have hindered private initiative.[8] Indeed, one can read Bliss's narrative as an examination of the role of risk-taking in the making of the transcontinental economy. Read this way, the Canadian nation was constituted not by the inanimate structural forces of geography, technology, and institutions, as Harold Adams Innis and his disciples have maintained, but rather by the attempts of "enterprising spirits [i.e., the risk-takers] to create wealth in the sprawling, thinly populated half of the North American continent."[9] Likewise, the self-confident subjects showcased in Andrew Ross and Andrew Smith's recent collection of *Dictionary of Canadian Biography* portraits, *Canada's Entrepreneurs: From the Fur Trade to the 1929 Stock Market Crash*, while diverse in terms of their language, country of origin, religion, and social heritages, all shared a capacity for risk-taking.[10]

Was this the case with John Kinder Labatt? What motivated him to enter the business of brewing in 1847? What entrepreneurial traits did he personally exhibit? What values did he establish that would guide the business over time? What did he do to grow the business during these formative years?

Early Life of the Founding Father

Born in 1803 of Huguenot stock, John Labatt was the eldest of seven children. His ancestors had come to Ireland from the Bordeaux region of France during the Battle of the Boyne. His great-great-great-grandfather, André Labat, had fought at the Boyne in a regiment of French émigrés for the Duke Prince, William of

Orange, against the deposed King James II of England.[11] After he and his wife, Mary, were crowned joint monarchs of England, Ireland, and Scotland in 1689, William was ordered by the English parliament to disband his army in Ireland. As a result, André Labat was discharged with the rank of captain. Lacking the money needed to return to France, he remained on the Emerald Isle. During the eighteenth century, André Labat's descendants settled in the small pastoral villages in the Irish county of Laois. They learned the English language and adopted the Anglican worship of the Church of Ireland.[12] It was here in the county of Laois, and specifically in the town of Mountmellick, that John Kinder Labatt was born and spent his formative years.[13]

For much of its history, Mountmellick functioned as a small, rural agricultural centre for the marketing of grain and livestock. During the twelfth century, sheep farming was extensively developed on the Cistercian monastic estates. Thereafter, it took hold in the limestone areas in and around Mountmellick, which provided for good grazing. One of the first cottage industries to emerge in Mountmellick was the woolens industry, which gave many households a secondary source of revenue to supplement their agricultural income.

During the late eighteenth century, Mountmellick was transformed into the "Manchester of Ireland" – a mighty title that did not truly reflect the town's relatively diminutive size and status. In the 1780s, a small number of textile mills were established in Labatt's hometown.[14] While the textile industry was the most significant component in the town's early industrial development, other infant industries were emerging. Among them were the tanneries, which turned animal hides into leathers, and the breweries, which turned malt grain into beer. In 1801, there were five breweries in Mountmellick, and although they were tiny in comparison to the massive cartel breweries in London, England, they produced enough beer to quench the thirst of the local population and those living in nearby towns. The ales and table beers produced in these Irish breweries were often poor in quality and relatively expensive. As a result, the Irish often preferred to drink porter – a well-hopped, dark-styled beer made from brown malt – which was imported from England, where it was all the rage among the working class.[15] However, the Irish appetite for English beer diminished after the government in Ireland imposed a tariff, in 1792, on imported beer in order to stimulate the growth of domestic brewing. By that time, Arthur Guinness had already begun producing porter at his brewery at St James's Gate in Dublin. The extension of Ireland's Grand Canal, which ran through Labatt's hometown of Mountmellick, was a boon to brewers like Guinness.

As a young boy walking to his grammar school in the centre of town, John Kinder Labatt was awestruck by the economic development that was taking place around him. The community in which he lived was in a state of profound economic and social change. While most of Ireland did not experience the rapid growth and development that accompanied the transition to mass industrialization, a few Irish towns, like Mountmellick, did. In these towns, the Industrial Revolution transformed people's lives. Virtually everyone was touched in one way or another – peasant and noble, parent and child, artisan and captain of industry. Members of the newly formed Anglo-Irish entrepreneurial class, made up of people like Arthur Guinness and distiller John Jameson, were making substantial fortunes. Eager to forget their humble origins, people of the "lesser classes" were climbing over each other as they scrambled up the social ladder. Seemingly any man with wit and foresight and a few good ideas could become wealthy and powerful. In reality, it was far more complicated than that.[16] The emerging capitalist system, spurred by rapid advancements in production technology, grew at an unprecedented rate. The substitution of machines – rapid, regular, precise, and tireless – for human skill and effort, fuelled the revolution in industry.[17] As a result, factory owners, who stood at the centre of the manufacturing process, enjoyed great gains in wealth and prestige. The developing capitalist class possessed the means of economic growth and thus quickly surpassed rural landlords in terms of influence and power. Therefore, the ultimate goal for any young man with ambition, like Labatt, was to take hold of the reins of production.

The transformation that was taking place before his eyes had a long-lasting effect on Labatt. Growing up in these revolutionary times led him to be comfortable with instability and change. Having witnessed only economic progress during his formative years, he was bullish about industry, the economy, and the future. Life in Mountmellick had taught him crucial lessons about the virtues of hard work, the value of transportation to local success in industry, and the direct relationship between manufacturing activity and prosperity at a time when the Industrial Revolution was reshaping the Western world. He might have stayed in Ireland, and pursued a higher education had he had the money – he was certainly bright enough. But the years after 1820 were marked by food shortages and social unrest.[18] Many Irish chose to emigrate even before the Great Famine of 1845–52.

Lacking the social connections of the more affluent Anglo-Irish and feeling the eastern pull of England, John Kinder Labatt packed his bags in 1830 and headed to the largest city on earth. Victorian London was the most spectacular metropolis in the world, and nothing like Mountmellick. While Britain was experiencing an industrial revolution, its capital was reaping the benefits and suffering the consequences of rapid economic development. In 1800, the population of London was roughly 1 million, but it had swelled to over 1.5 million people by the time Labatt arrived in 1830. England was soaking up Irishmen as the foot soldiers of industrialization. The London that Labatt entered was more diverse, dynamic, and dangerous than anywhere else in the Western world. "By seeing London," stated eighteen-century English poet, critic, and writer Samuel Johnson, "I have seen as much of life as the world can show." London was, indeed, a spectacle. Charles Dickens had gained a reputation as a writer by walking the streets of the city and drinking in its essence. In his earliest work, *Sketches by Boz*, Dickens wrote: "the streets are thronged with a vast concourse of people, gay and shabby, rich and poor, idle and industrious."[19] While fashionable areas like Regent and Oxford streets were growing in the west, new docks supporting the city's place as the world's trade centre were being built in the east.

It was here, in the east, that twenty-seven-year-old John Kinder Labatt found his first employment as a junior clerk with a timber merchant on Broadwall Street, just south of the river Thames, on the fringes of the notorious district of Bankside.[20] Once a playground for Elizabethan Londoners, where rich and poor alike adventured to debauch and tipple, or watch the bear-baiting and the plays of William Shakespeare at the Globe, Bankside was transformed during the Industrial Revolution into a hive of manufacturing activity.[21] Hundreds of foundries turned iron into coalhole covers, cartwheels, boilers, pokers, and eventually railway equipment. Thousands of hatmakers transformed Canadian beaver pelts into fashionable headwear. Glassworks like Pallatt & Green produced glassware that was sold all over the world. But the biggest manufactories in Bankside were the breweries.

Brewing had been taking place in the Bankside area since the fourteenth century. Before setting out for Canterbury in the 1380s, Geoffrey Chaucer and his time-honoured pilgrims met at the Tabard Inn on the east side of Borough High Street where they enjoyed the fine "ale of Southwark." During the fourteenth century, brewing was predominantly a small-scale, highly localized by-employment involving the brewing of un-hopped ale by women working from their homes.[22] But over the next two centuries, women were largely pushed out of the trade as brewing became more commercialized. By 1700, brewing was generally a large-scale, highly commercialized trade involving the brewing of beer in specialized brewhouses that were largely controlled by men.[23] Samuel Whitbread was one of the powerful men who came to control the brewing industry in Britain. Like John

Kinder Labatt, he had come to London to seek his fortune. Having apprenticed
for the brewer John Witman, he began brewing in 1742 with two partners, Godfrey
and Thomas Shewell. Eight years later, the operation was moved to the Chiswell
Street Brewery. Whitbread seized the opportunities of the Industrial Revolution,
investing heavily in steam power to create the first mass-production brewery in
Britain and one of the great brewing houses of the London porter boom.[24] By
the time that Labatt arrived in 1830, each Englishman was consuming on average
roughly thirty-three gallons of beer per year, and there were eleven breweries in
London that produced over 70,000 barrels per annum.[25] The biggest breweries,
like Whitbread and Co. Ltd and Barclay, Perkins & Co., which was located on
Park Street in Bankside, manufactured well in excess of that amount.[26]

By 1830, brewing stood on the threshold of modern manufacturing.[27] The
industry had assumed a pattern of heavy overheads, mass production, rationali-
zation, diminishing costs, and mass marketing – characteristics that are commonly
ascribed as "typically modern." Few could resist going to see for themselves all of
this industry and enterprise. The "vast establishment" of Whitbread on Chiswell
Street so impressed one German visitor that the only way that he could capture
its significance was to compare it to someplace holy. "Its buildings," stated the
Teutonic tourist, are "higher than a church."[28] When a German prince visited
the city in the summer of 1827, one of the first places that he went to was Barclay
Perkins & Co. The prince commented on "the vastness" of the brewery's dimen-
sions that rendered it "almost romantic." He observed that the steam engines that
drove the machinery were so powerful they could manufacture from 12,000 to
15,000 barrels a day, and the 150 horses that transported the beer were so big that
they were "like elephants."[29]

John Kinder Labatt worked just a few blocks away from Barclay, Perkins & Co.
He was in London when the massive brewery caught fire on 22 May 1832. Virtually
every Londoner was aware of the blaze. In an unsuccessful effort to put out the
fire, an engine pumped 2,000 barrels of beer onto the flames.[30] In the aftermath
of the "great burn," artists like Clarkson Stanfield visited the site to capture the
disaster for posterity on canvas. The brewery was subsequently rebuilt on an even
grander scale in order to meet the ever-growing demand for beer. For the ever-
observant Labatt, Barclay, Perkins & Co. – massive in comparison to the five small
breweries that augmented the grain trade in Mountmellick – was a constant reminder of London's immense size and complexity.[31] Perhaps the image of these
monuments to industry and modernity embedded itself in Labatt's subconscious.

But there is nothing in the written record to suggest that, at this stage in his life, he thought about becoming a brewer.

The price for London's explosive growth and domination of world trade was untold squalor and filth. Bankside was particularly dirty. Passing through Bankside in 1835, Charles Dickens observed that the "streets and courts dart in all directions, until they are lost in the unwholesome vapour which hangs over the house-tops and renders the dirty perspective uncertain and confined." Street sweepers attempted to keep the roads clean of manure, the result of thousands of horse-drawn vehicles, like the beer wagons from the Barclay, Perkins' brewery. The district's thousands of chimney pots constantly belched coal smoke, settling soot seemingly everywhere. In many parts of the city, raw sewage flowed in gutters that emptied into the Thames. In no way did London resemble the rural Irish town of Mountmellick.

But for Labatt there was no turning back. A defining characteristic of the young Irishman was that once he had made a decision, he stuck to it. Conservative by nature, Labatt did not make decisions rashly. He always carefully considered the consequence of his actions before acting. Nevertheless, he was slowly coming to the conclusion that perhaps London, England, was not the city in which to make his mark. He expressed his dissatisfaction with the city and his dead-end job to his two closest friends, John and George Claris. At a time when religious affiliation fostered social bonds, the Claris brothers were among the first to welcome Labatt to London. Of Huguenot stock themselves, John and George Claris were instrumental in getting Labatt his clerical job. The three often met after a long day of work at one of Bankside's many pubs to talk about their accomplishments and air their frustrations. None of them was fully satisfied with life in London. In addition to being frustrated with the fact that it was proving to be difficult for Irishmen to move up in the business world in London, Labatt lamented that he had not yet met a woman with whom he could share the rest of his life.

Just as the three began to think seriously about immigrating to British North America, John Kinder Labatt was introduced to Eliza Kell.[32] The daughter of a senior clerk at the Bank of England, Eliza Kell was tiny in stature and optimistic in outlook. At age seventeen, she was thirteen years John Kinder's junior, but carried herself in a way that did not reflect her tender age. She was immediately drawn to Labatt. Calm in character, Labatt was polite and kind. He dressed well, or at least as well as his clerical income would allow. He had a round face and almond-shaped eyes. Fair in complexion, he had a full head of dark-brown hair, which grew thick on the sides. His sideburns were long and bushy, in keeping with the fashion of the day. His downturned lips belied his good humour. Like Eliza, he was small in stature, standing roughly five feet eight inches tall. When he was introduced to Eliza, he carried a bit of extra weight around the mid-section, which made him look slightly stout.

From the moment they met, Eliza instilled in Labatt a new-found buoyancy. As the relationship developed, the two provided each other with a sense of security and emotional support. Not surprisingly, the two fell deeply in love. John Kinder Labatt often thought of marriage, but was concerned about his lack of material wealth. He felt he had little to offer the young Miss Kell. At the age of thirty, his only asset was his grammar school education and a few spare pounds that he had managed to tuck away from his minor clerical job.[33]

Given the undeveloped state of Labatt's finances, it is questionable if Eliza's family would ever have approved of a marriage. But then Eliza's father, Robert Kell, suffered a serious financial setback as a result of a speculative investment. At the age of forty-three, Robert Kell had a wife and three children, and the loss almost wiped him out.[34] With a debt of £1,150 and a yearly salary of only £300, he was in real risk of being thrown into debtors' prison – a common fate of debtors until the 1860s when the criminal code was reformed. Others had suffered this dreadful fate.[35] For example, Charles Dickens's father had been tossed into debtors' prison in the Marshalsea, Bankside, for spending beyond his means while entertaining his friends.[36] To avoid a similar outcome, Robert Kell decided to avail himself of his daughter's suitor. He openly encouraged the marriage of Eliza and John, and the two were wed in August 1833.[37]

Following the wedding, John Labatt assumed responsibility not only for his new wife but also for her mother and younger brother and sister.[38] Labatt realized that there was little chance that he could provide for his new family if he remained in London. His clerk's salary was barely enough for him to live on, let alone support a family of five. His thoughts returned to moving to a place where the acquisition of land was still possible for settlers lacking a large amount of capital.

At the time, word of cheap Canadian land was circulating in London. A series of public lectures in 1831 informed Londoners that the colonial government was virtually giving away land in 200-acre parcels. This presented a real prospect for gain for those wishing a new beginning based on a secure and profitable investment. Books like Charles Stuart's *The Emigrant's Guide to Upper Canada* (1820) and William Cattermole's *The Advantages of Emigration to Canada* (1830) painted a rosy picture of life on the frontier.[39] "In point of climate, soil and capability for advantageous settlement," stated Cattermole, "it [Upper Canada] is not exceeded, if equaled, by any country in the world."[40] The upper colony was thus entering the British consciousness as a stable and developing British colony where a man could acquire land with only a modest investment, while retaining the customs and language of his homeland.

Other books like *Authentic Letters from Upper Canada* allowed John Labatt to calculate the cost involved in making the move from England to the western part of Upper Canada.[41] From his discussions with the Claris brothers, Labatt was also aware that Upper Canada was becoming the destination of choice for many Irishmen. Indeed, so many Irishmen immigrated to the colonies in the first half of the nineteenth century that the Irish formed the largest non-French ethnic group in Upper and Lower Canada.[42] Unlike their counterparts in the United States, the Irish that settled in Upper Canada did not gravitate toward the urban centres. Rather, most of them settled in rural areas in order to farm.[43] Labatt was inspired by the success stories of those Irishmen that had gone before him, so in late 1833, he decided the time had come to risk everything for a new life in the New World.

Life in Upper Canada

John Labatt and the four Kells arrived in Upper Canada in January 1834. The journey from England had taken more than two months, but all five members of the family had survived the ocean voyage. They had managed to avoid boarding one of the coffin ships that too often arrived in Quebec City. None succumbed to the dreaded cholera – an acute infectious disease of the intestines acquired by consuming contaminated food or water – which was responsible for at least 20,000 deaths in British North America in the mid-nineteenth century.[44] From Quebec City, they made their way to York, soon to be renamed Toronto, where Labatt wasted little time in registering his claim for 200 acres of land at the offices of the Canada Company and the Commissioner of Crown Lands. He was joined by John and George Claris, who had also made the voyage from England.[45] Labatt was required to make a down payment of £35, which represented 20 per cent of the total cost of £175. The exact location of Labatt's new home was 120 miles to the west on Lot 18, concession 8 of Westminister Township, Middlesex County, in the recently created district of London.[46]

This London of the new world had been so named by the first lieutenant-governor, John Graves Simcoe, who selected the site in 1793 as the future capital of Upper Canada. Simcoe envisioned creating a "little England" in British North America. When the village was finally laid out in 1826, it had just 133 people. But London increased in size so fast that an additional survey was necessary within a few years. By the time Labatt arrived, the population of London was almost 1,200.[47] Even compared to Labatt's birthplace, Mountmellick, London was small. Nevertheless, the area could no longer be considered wilderness. By 1834, most of Westminster Township was a lightly forested frontier region in which the trees had been thinned by intermittent cultivation.[48] Within the limits of London itself, a local government had been established and a number of businesses had emerged. In 1834, there were seven merchant's shops, three milliners, six groceries, three drug stores, two provision stores, two watchmakers, one metal foundry, four saddlers, three blacksmith shops, one flour mill, two sawmills, one tannery, two bakeries, three cabinetmakers, sixteen master carpenters, one gunsmith, four wagon makers, seven licensed taverns, and one brewery.[49]

The real boom in London's early growth took place after the Rebellions of 1837–1838. When Labatt arrived in Upper Canada, the colony was in a state of unrest. The Family Compact, a small group of commercial elites that had dominated the government of Upper Canada since the 1790s, had implemented policies that benefited their own fraternal union of merchants at the expense of the yeomen of the colony. This outraged not only those who toiled daily in the fields with their plough, harrow, sickle, and scythe but also those who had ties to the agricultural community. For example, many brewers and barkeepers could not see the merit in spending taxpayers' money on infrastructure projects, like the Welland Canal, that only benefited those elite few engaged in exporting staple products to foreign markets.[50]

On the eve of the rebellions, there were twenty-five breweries in Upper Canada. All of them, including the eight in Toronto, were small-scale operations, producing at most a few thousand barrels of beer a year. Local brewers like John Sleeman, who in 1834 started brewing in Welland County, chiefly sought to supply the local community with English-style brews. They manufactured heavy ales, porters, and stouts and then transported them by wheelbarrow or wagon to the local taverns, inns, hotels, and grog-shops. Thus, most brewers derived their income from local sources, and many had no interest in policies being implemented by the Family Compact that sought to establish a commercial empire.

Not every brewer or farmer supported the rebel cause, however. For example, John Labatt defended the colonial government and rejected the republicanism of the leader of the rebel forces, William Lyon Mackenzie. His conservative ideology combined with his dedication to the Anglican Church caused him to be a staunch defender of law and order and the preservation of property. Along with George Claris, Labatt served in the militia on behalf of the established government during the 1837 rebellion.[51]

In the aftermath of the rebellions, the British government dispatched hundreds of troops to the colony in an effort to maintain the peace. As the new military headquarters of Upper Canada, London became home to many of these soldiers.[52] Between 1838 and 1853, eight regiments, including the 32nd British Infantry, were stationed in London. The military required provisioning, and thus enterprising individuals set up establishments to meet the military's need for leisure. Among the military's requirements was the demand for British-styled ales, porters, and stouts. Beer had long been part of the soldier's life. During the War of the Spanish Succession (1701–14), the commander of the British forces, the Duke of Marlborough, proclaimed: "No soldier can fight unless he is properly fed on beef and beer." British authorities accepted Marlborough's statement as gospel, and in the years following, British soldiers were given enough "beer money" to purchase five pints a day. This, along with the fact that the overwhelming majority of the polyglot population in London traced their ancestry to the great beer-drinking nations of England, Scotland, and Ireland, gave an immediate incentive to anyone looking to capitalize on their knowledge of the art and mystery of brewing.

The pronounced military presence and rising population were strong drawing cards for the handful of brewers who arrived on the local scene in the aftermath of the rebellions. In the past, successful brewers had been quick to tap into emerging markets. Men like John Molson in Montreal and Alexander Keith in Halifax had profited from setting up breweries in expanding cities, where raw materials were readily available and a healthy appetite for beer existed.[53]

But when it came to brewing, perhaps no city was more blessed by nature than London. The city had all the essential ingredients – barley, hops, and fresh water – to brew a quality beer. The rich alluvial flats, which extended from the Thames River to the northern branch of Bear Creek and southward nearly to the shore of Lake Erie, were remarkable for their great fertility. "It is not the city alone that deserves mention," proclaimed *The Canadian Agriculturalist*, a spirited agricultural newspaper, in 1855, "for around it, on every side is spread out farming country of great beauty and fertility."[54]

Between 1838 and 1855, London farmers grew a variety of grains, but often focused on wheat because it was a cash crop. By the late 1830s, Labatt had brought more than 16 acres of wheat under cultivation. His yield from this area was 4,000 bushels, which was easily sold through the market at St Thomas for $1 a bushel. But when local brewers began paying good money for raw materials, farmers turned their fields over to cultivating barley. A basic cereal grain, barley was not particularly good for milling into flour for making bread or bakery goods. But it was perfectly suited for making beer. The best barley grew in the northern hemisphere between latitudes of 40° and 55°.[55] Situated at 42.98° latitude, London was perfectly placed to produce barley crops. The fact that so many farmers in and around London began growing the grain brought the ire of those in society who saw John Barleycorn as a danger. It is "utter folly," stated James Haughton of the *Canada Temperance Advocate* in an open letter to Canadian farmers, to dispose "of a single grain [i.e., barley] to the brewer or distiller."[56] But the farmers of the county weren't listening. By 1851, London-Middlesex had been transformed into the colony's tenth most-productive barley county.

Hops were the last ingredient necessary for the production of beer. By the nineteenth century, they were widely used as a flavouring and stabilizing agent in brewing.[57] Previously, the vast majority of brewers had used a variety of bitter herbs and flowers (e.g., dandelion, heather, marigold, and burdock root) to offset the sweet taste of the fermented grains. But hops proved superior to these other additives because of their preservative powers. Hops contained resins that helped prevent contamination of the beer by bacteria and thus helped beer last longer and travel better.[58] Like barley, the hop plant grew best under specific climatic and soil conditions – all of which prevailed in London-Middlesex. A minimum of 120 frost-free days was needed for the flowering of the hop plant. Direct sunlight and long day length (15 hours or more) were also necessary. Thus, hop cultivation was limited to geographical areas, like London-Middlesex, that were situated between 35° and 55° latitude. In 1851, more hops were grown in London-Middlesex than anywhere else in British North America.[59] At the centre of it all, London was fast becoming the city of hops and barley.

Thomas Carling was the first to exploit the natural wealth of the Thames Valley in order to satisfy the local demand for beer. A farmer from the English county of Yorkshire, Carling had immigrated to Canada because of the availability of cheap farmland.[60] Once in London, Carling set about clearing his property. The custom at the time was to call on one's neighbours to help with the "logging." As author Susanna Moodie, who had herself moved from England to the Upper Canadian frontier in 1831, wrote in her classic Canadian work *Roughing It in the Bush*, one of the few ways to get frontiersmen to show up at these "logging bees" was to have plenty of alcoholic drinks available.[61] Thomas Carling offered his neighbours home-brewed ale, and word quickly spread of its "superior quality." His brew was made to resemble those produced by the great British breweries – Whitbread, Allsopp, and Barclay Perkins & Co. In the years that followed, he sold it to civilians and soldiers alike, and when Samuel Stansfield, a former sergeant in the 32nd Regiment, was granted a licence to keep a London inn, Carling provided him as well with ale and porter. At a time when the "roads" of London were constructed of dirt and wooden planks, Carling transported his beer to clients in a wheelbarrow. It grew so popular that in 1843 he abandoned farming for full-time brewing.[62]

The grist for Carling's brewery mill came from Labatt's barley fields. Even at this early stage, the two men were co-operating in business. It was a harbinger of things to come and would help explain why the London brewers subsequently became some of the largest and most successful in the nation. Like many London farmers, Labatt grew a variety of crops, but allocated a good deal of his land to the cultivation of wheat and barley. Local brewers purchased all of the golden grain that Labatt could harvest. He built up good relationships not only with Thomas Carling but also with John Balkwill, owner of London Brewery, and with Samuel Eccles, who ran a brewery in the neighbouring town of St Thomas. Of these three men with whom Labatt would have business dealings in one form or another for years to come, Samuel Eccles had the greatest influence upon him. Indeed, his relationship with Eccles was instrumental in determining his own entry into the business of brewing.[63]

Samuel Eccles and Pioneer Brewing

For much of his adult life, Samuel Eccles had worked at improving his Westminster farm. But when his cousin, William Peacey, died in 1842, he was called upon to operate the deceased's brewery in St Thomas.[64] The experience was not completely foreign to Eccles. Before settling in St Thomas in May 1832, he had worked at a brewery in New York where he learned the six essential steps in the brewing process: malting, milling, mashing, lautering, boiling, and fermenting. The art had remained fundamentally unchanged since Jean Talon had established Canada's first commercial brewery in the 1670s.[65] But before brewing academies emerged in North America in the 1880s, the knowledge of brewing was handed down from brewmaster – in essence, the chef of the brewery – to apprentice over the generations. To be sure, the art of brewing had been taught on a systematic basis in

centres such as Munich, Vienna, and Prague since the 1830s, but specialized brewing schools did not spread widely, even in Germany, before the scientific revolution in brewing occurred after 1870. Before such schools emerged, successful
brewing was often accomplished through trial and error. Early brewers relied on
their inspiration, intuition, and experience. Therefore, the trade that Eccles
learned was one of artful tradition.

As Eccles was taught, the first step in the brewing process was to make the barley malt. This was done by soaking the barley grain in water for about two days
and then spreading it out on the floor for roughly a week to germinate. Brewing
a good beer depended on gathering the finest ingredients. Therefore, the best
colonial brewers had often spent time on the farm, where they learned how to
judge the quality of the grain. During the germination process, the brewer would
occasionally turn the grains to prevent them from overheating or sweating too
much. They would carefully watch for the appearance of growth shoots, and
when they had developed enough, the brewer would halt the germination process
by increasing the temperature in the brewery. The resulting product, known as
the malt, was then milled – cracked and crushed – so that the grain more easily
absorbed water. As beer's principal ingredient, water was essential to making good
beer. The brewer would often pump water from his well into a reservoir (see figure 1.1). It would then flow down a wooden trough to the brew kettle below,
where it was boiled and then pumped into the mash tun for the mashing stage.
At this point in the brewing process, the milled malt was added to the hot water
in the mash tun to convert its starch into fermentable sugars. Mashing released
the sugars and flavours of the malt into the liquid. A brewer would stir the mash
for about one hour, or until the grain starches had changed and become sweet
to the taste. The next step – lautering – strained out the liquid, separating it
from the spent grain. This was usually done by pulling the plug in the bottom
of the mash tun to allow the wort – the sweet liquid extract produced from the
grains during mashing – to filter into the underback. The wort, or malt extract,
was the basis for the beer.

The brewer then began the boiling process to ensure sterility, thus reducing
the chance of infections. The wort was put into a brew kettle and the hops were
added. Once boiling was completed, the contents of the kettle were pumped into
the hop jack. A bed of straw in the hop jack filtered out the spent hops. The wort
became clear, flavoured, and ready to be changed into beer. The wort was allowed
to stand in the cooling pan until it was lukewarm before being drained into the
fermenter below. During the fermenting step, a special strain of yeast was added

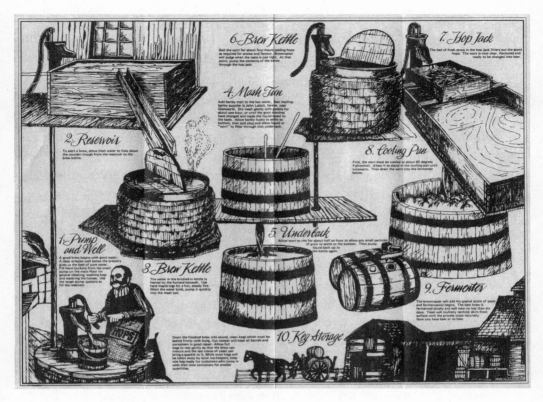

Figure 1.1 The pioneer brewing process.

to the wort. The yeast did the hard work for the brewer, making the liquid into beer. Part of the art of brewing was for the brewer to stop fermentation at precisely the right time. Halted at too high a gravity point, the beer went into a vigorous secondary fermentation in the cask, making it cloudy and acidic. Halted at too low a point, the beer became flat and lifeless – and the brewer's only recourse was to discard the bad beer and start again. If the fermentation stage went well, the beer was drained into clean kegs that were firmly sealed with a bung and then transported by wagon to local taverns, hotels, and grog-shops. This was the art of brewing that Eccles first learned in New York.[66]

After Peacey's death, Labatt continued to supply the St Thomas Brewery, which was now under Eccles's control. Over the course of the next five years, the two men became close. They had a good deal in common. Only a year apart in age, Labatt and Eccles had both lived in England before immigrating to the Upper Canadian frontier; each did so at the age of thirty. The two also shared a conservative ideology and had loyally served during the Rebellions of 1837–1838 in support of the established government, Labatt doing so in Captain Robinson's London Cavalry Company.[67] Both men were members of the Church of England and together had participated in founding the first Anglican Church at Glanworth in 1844. Each owned and operated a successful farm in the county, and both were committed capitalists who were looking to make the transition from farming to a profession that would make them part of the entrepreneurial class.[68] Eccles, however, was quicker than Labatt to realize that the way to the promised land was through brewing.

Eccles was inspired to choose brewing for economic as well as cultural reasons. Economically, London was booming and the population had a thirst for beer. If done with skill and attention to detail, brewing could be a profitable business. Culturally speaking, on the other hand, brewing would satisfy Eccles's desire for social status. In the middle of the nineteenth century, brewing was viewed by most as an honourable profession, and the brewers themselves were admired for their industry and contribution to the world in which they lived. When John Molson died in January 1836, an obituary in the Quebec City newspaper *Le Canadien* remembered him as "at all times a zealous supporter of every important commercial and industrial enterprise." "Few men," the obituary continued, "have rendered better service to their country in connection with its material development." Eccles and Labatt knew of the Molsons of Montreal. They also were aware of the great English entrepreneurs of beer – the "power-boom brewers" as they were called: men like Samuel Whitbread, William Bass, Samuel Allsopp, and John Perkins, all of whom, like Molson in Canada, had used their breweries to create commercial empires, which in turn gave them social standing and political power.[69] For men like Eccles, who were looking to make their mark on the world, brewing offered an economic means to a social end: a way up the social ladder.

Running the St Thomas Brewery had given Eccles the experience in business that he needed, and in February 1847, he purchased the London Brewery on Simcoe Street from its original owner, John Balkwill. Established in 1828, the London Brewery had started in a small log-and-plank building on the banks of the Thames River not far from London's core. A gambling sort, Balkwill had seen his fortune ebb and flow over the years, and he was often in desperate need of cash. Such was the case after the great fire of 1845, which devoured his brewery and 149 other buildings. Willing to take a chance once more, Balkwill rebuilt the brewery in stone the following year. It boasted a capacity of 50 barrels per week (or 2,500 barrels per annum), making it one of the largest breweries in the county. To be sure, there were much bigger breweries elsewhere in British North America. For example,

Figure 1.2 The London Brewery, c. 1828.

Alexander Keith's brewery in Halifax was producing 365 barrels a week during the eight cold winter months and 485 barrels a week during the four hot summer months.[70] In Montreal, Molson was mashing 2,500 bushels of grain a day, six days a week, in order to manufacture roughly 10,500 gallons of beer a month, or about 4,500 barrels per year.[71] But these breweries were servicing larger markets. Beer was a bulky, low-price commodity; in the context of mid-nineteenth-century conditions, its market had a geographical rather than a population limitation. Hence mass production could only subsist where there was a concentrated demand. Before the railway age gave rise to larger, regional breweries, brewing was a local business in which small-scale brewers slaked their neighbours' thirst. Therefore, the name of the game for Eccles was to better the local competition.

Soon after taking possession of the brewery, Eccles ran the following advertisement in the *London Times*:

> The subscriber [Samuel Eccles] … begs to acquaint his friends and the public that he is prepared to supply any orders for ALE they may favour him with. He flatters himself he will be enabled to give his customers as good satisfaction as when carrying on the St Thomas Brewery, and hopes by strict attention to business, and making a uniform good article, to obtain their support.[72]

Out of the "Blues": Labatt Enters the Business of Brewing

When this news reached John Kinder Labatt, who in the spring of 1847 was in England, he lamented that he was not somehow involved. "If I understood as much about brewing as Samuel Eccles," he wrote to his devoted wife Eliza, from England on 30 March 1847, "I certainly would try it."[73] Life on the farm was difficult for his family. Eliza, in particular, often felt the loneliness of rural life.[74] With a population of roughly 1,000 in 1846, St Thomas was virtually inaccessible to visitors during the winter due to the heavy snow and in the spring due to the mud on the roads. While Labatt had done well at farming, his success was dependent upon the weather and the environment; manufacturing, on the other hand, was theoretically independent of everything except the marketplace. His close friend George Claris had already made the transition from farming to business when he took over control of the Robinson Hotel in London. Fortunately, he had gotten out of that business before the hotel caught fire in 1845 and had invested his money in a large dry-goods store in St Thomas.[75] John Labatt was inspired by Claris and in the summer of 1846 made the bold move of selling his farm together with all his livestock and equipment. He had become restless and was determined to find an enterprise that would satisfy his desire to be in business.[76]

Labatt considered going into partnership with his younger brother-in-law, Robert Kell. Kell had recently returned to England from Paris and was eager to establish himself in a branch of textile industry, either in Huddersfield or in Bradford, where conditions had become substantially more stable since the decline of the Chartist movement, which aimed at gaining political rights for the working class.[77] But Labatt worried that his time roughing it in the bush had handicapped his development. "I am well aware of the disadvantages I labour under," he confided to his wife, "having been so long in the backwoods, away from the mercantile world, where I had not time to improve myself with books or in any way to fit myself to get through the world."[78] The confidence of his youth, which had carried him first to England and then to the New World, had vanished. He remained cautiously optimistic, however, that with the right partner to guide him, he could acquire the skills necessary to succeed in enterprise.

But Labatt did not find a partner or a business to his liking in England, and his affection for the old country was quickly fading. England had become an exceedingly expensive place to live, especially for a man like himself with a wife and seven children for whom to provide. "London is a very expensive place to bring

Figure 1.3 Labatt's London Brewery, c. 1847.

up a family," Labatt wrote to his wife in the spring of 1847, "and it will require a good business to keep our family there."[79] Establishing himself in Ireland, on the other hand, was out of the question because the Emerald Isle was in the grip of the Great Famine as a result of the failure of the potato crop in successive years. "People are dying in all directions from disease and starvation," Labatt wrote to his wife about his native country. "And almost everyone who can get out of the country is leaving for America."[80]

It did not take long, therefore, for Labatt's thoughts to return to his colonial homeland. "I often think when I am in the blues that I should be glad if I were settled in something amongst my old friends again and I am sure I don't know what to take up if I do go back … I fancy I should like brewing better than anything else."[81] Again, the idea of having a partner to share the burden of business appealed to him.[82] "For my part," he wrote, "I would never go into business in Canada or the States without a partner."[83] Engaging in enterprise in Upper Canada during the nineteenth century was risky business. Risks could be kept to a tolerable level, however, by judicious selection of a partner. On 16 April 1847, Labatt wrote to Eliza again, this time from Glasgow: "I have been considering this brewing affair for some time and I do think it would suit me better than anything else, for I fear very close confinement would not suit me after thirteen years of an active life in the open air."[84] The letter contained a detailed proposal for a partnership with his old acquaintance, Samuel Eccles.

When approached on the matter, Eccles was remarkably open to the idea. Taking on Labatt as a partner would reduce his exposure to a potential loss. Before the passage of legislation enacting limited liability in the 1850s, partnerships were a way of distributing the risks involved in business. As a result, Labatt was permitted to buy into the brewery for a sum of £2,350.[85] The investment received the ambivalent approval of Labatt's extended family. "We all think you are undertaking a great deal," Robert Kell wrote to John Labatt, "and if you were of a wild and speculative turn … we should tremble for you."[86] About half of the money that Labatt required to buy into the business was derived from Eccles, as the basis of their partnership, in the form of a personal loan on which Labatt made regular payments of interest over the next several years.[87] The rest came from the proceeds of selling his farm, mortgages on two pieces of land adjacent to the brewery, and members of the Kell family.[88]

Labatt's actions at this stage in his life revealed a capacity for cautious risk-taking – a value that would define his and his successor's business style in the years that followed.[89] With limited capital, he had to resort to borrowing, but he confined his source of those funds as much as possible to the Kell family. It would have been impossible for him to make the transition from farming to brewing in 1847 without borrowing. But by borrowing from his family, he avoided all the risks of becoming vulnerable to wealthy speculators or institutions that too easily and too often foreclosed on new colonial enterprises.[90]

Shortly after Labatt's investment in the brewery, he received a letter from Aunt Maria Kell. The sister of Robert Kell, Maria Kell had been one of the first to lend financial support to Labatt. In 1849, without being asked, she gave Labatt £500 from her life inheritance.[91] In return, Labatt agreed to pay her 6 per cent interest per year. Given her investment, she felt entitled to pass along some advice she had recently received from a family friend. In a letter to John Kinder Labatt, she quoted her friend as saying: "If they [Labatt and Eccles] give an honest, good article they will stand their ground; but the moment they deteriorate, they will sink."[92] It was sage advice. At a time when the market was local and word-of-mouth could make or break an enterprise, producing a *consistently* "good article" was critical to a firm's success.

Early Growth

In the years following the formation of the partnership, Labatt blossomed as a brewer and a businessman. He attentively listened to the advice that Eccles offered. Working twelve to fourteen hours a day, he helped to manage the six men on the payroll while learning about the process and perfecting the art of brewing. When he was not at work in the brewery, he was busy promoting his ales and stouts in and around the London-Middlesex area. Labatt's activities aided in the early growth of the brewery, and helped generate a rate of return on investment of over 10 per cent per year between 1847 and 1855.

But beyond the actions of the owners, the brewery's early success was due to the environment in which it operated. Labatt and Eccles had picked the right time and place to go into business. The county was growing at a healthy rate, and London was booming. By 1851, the population of Middlesex was 32,862, while that of the county's capital, London, was 7,035.[93] The population of London had increased almost sixfold since Labatt's arrival in 1833. The golden age of the military's stay was still underway. London had become one of just five towns in Upper Canada with a population over 5,000 – the others being Toronto, Kingston, Ottawa, and Hamilton. In 1853, a popular magazine summed up the reasons for London's astonishing development: "Much doubtless, of the prosperity, everywhere visible, and the rapid increase in the population, is to be attributed to London having so long a military station; but still, it is in the energy of the inhabitants and the productiveness of the adjacent country, that the real cause is to be found. The well-stocked shops and the expeditious yet safe mode of doing business, have long rendered London a place worthy of note in the far west."[94]

The appetite for beer was increasing as fast as the population. The census of 1851 revealed that 98 per cent of the town's residents could still trace their direct ancestry to the great beer-drinking nations of England, Scotland, and Ireland. Moreover, the majority of Londoners belonged to those religious denominations that were not prone to emerging temperance fervour. London had plenty of places where the beer of the London Brewery could be consumed. A number of hotels and taverns were within easy reach of the London Brewery by horse and wagon. In addition, as the London *Free Press* noted in March 1849, there were fifteen to twenty "beer shops" in every locality in the town, where there was "music and dancing, with other allurements to late hours."[95]

The drinking culture in London was not that much different than elsewhere in British North America. Most people imbibed during the mid-nineteenth century – men, women, and children. They drank at home, at work, and at play.[96] Colonial elections were often ruckuses with many candidates and electorates drinking before, during, and after the voting. Many people drank to excess. For example, Canada's future prime minister, John A. Macdonald, drank so much that on occasion he found it impossible to show up to work. "I suppose you were doing penance for the deeds of the previous day," wrote one client on a note that was pinned to the door of Macdonald's unoccupied Kingston law office in 1839.[97] Macdonald often spent time in colonial taverns during the 1840s and 1850s, along with other politicians, like Thomas D'Arcy McGee and George-Étienne Cartier, both of whom were heavy drinkers. But as Julia Roberts has demonstrated in her book, *In Mixed Company*, taverns were not just a place for elites. They were an important public space where men and women of diverse backgrounds – native and newcomer, white and non-white, capitalist and labourer – came to socialize and learn.[98] Upper Canadians also drank in inns, grog-shops, marketplaces, factories, and even churches. The Upper Canadian census of 1851 recorded there were 1,999 taverns, or one to every 478 people in the colony. London and Toronto had more taverns than streets. While the preferred alcoholic beverage of Canadians was hard liquor – specifically whisky, rum, and brandy – many drank beer, if it could be acquired, which wasn't always easy. When Sir Richard Bonnycastle visited Canada in 1846 he noted that whisky and "very atrocious brandy" were the only beverages excepting water that could be procured along the country roads.[99] But when quality ale and stouts could be had, Canadians merrily consumed them.

The London market was not saturated with brewers, at least not during these early years. At mid-century, there were only a handful of brewers in business ready and able to supply the thirsty people of London-Middlesex. The only other brewery, besides the London Brewery, operating within the town's limits was the Carling Brewery, which in the spring of 1849 had been sold to Thomas Carling's two sons, William and John. With keen commercial instinct – inherited from their father – the brothers embarked upon an ambitious phase of expansion in the fall of 1852.[100] Not ones to fall behind for long, Eccles and Labatt followed suit a few years later. The other three breweries in the county were located outside London's boundaries. The biggest belonged to Richard Rich who, in 1847, had opened the Blackfriars Brewery on the west side of Wharncliffe Road, just south of Oxford Street in what was then the village of Petersville. At half the size of the London

Brewery, the two-storey Blackfriars Brewery measured 60 feet by 30 feet and had the capacity to produce 3,600 barrels of beer per annum.[101]

This is not to suggest, however, that Labatt and Eccles did not face stiff competition. Realizing that the local population longed for a taste of "'ome," the merchants of London sometimes stocked imported beers from the British Isles. As early as the first decade of the nineteenth century, British beer had become a notable feature in the newspaper advertisements of Lower Canadian importers, and by the 1830s, foreign beer had found its way to Middlesex. In 1837, one store owner invited tavern-keepers to examine his stock of "1000 gallons of Cognac, Bordeaux, Spanish brandies, 500 gallons of Jamaican spirits; 300 gallons of Holland gin ... and imported ale."[102] Other London merchants routinely stocked Hilbert's Porter and Leith Ale. In 1845, the owner of a coffee house announced in the *London Times* that he had "just received per Great Britain ... thirty hogsheads Barclay and Perkins' London Porter, and now on draught."[103] The beers imported from the British Isles, however, often tasted flat and stale after sloshing around in barrels in the bottom of a ship for a couple of months. The beer produced at the London Brewery, by comparison, would have been delightfully fresh. Made to resemble the best British brands, Labatt's ale was a dark-amber brew tasting primarily of malt. And the beer drinkers of London-Middlesex relished it. In 1853, the *Anglo-American Magazine* noted that "Labatt's Brewery is too well known to all true lovers of malt to require particular notice; triple, double or single x, are all to be had, and of a quality that would almost shake one's belief in the exclusive excellence of Hodgson or Bass's pale East India."[104] The quality of Labatt's beer along with the favourable economic circumstances at mid-century permitted the brewery to prosper and grow.

Labatt Goes It Alone

With Labatt taking on an increasingly dominant role, Eccles gradually retreated from visible participation in the brewery. As a result, the London Brewery became associated in the public mind with Labatt.[105] And Eccles began looking to enter another business. "I have come to the conclusion," he wrote to his energetic and determined partner on 8 April 1853, "that the time has come to give up brewing and turn instead to something like tanning or soap making that does not heighten the emotions of others." Eccles had begun to worry that the cultural tide had turned against the "liquor traffic" – i.e., the brewers, distillers, and vintners of the nation. He had legitimate reasons for concern.

The temperance movement had recently arrived in London when Simeon Morrill, who was born in Vermont and raised in Maine, established the London Temperance Reformation Society. A tanner by trade, Morrill was elected town mayor in 1848 and held the office again in 1850 and 1851. Morrill was representative of a growing group of reform-minded businessmen who were helping to shape a more puritanical social order.[106] But it wasn't just progressive businessmen who were turning against the liquor traffic. After 1850, the Church of England, the army, and the police all began to endorse a more sober society.[107] Adding to Eccles's concern was the fact that the middle years of the nineteenth century had seen the first statutory implementation of the developing temperance movement, albeit in the United States.

In 1851, Neal Dow, the wealthy mayor of Portland, Maine, who was known to friends and foes alike as the "Napoleon of Temperance," gathered thousands of signatures on a petition demanding that the state legislature pass a law banning the sale of intoxicating beverages. Few Americans drank more than the lumbermen, mill workers, farmers, and fishermen of Maine. In Portland alone, there were 200 licensed liquor dealers – and perhaps 400 unlicensed ones – at a time when the city's population was less than 10,000. But due to Dow's tireless efforts, the bill passed on 2 June 1851. For the first time, a legislature of an American state voted to prohibit the sale and manufacture of intoxicating beverages.[108]

The significance of the event was not lost on those closest to John Kinder Labatt. "I would very much doubt whether you will get on long with the Maine Liquor Law," Robert Kell warned Labatt in July 1854, "which sooner or later, I expect, will be the law of Canada as it is fast becoming in the northern States."[109] Robert Kell had come to dislike the business of brewing. "There are many things about it I do not like," he wrote, "and in this I share his [Eccles's] opinion."[110] As a result, Kell advised his brother-in-law to again follow Eccles's lead. "Rather than separate from him I, if in your place, would have given up brewing and turned to tanning or candle and soap making."[111] But the insecurities that he had exhibited eight years before were now gone, and where others could see only adverse risk, Labatt perceived a business opportunity. Confident in the future, Labatt offered to buy out Eccles at a price that reflected the fair market value of the London Brewery.

Over the previous eight years, the business had increased in value by 13 per cent a year. In 1855, Labatt agreed to pay Eccles £5,368 for his share in the brewery

– more than twice the amount at which the share had been valued when the partnership was formed in 1847. Eccles, however, did not expect his friend to pay for his share of the brewery up front. As a result, the two settled upon an eight-year instalment schedule. Secured by a mortgage on the brewery land, Labatt agreed to remit £440 in 1856, £428 in 1857, £416 in 1858, £704 in 1859, £674 in 1860, £844 in 1861, £802 in 1862, and £1,060 in 1863. Once the ink dried on the bill of sale, John Kinder Labatt became the sole owner of the London Brewery.[112]

Conclusion

The founders of successful companies are often portrayed as self-confident individuals with a vision of what they want to do in business and how they will introduce new products and technologies with an eye on making themselves a profit. Not so in the case of Labatt. He exhibited no interest in brewing prior to buying into the business that would eventually carry the family name. In this sense, the decision to brew came out of the blue. In addition, he was motivated primarily by emotion rather than profit to become a brewer. At a time when he was away from home and "in the blues," he decided to brew in order to be back among his family and friends in the colony where he had spent much of his adult life. Rather than being self-confident, he was full of self-doubt after being "so long in the backwoods." His fear of failure and aversion to risk led him to seek a partnership with his old friend, Samuel Eccles. But rather than being a liability, his insecurity proved to be an asset once he began brewing and promoting his product. Aware of his own shortcomings, he listened to every word of advice that Eccles had to offer. He worked harder and longer than his partner and his competitors. And when it came to selling his products, he did so with a "pushiness" that would come to define Labatt as a businessman. His insecurity helped, rather than hindered, the growth of the firm.

Despite his own initial self-doubts, Labatt turned out to be an astute businessman and a gifted brewer. Perhaps the most sensible action that he took during these years was to not overextend himself by increasing his debt. It would have been tempting, given the profits that were being made, to expand the capacity of the brewery. But Labatt resisted the urge, focusing instead on consolidating his gains and producing ales and stouts that could compete with the best beers produced within the region and those imported from the British Isles. Profit maximization was not his principal consideration. These values – risk aversion, personal humility, pride in his product, fear of failure, loyalty to family and friends – came to define Labatt and would guide the business itself over time.

But beyond the actions of its principals, the success of the Labatt brewery during these formative years was determined by the environment in which it operated. London was perfectly suited for commercial brewing, with its rich supply of natural resources and a seemingly unlimited demand for beer. In the city of hops and barley, the composition of the civilian population was such that a strong consumer demand existed for British-styled ales, porters, and stouts. In addition, the military presence in the city created a stable market for beer, as soldiers gladly handed over their pay-packs to the brewers of quality ales, porters, and stouts, like Labatt's. While competition was stiff, the market was not saturated by any measure. In a region that was experiencing a substantial increase in population, there were plenty of customers and profits to go around. Labatt had started brewing in the right place and at the right time. Within eight years of entering the brewing business, John Labatt was the sole owner of the London Brewery and the foundation was laid for one of the most successful breweries in Canadian history.

Steaming into the Age of Rail
and Pale Ale, 1855–77

Of all the technological innovations of the Industrial Revolution, the railway had the most transformative effect on the Canadian brewing industry. With its relative speed and power, the railroad was able to overcome the seasonal difficulties of muddy roads and ice-packed waterways, and thus was far superior to traditional modes of transportation – i.e., wagons, stagecoaches, and boats – for getting products to market. As eminent Harvard University business historian Alfred Chandler has stated, the railroad "permitted a regularity and a certainty in travel and in the movement of goods that had never existed before."[1] In Canada, the advent of the railway meant it was finally possible to conquer the harsh winter and to keep trade and commerce moving year-long. In essence, climatic conditions were conquered, as were distance, time, and all the obstacles that geography put in the way of transportation by land. In his 1849 treatise *The Philosophy of Railroads*, engineer-cum-railroad promoter Thomas Keefer confidently stated: "it is *now* universally admitted, that distances are virtually shortened in the precise ratio in which the times occupied in passing over them is diminished. SPEED, ECONOMY, REGULARITY, SAFETY AND CONVENIENCE – an array of advantages unequalled – are combined in the railway system."[2] Profoundly aware of this, business and political leaders became obsessed with railway technology.[3] As a result, between 1852 and 1859, over 1,400 miles of railway were built in Upper Canada alone. By 1860, the railway system was capitalized at about $100 million and all the major urban centres in the colony were bound together with a ribbon of shining steel.[4]

Brewers quickly recognized the blessings of railroad transportation, especially after the introduction in the 1870s of the refrigerated boxcars that kept beer cold and fresh. But even before the advent of refrigeration, the brewers were among the first manufacturers in British North America to use the new mode of transportation to get their products to market. Aboard a railway, beer was less likely to spill, spoil, or go stale. A greater amount of beer could be transported safely and conveniently, resulting in a lower cost to producers and consumers. The railway broke down the old "tariff of bad roads" that protected artisanal brewers in small, local markets and laid the groundwork for the concentration of industrial production in a handful of metropolitan centres.[5] By extending the range of cheap overland transportation and by permitting the continuous flow of raw materials into and finished goods out of manufacturing establishments, the coming of the railway created the necessary conditions for the rise of mass production in beer making. As the most enterprising brewers found new consumers for their products, they expanded their plants to meet the new-found demand. The Canadian brewing industry shifted into a vigorous new era of industrialization and regionalization as this relatively small group of brewers came to dominate the central Canadian market. Ultimately, the railway turned a handful of local brewers into widely recognized names.

The advent of the railroad created opportunities and challenges for Canadian brewers. On the one hand, the railway gave brewers easier and cheaper access to distant places, thereby giving them the opportunity to expand their market. On the other hand, the railroad opened up their home market to competition. The question facing John Kinder Labatt was how to meet the challenges of the age of steam, steel, and rail.

Labatt Becomes a Railroader

John K. Labatt was one of the first to recognize that transportation was a key to industrial growth and the continued success of his nascent brewery. As a boy walking to school in Mountmellick, he had witnessed the positive effects of the canals on the development of industry in his Irish hometown. The connection between speedy and reliable transportation and steady economic development was further cemented in his mind during his time in England. On 15 September 1830, the world's first train steamed down the tracks from Liverpool to Manchester. The next day, the groundbreaking news was heard all over London. Labatt was thus present at the birth of the "railway mania" that would grip the English-speaking world for the next fifty years.

Figure 2.1 The Great Western Railway arrives in London, Ontario, in 1853, allowing John Kinder Labatt to ship his beer as far away as Montreal.

Even before the arrival of the railroad to his corner of the New World, Labatt had demonstrated his belief in the benefits to be derived from the expansion of transportation networks. As the area to the north of London became settled, Labatt found ways to penetrate this emerging market. He was helped in 1849 by the passage of colonial legislation that permitted private companies to build toll roads.[6] He and a number of other leading London businessmen, including Thomas Carling, formed the Proof Line Road Joint Stock Company to grade, macadamize, and bridge a road linking London and the northern hinterlands.[7] When completed, the road had three tollgates and followed the Richmond Street route north through Arva, Birr, and Elginfield. Several inns and taverns opened along the road, where travellers consumed Labatt's beer. The investment in Proof Line Road was significant for two reasons. First, it demonstrated Labatt's willingness to team up with his local competitors – in this case Thomas Carling – to promote the interests of the London brewing community. Second, it manifested his understanding that efficient and dependable modes of transportation were necessary in order to expand his business operations beyond the boundaries of London-Middlesex County.

In large part, Labatt was motivated to look to the horizon for new business opportunities because, in 1853, the golden age of the military's stay in London came to an end.[8] This external shock created a serious challenge for those at the old London Brewery. The military had been loyal customers of Labatt. The troops stationed in London were eager to hand over their disposable income to quench their thirst with quality English-styled ales and stouts. Many soldiers were heavy drinkers, and while there is no statistical data to indicate just how important they were to Labatt's survival, anecdotal evidence suggests that they were a significant and stable group of consumers.[9] But with the outbreak of the Crimean War, all of the regular troops were pulled out of London and sent to serve with Her Majesty's Imperial Forces in the Crimea. During the period 1853–60 not a single regular British regiment was located in London.[10] With the loss of these consumers close to home, Labatt aggressively sought out new markets.

In 1853, Londoners learned that Labatt was once again looking to bring a new communications route to the city of hops and barley, one utilizing the new technologies. What Labatt had in mind was an iron link connecting London and Port Stanley on the north shore of Lake Erie. As London's nearest port and one of the finest harbours on the Great Lakes, Port Stanley had strategic value for men like Labatt who were seeking export markets for their products. By horse-drawn wagon, it took a full day to transport goods the 25 miles from London to Port Stanley. By rail, it would take less than two hours. Thus, on 23 May 1853, the London and Port Stanley Railroad was incorporated with a capital stock of £150,000 and John Kinder Labatt, a long-time advocate of steam, steel, and rail, was one of its twenty-eight stockholders.[11]

Over the next five years, Londoners witnessed a whirlwind of activity. Even before the construction of the northern line to Port Stanley got underway, Londoners welcomed the arrival of the Great Western Railway from the east. Once the appropriate business structure had been put in place, it would be possible for Labatt to sell his beer in the largest central Canadian cities – Ottawa, Kingston, Hamilton, Toronto, and Montreal. As Labatt himself stated, "for the local man of business, a great opportunity has been presented [in the form of the railway]." The potential for men like Labatt was enormous. At a time when London's population was approaching 11,000, that of Kingston was almost 14,000, Ottawa's was closing in on 15,000, Hamilton's was nearing 20,000, and Toronto was fast approaching a population of 45,000.[12] The railway had changed these cities. Toronto, for instance, was transformed from a commercial port town into a thriving regional land-and-sea hub of economic activity.[13] So transformative was the change that, in 1853, the editors of the Toronto *Globe* proclaimed: "We question whether there is a town in the world which has advanced more rapidly than Toronto."[14] The *Globe*'s boosterism notwithstanding, Montreal was still the largest Canadian city, and it would remain so into the twentieth century. As early as 1865, Labatt was already thinking about how he might take on the competition in Montreal. But initially, at least, his focus was on those markets a bit closer to home.

Of course, Labatt would face competition from deeply rooted artisanal breweries in the villages, towns, and cities across central Canada. According to historical geographer James Gilmour, by the 1870s, every municipality with a population over 4,000 had at least one brewery.[15] Bigger cities, like Hamilton and Toronto, had many more, and some of the breweries were substantially larger than that owned by John Kinder Labatt.[16] The biggest in Ontario was Toronto Brewing and Malting Company. The brewery on Simcoe Street was capable of manufacturing 1,450,000 gallons (58,320 barrels) during the eight-month brewing session, leading one contemporary observer to state that those "who like a drop of good beer need not be afraid that it cannot be supplied fast enough to keep their whistles wet, or, at all events, damp."[17] There were other breweries that, while not yet as big as Toronto Brewing and Malting Company, were owned and controlled by men as ambitious and aggressive as any in the business of brewing, including John K. Labatt.

The Victoria Brewery, at the corner of Victoria and Gould streets, was one such establishment. After purchasing the 1,000-barrel-a-year brick brewery in 1861, Eugene O'Keefe increased production rapidly. Irish by birth, the former junior accountant at the Toronto Savings Bank had an aptitude for numbers, and he calculated that brewing was an industry with an almost unlimited capacity for expansion.[18] Within seven years, output had increased sevenfold to 7,000 barrels a year.[19] The expansion at the plant continued into the 1870s and 1880s, with further additions being made in 1872 and 1882. In 1883, O'Keefe's brewery manufactured 285,086 gallons (11,403 barrels) of ale.[20]

Labatt knew if he was to compete with the likes of O'Keefe, he, too, would have to increase the capacity of his plant. But to do so would be fatal if markets weren't first found. With the arrival of the railroad, Labatt now had the means to reliably reach distant markets. The question was how he would distribute and market his product once it was there.

A Network of Agencies

In January 1854, the Great Western Railway was pushed west from London to Windsor. Eager to be the first London brewer to exploit the markets to the west, Labatt immediately made a number of experimental shipments over the infant line. So pleased was Labatt with the results that, on 1 October 1856, regular shipments of his ales and stouts were inaugurated.[21] When the Great Western Railway between London and Sarnia opened in late December 1858, Labatt again quickly took advantage. On the first train, the *London Free Press* reported, was "a large quantity of freight … among which was 30 barrels of beer, and 50 dozen of ale, from the celebrated brewery of Mr Labatt, of this city."[22] By 1858, four railways had arrived in London, giving Labatt unprecedented potential to expand into new geographical markets.

Getting the beer to a distant market, however, was only the first step in Labatt's new strategy of expanding his operations geographically. In order to penetrate outlying markets, Labatt understood that he would have to modernize his business structure. He would need people to promote and sell his products in faraway places, and hopefully with the same zeal that he had exhibited when selling them in and around London.

At first, Labatt contracted small-scale merchants who were already in business (e.g., grocers and liquor dealers) to sell his products. This was the standard business practice in the mid-nineteenth century, and without any experience to prove the custom wanting, Labatt's initial impulse was to be conservative and follow suit. These independent merchants sold Labatt's ales and stouts along with a variety of other goods. No special treatment was given to Labatt's brands. At a time before the advent of modern advertising techniques, Labatt had to rely on the quality of his product and the subsequent word-of-mouth of his customers. The independent merchants had no incentive to promote Labatt's product over that of another competing manufacturer.

It did not take long for Labatt to become critical of this conventional system of beer distribution. He wanted a sales force devoted to the sale of his beer alone. So, beginning in the 1860s, Labatt hired specialized agents who were knowledgeable about his products and dedicated exclusively to promoting his brands. This system was already being used effectively in Britain, where Labatt often vacationed during the 1850s and 1860s.[23] For their services, Labatt paid his agents a basic salary plus a percentage commission on sales to encourage productivity. The new distribution system worked well. By the end of the 1870s, he had set up agencies

Figure 2.2 Portrait of John Kinder Labatt, c. 1864.

in Ailsa Craig, Bothwell, Brantford, Brockville, Chatham, Clinton, Cobourg, Collingwood, Exeter, Forest, Galt, Glencoe, Goderich, Ingersoll, Lucan, Newbury, Orangeville, Parkhill, Peterborough, Petrolia, Picton, Sarnia, Seaforth, St Marys, St Thomas, Stratford, Strathroy, Thedford, Trenton, Watford, Windsor, and Woodstock.[24] Every location was tactically important in the battle to dominate the regional beer market.

Although setting up and maintaining an agency network was the least capital-intensive task associated with gaining a presence throughout the region, expanding into new geographic markets required a good deal of money. Tying up money in barrels to be shipped to sales agents was tremendously expensive and, therefore, beyond the financial means of small operators. Compounding matters of capital strength, agency beer had to compete with the price of beer that was locally manufactured. For example, in Toronto, tipplers could buy locally made beer as well as beer made in Brantford, Guelph, Hamilton, Lachine, London, Montreal, Owen Sound, Port Hope, Walkerville, and Waterloo. The same was true in the larger towns and cities across the region. As a result, only those brewers who had achieved an optimum economy of scale could produce a product efficiently enough so that, after adding transportation costs, they could still be competitively priced with beer manufactured and distributed in the targeted market.

For those brewers, like Labatt, who could afford to supply a string of agencies, the benefits over time were multiple. By shipping beer to regional agencies, Labatt was able to increase his sales. This gave him access to greater capital, which he used to finance plant improvements, thus boosting his production efficiencies even further. Having recently added a second malthouse to the brewery, in 1863, Labatt embarked on his most ambitious renovation yet: a five-storey brick-towered brewhouse to replace the old stone brewery built two decades earlier. On 1 August 1863, John Labatt wrote to his wife, who was visiting her family in England, with an update on the brewery's expansion:

We continue to get on very satisfactorily with our new addition to the brewery. I think it will look very well, to say nothing about its advantages and usefulness, etc. I fear it will take longer to finish than I first expected. However, I am not at all fidgety or alarmed about it. If I should be spared a few years longer with God's blessing and help, I hope to see everything made right with all my creditors, who after all, are not very numerous nor are the amounts very or fearfully large. With the proper attention to business I can see my way clear through it all, and be able to have a nice, valuable property for you and your dear children. Everything I do about the premises is done well and substantial, and with ordinary care can be kept in good order for many, many years with very little expenditure.[25]

The letter reflected a new level of comfort with large and expensive undertakings. It also captured Labatt's continued dedication to family as well as his sense of obligation to his creditors. After fifteen years in business, he had become more confident about his talents as an entrepreneur. When the additions were done, the Labatt brewery was one of the largest in the region. In 1865, the *London Prototype* described the completed brewery in glowing terms: "The London Brewery is now a big pile of brick, solidly and compactly built."[26]

The expansion of the plant lowered the cost of each beer produced, and Labatt passed along the savings to his customers in the form of lower prices. The gap between large and small brewers thus widened, and many small local brewers broke under the strain of increased competition from larger firms with a regional reach. Between 1862 and 1892, sixty small locally oriented brewers were forced to close their doors.[27] By using the railway to ship his products to agents in distant regional markets, Labatt helped initiate a sharp turn toward market integration and essentially set the course for the rise of large industrial breweries and the gradual decline of small locally oriented ones during the last few decades of the nineteenth century.

John Labatt II

John Kinder Labatt never witnessed the full effect of his business strategy. On 26 October 1866, he died of a heart attack, the result of a condition that had afflicted him for some years. The obituary that appeared in the *London Free Press* gave a detailed account of his struggles during his dying days and concluded by noting that: "Throughout his career the deceased was remarkable for his energetic, shrewd and pushing business qualities."[28] The statement was fitting primarily because it was true. Labatt had come to Canada with very little. In 1833, he had borrowed to purchase his first piece of Upper Canadian land and, fourteen years later, sold his farm for a substantial profit. Making money came naturally to Labatt. At the time of his death, his estate was valued at $16,000.[29] As owner of the London Brewery, he never lost money. From the time that he entered the business of brewing, he had been single-minded in his pursuit of profit, which

entailed expanding the scale and scope of his business. His artistry for making
ales and stouts was only eclipsed by his ability to aggressively promote his products in an increasingly competitive marketplace. Before any other brewer, Labatt
realized that growth and prosperity in the brewing industry depended upon one's
ability to utilize new technologies and penetrate outlying markets. For this, the
London Free Press concluded that Labatt was "a man of business who had become
known in all parts of the Province ... few obstacles appeared to him insurmount-
able, his motto being to overcome them all if possible."[30]

In his last will and testament, John Kinder Labatt sought to structure his affairs
so that the brewery that he had founded would remain prosperous and in family
hands after he was gone. The will laid out the principles that Labatt felt should
guide the family enterprise into the future. "After my decease," the handwritten
will read, "I will and direct that the business I now carry on at the London Brewery shall be continued by my wife Eliza Labatt."[31] According to the will, Eliza was
entitled to retain the brewery, sell it, or lease it out to another brewer, if she so
decided. But if Eliza chose to rent or sell the brewery, the offer must first go to
their third son, John Labatt. "And I further will and direct that in the event of
selling or renting my said brewery, preference shall be given to my son John
Labatt to be purchaser or tenant."[32] Only if John declined the offer would the
option to rent or buy the brewery be extended to the elder two sons, Robert and
Ephraim Labatt. As historian David Landes notes, the willingness of family business owners to single out the most capable of their offspring – regardless of age
or emotional attachment – to guide the enterprise into the future is a key determinant of success.[33] Before his death, John Kinder Labatt had concluded that the
London Brewery could not support four owners, nor could the business survive
a potential four-way quarrel over day-to-day operations. Thus, he singled out
Eliza and, ultimately, John Jr to run the brewery that he had built. Eliza and John
Jr immediately entered into a partnership. In one of his final and most significant
acts, he structured his affairs so that the brewery would end up in the hands of
his most able son, his namesake, John Labatt.

In terms of his approach to business, John Labatt Jr was his father's son. Pragmatic, principled, and forward-looking, he was paternal to his employees and
loyal – as time would tell – to a fault. He was disciplined, determined, quick on
his feet, and rarely ran from the competition. In this regard, he shared his father's
"shrewd and pushing business qualities." But above all, like his father, he was
proud of the quality of the beer that was being produced at the London Brewery.
In his opinion, "it was the finest in the Dominion." He differed from his father,

Figure 2.3 Labatt advertising poster from around the time of John Kinder Labatt's death in 1866.

however, in his willingness to take chances, and he rarely, if ever, exhibited any self-doubt.

Growing up in the house situated on the brewery grounds, John Labatt was constantly surrounded by beer, brewers, and beer drinking. While he received a formal education – first at Caradoc Academy, just west of London, and then at a secondary school closer to home – he never went to university, although he was intellectually capable enough. His first job was with a wholesaler in London. Then, in 1857, at the age of nineteen, he took up full-time employment at the London Brewery.[34] So impressed was John K. Labatt with his son's work around the brewery that, in 1859, he decided to send him south of the border to perfect his craft as a brewer. John Jr's exact destination was Wheeling, Virginia, where an old acquaintance of John Kinder Labatt, George Weatherall Smith, owned a thriving brewery.[35] John Jr remained in Wheeling for five years, living with the Smiths and receiving an excellent education in the art and mystery of brewing. Like his father, he was quick to take direction from those he respected and believed had something valuable to offer. But he did not suffer fools gladly. Of all the things that Smith had to teach the young Labatt, the recipe for India pale ale was the most important.

India Pale Ale

George Smith had made a fortune selling India pale ale to the beer drinkers of Virginia. India pale ale, or IPA, was first made popular in India by George Hodgson, who opened a brewery near the East India Dock on the River Thames in East London, England, in 1752. At a time when the British Empire was at its height, Hodgson sought to ship his beer to distant markets like India, where large numbers of British troops were stationed. The perennial problem for brewers at the time was that beer did not keep well on long ocean voyages, especially to hot climates like India. These trips often resulted in flat, sour beer. To solve the problem, Hodgson took his pale ale recipe, increased the hop content considerably, and raised the starting gravity by adding extra grain and sugar. The result was a top-fermented beer that could withstand the rigors of travel and shelf life in India. When the railway boom swept the western world beginning in the mid-nineteenth century, IPA was the ideal beer because it travelled better than heavy ale and stout. In the words of historian R.G. Wilson, "it was the high-fashion beer of the railway age."[36] In terms of its taste, IPA was hoppier, more bitter, and more alcoholic than other ales. When bottled or poured into a beer glass – an act that became increasingly common in the latter half of the nineteenth century, as glassware became more affordable – IPA appeared enticingly golden.

In 1864, John Labatt returned to London, to help his ailing father and to escape the Civil War that was having a disastrous effect on Smith's business. The war soured the overall commercial climate in Virginia, and military demands for grain caused the price of barley to skyrocket. To make matters worse, Smith sympathized with the rebellious South and consequently ran into sales troubles with the generally pro-Union northwestern counties of Virginia. Sensing that life would be better elsewhere, Smith liquidated his assets in Wheeling and purchased a 6,000-barrel-a-year brewing business in the town of Prescott on the St Lawrence River between Brockville and Cornwall. At the time, Prescott was a relatively stable agricultural community with the potential of becoming a major river port because of its proximity to the United States.

As the civil turmoil started to settle south of the border, Smith returned home to West Virginia, arriving just in time for the 1864 fall brewing season. With no need for two breweries, he offered to lease the Prescott Brewery to his one-time apprentice, John Labatt. While John Labatt was not interested, his two older brothers, Robert and Ephraim, were itching to be their own men. In 1864, they purchased the Prescott Brewery from Smith and ran it in partnership until 1867.[37]

With his two elder brothers attending to their new business in Prescott and his father's health failing, John Labatt was the obvious person to take over as brewmaster at London Brewery. In 1864, he assumed the task with youthful enthusiasm and attention to detail. As brewmaster, John Labatt crafted every beer down to its last detail, ordered the ingredients, made sure that the brewery's equipment was functioning properly, kept the costs of production in line, supervised the packaging of the beer, and followed the product out into the marketplace to make sure it met or exceeded his customers' expectations.[38] Labatt's skill as a brewmaster was soon widely recognized and celebrated. In 1865, the *London Prototype* reported that "Mr John Labatt, jr, is the brewer of the establishment [in London], and his skill and ability in the duties of his office are such that to him, in large measure, is due the high character and good name and celebrity which Labatt's ales and beer have attained throughout the Western Province."[39] He was quickly proving to the public that the younger generation of Labatts were just as committed to excellence in brewing.

In the year prior to his father's death, the junior John convinced the senior one that the business would benefit from brewing an IPA based on the formula that he had learned in Wheeling. John Labatt II had a sense that tastes were changing. He knew from various sources that in Britain there was a shift away from the consumption of heavy ales, porters, and stouts. In Victorian Britain, pale ale was increasingly becoming the beer of choice.[40] This was reflected in the ascendancy of the Burton brewers – firms like Bass, Worthington, and Samuel Allsopp & Sons that specialized in the production of IPA[41] – that began to challenge the supremacy of London brewers. Output at Bass, for example, increased from 130,000 barrels in 1853 to 900,000 barrels in 1876.[42] Conversely, the London-based Truman Brewery, which had risen to prominence during the porter boom of the late eighteenth century, had fallen from the "top of the tree" due to its inability to produce pale ale to the same standards as the Burton brewers. Production at Truman's fell from 606,000 barrels in 1872 to 510,000 barrels in 1886–87.[43]

John Labatt also had a sense that his water was well suited for the production of IPA. The chemical composition of the water of Burton upon Trent was central to the success of the Burton brewers' IPA.[44] Burton water was infused with alkalinity and had moderately high permanent hardness. It also contained sulfates.

Labatt suspected that London's water had some of the same qualities; just to be sure, he had it analyzed. It turned out that he was right.[45] As a budding brewmaster, he placed a high value on the quality of the water from his two wells, declaring it to be superior to the water of Toronto. "Now it is well known that the Toronto water is very bad," Labatt stated, "so much so that I never think of drinking water in Toronto unless it is boiled in the shape of a cup of tea."[46] After considerable experimentation and several trial runs, in 1867, John Labatt declared that his India pale ale was ready for market. As manager and brewmaster of the newly named Labatt and Company, John Labatt II made all the important strategic decisions and was sure that the investment in India pale ale would pay off. He was more willing than his father to take big risks in order to sustain and grow his business. He was also more confident than his father in his own abilities as businessman and brewer. Indeed, his belief in his own talents bordered at times on arrogance. Nevertheless, when it came to making IPA, his business instincts were exceptionally sound.

Labatt's IPA was an instant success. The virtues of London water enabled John Labatt to manufacture a product that eclipsed the one he had helped produce in Wheeling. Added to this, Labatt had read the market correctly. Beer tastes in Canada, as in Britain and the United States, were changing. Starting in the late 1860s, the dark brews began to lose significant ground to the pale and amber ales. By century's end, pale and amber ales constituted not quite one-half of the Canadian beer market.[47] At Labatt and Company, India pale ale constituted the bulk of production during the 1870s. Labatt was well positioned to prosper in the age of rail and pale ale.

The popularity of IPA led to a great leap in production. Between 1861 and 1870, annual production at the London Brewery doubled from 75,000 gallons (3,000 barrels) to 150,000 gallons (6,000 barrels) of beer. The level of production was substantially higher than at most other breweries in the province, which averaged roughly 22,000 gallons (880 barrels) of beer a year.[48]

In 1870, Labatt sold his standard barrels of beer for between $6 and $8 and his bottled "quarts" for fifteen cents. This translated into a gross income of $39,655, which was the seventh-highest return from a brewery posted in Ontario.[49] Out of that sum, John Labatt paid his fifteen employees wages in the amount of $4,500. Wages ranged from roughly $250 for the cooper to $800 for the general manager. Labatt's new apprentice brewer, Denis Mason, was given $350 and a place to stay in the Labatt household on the brewery site.[50] Labatt also paid for roughly 20,000 bushels of barley, 20,000 pounds of hops, the wood needed to fuel the ten-horsepower steam engine, as well as the hay and oats needed to feed the three teams of horses.[51] Finally, he paid the capital costs for the buildings and equipment, together with repairs, maintenance, and taxes, which included municipal taxes and an excise duty of one cent per pound of malt.[52] In total, his expenses in 1870 were about $30,000, giving him an operating profit of just under $10,000.[53]

The profit was substantial enough to stimulate talk about changing the ownership structure of the firm. The positive cash flow was now such that John Labatt could purchase his mother's half share in the brewery and pay her a stable monthly income. The partners agreed that the brewery had significantly appreciated in value since 1866 and was now worth, in their estimation, $87,280. At the age of fifty, Eliza Labatt agreed to lend her son the money necessary to purchase her half share in the brewery, in the form of two mortgages at 8 per cent interest per annum.[54] As a result, on 15 August 1872, after six years of partnership, John Labatt became the sole owner of the brewery that he had so efficiently managed since his father's death.

World's Fair as an Advertising Instrument

One of the biggest challenges brewers faced during the late nineteenth century was getting the word out about their products. The advent of the railway increased the geographical scope of the market and made it easier for brewers to ship their brands to distant places. This, along with brewers introducing new types of beer, meant beer drinkers had an unprecedented number of brands, ranging in quality and consistency, to choose from. One way to get recognition for one's brands was to have them judged "best in class" at a world's fair. Companies from around the globe were attracted to these exhibitions by the prospect of winning prizes and drawing attention to their products.[55] In a world that had not yet witnessed the advent of electronic media, expositions like this offered manufacturers a medium through which to situate their products, and the image of themselves, in the hearts and minds of a large public audience. Cyrus McCormick, for example, had been using the apparatus of world's fairs since the Crystal Palace Exhibition of 1851 to promote his harvesting machines at home and abroad. While his reaper was associated with science and progress and industrial might, McCormick himself posed as a heroic figure: the celebrated inventor-manufacturer whose name was known on every continent.[56] In the immediate aftermath of the exhibitions, he dispersed his agents, armed with tales of testimonials, awards, and honours from the fairs, to sell the reaper.[57] Like McCormick, the most avid competitors were those who sought greater reputations and markets for their goods. Manufacturers entered their products in various competitions for judging, placed them in the exposition's resting and eating places, built lavish exhibits for their promotion, and passed out souvenirs – all to court the public.

Of all the events of the Victorian era, perhaps none was more spectacular than the first world's fair that was held in the United States. Conceived to commemorate the 100th anniversary of American independence, the exposition took place in Philadelphia between May and November 1876. As with other world's fairs, the Centennial Exposition was designed to be a spectacle of progress.[58] In his opening address, U.S. president Ulysses S. Grant stated the official purpose of "this Centennial occasion" as being "to bring together in Philadelphia, for popular inspection, specimens of our attainments in the industrial and fine arts, and in literature, science and philosophy, as well as in the great business of agriculture and of commerce." It was a heady purpose for a gilded age.

The built environment alone was enough to amaze fair-goers. The exhibition occupied 236 acres of the most beautiful portion of West Fairmont Park.[59] On the grounds were 250 buildings, of which the biggest were the Main Exhibition Building, Machinery Hall, Agricultural Hall, Horticultural Hall, and Memorial Hall and Art Annex.[60] Within these buildings was an assortment of man-made items, from tasty new delights, like popcorn and soda pop, to new innovations such as the typewriter and the telephone. There were also powerful new products like the 1,400-horsepower Corliss steam engine that left more than one spectator dumbfounded.[61]

Symbolizing the fact that this was still very much the railway age, the Pennsylvania Railroad and the Reading Railroad constructed rail tracks from downtown Philadelphia to the site of the exhibition. During the 159 days of the exhibit, 5,907,333 passengers were carried on 66,467 train trips in that local commute for the one-way fare of ten cents. In total, almost 10 million paying guests attended the fair and more than 30,000 firms exhibited their goods at the exposition.

Among those companies that were drawn to the exhibition by the potential of advancing their material self-interests were the breweries of the attending nations. Despite the presence of a number of temperance societies, indeed arguably because of it, the brewers proudly and extravagantly celebrated their profession and promoted their products. In the northeast corner of the exhibition grounds, beside Agricultural Hall, they erected the Brewers' Building at a cost of $30,000. The building was 272 feet long by 96 feet wide. Perched on the crest of the roof was a beer barrel of immense proportions adorned with flags from all the brewing nations of the world. Signifying the rising popularity of another lighter beer, lager, the main entrance on the south side of the building was crowned by a statue of jolly King Gambrinus, the alleged inventor of this bottom-fermented beer.[62] Hop vines trailed along the south side of the building. Over the eastern entrance was a large trophy surrounding a medallion on which was inscribed the statement: "In the year 1863, 1,558,083 barrels of beer were brewed in the United States; in 1875, 8,743,744 barrels were produced from malt liquors, on which a tax was paid of $9,144,044."[63] The U.S. brewers were demonstrating their economic value to the nation, and not so subtly refuting the criticisms of the prohibitionists that the brewers, along with their conspirators in the liquor traffic – the vintners and distillers of the nation – were a detriment to society.

Inside the Brewers' Building were displays of every manner of product and implement used in the brewing trade. Perhaps the most spectacular exhibit was the "Centennial Brewery," which was erected at great expense by Charles Stoll of New York. He had installed a working brewery with a capacity of producing 150 barrels of beer at one time.[64] Opposite the brewery was a complete malt house with equipment provided by Hughes and Bergner of Philadelphia. Architectural and engineering firms displayed models of breweries and equipment. In all, there were 207 exhibitors that represented firms selling raw materials, refrigerating equipment, sheet metal implements, elevator buckets, cooperage, steam pumps and engines, and any other product that brewers might desire.

When Labatt arrived at the exhibition, he immediately made his way to the Brewers' Building as he was eager to see the latest and greatest developments in the field. Having examined some of the more remarkable innovations, like Frederick Schlich's patented automatic bottle-washing machine, he walked over to the "Ice House" where all the ales, lagers, and stouts were stored for the contest. He had entered his XXX Stout and India pale ale in the Centennial competition. Both of these brews had recently won silver medals at the Dominion of Canada Exposition. He was not, however, the only Canadian brewer to make the trip to Philadelphia. In total, seven Canadian brewers entered the competition. Along with Labatt, William Carling and Robert Arkell had travelled by train from London. A one-time hotelkeeper and independent maltster, Arkell had entered the business of brewing in 1872. His India pale ale, amber ale, and XXX Stout had taken the local market by storm, leading the *London Free Press* to declare that his brews were "all the rage" in and around London.[65] From Toronto came Eugene O'Keefe and the Davies brothers. In 1869, Thomas and Joseph Davies had inherited their father's Don Brewery on the west bank of the Don River, north of Queen Street West and east of River Street, and turned it into the most productive brewery in Canada.[66] They continued to manufacture their father's brand of Sparkling Cream and XXX Ale, in both pale ale and porter varieties. Labatt had long considered the Davies clan cutthroat competitors and knew they would be tough to beat in the City of Brotherly Love. Joseph Waterhouse from Chatham had also ventured to Philadelphia, seeking to make his mark. And finally, there was Samuel McLeod and his partner J.C. McNaughton, who owned and operated a brewery in Montreal.[67] All of these brewers entered the highly contested competition, hoping to be singled out as the manufacturer of the world's best ale – an objective judgment that they could subsequently use to promote their product.

In addition to the Canadian entries, there were seven of the "well-known breweries of Great Britain"; the Marree Brewery from Punjab India; seven breweries from Australia, which submitted ten samples of ale for judging; as well as breweries from Sweden, the Netherlands, Portugal, Chile, and the Argentine Republic.[68] Competition was stiff – far stiffer than at past world fairs – and Labatt found himself embroiled in internecine warfare among an international brotherhood of brewers in pursuit of common goals. While the immediate goal was to win gold, the ultimate prize was to win over the hearts, minds, and pocketbooks of consumers at home and abroad. As Labatt was profoundly aware, his market fortunes rode on his showing in Philadelphia.

When the judging was complete, all of the Canadian brewers could take a great deal of pride in being congratulated by the Centennial commission for "careful and intelligent brewing."[69] But it was Labatt who was singled out for special praise. While his XXX stout beer was pronounced by the international judging panel to be "first-rate," his India pale ale was awarded a gold medal.[70] In addition, he received a certificate of excellence for his malt.

Winning the award extended the reputation of the London Brewery beyond Canada's boundaries. Labatt used the world's fair to build respectability for his products and to support his sales. At home, he seized the advertising opportunity that the victory gave him. In a series of advertisements that appeared in the regional press, he trumpeted the news of his success in Philadelphia. For example, an advertisement for Labatt's ale and stout that appeared in the *Globe* in December 1876 started with the line: "The Centennial Prize!"[71] Another advertisement in the same paper that appeared a year later stated that the "highest international and Canadian medals were award to John Labatt."[72] By March 1877,

Figure 2.4 Labatt's India Pale Ale label featuring the medals that Labatt won at the International Exposition in Paris, c. 1885.

Labatt was including images in his ads of the medals that he had won.[73] In the following years, he placed his ads in directories, newspapers, and magazines that ranged in size from small community pamphlets such as Gore Bay's *Algoma Conservator* to newspapers like the *Toronto Empire*.[74] He also targeted specific audiences on a regular basis by advertising in such market-specific serials as the *Farmers' Advocate* (the nation's most popular agricultural journal), the *Labor Advocate* (the official magazine of the Knights of Labor), and the *Irish Canadian* (an Irish-Catholic periodical).[75] Further demonstrating his ingenuity in the art of product promotion, in December 1885, Labatt became the first brewer in Canada to use a label facsimile as a regular feature in his advertisements. The label featured images of the medal that his IPA also won at the International Exposition in Paris in 1878. In addition, Labatt's ads often featured an image of the brewery, which appealed to consumers at a time when factories were symbols of modernity, progress, and standardization. It was not until the 1890s that other Canadian brewers followed suit.[76]

John Labatt was in the vanguard of the advertising revolution in Canada. At a time when other Canadian businessmen were beginning to employ the advertising services of others, Labatt oversaw his own advertising campaigns. His marketing was unique among the brewers. One of the first to engage in brand-driven marketing, he crafted his advertisements to highlight the qualities of a particular brand. The ads clearly identified the product, the manufacturer, and why the product was worth purchasing – the essential themes of brand-driven marketing. The tactic encouraged product recognition and kept Labatt's advertisements from disappearing in the cluttered newspaper pages of the Victorian age.[77] This simple yet clever innovation proved valuable in the struggle to distinguish his ales and stouts from others in the increasingly integrated markets of south Ontario.

Conclusion

Labatt had steamed into the age of rail and pale ale. Between 1855 and 1877, production increased almost tenfold in response to the rising demand for Labatt's ales and stouts. In meeting the challenges of the period, Labatt developed a number of firm-specific advantages over the competition. Sensing the shift in consumer tastes away from heavy porter, ales, and stouts, John Labatt II took a calculated risk and began producing and promoting India pale ale. Appreciating the value of keeping one's brands in the public's eye, he ploughed whatever money he made from his beer sales back into heavier advertising in an effort to maintain market share. His utilization of brand-driven marketing fostered brand loyalty and added to the brewery's economies of scale. One effect of this was to increase the gap between large and small brewers.

By 1877, Labatt was one of a select number of big regional brewers who were selling their products all over Ontario. The end of the military's stay in London had caused Labatt to become one of the first brewers in the colony to use the railroad to transport his beer into the villages, towns, and cities of the province with "speed, economy, regularity, safety and convenience," just as Thomas Keefer had promised. The railway transformed the business of brewing in Ontario from a locally oriented cottage industry to a modern industrial enterprise, utilizing the latest technologies and production and distribution techniques.

Having formulated a strategy of geographic expansion into those areas linked to London by a ribbon of steel, Labatt adjusted the organization of his business to more effectively distribute and market his goods in distant places. The agency system that he pioneered was the most significant feature of beer distribution in Victorian Canada. Agencies became the lifeblood of the brewing industry. Some "fast followers" quickly copied Labatt's move. The price was high for not doing so. Breweries that didn't expand their scale and scope increasingly found themselves falling behind in the competitive business of Canadian brewing.

"More Money than Since or Before"

How John Labatt's Brewery Prospered during the Canada Temperance Act, 1878–89

Judge Macdonald: "Did you find the manufacture of malt liquors decrease?"
John Labatt: "No, I made more money during the Scott Act time [the period
of the Canada Temperance Act, 1878–89] than I ever did since or before."
~ Royal Commission on the Liquor Traffic,
Minutes of Evidence[1]

On 8 May 1878, the Canadian federal government of Alexander Mackenzie attempted to restrict the production and consumption of alcohol by passing the
Canada Temperance Act. Known popularly as the Scott Act for its sponsor,
Richard William Scott, leader of the government in the Senate, it gave municipal
and county governments the legal authority to go "dry" if a majority of local inhabitants voted in favour of prohibiting the retailing of "intoxicating liquors."
Supporters of the Act hoped that the law would put brewers of the nation out of
business. While the Act remained law until 1946, when it was successfully challenged and deemed unconstitutional by the Judicial Committee of the Privy
Council, it was only widely embraced during the period 1878 to 1889. The Scott
Act represented an unprecedented external shock to those, like John Labatt, who
made a living from liquor trafficking. How did John Labatt manage to not only
survive but also prosper during a period of local-option prohibition?

Teetotalism and the Canada Temperance Act

During the second half of the nineteenth century, the temperance movement gained ground in North America, Scandinavia, and Britain.[2] While the temperance movement in each of these geopolitical regions varied, it was generally committed to bringing about a reduction in the consumption of alcoholic beverages. At an earlier point in the temperance movement's evolution, the means to the glorious end of dry heaven on earth was moral suasion.[3] But as the movement evolved and the apparatus of the state became more developed and pronounced, the drys in society began to argue that moral regulation was the means to ending the reign of "King Alcohol."[4] "Righteous laws" should be enacted, proclaimed Canadian temperance advocate Francis S. Spence, "for the suppression of intemperance." Like temperance advocates elsewhere in North America and in Europe, Spence believed that by wiping out the liquor traffic, all of society's troubles would be washed away.[5] He joined the chorus of dry voices in calling for the state to use its vast legislative powers to prohibit the production and consumption of John Barleycorn.

In an effort to have the state pass such laws, the prohibitionists began pressuring politicians and the public alike. In North America and Northern Europe, they came together to form lobby groups.[6] In Canada, the most powerful of the groups was Francis Spence's Dominion Alliance for the Total Suppression of the Liquor Traffic. At the Alliance's inaugural convention in 1875, Canadian prohibitionists laid out their strategy for putting brewers like Labatt and the rest of the liquor traffic out of business.[7] The decision was made to lobby the government for legislation prohibiting the production and consumption of booze and simultaneously to change the culture around imbibing. With this two-pronged approach spelled out, the Alliance began pressuring Prime Minister Alexander Mackenzie and his Liberal government for dry legislation. Unlike the man who previously held the highest elected office in the land, Canada's first prime minister John A. Macdonald, Mackenzie abhorred drink. Nevertheless, he felt that on this issue each local populace should decide. Consequently, in 1878, his government passed the Canada Temperance Act.

John Labatt and the rest in the Canadian brewing community had hoped that beer would be excluded from the legislation. After all, they pointed out, beer was a less alcoholic beverage and thus far less damaging than hard liquor. "My contention is that if the Government would do all they [sic] could to encourage the use of these malt beverages to the exclusion of the stronger ones," stated Toronto

brewer Eugene O'Keefe, "it would be better for the people."[8] Labatt shared
O'Keefe's view.[9] Indeed, the brewing community generally believed that beer was
a benefit to society. They had long maintained that beer was a "temperance drink,"
and much safer to consume than either water or high wines. As early as 1821,
Kingston brewer Thomas Dalton had told the people in his community to "avoid
stagnant water, and ardent spirits, drink copiously of genuine Beer, and you may
confidently bid defiance to that pest of all uncleared Countries, the Fever and
Ague."[10] During the first half of the nineteenth century, this view captured the
popular imagination, so only the most radical drys advocated prohibiting the manufacture or retail sale of malt liquor.

But a number of developments took place during the last quarter of the nineteenth century that shifted the popular perception around beer, brewing, and
beer drinking. First, by the 1870s, Canadians had a new variety of relatively safe
and affordable beverages available to them. As early as 1857, the *Abstainer*, a Halifax temperance periodical, had argued that coffee should take the place of beer
"as the working beverage."[11] With the decline in the price of coffee and tea after
1870, thousands of families of all levels of society began brewing these hot, aro-
matic, non-alcoholic beverages on a daily basis. Milk was also widely available in
towns and cities.[12] As well, the soda pop that Labatt had first seen and sampled at
the Centennial Exposition in Philadelphia in 1876 was slowly making its way into
Canada. And finally, the water supply was generally becoming more sanitary –
notwithstanding the comments of the *Globe* in 1882 that Toronto's water was
"drinkable sewage."[13] Thus, a number of material developments taking place
served to undermine beer's traditional role in society as *the* temperance drink.

The second development that caused a shift in the culture of beer related to
the first, but took place at the level of perceptions and ideals. In the battle between the wets and the drys, the latter were winning the propaganda war.[14] In
their minds and messaging, no distinction existed between the brewers, vintners,
and distillers of the nation. Together they were the "merchants of misery and de-
spair," each as guilty as the other at causing intemperance and social decay.[15] The
point was driven home in a cartoon published in the satiric magazine *The Grip*.
The drawing, by cartoonist and staunch prohibitionist John Bengough, was of a
hellish-looking tavern – dark, unclean, impure, and dangerous. Standing beside
the barmaid, "Miss Canada," was her partner in the immoral business of booze
peddling, the devil. As Miss Canada worked the taps of the beer keg, Satan
tempted his patrons to sin, pouring them "murder malt," "crime rum," and "riot
gin." Like other prohibitionist propaganda of the period, the message of this

cartoon was clear: drinking *any* intoxicating beverage, be it beer, wine, or hard liquor, would condemn one to an impure, unchristian life in a living hell.[16]

As a consequence of the prohibitionists' propaganda campaign and the resulting shift in perceptions of beer, brewing, and beer drinking, the brewers were not exempt from the Canada Temperance Act. They found themselves bound by clause 96 of the Act, which stated that "no person ... shall, within such country or city [that has invoked the law], by himself, servant, or agent ... sell or barter ... any spirituous or other intoxicating liquor, or mixed liquor capable of being used as a beverage."[17] Any lingering doubt about beer's inclusion in the new legislation was laid to rest by the following section of the Act.[18] In the eyes of the law, "intoxicating liquors" included "brandy, rum, whiskey or spirituous liquors, wine, ale, beer, porter, cider, or vinous or fermented liquors."[19] In short, the law suppressed the regular retail trade in beer in those areas where the Canada Temperance Act was in force.

The passage of the Act was the first federal legislative salvo launched in the battle over the bottle and it came as a wake-up call for those like Labatt who had made significant investments in their breweries. Immediately after the passage of the Canada Temperance Act, the Dominion Brewers and Maltsters Association (DBMA) was formed with John Stevern, a brewer from Belleville, as its first president. John Labatt was one of the principals agitating for a collective reaction on the part of the brewers of the nation to the passage of the Scott Act. He was also one of the first to make a sizable financial contribution to the DBMA's war chest, which would be used to influence those in power.[20]

At the first meeting of the DBMA, the decision was made to lobby the federal government for the Scott Act's repeal. The DBMA believed such an action was possible since John A. Macdonald was back in power. Too moralistic, too Ontario-centric, too ideological, and far too dry, Mackenzie was unable to achieve re-election in 1878. Macdonald, on the other hand, was a pragmatic politician with an astute sense of the Canadian condition.[21] While in opposition, he had formulated the National Policy, promising Canadians that if returned to power, he would implement a tariff to protect domestic manufacturers from foreign competition, which, in turn, would create jobs, stem the tide of immigration to the United States, and create an internal market for the farmers of the nation.

The idea of a National Policy to stimulate economic development and restore economic prosperity resonated with a majority of Canadians. At a time when the laissez-faire economic doctrines of Adam Smith were being critically questioned by philosophers and public policy-makers in industrializing nations, Canadians viewed the nationalist economic stance of Macdonald as progressive and modern.[22] As a consequence, they rewarded him in the federal election of 1878, giving his Conservatives a majority of the seats in the House of Commons.

As part of the National Policy, the duty on imported ale, porter, and stout was raised to eighteen cents per imperial gallon, thus protecting domestic brewers like Labatt from foreign competition.[23] Simultaneously, Macdonald lowered the tax on malt manufactured in the country back to the level that it had been before Mackenzie and his Liberals had come to power.[24] This led many to believe that the Conservative government was a friend of the brewing community.[25] Critics also pointed to the presence of brewer John Carling in the federal Cabinet. As a member of Parliament, Carling represented London more or less continuously between 1867 and 1895. The only time he was out of politics was during the Liberal-government years of 1874–78 – the very period that saw the formation of the Dominion Alliance, a tax increase on manufactured malt, and the ratification of the Canada Temperance Act. With the Conservatives back in power, Labatt and the rest of the beer lobby were optimistic that the Act's days were numbered.

To hasten that end, Labatt was asked to write to the prime minister on behalf of the brewing community.[26] Whether or not he did so remains a mystery. But it would not have mattered, even if he did. On Parliament Hill, there was no desire to revisit the liquor question. Despite his own fondness for drink, Macdonald was unwilling to come to the defence of the liquor traffic. With his federal Cabinet divided on the liquor question along religious, regional, and linguistic lines, "Old Tomorrow" recognized the political advantages of inaction and defended the status quo. By allowing counties or municipalities to prohibit the retail sale of liquor by majority vote, the Canada Temperance Act relieved the federal government of responsibility for the law. Having passed the Act, the government had no real reason to pay any attention to Labatt or any other brewer. Until his death in 1891, Macdonald did little to further the interests of the brewing community. The questions surrounding alcohol and its place in society split Canadians more or less down the middle. In Quebec, for example, there was very little support for the Scott Act and even less for the idea of full-fledged prohibition, whereas in the rural communities across the rest of Canada with strong Anglo-Protestant populations, support was relatively high. As a man whose paramount concern was always unity, Macdonald was unwilling to take any action that might divide his party and, more importantly, fracture the nascent nation.

The Canada Temperance Act gave a new sense of purpose to the dry forces across the country. Under the guidance of the Dominion Alliance for the Total

Suppression of the Liquor Traffic, local Scott Act associations orchestrated petition drives to get signatures from the requisite 25 per cent of the electors in each
town or county to force a referendum on the liquor question. When that was accomplished, the associations worked at winning over local populations to their
cause. By the mid-1880s, their zeal had paid off. Much of the Maritimes, parts of
Quebec, and two counties in Manitoba went dry. In John Labatt's home province,
where the bulk of his sales were made, the Canada Temperance Act was adopted
in twenty-five counties and two cities.[27] If there was any consolation for Labatt,
it was that London never held a Scott Act vote. The tradition of beer making and
beer drinking was too deeply rooted in the community. As other cities and communities went dry, London, Ontario, remained wet.

The problem for Labatt was that, by 1878, a healthy portion of Labatt's sales
was outside of London. This was not the case for most of his main competitors.
As Eugene O'Keefe told the Royal Commission on the Liquor Traffic in 1895,
"my business was principally in the city [Toronto] at that time."[28] The Royal
Commission had been struck in 1892 to review the operation of the Canada Temperance Act and to consider the merits of enacting a new federal law prohibiting
the manufacture of intoxicating liquors. Labatt also gave testimony before the
Commission reporting that his business had fallen off slightly following the enactment of the Act.[29] The pressing need to compensate for the initial decline in
sales in Ontario prompted Labatt to look to those places that had held the temperance forces at bay. He was motivated to move before his main competitors
needed, or thought, to.

Expanding East and West

No province received the Canada Temperance Act more coolly than Quebec. The
Protestant moral urge toward prohibition that existed in English Canada was
simply not evident in the predominantly French-speaking and Roman Catholic
province. In addition, the brewing lobby was far more potent in Quebec than
elsewhere in Canada. As a result, referenda were held in only eleven counties; nine
of these were in the Eastern Townships, where a strong Anglo-Protestant population existed. In the eleven plebiscites, only five returned majorities in favour of
the law, and only one of these – in Chicoutimi – was in a county that was French-
Canadian.[30] Thus, most of the province remained wet during the Scott Act era,
leading John Labatt to fix his sights on the beer drinkers of Quebec.

Of all the markets in *la belle province*, Montreal was by far the most attractive. With a population of over 150,000, of which 20 per cent were, like Labatt himself, of Irish ancestry, Montreal was Canada's largest urban centre. In 1878, Montreal had a population that was almost double that of Toronto and five times that of London, Ontario.[31] Despite being home to one of the first temperance societies in North America, Montrealers had decided to remain wet during the Scott Act period. As a result, the number of places to tipple increased substantially, although the quality of the establishments, in the eyes of some, diminished accordingly.[32] Between 1879 and 1887, the number of liquor licences handed out in Montreal to hotels, restaurants, saloons, and groceries increased from 723 to 1,273. According to William B. Lambe, collector of provincial revenue for the city and district of Montreal, in addition to these legal drinking establishments, there were between 2,000 and 4,000 establishments in the city selling liquor without a licence during these years.[33] By 1887, there was roughly one legal drinking establishment for every 130 inhabitants, leading one temperance advocate to lament that Montreal was "the most drunken city on the continent."[34]

People of every social stratum drank – rich, poor, and those in between. But increasingly, the tavern was becoming the workingman's social club, and as Labatt was profoundly aware, beer was becoming the worker's beverage.[35] That is not to say that the alcoholic drink of choice of Canadians was malt liquor. That would come later, on the heels of the noble experiment and as a result of the brewing lobby's creation of a cult of moderation. But the trend toward lighter, more moderate beverages was certainly apparent during the 1880s.[36] At a time when Montreal was experiencing its own industrial revolution, members of the working class poured into such taverns as the Crown and Sceptre, the Horseshoe, the Suburban, French Marie's, and Joe Beef's Canteen on the corner of Rue de la Commune and Rue de Callière in the port district.[37] In 1882, visitors to Joe Beef's Canteen consumed 480 gallons (20 barrels) of beer each week.[38] Across the province, yearly per capita beer consumption increased from 1.51 gallons in 1879 to 2.82 gallons in 1889.[39] Total beer consumption in the province doubled during the same period from 2,092,521 gallons (87,300 barrels) to 4,144,904 gallons (165,796 barrels) of beer.[40]

Meeting much of this demand were some of the oldest and largest breweries in North America. If a brewer could make it in Victorian Montreal, they could probably make it anywhere. A great beer-making tradition had existed in Montreal since the Conquest of New France in 1763. A century after the Conquest, there were ten breweries in Montreal producing 1,660,000 gallons (66,400 barrels)

Figure 3.1 Labatt's agency on De Lorimier Avenue in Montreal, c. 1885.

of beer.[41] The largest of the existing Montreal breweries was not, however, the oldest. That distinction went to the Molson Brewery, which was established in 1786 in Montreal. But brewing at this venerable firm had, by the 1850s, become "a secondary enterprise," and production in 1863 was only 150,000 gallons (6,000 barrels).[42] This was substantially less than the brewing taking place at Montreal's largest brewery, Dow and Company.[43] By 1878, Dow was producing almost a million gallons. By comparison, Labatt's brewery was relatively small. While the capacity at the London Brewery was 750,000 gallons (30,000 barrels), production in 1878 was far below that amount. Nevertheless, the 250,550 gallons (10,022 barrels) that Labatt produced that year earned him a profit of almost $30,000.[44] Always confident in his abilities as a brewer and a businessman, Labatt ploughed the profits back into the business and headed to Montreal to take on the likes of Dow, Dawes, and Molson.

Given the excess capacity at the London factory, John Labatt would probably have made his way to Montreal eventually. But the passage of the Canada Temperance Act accelerated his push east. In 1878, he opened an agency in Montreal to distribute his product and began shipping his beer in barrels via the Grand Trunk Railway. Initially, he was forced to hire an independent merchant to sell his beer. He had disliked doing this in the past, for all of the reasons that manifested themselves after J.B. Richer began peddling Labatt's beer in Montreal.

A wholesale grocer located at the corner of La Gauchetière and St Charles Bor-
romée streets, Richer was an experienced distributor of perishable goods. During
his years in business, he established a network of valuable contacts in the city,
many of whom were engaged in the local liquor trade. While Richer approached
his new job with an admirable level of professionalism, his other commercial
commitments drew heavily on his time. This concerned Labatt, who preferred
having a sales force made up of men dedicated to selling his beer and his beer
alone. Consequently, in 1885, he transferred the agency to P.L.N. Beaudry, who
agreed to devote all of his energy to promoting Labatt's ales and stouts. In return,
Labatt paid Beaudry a salary of $2,500 a year plus $5 for each railway car of beer
(roughly 1,650 gallons) he sold until his remuneration totalled $3,000 per year.[45]

Labatt was determined to make a mark in Montreal. On 30 December 1885, he
wrote Beaudry, stating "push it [India pale ale] all you can and if you find it takes,
as you expected it should, push the draught ale business for all you are worth."[46]
Success in the business of brewing has long been determined by the ability to get
one's products into the hands of consumers. In Victorian Montreal, this meant
first getting one's draught beer into a tavern, saloon, or hotel. Ordinarily, the owners of these drinking establishments, even one as popular as Joe Beef's, could only
afford to have one or two brands of malt liquor on draught, due to the perishable
nature of the beverage in the tapped keg and the cost of the draught equipment.
Therefore, competition for outlets was fierce.

In order to get their beer on tap, brewers offered a variety of inducements to
those in the licensed trades. These inducements included spending money at the
bar treating the customers, discounts on the per-barrel price of beer, easy credit
terms, and paying for the cost of the draught equipment. The first of these,
known as "spending," was generally regarded as the most unfortunate practice in
the brewing business, yet all the major Canadian brewers engaged in it. The
spending system was pretty straight-forward: in exchange for a tavern-, saloon-,
or hotel-owner agreeing to put a brewer's beer on draught, the brewer agreed to
treat the regular clientele to rounds of drinks whenever he or his representative
visited the bar. This was an expensive way to gain a share of the market, not only
because the beverages of other manufacturers had to be purchased during the
spending spree but also because representatives like Beaudry felt obliged to drink
with customers in one establishment after another.

Sometimes the practice of spending undermined the constitution and efficiency of Labatt's agents. At the Royal Commission on the Liquor Traffic, Labatt
told his examiners that "there was not an unsteady man about the brewery."[47]

The statement may have been true. But what Labatt did not share with the examiners was that many of his agents were drinking to the point that it was compromising their health. For example, his representative in Ottawa, Mr Blackburn, was experiencing bouts of delirium tremens, a severe form of alcohol withdrawal resulting in such symptoms as confusion, diarrhea, insomnia, nightmares, disorientation, agitation, and other signs of severe autonomic instability. Labatt found Blackburn's situation unacceptable, writing to Blackburn that he had no doubt it was "brought on by drinking too much and getting your blood out of order."[48] Labatt paternalistically warned Blackburn that if he continued to drink and spend the way that he had in the past "it would end fatally."[49] Labatt's general manager, Fredrick William Raymond, sought to terminate Blackburn's employment. Raymond had joined the Labatt brewery in 1884, agreeing to supervise the accounting and administration of the firm in return for an annual salary of $800 in the first year and $900 in the second. He promised to serve John Labatt "faithfully and diligently" and, in the event of his departure, not to practice the "art and mystery" of brewing with another person anywhere in the provinces of Ontario or Quebec.[50] Raymond was not a brewer by training, but rather an accountant. He was a man of business, a man of numbers. But what he lacked in artistic flair, he made up for in commercial acumen. He was far more ruthless, skeptical, and profit-oriented than his boss. He wanted Blackburn fired. Labatt, however, felt differently, given that Blackburn had promised to quit his excessive drinking. Labatt understood that the practice of spending was necessary in order to get one's barrel behind the bar. But when the drinking and spending became excessive and compromised the constitution of his employees and the integrity of his firm, he demanded that the practice stop.

Labatt, however, never had any reason to offer Beaudry such advice. The Montreal agent drank only in moderation and never lost self-control in public. Despite various accords between Labatt and other brewers not to undersell one another in each other's markets, price-cutting occurred. However, Labatt did not like this to be publicized. He believed there was an intrinsic link between price and quality, and by selling his beer at a lower price than his principal competitors, "it will be considered an inferior ale."[51] Nevertheless, out of the public's view, Beaudry offered discounts of up to 15 per cent in order to get Labatt's barrels on tap in Montreal.[52] He also was willing, when pushed, to pay for the bar owner's costs of putting the beer on tap. This strategy proved expensive in the long run: bar owners demanded that Labatt also pay for the maintenance and repair of the pumps and pipes that had been installed. "This might go on indefinitely," wrote a frustrated F.W. Raymond to John Labatt, "[since] they not only ask us to put in the pumps but are continually at us to keep them in repair."[53] Nevertheless, in the short run the practice was effective.

Labatt's inducements led to success in Montreal.[54] By the end of the period under review, Labatt was sending fifty-three railroad cars of ale (3,498 barrels), or roughly 15 per cent of his total production, to Montreal for distribution and consumption.[55] So much beer was pouring into Beaudry's agency that a new building was needed. The two-storey, 10,000-square-foot structure at De Lorimier Avenue near St Catherine Street was one of the largest of its kind in Canada. Labatt financed the construction and thereafter retained ownership of the building, which was "fully supplied with every convenience."[56]

Simultaneously with his geographic expansion to the east, Labatt pushed west. In the newly minted province of Manitoba, beer consumption increased almost eightfold during the period 1878 to 1889. This was attributed to the population of Manitoba more than doubling during the period and to the fact that, on average, each person drank twice as much beer at the end of the period as at the beginning.[57] As early as 1882, Labatt had sensed that the west was a land of opportunity. His business instincts proved sound that summer when two of his "travellers" (i.e., travelling salesmen) returned from Manitoba with the news that there was a market for Labatt's ales and stouts. They also reported that a total of seven small, local brewers, four of whom were in the province's most-populated city, Winnipeg, were meeting the demand.[58] The opportunity was too good for John Labatt to pass up. He told his travellers to return to the west and to be aggressive in finding buyers for his stock. His instructions, and their subsequent actions, paid off the following summer. From Port Arthur came an order for "84 casks bottled and 31 barrels draught"; from Portage La Prairie, an order for "100 casks bottled"; from Brandon, an order for "one freight car" of beer. At twenty-eight cents per gallon, Labatt grossed $462 from the Brandon order, about half the amount he would make from an order twice the size that he had received from licensed trades in Winnipeg.

The completion of the Canadian Pacific Railway (CPR) opened up a whole new market for businessmen like Labatt, who were constantly looking for new places to peddle their products. "In 1886 when the line opened," notes historian Michael Bliss, "it became possible to travel and ship from one end of Canada to the other via the Canadian Pacific Railway, the largest and most important business in the country, the first pan-Canadian corporation."[59] From Labatt's brewery in London, the CPR stretched west, across the Prairies, to British Columbia, where a strong

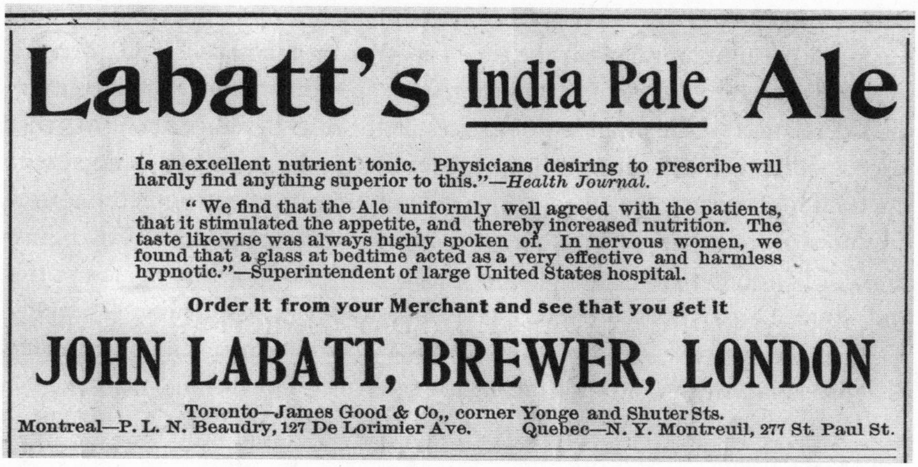

Labatt's India Pale Ale

Is an excellent nutrient tonic. Physicians desiring to prescribe will hardly find anything superior to this."—*Health Journal.*

" We find that the Ale uniformly well agreed with the patients, that it stimulated the appetite, and thereby increased nutrition. The taste likewise was always highly spoken of. In nervous women, we found that a glass at bedtime acted as a very effective and harmless hypnotic."—Superintendent of large United States hospital.

Order it from your Merchant and see that you get it

JOHN LABATT, BREWER, LONDON

Toronto—James Good & Co,, corner Yonge and Shuter Sts.
Montreal—P. L. N. Beaudry, 127 De Lorimier Ave.   Quebec—N. Y. Montreuil, 277 St. Paul St.

Figure 3.2 During the Scott Act period, Labatt often used typewritten ads to communicate the message that the consumption of beer was beneficial to the health of both men and women. This ad, which was placed in the *Canadian Churchman* in 1889, used the testimony of medical professionals, which was often sexist and gendered, to make the case for beer.

beer-drinking culture existed. Even before the ratification of the Canada Temperance Act, B.C. had the highest per capita beer consumption in the nation. The passage of the Scott Act seemed only to exaggerate the pattern. In 1878, beer consumption in British Columbia was 152,621 gallons (6,104 barrels), meaning that each man, woman, and child was drinking on average 3.39 gallons of beer per year, between three and six times the amount they were drinking at the same time on the opposite coast.[60] By 1889, British Columbians were drinking on average 5.944 gallons of beer per person, resulting in a province-wide consumption of 515,103 gallons (20,604 barrels).[61]

Meeting this demand were a number of local brewers. Commercial brewing had existed in British Columbia since the gold rush. The moral impulse to brew a "weaker drink" did not exist on the west coast the way that it had in New France during Jean Talon's intendancy (1665–75).[62] There was no premature birth of the industry on the west coast as there had been in Quebec. Furthermore, unlike on the east coast, or in Ontario, brewing did not emerge out of a desire on the part of budding brewers to drain soldiers and sailors of their pay packets. Instead, brewing in B.C. emerged out of an existing demand for beer from those engaged in B.C.'s primary-product industries – fishing, lumbering, and especially mining.

Between the 1858 Fraser River gold rush and 1890, breweries operated continuously in British Columbia.[63] By the time Labatt arrived in 1886, the B.C. brewing industry was on the verge of a transition, from an industry made up of privately owned, relatively small providers of a necessary frontier beverage to one in which large, modern breweries owned by multiple shareholders began to compete with the traditional, privately owned plants.[64] Local brewers faced competition from imported products from the very inception of the industry. As in Labatt's hometown of London, the B.C. population preferred the taste of British ales, porter, and stouts. Large British brewers, like Allsops, Younger, and Tennants, supplied B.C. drinkers with beer, in bottles and barrels, through the many liquor importers established in British Columbia during the gold rush.[65] By the mid-1880s, British Columbians could also purchase Bass ale and Guinness stout, as well as Val Blatz Milwaukee beer.[66]

For Labatt, freight rates and the cost of advertising a brand name new to British Columbia meant that it was much more expensive to do business on the west coast than closer to home. In Victoria, for example, his pale ale sold for $12.80 per "slack barrel" of five dozen quart bottles.[67] The price was roughly twice his selling price in Ontario and Quebec. And also about twice as much as the best imported brands from the United States.[68] Therefore, unlike in Manitoba and Quebec, Labatt found it impossible to gain a permanent presence and generate any sort of profit in British Columbia.

Industry and Firm Specific Outcomes

The evidence given at the Royal Commission by Labatt and other brewers from across the country demonstrated the extent to which the brewing industry had been transformed during the period. In 1878, there were 134 breweries in Canada producing 8,658,356 gallons of malt liquor. In 1890, the number of breweries had been reduced to 129, but the amount of beer and ale being manufactured had almost doubled to 17,196,155 gallons.[69] Admittedly these numbers paled in comparison to those of the great beer-producing nations. By 1894, brewers in the United Kingdom produced over 1 billion gallons of beer.[70] A year later, 1,771 brewers in the United States manufactured 1.04 billion gallons of the beverage, while German brewers produced 1.2 billion gallons of malt liquor.[71] Nevertheless, by the early 1890s, brewing in Canada was playing an important part in Canadian

Figure 3.3 Workers in front of the Labatt brewery, c. 1890. For brewery workers, life was often difficult. The work generally began before dawn, and when the day was done after dusk, the men were absolutely exhausted. Brewery work at the end of the nineteenth century required muscle, dexterity, and skill, as men lugged burlap sacks of hops and barley, and heaved kegs and bottles of beer as part of their daily routine. Two dozen quarts of bottled beer in a wooden case weighed about ninety pounds and had to be lifted by hand, one after another, hour after hour, onto horse-drawn wagons. For those who were given the bone-jarring task of delivering the beer to market over rough roads, the work ran from Monday to Saturday; on Sunday, the wagon "drivers" were expected to feed their teams of horses. At a time when the industry was only semi-automated, many other operations – like bottle- and keg-washing – had to be done by hand. Boys usually did the mind-numbing work of putting the labels and tin-foil tops on the bottles. In return for their labour, brewery workers received only a modest wage and there were no pension plans, medical services, paid holidays, or sick leaves to make the job more appealing. When employees did not show up for work, others were expected to pick up the slack.

economic life. In 1893, the Canadian brewing industry was providing direct employment to 1,724 workers and was paying $774,411 in annual wages.[72] The majority of plants were still in Ontario, where 82 breweries employed 1,047 people and manufactured $3,578,874 worth of malt liquor.[73]

One of the most striking developments of the period was gradual concentration of the industry in a few production centres. By 1891, London and Toronto were the principal hubs of the trade. These two cities were home to the fourteen largest breweries in Ontario.[74] Labatt was one of them. Together, the "Big Fourteen" produced over 50 per cent of all the beer, by value, in Ontario.[75] They dwarfed the breweries at the other end of the spectrum. Whereas, on average, between six and seven people were working at each of the smallest forty-five breweries in the province, the workforce at the Big Fourteen numbered thirty-eight or thirty-nine people. John Labatt helped bring up the industry average by employing seventy men and boys.[76]

The other notable microeconomic development of the period was that the big breweries were producing far more beer than could be locally absorbed.[77] This was clearly the case in London, Ontario. In combination with Carling, Labatt manufactured approximately $500,000 worth of ale and stout in 1891, yet the local population consumed only $54,361 worth of beer that year.[78] When Thomas Alexander, an Inland Revenue officer, appeared before the Royal Commission on the Liquor Traffic, he was asked specifically about the nature of the London-Middlesex brewing trade. "Have you any means of knowing whether the malt liquor made in these years [1878 to 1889] was sent out of the district, or consumed in it?" the Commissioners asked. "Breweries like Carling and Labatt shipped a great deal away from here to Montreal, Hamilton, Ottawa, and Toronto," he responded, "but with the other breweries it is mostly local consumption."[79]

While the Scott Act was in force, Labatt seized the opportunities of the railway age and expanded his distribution network in order to tap into the growing demand for beer in distant places. As the railway expanded across the nation, and new regions of the country became settled, Labatt's boxcars laden with beer followed swiftly behind. Ironically, the Scott Act, which was designed to do harm to those in the liquor traffic, had the reverse effect on Labatt. Between 1879 and 1889, Labatt recorded unprecedented profits (see table 3.1). Like the successful banks of the age, Labatt first grew by aggressively getting established in new territories and then consolidated his position by wiping out the competition and absorbing their market share.[80]

Table 3.1

Beer production and net profit at Labatt, 1878–89

Year	No. of barrels brewed	No. of barrels used to fill bottles	Net profit
1878	10,022	1,922	$29,415.36
1879	13,482	2,516	$49,851.03
1880	15,162	2,628	$62,866.11
1881	17,290	2,472	$57,126.01
1882	21,104	4,204	$66,250.08
1883	22,673	3,980	$47,315.34
1884	22,907	4,384	$66,892.69
1885	19,702	3,298	$51,432.26
1886	20,999	4,614	$72,574.72
1887	22,855	5,380	$74,078.76
1888	22,518	5,108	$70,391.59
1889	21,611	6,728	$55,117.15

Source: Letter Book, vols. I and II, *Labatt Collection*.

When he appeared before the Royal Commission in 1895, Labatt was asked to explain how he had made so much money during what were supposedly temperance times. "How do you account for that?" he was asked. Labatt told the commissioners that an increasing proportion of his beer sales were "all over the country in bottles," which Labatt admitted was "something more" profitable than draft ale.[81] Prior to the onset of the Canada Temperance Act, wood barrels were the most frequently used containers for packaging beer. Due to the combination of their relatively high cost and breakability, glass beer bottles were not widely used prior to the 1870s. Admittedly, John Molson had sold his beer in bottles beginning in the early 1800s, but bottled beer from the historic Montreal brewery, as at breweries elsewhere, represented only a small percentage of total sales until the last quarter of the nineteenth century.[82]

But during the 1870s, a number of technological and economic developments changed beer packaging. Advancements in glassmaking technology enhanced bottle strength and lowered the unit cost, and bottle closures improved significantly.[83]

With these technological improvements and attending economic advantages, Canadian brewers proved more willing to bottle their beer.

As important as these technological advances were to the growing popularity of bottled beer, so too was the passage of the Canada Temperance Act. When a city, town, or county went dry, brewers could no longer legally sell their beer in those areas. But in spite of the law, some did. Labatt thought the Act "was a big humbug."[84] As he told the Royal Commission, he had no moral qualms about contravening the law, which in his opinion "did more harm than good."[85] Time and again, men would show up at his plant in London or at one of his agencies across the land and purchase beer in bottles. Bottles were smaller than barrels, so it was easier to hide, camouflage, and conceal the beer. Furthermore, beer bottles were somewhat unidentifiable; many were identical to those used in mineral water and soda water businesses. Also, Labatt never asked his clients where they were from. He would take their money and see them on their way. If they chose to smuggle the beer into the areas that had gone dry, that was their decision.[86] He took comfort in the fact that, strictly speaking, he was not doing anything illegal. By 1889, Labatt was selling three times as many bottles of beer at his London plant as he was in 1878. The demand for bottled beer was so great that Canadian brewers were forced to import bottles from as far away as Germany.[87] However, the statistics in table 3.1 do not fully capture the total number of bottles sold during the period. This is because Labatt's practice was to ship his beer to his agencies in barrels and then have some of that beer bottled for local distribution. Existing records do not indicate what percentage of the barrels shipped from London were subsequently bottled at Labatt's agencies. We can safely assume, however, given Labatt's testimony on the source of his profits during the 1878–89 period, that it was not an insignificant amount and was certainly substantially more, as a percentage of total output, than the numbers in table 3.1 suggest.

Conclusion

To the lament of those in the temperance movement, the Scott Act actually made a number of robust brewers even stronger. Survival in business has often been determined by how well and how fast company managers respond to external shocks. Labatt was certainly quick on his feet during the Scott Act period. When markets near home dried up, he further expanded the geographical scope of his operations. The urgent need to compensate for the initial drop in local sales prompted Labatt to transport his beer to those places that had held the temperance forces at bay: he became one of the first Ontario brewers to gain a presence in the neighbouring provinces of Manitoba and Quebec. Given his earlier expansion, Labatt would probably have sought out these distant markets at some point in the firm's evolution, but the Scott Act accelerated his push to the east and then the west. Often, the quantity of beer shipped and the profits made were small (or, as in British Columbia, non-existent). Nevertheless, from a long-term perspective, he was making the Labatt name more widely known, establishing markets from a well-defined centre, and weaving a rudimentary east–west network that would enable him to survive when other brewers succumbed to the competition, declining and disappearing as viable enterprises in their confined regions.

The Scott Act also changed the way that Labatt did business. On the production side, a shift away from kegs to bottled beer meant Labatt's sales were no longer overwhelmingly in barrels. Due to the need to transport beer in containers small enough to elude the authorities, bottling beer became increasingly popular during the period of the Scott Act. Given that there was "more money" to be made from bottled than barrelled beer Labatt's profits during this time were more than "since or before." From a cultural point of view, Labatt's operations during the Scott Act period reflected the emergence of a new set of values. Until that point in the brewery's history, loyalty to family, duty to creditors, paternalism toward employees, respect for customers, and pride in profession and product had defined the business culture at Labatt. But now pride was verging on arrogance, and a moral ambiguity toward the law was evident. If a law "was a big humbug," as Labatt had stated, did one have an ethical obligation to abide by it? Labatt didn't think so. During the Scott Act period Labatt constantly violated the law. And he had no moral qualms about so doing. This value – specifically and solely a moral ambiguity toward dry legislation – became firmly rooted in the culture of the firm. On other matters, as the next chapter demonstrates, John Labatt was moral to a fault.

John Labatt Blows In and Out of the Windy City

*Entrepreneurship and the Legacy
of a Failure, 1889–1913*

The last decade of the nineteenth century witnessed an unusually high level of Canadian risk-taking abroad. Canadian businessmen, who had already made their mark in Canada by building national firms with competitive advantages derived from economies of scale and scope, searched for growth opportunities beyond the national border. Bursting with energy, confidence, and capital, they exploited their international comparative advantages in order to turn a profit. Sometimes these entrepreneurs took their managerial and technological expertise as well as their venture capital to foreign markets in an attempt to duplicate the success they had achieved at home. In pursuit of a rich return on their investment, a cabal of Toronto capitalists, for instance, established power utilities and built railroads in Latin America and the Caribbean.[1] On other occasions, Canadian businessmen opened up branch offices in other lands to extend to foreigners the services they offered Canadians.[2] From Canada's financial sector, the Merchants Bank of Halifax (renamed the Royal Bank of Canada in 1901) proved to be quickest to the frontier, gaining what eminent business historian Alfred Chandler has termed a "first-mover advantage."[3] These entrepreneurs were often "pushed" by maturing markets and increased competition at home, and "pulled" by the relatively regulator-friendly, cash-strapped, and technologically deficient markets abroad.

John Labatt had the distinction of being the only brewer among this group of enterprising spirits who embarked upon a southerly quest. At the dawn of the twentieth century, the Canadian brewing industry was still dominated by owner-entrepreneurs who focused on maintaining their share of the home market, rather than seeking out opportunities for growth abroad.[4] Many Canadian brewers were risk-averse. Instead of taking on the competition outside their national boundary, they chose to cater to the local beer market and diversify into related and unrelated areas of domestic production.[5] For instance, John Labatt's contemporary, Calgary-based brewer A.E. Cross, not only brewed but also raised livestock and produced electricity, as well as oil and gas on a minor scale.[6] John Labatt's strategy was different.

What was it about John Labatt II that set him apart? What pushed and pulled him southward at the end of the nineteenth century, when everyone else in the Canadian brewing industry was content to stay at home? What were the cultural values or personal traits that led him to believe that he could succeed south of the border? Who or what was to blame for his failure in the Windy City?

Push Factors: Cartels, Cheaters, and Profit Squeezes

During the last decade of the nineteenth century price-cutting insidiously crept into the Ontario brewing industry, making it very difficult for John Labatt to generate a "living profit" – i.e., a reasonable return on his capital – solely from domestic beer sales. The nature of the business of brewing was such that fixed costs were relatively high. Brewery equipment was expensive. As a result, the big-fourteen Ontario breweries had to have substantial gross sales before a profit could be made. But once the break-even point was reached, the percentage of profits on the remaining sales was large. In an effort to cover their fixed costs or improve their market share in one place or another, the big brewers often cut their selling price below those of their rivals. Anxious to fend off such an assault, competitors would respond in kind, cutting the price of their products.

Price-fixing was seen as the solution to these price wars.[7] In London, Ontario, the two largest brewers, John Labatt and John Carling, tacitly agreed not to undersell one another in the local market. The long, cordial relationship between the Carlings and Labatts, dating from the 1840s, prevented a ruinous price war and was one of the reasons why both breweries managed to survive despite the relatively small size of their plants and of the local market. As they expanded their sales beyond the boundaries of the county of London-Middlesex, they continued to maintain prices in markets where they both competed. When either Labatt or Carling was forced to lower prices to take on the competition, a warning and explanation was always sent to the other.[8] This remained the case into the twentieth century.

More often than not the price-cutting was initiated by one of the Toronto-based brewers, who catered to a larger local market and on occasion found themselves with excess supply, which they often dumped into nearby markets, sometimes selling at a loss. A handful of Toronto brewers enjoyed economies of scale superior to those of Labatt. Still, this kind of behaviour was generally frowned upon: price-cutting prevented businessmen from making a living profit. Many rejected the maxim that competition was the lifeblood of trade, and justified price-fixing as being good for both producers and consumers.[9] In the late Victorian Age, seemingly everyone in Canada fixed prices: railway men, steamship owners, sugar refiners, wholesalers, grocers, druggists, jewellers, shoemakers, flour millers, stove founders, oil refiners, physicians, lawyers, bankers, and brewers.[10] Once prices were fixed, it became the responsibility of the various trade cartels (e.g., the Canadian Bankers Association, the Dominion Wholesale Grocers' Guild, the Retail Merchants Association of Canada) to ensure that no one violated the price-fixing accords. Regulation of competition was deemed necessary to preserve the ethical as well as the material bases of business success.

In 1891, the Ontario Brewers' Association fixed the price at which beer would be sold within Canada's most populated and prosperous province. While there was a good deal of debate about the price point, an agreement was reached, and from then on, draught beer would sell at $16 per hogshead, or thirty-two cents per gallon. It was further agreed that a dozen quarts of ale would sell for no less than $1, and a dozen pints for a minimum of seventy cents.[11] John Labatt felt these prices should be higher, but was willing to compromise for the sake of solidarity.[12] To be sure, he and right-hand man Fredrick W. Raymond were skeptical that the agreement would hold. Specifically, they felt that the Toronto brewers would be "discounting on the sly."[13] They were wrong in one respect: it was not only the Toronto brewers who violated the terms of the accord.

The problem with cartels is that they virtually always breed cheaters. Just a few months after the price-fixing agreement was signed, Labatt learned that a number of brewers were slashing prices in violation of the accord. In July 1891, Raymond wrote to Labatt to report the depressing news: "The Toronto men have been selling in London at $14.00 per Hhd" – i.e., at a 12.5 per cent discount.[14] The underselling continued thereafter. In 1894, Labatt compiled a list of price-cutting infractions in Ontario.[15] At a time when brewers had committed not to sell at less than $1 per dozen quarts, many brewers were selling at a 20 per cent discount (see table 4.1).

Table 4.1

Price-cutting of beer below $1-per-dozen-quarts commitment of brewers, various Ontario locations, 1894

Location	Price per dozen quarts	Brewer
Arnprior	$.80	Ontario Brewing and Malting Co.
Aylmer	$.80	Dominion Breweries
Brantford	$.85	Toronto Breweries and Others
Carleton Place	$.80	Dominion Breweries
Chatham	$.80	Dominion Breweries and Carling
Ingersoll	$.80	Grant and Dominion Breweries
Madoc	$.80	Ambrose & Winslow
Niagara Falls	$.80	Carling and Toronto Breweries
Picton	$.80	Prescott Brewing & Co
Pretoria	$.80	Carling and Thomas Davies
Sarnia	$.80	Carling and Thomas Davies
St Thomas	$.80	Toronto Breweries and McCoy
Trenton	$.80	Ontario Brewing and Malting Co.
Tweed	$.80	Thomas Davies

Source: "Sample of Cut Prices" (24 April 1894), Letter Book, vol. II, 159, *Labatt Collection*.

For example, R.T. Davies' Dominion Breweries Ltd was selling a dozen quarts of its ale for eighty cents in Chatham, Aylmer, Ingersoll, and Carleton Place.

In addition to the discounts on the price of bottles by the quart, various brewers offered discounts by the barrel. Labatt also compiled a list of these brewers. Many of the same names appeared on the list. For example, the Ontario Brewing and Malting Company built a state-of-the-art 125-square-foot brewery in Toronto in 1884, and was selling its beer at the discounted price of twenty-five cents per gallon in Kingston, Ottawa, and St Mary's.[16]

In May 1894, Labatt met with John Carling to discuss cutting their prices in order to compete with the Toronto brewers, who were underselling them in London by at least ten cents per dozen quarts. Labatt was furious, given that he and Carling had lived up to their promise not to undersell the Toronto brewers in their home market with the expectation that those brewers would show the same consideration when it came to selling Toronto-made beer in London. "At our Toronto meeting when this thing was spoken of," Labatt wrote to Ontario Brewers' and Maltsters' Association president James Lotridge, "Mr O'Keefe said, 'oh there is honour among thieves.' I believe myself he was right, but there is no honour among some of our Ontario brewers."[17] Labatt also wrote directly to Eugene O'Keefe, de facto leader of the Toronto brewers, about the "unfair practices."

> As soon as we agreed to keep up prices in Toronto, the Toronto brewers came to London and offered their ale $.10 per dozen under us, we were getting $1.00 per dozen [quarts], we then came down to $.90 and then they dropped to $.85, and since then both the Toronto Brewers and Sleeman have offered $.80 if [bought] by the car load and I believe in one case they even offered five percent for cash off the $.80. This is certainly a mean way to treat us. They have ruined our prices without benefiting themselves … I doubt if they have cleared expenses.[18]

The statement reflects that Labatt was blind to the riptides of competition that flowed beneath the surface of the marketplace. It was proving impossible to maintain the cartel in the expanding Ontario marketplace. Too many brewers were succumbing to the temptation to increase market share or dominate new markets by slashing prices on the sly. Nevertheless, given the business culture of the times, Labatt's comments were not unusual. An agreement had been reached on prices. To break such an agreement was widely seen as bad behaviour, not only by those within the brewing community but also by businessmen in virtually every industry across the nation. As the *Canadian Grocer* reminded readers, throughout the 1890s, "price-cutters lacked the courage to meet rivals on fair ground and succeed"; their business life was "conceived in selfishness and nurtured by methods, the very antithesis of business-like [behaviour]."[19] Men in finance, industry, commerce, and agriculture expressed similar sentiments.[20]

Unfortunately for Labatt, his appeals were directed at one of the greatest price-cutters in the business. Eugene O'Keefe owned one of the biggest breweries in the nation and was on the verge of being installed as the new president of the Ontario Brewers' and Maltsters' Association. O'Keefe had little sympathy for Labatt's predicament, so the underselling continued.

The price war started by the Toronto brewers bore heavily on Labatt's bottom line (see table 4.2). During the 1880s, his net revenue reached new heights, and in 1890, Labatt recorded very respectable profits of over $70,000. But thereafter profits declined. Labatt production had ebbed and flowed in the past in response to

Table 4.2

Number of barrels and bottles brewed and bottled, and net profit at Labatt, 1886–96

Year	No. of barrels brewed	No. of barrels used to fill bottles	Net profit
1886	20,999	4,614	$72,574.72
1887	22,855	5,380	$74,078.76
1888	22,518	5,108	$70,391.59
1889	21,611	6,728	$55,117.15
1890	23,165	2,436	$70,214.92
1891	18,575	n/a	$42,422.91
1892	19,946	2,759	$37,627.28
1893	20,460	n/a	$26,704.51
1894	23,665	3,028	$48,828.57
1895	24,306	n/a	$59,983.26
1896	26,152	n/a	$47,477.34

Source: Letter Book, vols. I and II, *Labatt Collection*.

the rhythms of the business cycle. What he had not experienced was the decline in prices and profit margins. In 1893, Labatt produced almost as much beer as in 1886, yet his profits were approximately one-third. It was a similar story in 1894: Labatt produced twice as much as he had in 1879, yet earned similar profits. He could hardly believe it: "My output was larger than the largest year I have ever had, yet my profits were at levels not seen since the onset of the Scott Act [in 1878]."[21] Labatt was motivated to escape the profit squeeze in Ontario by seeking out external markets that promised a healthy return on investment and a long-term prospect for growth.

Pull Factors: Markets, Profits, and Prestige

With the price war raging in Ontario, Labatt joined those enterprising Canadians looking abroad for opportunities for growth. He was driven by the allure of the potential profits and prestige to be gained from selling his beer in the American market. Labatt had long believed that his beverage was second to none, and that once beer drinkers south of the border had tasted it, they would become loyal consumers. Profits, he confidently concluded, would flow naturally thereafter.[22]

The U.S. beer market was gigantic – a function of a population that was thirteen times the size of Canada's, consuming four times the amount of beer on a per capita basis. In 1893, Americans consumed 989 million gallons of beer or, on average, 14.8 gallons for every man, woman, and child.[23] In comparison, that same year, Canadians consumed only 17.28 million gallons of beer or, on average, 3.495 gallons per person.[24] Labatt knew "the value of the U.S. trade" and was certain that he could gain a slice of the larger American market, in part because of the time that he had spent south of the border in the late 1850s and early 1860s apprenticing for his father's friend, Virginian brewer George Smith. "I know what it is to start up a business in a new place where you are not known," he presumptuously wrote in 1893. "I have tried it before in the States and I lived in the States and did business there for four or five years."[25]

Labatt was particularly interested in establishing his business in Chicago, "seeing that it has a population equal to about one fifth of the whole of Canada," he noted in 1893, "and we can make shipments from there to such points as will pay us to do so."[26] Per capita beer consumption in Chicago was more than three times higher than the American average. In 1890, Chicagoans consumed 52.72 million gallons of beer. *The Saloon Keeper's Journal* proudly proclaimed that every man, woman, and child in the Windy City was annually consuming 49 gallons of beer – twice as much as the average German.[27] Chicago would act as a base for Labatt's expanding U.S. operation. After establishing a bottling plant and a clientele in the Windy City, he planned to expand outward, using the national railway network to ship his beer, first to nearby cities such as Kansas City, Omaha, and St Louis, and then to any other city in the Union where there was a demand for his drinks.[28]

Labatt had long recognized the benefits of railway transportation.[29] With Chicago linked to London by 650 kilometres of rail, he calculated a $1.28 per hogshead cost to ship his beer by rail to the Windy City. That was a third of what he paid for transport to Saint John, New Brunswick and less than one-fifth what he paid to Victoria. Labatt was understandably attracted by the size and proximity of the Chicago market.

But it was not just freight rates that Labatt had to consider when shipping to the United States. He would also have to pay the U.S. duty on imported ale. The America tariff on ale, porter, or beer in "bottles, or jugs of glass, stone or earthen ware" was thirty-five cents per gallon.[30] At that rate, Labatt could not make money. However, the duty on imported draught ale, porter, and beer was lower, amounting to twenty cents per gallon (or \$12.60 per hogshead). While substantially less than the imported bottled-beer tax, the draught-beer tariff was still more than 90 per cent of Labatt's discounted price of twenty-two cents per gallon (\$13.80 per hogshead).

Nevertheless, Labatt determined that he could make a profit by bottling his beer in Chicago. "I believe if my bottling of ale and stout is gone into properly in Chicago," he stated in 1889, "that it would in time pay well, though perhaps not in the first year."[31] Labatt decided to ship his beer in 54-gallon barrels (i.e., 1 hogshead) to Chicago and have it bottled there. Considering freight rates, the U.S. duty, and the normal costs of bottles, corks, labels, brushes, wages, and office expenses, Labatt calculated the total cost of shipping and bottling 1 hogshead in Chicago at \$26.66, or \$1.08 per dozen pints.[32]

Believing in the superiority of his product, Labatt concluded that his ale would sell for slightly more than the best American ale and slightly less than the finest British imports. Of all the beers that Labatt compared his to, Britain's Bass was top of the list. Labatt had long admired the British brewer. Indeed, he used a red triangle logo that very closely resembled Bass's logo until he was instructed to cease and desist by Bass. He subsequently used a red spearhead instead. Despite his admiration for the British brewer, Labatt felt his beer was actually better than Bass – or at least more popular with those who had tried the two brands. "A good many people, especially ladies," he boasted, "like my ale better than Bass!" "You will find ladies will like our ale," he wrote to a potential distributor in Chicago, "and they make their men get it and use it also ... At least, that is my experience in large Canadian towns."[33] Given that the best American ale was selling in Chicago for between \$1.65 and \$1.75 per dozen pints, and Bass ale was selling for between \$1.85 and \$1.90 per dozen pints, Labatt felt confident that he could get \$1.83 for a dozen pints of his beverage.[34] At that price, each twelve-pack sold would generate a seventy-five-cent profit.

But the profits never materialized, and Labatt was forced to retreat from the American marketplace. Labatt had always maintained that it would take time to generate sales south of the border. "If business is going to pay it will make its way gradually," he wrote shortly after beginning operation in Chicago in 1893. "It can not be done in a rush."[35] But by 1896, his patience had worn thin, and he gave up on efforts to join the ranks of the beer barons in the United States.

Figure 4.1 Labatt advertisement, c. 1895. By this time, John Labatt had reworked his logo into a red arrowhead that less resembled Bass's famous red triangle.

Accounting for Failure

What went wrong? Who or what was to blame for Labatt's failure in Chicago? At a structural level, the industry had changed substantially since Labatt's initial stint in the United States thirty years before. By 1890, brewing in the United States was a significant industry, and beer was a mass-produced and mass-consumed good. Several factors caused the transformation in the American industry. First, widespread emigration from strong beer-drinking countries such as Britain, Ireland, and Germany contributed to the creation of a strong beer-drinking culture in the United States.[36] Second, the United States had increasingly industrialized and urbanized since the Civil War, and saloons and beer drinking had become central to working-class culture, with many labourers consuming beer during and after work. Third, rising incomes allowed workers to buy more beer. Fourth, the brewing industry benefited from a temperance movement advocating the consumption of lower-alcohol beer over higher-alcohol hard liquor. Fifth, a series of technological and scientific developments fostered greater beer production and the brewing of new styles of beer.[37]

An equally impressive transformation was underway at the firm level. Before 1870, American breweries were essentially small-scale local operations. But by the 1890s, a handful of large brewers, with highly mechanized factories and merchandising chains extending beyond their hometowns, emerged to dominate the U.S. marketplace. When Labatt was cutting his teeth in the United States during the 1860s, each brewer had known the exact confines of their market and been able to maintain their market share without much competition. But the development of a national web of railroads had drawn the whole country closer together, and the great advances in technology made it feasible for individual brewers to chase customers further afield. The emergence of these national brewers changed the whole complexion of the American beer market.[38]

The national brewers were usually based in medium-sized cities – e.g., Pabst, Schlitz, Miller, and Blatz in Milwaukee; Anheuser-Busch in St Louis; Stroh in Detroit; and Christian Moerlein in Cincinnati. Like Labatt in London, the national brewers expanded into distant markets because there simply were not enough local customers to drink all that they produced. In 1893, Pabst Brewing became the first American brewery to produce and sell more than 1 million barrels of beer in one year. Soon after, Schlitz and Anheuser-Busch joined the million-barrel-a-year club.[39] In comparison, Labatt's averaged under 22,000 U.S. barrels annually during the 1890s. The American "shipping brewers" came to dominate the national market because they utilized railroads, refrigeration, advertising, and, above all, economies of size.[40]

All the shipping brewers already had a significant American Midwest presence by the time Labatt arrived in the early 1890s. Chicago had survived the Great Fire of 1871, albeit not without significant damage. The fire had destroyed about one-third of the city, including the entire central business district. Nineteen breweries had gone down in flames, including William Haas's 1833 brewery, the first established in the city.[41] Haas and fifteen other brewers never reopened their doors. Outside brewers quickly took advantage of the diminished supply yet stable demand for beer. By 1879, Pabst and Schlitz, combined, sold 95,000 barrels of beer in Chicago.[42] In the years that followed, they went one step further, using Chicago's strategic railroad freighting position to open up their business throughout the United States. By 1890, the Milwaukee brewers had sales in Chicago of close to 325,000 barrels.[43] Despite the omnipresence of outsiders, independent Chicago brewers survived for a time, making Chicago one of the most competitive places in the United States to do business. By 1894, Chicago had a total of fifty-three breweries and ranked third in the nation, just behind Philadelphia and New York respectively. Competition was stiff in Chicago. Unlike Brazil, where the Canadian utility imperialists used their huge pool of surplus capital to sweep away existing enterprises and potential competitors, in Chicago, Labatt had to contend with both large and small brewing firms for a share of the market.[44]

As is often the case, intense competition put downward pressure on prices. For a time, brewers in Chicago attempted to stabilize prices through a string of cartel-like market-sharing and price-fixing agreements. Without the force of law behind them, these "pools" and "trusts" usually fell apart in a matter of months. The failure of these arrangements led to the merging of a number of firms. During the late 1880s, with a widespread industrial depression limiting investment opportunities in Great Britain, English investors began to eye the profitable American brewing industry. Later, the same forces would bring these venture capitalists to Labatt's door. In 1889, English investors made an offer of $16.5 million for the combined Schlitz, Pabst, and Blatz breweries in Milwaukee. Schlitz and Pabst were experiencing unprecedented growth – much of it due to the booming Chicago market – and turned down the proposal. But a host of other brewers found the English offers too good to refuse.[45]

With hopes of securing a larger market share and, if need be, squeezing out the remaining Chicago brewers, the English-controlled breweries abruptly started to bring down the wholesale price of their beer. The Milwaukee brewers were forced to participate in this price war, selling their products in 1890 for as low as $4 per barrel (roughly $8 per hogshead) – $4 less than the going rate of a barrel of beer in Milwaukee.[46] There was talk in the Chicago brewing community that the price would eventually fall to the inconceivable figure of $2 a barrel.[47] Even at $4 per barrel, beer was selling for just under thirteen cents per gallon – far below Labatt's price in Ontario and nowhere near enough to cover his costs in Chicago. In response to this situation, some innovative brewers tried lowering their costs through the efficiencies of vertical integration by bottling their own beer to generate higher profit margins. This strategy proved tremendously successful for a few firms. For example, Anheuser-Busch reported a profit of $750,000 in 1892, despite the declining prices for beer in Midwest markets.[48]

But price-cutting and vertical integration were only some of the aggressive practices used by American brewers to effectively compete against the likes of Labatt in the Midwest market. Ultimately, success in brewing was determined by the ability to get one's beverages into the hands of consumers. During the 1890s, Chicago's biggest brewers began spending huge sums to purchase saloons to exclusively funnel their beer. For example, Joseph Schlitz spent millions building fifty-seven saloons in Chicago. Some of them, like O'Leary's Horn Palace across from Chicago's Union Stockyards, were spectacular. O'Leary's had an ornate bar room, a billiard parlour, and a concert hall that could seat 1,000 patrons, as well as a clandestine faro and roulette area.[49] Shortly thereafter, the Chicago Brewing and Malting Company, which controlled five of Chicago's leading brewing and malting companies, and Milwaukee and Chicago Breweries Limited, which absorbed the United States Brewing Company in 1891, allocated $6 million for the purchase of saloons in the Windy City. By 1893, brewers had an interest in approximately half of the 7,000 saloons in the city.[50]

By adopting the British practice of "tied houses," the American brewers hoped that profits would rise as they seized control not only of the saturated beer market but also of the retailers themselves.[51] Unlike his large American counterparts, Labatt did not have the cash, access to credit, or experience necessary to tie American saloons to his brewery. "I have not a single tied house," he later reported, "and have always refused that kind of business."[52] He would have been familiar with the practice, however. Many Canadian brewers held loans and mortgages on hotels and taverns.[53] Unwilling and unable to capture his own string of retail outlets, Labatt had to rely on agents to get his beer into the hands of consumers.

Unfortunately for Labatt, finding an agent willing to distribute his beer in the Windy City proved problematic. Due to the small quantities of beer and profits involved, Labatt could promise only a tiny salary for a salesman working on commission. As a result, in 1892, he was forced to hire men whom he would not have hired under normal circumstances. Almost as soon as "Mr Low" and "Mr Rogers" began distributing Labatt's products in Chicago, problems arose. The two men quarrelled incessantly, and Low turned out to be particularly unreliable.[54] Eventually, Rogers was given sole control of the agency.

Sadly, however, Rogers quickly proved to be as delinquent in his duties as Low. He worked too little, or, at least, to little effect.[55] While Pabst's agents were on the road 350 days a year visiting saloons and buying rounds for the house, listening to bartenders' woes, wooing agents, and scolding recalcitrant customers in a sixteen-state territory that stretched from New York to California, Rogers was having a hard time dealing with business in a single city.[56] Added to this, he was too much committed to the practice of spending and continually asked Labatt for extra expense money. As early as March 1893, John Labatt was showing signs of frustration with his Chicago agent. "If you require more [money] than this you will have to make it by selling more goods and getting it out of commissions."[57] To make matters worse, Rogers was drinking to excess. This caused Labatt to rebuke his "Chicago man."

> I know some brewers' agents spend a lot of money and drink heavily, but it is not necessary with an article like ours which is on par with Bass, and if it will not sell on its own merits, I do not want anyone to kill himself by swilling on my account. I would sooner go out of business. You can easily show samples without drinking yourself. You can say you are pledged to me or the Dr has forbidden it [drinking] on account of your nervous tempera-ment or make any excuses you like and you will find you will be much more respected in the long run. If the ale suits and is wanted, the client will keep it ... regardless of your spending a few quarters with them or drinking with them. It comes down to dollars and cents and if it does not pay them to keep it, it won't matter what you do.[58]

Despite his assurances that he had "put the plug in it," Rogers kept on spending and tippling. Labatt's manager, F.W. Raymond, wanted him fired for it. "It seems to me the sooner we part with Rogers the better for us," Raymond wrote to Labatt in October 1893. "We have to write off some $6,000 as a net loss to date on our United States business, and in the face of his last statement where expenses and salary are continued and no sales of any consequence being made, it would be better to abandon the field altogether than go on as we were."[59] But a combina-tion of moral rectitude and benevolent paternalism prevented Labatt from letting Rogers go. Back in Canada, this type of paternalism was on display when other agents, like Mr Blackburn in Ottawa (see chapter 3), drank immoderately. Benev-olent paternalism was a defining element of John Labatt's managerial style. It was evident at company picnics, dances, and Christmas parties – all of which were initiated and paid for by Labatt. He also gave his men bonuses and gifts based on his own arbitrary evaluation of who was deserving. "Purchase at my expense for yourself," he instructed one of his employees, "a nice turkey and take a couple of dozen ale each for Christmas and charge same to me."[60] Labatt acted like most

Figure 4.2 During the Gilded Age, Labatt framed its products as upstanding and respectable, as in this famous advertisement featuring two gentlemen in a parlour, c. 1895. What Labatt's ads did not do, however, was appeal directly to members of the working class. This was a missed opportunity because the working class was emerging as a significant drinking group. To be sure, the working class still had its share of teetotallers, but increasingly, the workers of the nation were choosing to drink moderately and responsibly by downing a pint or two of beer.

self-made men of the Gilded Age, displaying a strong paternal identification between company and personal property.[61] And also reflecting the Gilded Age view of the relationship of master and men: Rogers was "his man" and he felt an obligation to take care of (and control) him. Labatt's paternalism, however, prevented him from doing what needed to be done to successfully compete in the Windy City.

Perhaps, in due course, Labatt would have made a profit in Chicago, if time and tastes were not working against him. But they were. As a brewer of British-styled ale, porters, and stouts, Labatt found himself on the wrong side of the revolution in consumer tastes taking place in North America during the nineteenth century's final decades. The German-American brewers (e.g., Pabst, Stroh, Miller, Blatz, Busch, Coors, and Schlitz) employed a different method of beer making than Labatt. Brewed, stored, and served at a cool temperature, their lager beers appeared light and clean, and tasted crisp and refreshing. In contrast, Labatt's British-styled beverages looked dark and cloudy, and often tasted heavy and malty. As a result, concludes business historian Austin Kerr, lager beer "proved much more popular than the traditional British ales in the American market with its warm summer climate."[62] Even Bass was finding it impossible to compete in markets like Chicago, which had no existing colonial connection.[63] While other Canadian brewers were slowly adding lager beer to their product lines to meet growing demand at home, Labatt held firm to his belief that his British-styled ales, porters, and stouts were far superior in terms of flavour.[64] "I do not make lager ... as an ale and stout brewer," Labatt obstinately pronounced in 1898.[65] Labatt was trapped in the cage of tradition.

Figure 4.3 *Opposite* At the dawn of the twentieth century, John Labatt II continued to portray his product as gentlemanly. In this piece of promotional material, he associated beer with the outdoor life. Bourgeois men had come to reject the prim, restrained, soft masculinity that had previously dominated the upper and middle classes. The new "manliness" celebrated vitality, health, strength, and contact with "nature." They joined gymnasiums and amateur sport clubs to develop their muscles, which were now seen as an outward expression of an inner fortitude. At the same time, a cult of wilderness emerged around hunting and fishing clubs, national parks, and cottages – like the one that Labatt owned in Muskoka. In this ad, Labatt associated its beer with leisurely activity and "healthy" outdoor pastimes. This ad from 1900 demonstrates that John Labatt II was again trapped in the cage of tradition, unable to break with the perception that his product was for white, middle- and upper-class men rather than for working-class immigrants or others of diverse backgrounds.

Thus, a mixture of entrepreneurial and structural factors prevented Labatt from gaining a presence in the United States at the end of the nineteenth century. Entrepreneurially, Labatt proved unwilling to adopt the morally ambiguous business practices of his American counterparts. Chicago, at the end of the nineteenth century, was one of the most competitive and corrupt places in the United States to do business, and Labatt naively thought that his Canadian strategies for growth and survival would work equally well south of the border. He arrogantly thought that once beer drinkers tasted his award-winning brews, a robust market would develop for them. He felt so strongly about being moral in business that he preferred to fail – "go out of business," as he put it – rather than succeed by unethical means. The spirit of late nineteenth-century Canadian capitalism did not leave him when he left Canada. The same Victorian moral rectitude that barred him from taking on the cheaters in Ontario prevented him from doing what was necessary to compete in Chicago. Like many of the Canadian entrepreneurial elite, Labatt was honest and loyal. But unlike Labatt, most Canadian entrepreneurs were not loyal to a fault. Perhaps if he had had a more perfect knowledge of the brewing business south of the border – rather than one based on his short stay in Virginia over thirty years before – he would have thought differently about taking on the cutthroat competition in the Windy City. But success in Canada had made him overconfident – a common failing of unsuccessful entrepreneurs.[66]

While these personal traits – overconfidence, loyalty, arrogance, and naivety – played a critical role in Labatt's decision to head south and a supporting role in his failure in Chicago, structural factors played the most important part in his inability to capture a share of the Chicago market. Labatt had neither a first-mover advantage nor the necessary size to successfully challenge the dominant players in the Chicago market. His relatively small brewery meant that he could not achieve the manufacturing efficiencies of his American counterparts or attract the industry's top talent – although this did not stop him from trying throughout the 1890s to find "men of experience and robustness of body and mind to carry out my business successfully."[67] The tariff on imported Canadian beer made it impossible for Labatt to compete with American brewers on price, especially after the onset of the Windy City price wars in 1890. Moreover, Chicago's distribution system privileged wealthy brewers who captured retail outlets, insuring that their products found their way to consumers. While aware of the practice, Labatt lacked the will and means to tie saloons to his brewery. Finally, Labatt's failure was ensured by the taste shift away from his heavy English-styled ales and stouts to lighter German-styled lagers.

Given the structural factors that were working against him, Labatt was destined to fail in the Windy City. Even if he had possessed all the characteristics of Schumpeter's "heroic" entrepreneur, he would not have succeeded in Chicago. The fact that he did not possess these characteristics made a bad situation worse and hastened his U.S. agency's collapse. Unlike contemporary Canadian bankers and utility imperialists who had success in Latin America and the Caribbean, Labatt lacked the international competitive advantages necessary to survive and prosper in an environment as spirited as Chicago. The early history of Labatt is a record of domestic success followed by international failure.

Conclusion

After failing to break into the United States, John Labatt lost interest in building a brewing empire. He would have sold the brewery in 1897 had he been able to reach an agreement with Eugene O'Keefe.[68] With his attention often elsewhere, he gave serious consideration to stepping down as president and handing over control of the company to one of his offspring. Like the leaders of other long-lasting family enterprises, John Labatt was philoprogenitive.[69] His two marriages produced twelve children, of which nine survived. The oldest of John Labatt's seven girls was Catherine, who was born in 1867, followed by Frances, Selina, Elizabeth, Dora, Ismena, and Jean. While many of his daughters, particularly Catherine and Frances, possessed the necessary qualities to manage the brewery, the late Victorian Age was not a time when women controlled companies. This left his two sons, but unfortunately neither was ready to take over. His younger son, Hugh, had only turned fifteen in October 1898 and was attending Lakefield Preparatory School, just north of Peterborough. John S., on the other hand, was eighteen and had recently begun studies in chemistry at McGill University. John's choice indicated that he was considering entering the family business someday, assuming there was still a business to run. It also demonstrated that the art of brewing was becoming less a mysterious art-and-craft to be handed down from brewmaster to apprentice, and more an applied science to be learned at university or one of the brewing academies that were emerging south of the border. To be sure, there were other family members who could have run the brewery until the boys were ready. Two of the most capable candidates were the husbands of John Labatt's eldest daughters, Catherine and Frances. But neither Alan Dunbar Scatcherd nor Hume Cronyn – both successful lawyers – showed any interest in the brewing business.[70] As a result,

John Labatt, who turned sixty on 11 December 1898, felt he had no choice but to stay on as president of the brewery that he owned and controlled.

The failure in Chicago stripped Labatt of his arrogance. His cocksure belief in the superior quality of his products vanished. He no longer believed that once people tasted his beer, they would buy it not once but forever, loyally, and at virtually any price. A new humility and focus took root in him. The failed foray also brought to light the difficulties of making money at a distance. As a result, Labatt initiated a retrenchment program that saw him close a number of agencies in order to concentrate on business in Ontario. Over a ten-year period he shut down all of his operations outside of Ontario except for the agency in Montreal. Then finally, in 1908, he closed the Montreal agency as well. The cost of doing business in Montreal was substantially higher than it was in Ontario. Labatt's margin of profit was just over 1 per cent in Montreal. That was dismally low compared to the 28 per cent profit margin being generated in Toronto, or the 18 per cent in Hamilton. The long haul to Montreal was crushing him at the margins. But freight rates alone did not tell the full story. Wages and licensing fees were also higher in Montreal than elsewhere. The cost of operating the Montreal branch was 50 per cent higher than running the branches in Ottawa and Hamilton, and more than double the cost of operating the Toronto branch. "The way of doing business down there," Labatt lamented about business in Montreal, "is quite different from the way it is down in Ontario."[71] To make a bad situation even worse, prices were "unreasonably low" in Montreal and throughout the province of Quebec. It was all too much for Labatt. Having sold only thirty-five railcars of beer in Montreal in 1908, Labatt concluded that it was "foolish to try to struggle any longer where there is so much capital tied up in the Montreal branch including accounts which we very much need here."[72] The only question left was: "How to wind it [the Montreal branch] up in the best and most economical way to get the most out of it and as quickly as possible."[73] Over the next six months, he and his new agent in Montreal, J.W. Moffat, sold off assets and collected money owed. During the liquidation process, Labatt lost another $17,362.45 on his Montreal operations.[74] Still, he was glad to have escaped when he did. "I am happy to be out," a humbled Labatt wrote in January 1910.[75] The retrenchment strategy had its desired effect: profits in 1911 returned to levels not seen since the Scott Act days.

That year, John Labatt turned seventy-three. He had visibly aged since his failure in the Windy City. His beard and hair were now snow white (see figure 4.4). His eyes had lost the spark of youth and often looked tired and lifeless. The tragic loss of his second wife, Sophia, in 1906 from poisoning due to a druggist's mistake

Figure 4.4 Portrait of John Labatt II, 1911.

on a prescription and the troubles at the brewery had taken their toll.[76] Grief was often etched on his face. His two sons John and Hugh were now aged thirty and twenty-seven, respectively. Since both had worked with him for a decade, John Labatt had some assurance that the old London Brewery would remain in family hands for the foreseeable future.[77]

The failure in Chicago that led to a crisis in confidence ultimately precipitated a defensive move to protect against loss through bankruptcy and to ensure continuity of ownership: incorporation of the family firm. When John Labatt finally decided to incorporate in April 1911, he was the last of the big Ontario brewers to do so. When a public corporation was created, it did away with private ownership and normally, but not always, separated ownership from management. This was the hallmark of a new type of capitalism that Harvard business historian Alfred

Chandler termed "managerial capitalism," which transformed the American economy during the last half of the nineteenth century. Chandler maintained that
managerial capitalism was superior to personal capitalism because the economic
reasoning of specialized managers trumped the emotional impulses of family operators. Certainly, Labatt was driven by emotion rather than sound economic
reason when he expanded to the United States. However, John Labatt II showed
no interest in having his firm participate in the managerial revolution. As late as
December 1910, Labatt was still expressing his pride in the fact that the old London
Brewery was family-owned and -controlled. "No manager's salary has been paid,"
he crowed, "as the whole business has been under my personal superintendence."
He remained wedded to his version of personal capitalism. He was not about to
hand over the decision-making process to a team of salaried managers who had
little or no equity ownership in the enterprise.[78] But now, only a few months later,
he would restructure the ownership of the firm.

On 11 April 1911, the Secretary of State in Ottawa sealed the letters of patent
for "John Labatt Limited." Under the terms of the amended Companies Act of
1906, the board of directors – or "The Body Corporate and Public," as it was then
termed – had to consist of a minimum of five members.[79] In the months leading
up to submitting the application for incorporation, Labatt struggled with whom
to appoint to the brewery's "body corporate and public." Some were easy choices.
It was obvious from the start, given Labatt's dedication to family, that his two
sons would hold prominent positions in the new corporation. In addition to des-
ignating himself as president, the application named John Sackville Labatt as
vice-president and Hugh Francis Labatt as secretary. The other two positions on
the board were more difficult to fill. It wasn't that he lacked a deep pool of talent
to draw from. There were plenty of very capable family members to appoint to
the last two positions on the board, but most were committed to other enterprises. Labatt decided to appoint those who were readily available, specifically,
his nephew Robert H. Labatt and his brother-in-law Sydney Chilton Mewburn.[80]

Although the retrenchment program was having positive results, after Chicago, Labatt no longer felt invincible in business. In an effort to further safeguard the family firm, he also created a trust in his will so that in the event of
his death, the ownership of the brewery would pass to his nine children, with
the day-to-day management of the brewery passing to his two sons, John and
Hugh.[81] There was no question, however, that, at least for now, this was still John
Labatt's brewery and that he would continue to have full control when it came
to determining the direction of the firm. Labatt made the decisions on the roles

of his sons and how the shares were to be distributed. Working with F.W. Raymond, whom he appointed as auditor, Labatt calculated that the firm's total assets were slightly over $485,000, against which he had liabilities of $235,000. The net assets were thus valued at $250,000, represented by 2,500 shares worth $1,000 each.[82] Of the 2,500 shares, one went to each of his sons and one each to Sydney Mewburn and Robert Labatt, a necessity to qualify them as members of the board. The remaining 2,496 shares were the property of John Labatt.

Thus, the failure in the Windy City had a long-lasting and multi-faceted effect on Labatt. It led to a retreat back to homeland Ontario, as retrenchment became the primary strategy for growth. At the same time, a crisis in confidence fostered a culture of risk aversion at the firm. A diminished faith in his abilities to take on the competition led John Labatt II to finally incorporate the company that he had owned and controlled for over four decades.

"No Frolic about This Contest"

At War with Labatt, 1914–18

On the evening of 4 August 1914, word spread through the first-class lounges of the ocean liner that was carrying John Labatt home from England: "We are at war." The tensions that had been brewing in Europe for years erupted with the assassination of the heir to the Austro-Hungarian throne, Archduke Franz Ferdinand, by a young Serbian nationalist. In response, Austria declared war on Serbia, which had an alliance with Russia. The rest of the diplomatic dominoes then fell with alacrity. When Russia came to the aid of Serbia, Germany entered the war on the side of Austria, leading France to come to the defence of its Russian ally. Britain, a friend of France, had promised to defend the neutrality of Belgium so when German forces invaded Belgium as part of an attack on France, Britain also entered the conflict. As a member of the British Empire, Canada automatically joined the struggle. Prime Minister Robert Borden believed that Canada's interests were inextricably tied to those of the "mother country" and so he pledged "to put forth every effort and to make every sacrifice necessary to ensure the integrity and maintain the honour of our Empire."[1] This initial paroxysm of patriotism would soon be displaced by the grim reality of total war.

When John Labatt heard the news that Canada was at war, his thoughts immediately turned to what the conflict would mean for his family and the brewery. He was now seventy-six years old and in poor health. While he was too old and frail to fight, many in his family were of fighting age and might see combat overseas. In addition, there were the many young men working on the factory floor who also might see action. And what about the brewery itself? What would the war do to business? To be sure, war had historically been good for the Canadian economy. From King George's War in the 1740s to the Franco-Prussian War in

the 1870s, Canada had benefited from international conflicts, largely as a consequence of the demand for Canadian supplies.[2] Nevertheless, few people were
ready to predict in 1914 that history would repeat itself this time around. This
war was shaping up to be – in the words of the doyen of Canadian economic historians, Adam Shortt – "incomparably greater than anything this world has
known."[3] Closer to home, John Labatt's eighteen-year-old grandson, John Labatt
Scatcherd, was given a similar message. "You cannot appreciate what this war
means," Robert Colin Scatcherd soberly warned his nephew, who was itching to
enlist. "It is one of absolute extermination, and is far different from anything that
any Canadian or Englishman, or in fact anyone, ever dreamt of, as is daylight and
darkness … There is no frolic about this contest."[4]

For those in the business of brewing, war often led to increased sales. Beer had
long been associated with the military; Labatt's signature India pale ale had mar-
tial origins. As an ingrained part of British tradition, beer had flowed to the Canadian troops who fought under British command in the South African War from
1899 to 1902. But war was a double-edged sword for the brewing industry: it also
regularly occasioned increased taxation and regulation. For example, during the
South American War, the Conservative government of Gascoyne-Cecil in Britain
raised the duty on beer by 1 shilling per barrel to help pay for the conflict.[5] Would
the Canadian government do the same during the Great War? At a time before
income tax, the Canadian government only had so many ways to pay for the conflict, thus a new tax on the industry seemed likely. And what about prohibition?
Those who had dreamed of a dry heaven on earth had never gone away. In fact,
they were more organized and committed than ever to ending the reign of King
Alcohol. If they finally got their way, what would happen to those who made a
living from making and selling beer?

The Buddenbrooks Effect

On 17 April 1915, John Labatt returned home from an afternoon stroll feeling
under the weather. For the next ten days, he remained in bed at home, attempting
to nurse himself back to health with the aid of Catherine and the family doctor.
Friends and family members dropped by to check on how he was doing. His
brewmaster, Denis Mason, came by every day to see the man for whom he had
worked for over forty years. For Mason and many others, Labatt was the only boss
they had ever served. For a while it looked like John Labatt would pull through,

but then on 26 September, his condition worsened and he died the following afternoon. The headline in the *London Free Press* on 28 April 1915 read, "MR JOHN LABATT SUCCUMBS AFTER TEN DAYS' ILLNESS."[6] The *Toronto Star* and the *Globe and Mail*, which were no friends of the liquor traffic, had nothing to say. The funeral was a low-key event attended by the family and a few close friends.

At the time of his death, John Labatt was seventy-seven and still president of the firm that bore his name. He was one of London's oldest businessmen as well as the oldest continuing member of the Anglican congregation at St Paul's Cathedral on Richmond Street in the city that he and his father helped put on the map. He had devoted fifty years to growing the family business, but in the later stages of his life, he was somewhat naive about emerging business practices and market trends. This cost him dearly. Having once dreamed of becoming the North American equivalent of great British brewer Bass, by the time of Labatt's death, his company was reduced to essentially a regional brewery with agencies in Toronto, Hamilton, and Ottawa and a subagency in Chatham. In many ways, the enterprise was still locked into a nineteenth-century code of business leadership and family ownership.

Nevertheless, at a cultural level, John Labatt's legacy was secure. Almost singlehandedly, he had changed the world of beer advertising in Canada. He had introduced IPA to a large segment of the beer-drinking public. Closer to home, he paternalistically taught those on the brewside of the company the value of making a quality product. For those in administration, he had left them with a sense of how to manage the company in good times and in bad. "Never be in a hurry to spend money," he had once instructed his son John Sackville Labatt, "and always try to avoid taking on debt." The same message was conveyed in a thousand different ways to the others who helped administer the old London Brewery.

In early May 1915, members of the Labatt family gathered at the office of John Labatt's son-in-law, Hume Cronyn. A lawyer by training, Cronyn had drawn up Labatt's last will and testament in 1911. Now it was time for the will to be read. The document reflected the nature of John Labatt himself: firm but fair, clear and concise in language, authoritative in tone, and conservative in nature.[7] Like his father before him, John Labatt wanted to support his unmarried daughters. "I desire to provide a permanent income for the benefit of each of them," his will read.[8] The provision was rooted in the turn-of-the-century belief that unmarried women needed to be supported by an inheritance. The sum was set at "not less than one thousand dollars a year," which was equal to nearly twice the average annual wage of a workman at the brewery and was intended to keep his daughters in a style that accorded with accepted upper-middle-class standards.[9]

The will further specified that the company was to be carried on under the management of John Labatt's two sons, John Sackville and Hugh Francis, and that their remuneration was "to be fixed by the other Trustees and not to exceed Two Thousand Dollars a year to each for the first four years after my death."[10] In yet another attempt by John Labatt to manage the affairs of the firm from the grave, the will stipulated that "no dividends shall be paid upon the capital stock … until all direct liabilities have been fully satisfied." Even in death, he was taking care of the right side of the balance sheet. But it was the following clause that would determine the nature of family control over the next thirty-five years:

> After the expiration of ten years from my death, I desire that all my estate including the proceeds of my life insurance and of my residence when sold shall be divided so that each of my children then living shall receive one share and the children of any deceased child shall receive the share which the parent would have received if living … And it is my desire that in making the said division of stock, which my estate then holds in the said John Labatt Limited, it shall be distributed among my children and grandchildren in the proportions aforesaid.[11]

The will thus guaranteed that his sons would receive no more income from their stockholdings than each of their seven sisters. However, they would have a greater direct role to play in the day-to-day operation of the firm. By stipulating that the firm remain in family hands, John Labatt safeguarded the company from a possible takeover. In the alcoholic beverage industry, the concentration of ownership, particularly in family hands, was a critical factor in the survival of firms.[12]

John Labatt's death could not have come at a more inopportune time. While many sectors of the economy had bounced back from the 1913 recession, inflation was on the rise. As a result, the union was demanding higher wages. In addition, the government was seeking to increase its revenue by imposing new taxes. To make matters worse, the brewery was losing workers to the front, and the "dry army" was on the march to kill King Alcohol. At a time when the company was in desperate need of direction, there was a vacuum in leadership. The two men assigned the task of keeping the company safe during this precarious time lacked the dynamism of their father.

At the time of his father's death, John Sackville was thirty-five years old, while his younger brother, Hugh Francis, was thirty-two. Neither man possessed the business or brewing talents of their father. Mild-mannered and lackadaisical in temperament, they had lived far too long under their father's secure tutelage to make their own mark on the world.[13] Both men were much more content to follow rather than lead. They lacked the stomach for confrontation and were easily influenced by the thoughts of others. Rarely did they express their own opinions around the boardroom table.[14] But having no other sons, John Labatt II could not exile John and Hugh to some lesser station.

John Sackville was the more avuncular of the two.[15] His post-secondary education in science at McGill University made him better educated than his younger brother. He was an average-looking man, with dark hair, dark eyes, and thick eyebrows. Like so many fashionable men during the war, he was clean-shaven. Later in life, he wore glasses, which made him look even more benign. He stood about five-feet-eight-inches tall and, in his thirties, weighed roughly 170 pounds. His outward appearance reflected a soft, gentle interior. By his early thirties, John Sackville had developed an air of utter harmlessness. He had a meek benevolence about him. He enjoyed the outdoors, vacationing in the Muskokas, and riding his horse at the London Hunt Club. In his mid-thirties, he had lent his steed to another club member and rode a borrowed horse that was recovering from an upper respiratory tract infection and still quite weak.[16] When John Sackville attempted to guide his mount over a stone wall, the pair fell short and came crashing to the ground. John's leg was broken in nine places. He underwent multiple surgeries but was never the same. For the rest of his life, he walked with a limp and a cane.[17] Before the war, John Sackville occasionally enjoyed a cigar in one of the salons at the Hunt Club. But during the war, as cigarettes came to be seen as more "manly," he switched to smoking those instead.[18] He smoked for the rest his life. His drink of choice was a scotch and soda rather than beer. In fact, he only sipped beer when greeting visitors at the brewery. As with running the business, he drank beer out of a sense of obligation rather than to quench a personal thirst.

Like his brother, Hugh lacked his father's imaginative skills and attention to detail. A handsome man, he was slightly taller than his older brother. His wide smile and disarming demeanour made him very approachable. He displayed none of his father's mid-life self-confidence and majesty. Workers and managers alike freely engaged with him at the brewery. Paradoxically, he was shy by nature – a characteristic that was intensified by a stutter that he possessed from infancy. Despite his handicap, he completed his secondary education at Trinity College

School in Port Hope, but without the grades needed to get into university. After entering the family business in 1900, he did a variety of jobs, from rolling out the barrels of beer to holding talks with the union. Still, when it came to the most pressing problems confronting the brewery during the war, he turned to others for guidance. Gone were the days when a direct descendent of John K. Labatt determined the direction of the firm.

Just a few days after the Germans released poison gas against two Canadian brigades on the front line of the Second Battle of Ypres, the Labatt family members met to discuss the new composition of the board of directors. All involved agreed that the board should continue to be made up of five family members.[19] The obvious replacement for their father was their brother-in-law Hume Cronyn, who at the age of fifty-one had well-established connections in Canadian business, law, and the Liberal Party. He was also well known in military circles, having served with the Queen's Own Rifles of Canada during the North-West Rebellion of 1885. Upon leaving the army in 1907, he took up a post as general manager of the Huron and Erie Mortgage Corporation, where he gained a reputation for being a sensible and straight-talking businessman. Col. Robert Labatt, who was wounded on the western front in the summer of 1915 and had subsequently returned to the board of directors, thought that Cronyn's connections might well prove useful in these "hazardous times."[20]

The Labatt family also had to find a replacement for Sydney Mewburn, who had left the board of directors as soon as the war broke out and was now the assistant general of the military forces in Canada. Major-General Mewburn would be difficult to replace. Few had his powers of observation and his ability to get things done. When another brother-in-law, William T. Whitehead, was appointed as Mewburn's replacement, he was the first to admit that he had big shoes to fill. Nevertheless, Whitehead was confident in his own capabilities. He came from a prominent family in Montreal that dealt in real estate, textiles, and insurance. Before marrying Selena Labatt in 1911, he worked as a senior executive with Dominion Textiles where he proved that he could make tough decisions and find sensible solutions to practical problems. He brought these talents as well as a spirit of vigorous enterprise to the Labatt board. By the fall of 1915, these five board members agreed to appoint John S. Labatt as president, Col. Robert Labatt as vice-president, and Hugh Labatt as secretary-treasurer.[21] These five men had the tricky task of formulating a strategy to keep the firm afloat during the first two years of the war.

Wartime Regulation and Taxation

Robert Borden's Conservative government had a long tradition of tiptoeing around the liquor question. During the First World War, the governing federal party was divided over the liquor question. There were those like the charismatic Sam Hughes who advocated total abstinence, especially for those in the military. A Presbyterian turned Methodist, Hughes believed that alcohol was holding soldiers back from reaching their full potential. The founder of the Methodist Church, John Wesley, warned against the dangers of drinking in his famous sermon, "The Use of Money." In English Canada, Methodists were the leaders of the movement to cure society of its "addiction" to alcohol. During the Great War, Methodists like Hughes worked hard at hammering their ploughshares into swords.[22] Vain, colourful, and often charming, Hughes made a thirty-year public career of politics and militia service. While Borden thought that Hughes was a bit of a crank with an "unbridled tongue," he could not deny his boundless energy and dedication to the military. Thus, Borden made the dry Hughes his minister of militia and defence.

One of Hughes's first wartime acts was to prohibit the consumption of alcoholic drinks in Canadian training camps, even those overseas. For this, the soldiers dubbed him the "Foe of Booze."[23] With no alcohol on base, Canadian soldiers began visiting the pubs in the little villages around Salisbury Plain, in southern England, where the Canadian Expeditionary Force was stationed at the beginning of the war.[24] They poured into the drinking establishments with the same force they later displayed on the battlefields of continental Europe. But too many times the troops drank to excess, which brought both local criticism and attention from those in command.[25] Worried that the drinking was getting out of hand, General Edwin Alderson, who commanded the Canadian Expeditionary Force during the first half of the war, sent a dispatch to the War Office. "I have just arrived back here from Plymouth," he stated in October 1914, "and find that it is absolutely necessary that there should be canteens for the sale of beer in camp. The men, as I anticipated, finding no liquor in camp canteens, go to the neighbouring villages and get bad liquor, and become quarrelsome."[26] Alderson felt that if the men had beer on base, they would not be given to the debauchery that they had displayed under the spell of "the all-powerful stuff." In the military, at least, beer was still seen as a temperance drink. As those at the old London Brewery had long known, beer was the soldier's dear friend. When the news was announced that Alderson was ending Hughes's "teetotal rule" for canteens, the enlisted men celebrated with "prolonged cheers."[27]

Borden did not share Hughes's faith-based loathing of the liquor traffic. He was committed to helping Britain win the war. That objective trumped everything else, even party politics.[28] Nevertheless, he was willing to meet with temperance advocates. Some of them demanded that he do something to end the tyranny of drink at home, while others begged him to protect the boys from the scourge of booze overseas. On 31 May 1915, he greeted a delegation of women who impressed upon him the many dangers of Alderson's policy of having wet canteens in the army. They warned against "young men unaccustomed to the use of intoxicating liquors who are exposed through the medium of wet canteens to a strong temptation of which they are often unable to resist."[29] Borden described them to his overseas minister Sir George Perley as "very earnest in the expression of their views," and remarked that they warned: "the knowledge that their sons will be exposed to such temptations deters mothers from permitting them to enlist."[30] In churches across the nation, congregations pressured young men intent on enlisting to first sign pledge cards promising to resist the lure of John Barleycorn. Yet Borden did nothing to stop the flow of booze to the boys overseas, where alcohol played an important role as a sedative, a means of escape, a medicine, and a form of liquid courage.[31]

Instead, Borden pragmatically implemented policies and regulations similar to those enacted in other Allied countries. In Britain, the Liberal government of Herbert Henry Asquith raised the tax on beer, curtailed drinking hours, and restricted the production of beer.[32] British war secretary David Lloyd George, who succeeded Asquith as prime minister in 1916, was against the consumption of booze during the war. As he famously stated: "We are fighting Germany, Austria and Drink, and as far as I can see the greatest of these three deadly foes is Drink." By the midpoint of the war, British brewers were allowed to produce only one-third of the quantity of "standard" beer that had been brewed during the year leading up to the war. Since restrictions were based on strength, the brewers attempted to keep volume up by making weaker beer, which used less grain. Nevertheless, production fell from 30 million barrels in 1914 to 19 million in 1917, and the resulting weaker "Government Ale" was mocked in the press and the music halls. "Oh they say it's a terrible war, oh lor' – And there never was a war like this before," went the lyrics of one popular wartime song. "But the worst thing that ever happened in this war – Is Lloyd George's Beer."[33] In some areas where munitions were produced, such as Gretna Green in Scotland, the government nationalized the pubs and breweries to ensure it had direct control over local drinking habits. In France, the licensing system of cafés was revised in 1915 with the aim of reducing their numbers, and public intoxication was deemed a crime for the first time. That same year, absinthe was banned. The nation could ill afford to lose potential soldiers to the debilitating influence of *la Fée Verte*. In Australia, wartime rationing allowed the government to impose stricter limits on the consumption and distribution of alcohol.[34]

In Canada, the federal government could only do so much to curb the use of alcohol since the constitution gave the provinces jurisdiction over the retail sale of intoxicating beverage. However, the federal government did have the authority to regulate the manufacture of booze. Borden first used this power in 1915 to divert resources away from the production of alcoholic beverages and to the production of essential wartime materials. That same year, he doubled the duty on the malt needed to make beer.[35] That increase hit the Labatt brewery hard. "The excise duty alone," lamented Labatt's board of directors in September 1915, "will make for greatly reduced net profits for the current year."[36] To make matters worse, that same year, the government raised the excise duty on beer from ten to fifteen cents per Imperial gallon.[37] At a time when the tariff was the foundation stone of the government's financial structure and the most important source of revenue, the increased duty on beer helped the government pay for the war. For those at Labatt, however, the higher duty when combined with the skyrocketing price of barley – which increased by almost 50 per cent during the first year of the conflict – further eroded profits, which declined by more than 30 per cent between 1914 and 1915 (see table 5.1).[38]

The government's wartime policies also made it difficult for Labatt to find replacement workers for those it was losing to the front or to retirement. Due to Borden's wartime regulations, Labatt could not hire anyone whose ancestors were from the belligerent nations. This meant that Labatt could not hire Austrians, Germans, or German-Americans.[39] When Labatt's long-time brewmaster, Denis Mason, retired, the company had to go to great lengths to obtain a replacement. Finding a suitable substitute for Mason was essential because, as brewmaster, he secured the reputation of any successful beer. At the time of his retirement in 1916, Mason was seventy-two. Since the 1870s, he had diligently managed the brewside of the operation and, with the exception of F.W. Raymond, had done more than any other non-family member to further the success of the Labatt brewery. But even before the death of John Labatt II, Mason was becoming frustrated with the

Table 5.1

Sales, selected expenses, and net profit at Labatt's London Brewery, 1914–18

Year	Net sales	Materials consumed at London	Wages and salaries paid at London	Duty and licences paid	Freight paid from London	Net profit
1914	$418,049	$231,867	$48,901	$51,702	$26,768	$85,027
1915	$413,998	$233,272	$44,872	$59,456	$22,356	$57,058
1916	$328,451	$130,920	$41,732	$34,574	$19,715	$30,180
1917	$191,632	n/a	n/a	n/a	n/a	$22,211
1918	$299,262	n/a	n/a	n/a	n/a	$31,654

Source: John Labatt Ltd, *Balance Sheets*, 1914–18.

changes taking place in the world of brewing. His artistic temperament was often on display as the firm struggled to produce a quality lager and temperance brew. The pressures of brewing during the war only added to his aggravation. Still, while John Labatt was alive, he soldiered on.

Finding a replacement for Mason would be difficult in the best of times, but doing so during the war presented even greater difficulties. Unable to find anyone capable closer to home, in 1916, Robert Labatt travelled to the renowned brewing academy, the Wahl-Henius Institute, in Chicago. The city was still a mecca of brewing. Labatt's contacts there told him about a young Swedish brewer with "exceptional taste and judgment."[40] At the age of thirty-two, Werner Jonason was forty years Mason's junior. But he already had a good deal of experience. Jonason had spent much of his childhood in his father's bakery and brewery in Karlshamn, learning the ancient craft of Swedish brewing.[41] Thereafter, he was taught how to brew on a larger scale at a succession of German and Swiss breweries. Having immigrated to the United States just after the turn of the century, he found work at a Chicago brewery. While the salary was not good, he managed to save $500 to pay for additional training at Wahl-Henius. After graduating with distinction from the academy, he went to work at the P.H. Kling Brewery in Detroit. The Kling brewery was one of the most successful in the city, in part because of the popularity of its lager, which was promoted as the "beer with the taste that satisfies."[42] Jonason's experience making extra pale ales and lagers as well as porters and stouts impressed Labatt. As a result, when he returned to London, he immediately recommended Jonason to take over from Mason.[43]

Despite the shortages of men and materials and the increased cost of doing business during the war, Labatt was still solvent. This was an accomplishment in and of itself. Many brewers had already surrendered under the pressure of doing business during the conflict. But for those who remained in business, the greatest challenge was yet to come.

The Onset of Prohibition

As the first contingent of Canadian recruits went abroad, the prohibitionists seized a once-in-a-lifetime opportunity to end their long war with the wets.[44] For decades they had made the claim that alcohol was the root of all evil. But despite the passion of their pleas, they had been unable to win over a significant majority of the population to their cause prior to the First World War. The late nineteenth-century topic of prohibition split Canadians more or less down the middle. Only distant Prince Edward Island toyed with full-fledged prohibition before 1914.

But the Great War changed everything. The prohibitionists had long maintained that in order to have a dry heaven on earth, the government would have to take redemptive action because society had lost its moral compass. Prior to the onset of hostilities, the prohibitionists' position alienated wets and civil libertarians alike. But during the war, reticence about state intervention receded as the federal government slowly moved beyond military mobilization into wider and deeper regulation of economic and social life. The war unleashed a moral fervour in Anglo-Canadian society to remodel the social order. The state became more than merely a tax collector and polling clerk as it grew into an institution capable of vigorous, positive, and, at times, intrusive action.

During the war, the prohibitionists added another layer to their argument to banish the bottle, associating their cause with the war effort and stressing the need for efficiency, duty, and self-sacrifice. "Is it asking too much, is the sacrifice too great for Canadians," catechized Ontario's recently elected teetotalling Conservative premier, William Hearst, "to abstain at this time from the reckless waste of money that is now incurred for intoxicants – money that could be so well used for the purchase of munitions, for the aid of the wounded, and for other purposes in connection with the cause for which we are now fighting?"[45] Prohibitionists like Hearst also argued that precious time was being wasted in the taverns of the nation. Public drinking establishments, the drys argued, did not serve any worthy purpose. The tavern was at best an unnecessary distraction, which fostered "lolly-gagging" that was weakening the war effort and, at worst, a "meeting place for Canada's enemies and a breeding-centre of sedition."[46] In addition, the beer drinking that was taking place in the tavern was undermining the efficiency of the worker and making the nation's warriors less effective. Who could deny, asked the *Christian Guardian* in 1914, that "the beer-befuddled soldier is a poor defence to his country?"[47]

Brewers like Labatt had long been portrayed by the prohibitionists as "home breakers"; now with the war raging on the front lines of Europe, they were also depicted as a detriment to the collective cause of defeating Germany. At a time when anti-German sentiment was on the rise – when places like William Lyon Mackenzie King's hometown of Berlin, Ontario, were changing their names to honour British heroes, like Lord Kitchener – the liquor interests were said to be allies of the Germany's Kaiser Wilhelm II. Brewers like Labatt were "the worst pro-Germans we have in Canada today, the most treasonable persons," stated the *Christian Guardian* in 1915.[48] The beer maker was the Kaiser's "dear friend" and "chief ally."[49] Within this highly charged environment, those who defended the liquor interests were portrayed as unpatriotic and hostile to the war effort. Any-one who sided with the likes of Labatt "might as well enlist under the Kaiser as far as patriotism goes," one Prairie newspaper insisted.[50] Virtually everyone un-derstood that the war demanded a greater degree of collective commitment to the cause and a higher level of personal sacrifice. The only question was: how far should the government go in restricting the liberties of some to protect and pro-mote the security and strength of the nation at war?

As the dry army enlisted new people, state-imposed prohibition began to look more likely. In Ontario, a number of prominent businessmen were leaders of bi-partisan organizations dedicated to cutting off the flow of booze for the duration of the war. For example, Toronto businessman and millionaire Joseph Flavelle became the chairman of the powerful Ontario Board of License Commissioners.[51] As a boy growing up in Peterborough, Flavelle had watched his father "waste" most of his breadwinnings on alcohol at the local tavern. Too often, one nickel-shot of rye led to another, and to another. "It was not that my father meant to conduct himself the way he did," Flavelle charitably later stated, "but the appetite for liquor became a desire which would lead him to drink week after week until he would have to go to bed ill for two or three weeks."[52] With his father often absent or incapacitated, Joseph was raised by his mother. The daughter of a

Methodist minister, she instilled in him the value of hard work, self-discipline, self-denial, and a relentless rejection of temptation.[53] Unlike his father, Flavelle did not drink – not a drop. His father's behaviour and his Methodist upbringing had taught him that prohibition was the only way to achieve temperance. Like many businessmen of the age, he worked hard for a new world in which "good men" would not be lost to drink.

For the first time, too, the drys in society were joined by elites in the Anglican Church. Beyond their immediate family and close friends in the London brewing community, the Labatts had always found comfort among those in the Anglican Church. But now many of their own flock were against them. The shifting culture around alcohol played on the self-perceptions of those in the brewing community, as they too internalized the gaze of their critics. Across the country, respected businessmen and politicians organized a Committee of One Hundred in their locale to spearhead the drive to eradicate Labatt and the rest of the liquor traffic. Each committee was linked to a network of activists with thousands of zealous volunteers. In every province across the land, they organized huge demonstrations and brought in prominent speakers like U.S. temperance orator Billy Sunday and Canada's own Nellie McClung to denounce the likes of Labatt and to promote prohibition. Petitions with thousands of signatures calling for full-fledged prohibition poured in to provincial governments, and the newspapers offered almost unanimous support for the prohibitionist cause. "The local option has proved itself to be inadequate to meet the situation," stated the *Toronto Star* in April 1915. "The situation could only be met by a Province-wide measure."[54] The spectre of prohibition loomed.

As Canadian troops made the cold march toward the small village of St Eloi in Belgium during the winter of 1916, back in Canada all signs were pointing toward prohibition becoming a reality in Ontario. Prince Edward Island, Manitoba, Nova Scotia, and Alberta had already crossed the prohibition watershed, and the governments of Saskatchewan, New Brunswick, British Columbia, and the Yukon Territory had signalled that they would soon be moving in the same direction. In the opinion of Ontario's premier, William Hearst, prohibition was a morally and economically necessary wartime measure. "My contention is that if prohibition would bring no benefit to the province from a moral standpoint, if the results that follow its enactment would add nothing to the health and happiness of our people, as a war measure, for the purposes of adding economy, thrift and efficiency, it is justified."[55] A Methodist, Hearst rarely drank. Like Joseph Flavelle, he felt that alcohol stood in the way of personal progress as well as the collective war

Figure 5.1 Labatt salesmen at the launch of the brewery's new non-intoxicating beer, Old London Brew, 1918.

effort. He was set on prohibiting its use. So too was the Liberal opposition leader in Ontario, Newton Wesley "Ban the Bar" Rowell. However, due to the division of powers in Canada between the federal and provincial governments, the Ontario government could only prohibit the retail sale of alcoholic drinks. Brewers like Labatt would be still be allowed to produce full-strength beer, but they would not be allowed to sell it in the province.

Unlike his provincial counterparts in the west, Hearst decided that he would not waste the time, nor spend the money, on a province-wide referendum.[56] Besides, without the voice of the soldiers who were serving overseas, it could be, he said, only a partial expression of public opinion. Plus, he felt sure enough of the general sentiment across the province. His political calculus was correct, but there were still people who opposed full-fledged prohibition, even within his own Cabinet. Few of them, however, were willing to express their views in public for fear of being admonished by the premier or labelled as "unpatriotic" by the drys. As

Stephen Leacock satirically stated, being opposed to prohibition during the war was like "being in favour of burglary."[57] Still, several labour organizations went on record as stating that prohibition would be detrimental to the public good.[58]

On 22 March 1916, Hearst introduced the Ontario Temperance Act to the House. The bill was more draconian than even the government supporters had expected. Once ratified, the legislation would close all bars, clubs, and liquor shops for the duration of the war. Liquor would no longer be allowed in hotels, boarding houses, offices, or other places of business. Only private homes and some private clubs would be exempt from the supervision. While the act did not define what constituted an alcoholic beverage, the License Act enacted prior to the Ontario Temperance Act stated that any beverage with more than 2.5 per cent proof alcohol (roughly 1.5 per cent by volume) was intoxicating and therefore an "alcoholic beverage": it could not be sold within the province.[59] The provincial liquor commission would be charged with administering the act. The measure would be in force for the duration of the war. Only when the soldiers had returned from the front and been absorbed back into civilian life would the matter be submitted to the voters as a subject for referendum.

When the Ontario Temperance Act unanimously passed the House, parliamentarians stood and sang "God Save the King." In the opinion of the *Toronto Star*, the act represented "real progress and it reflects credit upon those public men of both parties and temperance workers to whose efforts it is due."[60] Outside of the legislative assembly, a few dissenters like Stephen Leacock argued that the Ontario Temperance Act was tilted against the working class – the working man could not be trusted with a glass of beer but the well-placed patrician might draw a bottle from his private cellar or retire to his private club. In Leacock's mind, the act was flawed from the start.

The passage of the act was even commented upon in England, where the *Times* of London considered it a "drastic war measure."[61] Prohibitionism never gained the same momentum in Britain as it had in North America, in part because of the efforts of the nation's brewers. In reaction to vehement attacks by temperance reformers in late Victorian times, British brewers and publicans – a potent combination in terms of lobbying – formed "the trade." In a relatively short period, the trade gained a formidable reputation, which other pressure groups could only envy.[62] Having reached out to working-class drinkers and moderate reformers, the trade was able to resist government support of anti-drink legislation.[63] Prohibition failed to become a reality in Britain. The success of the trade might well have served as a model for brewers in Ontario, but Labatt and the others took no notice. There was no effort to demonstrate the economic contribution the brewers made to the growth of the economy and no effort to convey to the public beer's historic role in maintaining morale in the military. In fact, there was no coordinated counterattack at all. Like it or not, the great adventure in aridity got underway.

Mail-order Beer

In the summer of 1916, those at the old London Brewery decided to exploit the loopholes in the Ontario Temperance Act. It was common knowledge that the act did not prohibit the manufacture of full-strength beer, just the public possession of it for the purpose of retail sale.[64] Also widely known was the fact that brewers like Labatt were legally allowed to sell their products to residents outside of Ontario.[65] Furthermore, given that the jurisdiction over the interprovincial traffic in liquor rested with the federal government, provincial governments could not prohibit the importation of intoxicating beverages by their own citizens for personal consumption at home, even if the province in question was legally dry. "I believe we are presented with an opportunity," Hume Cronyn coolly stated to the board after relaying these facts. What Cronyn had in mind was a mail-order business that would see Labatt's full-strength beer exported to places where prohibition was not in force and then – this was the ingenious twist – shipped back into Ontario for private consumption. The innovative scheme complied with the letter, if not the spirit, of the law. Moral ambiguity again reigned at Labatt.

For this plan to work, however, Labatt would have to have a physical presence in a wet territory. At the time that the board of directors was considering Cronyn's clever plot, five provinces did not have prohibitionist legislation on the books; but four out of the five had indicated it was only a matter of time before they too went dry. Quebec was the only province where the issue was really still in question. Quebec had always represented an exceptional case in Canadian history. The Protestant moral urge toward prohibition that existed in English Canada was simply not evident in the predominantly French-speaking and Roman Catholic province of Quebec. This was due in part to the fact that alcohol was consumed in celebration of the Eucharist. In addition, some Quebecers saw prohibition as anti-Catholic because Protestant groups like the Ku Klux Klan strongly supported it. Finally, prohibitionism never took hold in Quebec the way it did in the rest of Canada because of the efforts of the brewers in the province.

The Quebec brewers were better organized, more united, and far more strategically minded than the brewers in the rest of Canada when it came to battling
the prohibitionists. Leading the wet campaign in Quebec were Herbert Molson,
president of the oldest continuous brewery in North America, and Norman
Dawes, vice-president of National Breweries. Molson and National Breweries were
two of the largest beer manufacturers in Canada, and they had more than most
to lose if prohibition became a reality in Quebec. As part of their crusade to keep
Quebec wet, they reminded the public that brewing was a part of the nation's
cultural heritage. "For more than a century," read an advertisement that appeared
in the press, "[the brewers] have promoted temperance in its truest form ... [And]
the men who founded these breweries played important parts in the affairs of
the early history of Canada."[66] In another advertisement, they made the case that
prohibition would not only cost jobs "by throwing hundreds of workers out of
employment" but also deny the workers their favorite alcoholic beverage. "Beer
has been for centuries a part of the daily diet of our working classes," the Quebec
brewers reminded the public in another ad.[67] At the same time that they were
lobbying the public, the brewers were pressuring the provincial government of
Jean Lomer Gouin to reconsider its proposed dry legislation.[68] In the end, the
pressure tactics worked. Quebec's experiment with banning the sale of all alcoholic drinks lasted only a few months, after which Gouin moved back to a system
of partial prohibition that permitted the sale of beer and wine.[69]

Quebec's relatively favourable attitude toward alcohol led to Labatt's return to
the province after an absence of more than a decade. In the summer of 1916,
members of the board unanimously agreed to "proceed without delay to obtain a
wholesale licence from the Quebec Government." At the same meeting, the decision was made to "secure premises on lease in the City of Hull for the purpose of
warehousing and shipping booze." Hugh Labatt was assigned the task of managing
the mail-order business, first in Hull and Montreal and later in Buffalo, New York.
Within a year, the Ottawa agency business was almost entirely transferred across
the river to 275 Rue Street in Hull. For a time, the mail-order business worked almost as well as Cronyn had imagined. Full-strength beer was manufactured at the
Labatt's plant in London and then shipped to its branch office in Montreal. When
the mail orders were received from thirsty Ontarians, the same beer was simply
returned to Ontario for local consumption. Sales at the Montreal branch soared.
Between 1 October 1916 and 30 September 1917, the Montreal branch did over
$275,000 in business, while combined sales at the Toronto and Hamilton branches

totalled roughly $65,000.[70] There was a lesson to be learned from all of this: the real money was to be made in selling full-strength beer.

The prohibitionists could hardly restrain themselves. Labatt's violation of the spirit of the law was a "disgrace," an "abomination," an "outrage." One indignant prohibitionist explained the Labatt's shell game in the following way: "The liquor is first put on a joy ride on a freight train to Quebec to become Frenchified and then it is sent back again to Ontario."[71] "What a farce!" Something had to be done, the prohibitionists proclaimed, to stop the interprovincial transaction in liquor.[72] In the autumn of 1916, as the bloody Battle of the Somme was being waged in Europe, the prohibitionists began pressuring the federal government of Robert Borden for a law to stop the mail-order business of liquor men like Labatt. Belatedly, the brewers also sent a delegation to Ottawa. As the dry editors of the *Toronto Star* noted with malicious joy, the brewers "are in a fight for their lives."[73] But, for the brewers, it was too little, too late. In late 1916, the Borden government passed legislation outlawing the export of liquor into provinces where prohibition was in force. The mail-order business dried up.

Near Beer

At the old London Brewery, the board of directors worried that the Ontario Temperance Act would place "the company in a very bad position." The previous year had been tough enough. Wartime shortages of men and materials along with rising government taxation had led to increased expenditures, which had taken a toll on the company's bottom line.[74] Added to this, a great many of the company's debts, which had always been considered good, were now classed as "doubtful."[75] However, there was a sense that if the company could endure the dryness of war, peace would bring a wetter oasis. The question was how to survive the remainder of the war.

On 27 September 1916, the board of directors met at the King Edward Hotel in downtown Toronto and agreed that "the only way to continue the business would be to adapt the brewery to the manufacture of Temperance Beer and Porter."[76] Virtually every brewer that survived the dry regime produced these temperance drinks – i.e., non-intoxicating beer – with no more than 2.5 per cent proof alcohol. Initially, the demand for these "near beers" was unexpectedly strong. "I have been surprised at the demand for Temperance Beer," wrote A.E. Cross of the

Figure 5.2 Labatt advertisement promoting its three temperance brews – Old London Brew, Cremo Lager, and Special Porter – and emphasizing their thirst-quenching qualities, 1919.

Calgary Brewing and Malting Co. in September 1916. "Although there is not much profit in it, we are able to pay our debts, which is a good deal better than going broke."[77] Members of the Labatt board felt the same way. Labatt had the advantage of having already moved into the production of non-intoxicating beer. In 1910, John Labatt II had overseen the introduction of Comet beer. The brand was named after Halley's Comet, which had passed especially close to Earth that year. Before the war, virtually nobody chose to drink these temperance beers. Why would they? They were less alcoholic and tasted worse than regular brews. But during the war, when Canadians were in a mood to make personal sacrifices for the collective cause – and full-strength beer was not available for retail sale – more people bought these beers.

Nevertheless, there were a few problems with production after prohibition came into effect in 1916. One recurring difficulty related to the alcoholic content of Labatt's draft temperance beer. While the beer contained 2.5 per cent alcohol at the plant, on occasion the percentage was higher by the time it reached the consumer. While this did not displease the province's beer drinkers, who often yearned for "the real stuff," it greatly annoyed the province's liquor inspectors. As a result, in October 1916, Labatt was charged with violating the Ontario Temperance Act. The company agreed to immediately stop production until it "could guarantee its draft beer did not exceed two and half per cent."[78] Once Labatt determined that the higher alcohol content resulted from additional fermentation after the beer was kegged, corrections were made and production got back on track.

During the war, Labatt vigorously pushed its temperance beer, which led the company to use trucks for the very first time. Trucks allowed for flexibility in deliveries and freed the brewers from the monopoly of the railways. Now brewers could take smaller orders and deliver their product directly to the purchaser's door – as had previously been done in wagons, but now with much greater speed and efficiency. During prohibition, trucks were especially critical to the survival of breweries because, as John S. Labatt noted, "it is hard to market 2.5% beer except by peddling." What he meant was that the temperance beers of the age were poor substitutes for the real stuff. Few, if any, of the brands on the market were sought after by consumers. Fewer still were asked for by name. With very little brand recognition, temperance beers had to be continually pushed. Labatt's agents made regular calls on hotels throughout the province to promote the firm's near beer and enhance goodwill among the hotel operators.

During prohibition, the temperance beer market was almost as competitive as the regular beer market had been before the onset of the dry regime. In part, this was because there were few places to imbibe during the war. The number of hotels in operation was falling fast. Without the added income from liquor sales, many hotel operators found it impossible to pay their bills. This pleased few in the liquor trade. At George J. Foy Limited in Toronto, a hard-nosed Irishman by the name of Edmund M. Burke was given the unenviable task of collecting the debts owed by those in the hotel industry. His charm was only exceeded by his ruthlessness. His exploits were legendary and well known to everyone in the industry, including those at Labatt. Burke did not think much of the dry regime. But he knew there was no use in complaining. All one could do was soldier on and try to stay afloat until the ebb of the prohibitionist tide.

In October 1916, the board of directors was able to report that the sales of temperance beer "were encouraging for this time of the year, [and] for this class of goods."[79] Nevertheless, there was a problem in that production was on pace to reach only 8,000 barrels for the year. That was far too low to generate an overall operating profit. The board of directors decided to double-down on their near beer bet.[80]

But in order to increase production, a major investment would have to be made. The firm would need a long list of new and expensive factory equipment: an insulated cellar, an ice machine, a brine cooler, pressure tanks, and bottling-cellar equipment. To determine how much all this would cost, Labatt arranged for C.F. Hettinger, a Boston-based engineer and brewery architect, to visit the plant in London. Hettinger was highly regarded in the brewing industry, having previously worked for both Molson and O'Keefe. After looking over the Labatt plant, Hettinger concluded that it would cost approximately $125,000 to increase the capacity of the brewery to 25,000 barrels of temperance beer per annum. This was a huge sum for Labatt to spend in the midst of the war. Nevertheless, the company borrowed the money it needed from the Bank of Nova Scotia and began to retrofit the brewery.

When the renovations were complete, Labatt launched two new temperance beers: an ale called Old London Brew and a lager called Cremo, which the label warned was "best served cold." The advertisements that followed emphasized the thirst-quenching qualities of these new brews and promised "a measure of satisfaction" (see figure 5.2). But many Canadians were not impressed. As the soldiers began returning home from overseas in the final years of the war, they voiced their displeasure with these non-intoxicating beers. "We thirsty souls are craving an old-

Figure 5.3 During prohibition, Labatt used trucks for the very first time to transport its beer. The restored truck featured here was used in 1919. Trucks offered flexibility in deliveries and freed the brewers from the monopoly of the railways. Brewers could take smaller orders and deliver their product directly to the purchaser's door. This had previously been done in wagons, but could now be done with much greater speed and efficiency.

time 'schooner' of beer of moderate strength," stated Lieutenant-Colonel A.T. Kelly Evans. In the opinion of Canada's veterans, the temperance brews were "sickening and damaging to the constitution"; "unhealthy, unwholesome, indigestible and nauseating to the drinker"; and "not even fit for a Teuton." Lieutenant-Colonel Evans agreed and blamed the prohibitionists for inflicting tortures upon Canadian drinkers, "worthy to be classed with the atrocities inflicted on the early Christians in Rome, or the Huguenots in France."[81] As sales plummeted, the temperance beer plant took on the appearance of a white elephant.

Conclusion

On 23 May 1917, members of Labatt's board of directors met at the office of William Whitehead on St James Street in Montreal. They were there to discuss the ongoing difficulties of operating a brewery during the war and prohibition. Whitehead was particularly worried. "We are running the business at a considerable monthly loss," he stated.[82] Later that day, Whitehead repeated the troubling news to the other shareholders of the company at his home in Montreal.[83] The family firm had never been in such a precarious position. John S. Labatt blamed "the disorganized situation" on "legislation and war conditions."[84] He pointed to the fact that other brewers were also struggling. The war had upended normal industrial calculations, constricting capital and introducing short-term variables into what were usually long-term capitalization strategies. There was no denying this. During the war, Canadian breweries were going out of business on a regular basis. On the eve of the conflict, the industry had boasted 117 breweries. By 1917, 67 of them had been wiped out. The greatest damage had been done in Ontario, where the number of breweries declined from 49 in 1915 to 23 just two years later. Some of the brewers whose doors went dark were among the province's oldest. For example, Labatt's long-time rival, George Sleeman and Sons, which had been making beer in Guelph, Ontario, since 1847, was forced to close in July 1916.[85]

To be sure, circumstances had played a big part in determining the fate of firms. But so too had leadership, and Labatt was lacking it during the war. For John and Hugh Labatt, the war was a baptism by fire. They were often overwhelmed and idea-less in the face of wartime challenges. Too often they acted as though things were out of their control, baffled by the "disorganized situation" of war. Their performance at the helm of the firm lends further support to the argument that successful family firms quickly lose their creative energy as control passes from the founder to his/her heirs. The third generation lacked the initial generation's hunger to succeed. They were unable to build new competencies in addition to the old. The best they could do was let others lead. Lacking the contempt that their father and grandfather had for those who would judge brewers for making a living profit, they proved unwilling and unable to take on the cold-water army. Because they didn't see the brewery as a living symbol of their own achievements, they were unwilling to do *whatever* needed to be done not just to survive but also grow the firm during a dry regime.

PART TWO

**State
Regulation
and
Expansion**

"Something Very Unforeseen"

How a Bootlegging Manager-Entrepreneur Saved Labatt from Prohibition, 1921–28

At a hastily arranged meeting at the home of Hume Cronyn in London on 17 June 1921, Labatt's directors "resolved that unless something very unforeseen occurs, the Board has decided to wind up the business on September 30th next."[1] The company had been hemorrhaging money for months under the colossal weight of prohibition. Every branch of the company was operating at a loss.[2] In all likelihood, the firm would be bankrupt in about a year – the latest casualty of the dry regime. All the family members on the board were there that day as well as the one outsider, Labatt general manager Edmund Burke. Having listened to what the board had to say, Burke made the board an offer that it could not refuse. "Keep making full strength beer, don't ask any questions and let me run things," Burke urged the Labatt family, "and your brewery will not only survive but thrive during prohibition." All Burke wanted in return was 10 per cent of the profits.[3] The Labatt family agreed.[4]

In the decade after the war, prohibition continued to be a fact of life in most parts of Canada and in the United States. The majority of provinces that had gone dry during the war remained so after the armistice. Saskatchewan, for example, joined the dry column in 1917 and remained there until 1925. Next door, in Alberta, prohibition stayed in effect until 1924; New Brunswick was dry until 1927, and Nova Scotia until 1930. Given the bulkiness of beer, and the difficulties of making beer money at a distance, the only market that really mattered to those at Labatt was Ontario, and it remained dry until 1927. The laws in these places continued to prohibit the retail sale of intoxicating liquor. But unlike in the United States, where the Volstead Act (officially, the National Prohibition Act) prohibited both the production and consumption of alcohol between 1920 and 1933, Canadians were still allowed to manufacture intoxicating beverages.

As in Canada, prohibition in the United States had a devastating effect on the brewing industry, cutting the number of breweries roughly in half. Those brewers that survived generally diversified into other businesses. For example, Anheuser-Busch and a handful of other brewers turned to making soft drinks and ice cream, cheese and yeast, and non-alcoholic beer with brand names like Hoppy and Bevo, Besto and Pevo. In St Louis, the Falstaff Brewing Company started making smoked hams in an effort to survive. In Allentown, the F. & M. Schaefer Brewing Company concentrated on making and selling ice.[5] Other brewers survived by making malt syrup that was advertised as an ingredient for baking cookies, but was primarily used for making homemade beer. Still other breweries endured by disposing of their assets, selling off branch properties and saloons in an effort to kept their creditors at bay.[6] But Edmund Burke's strategy for survival was different.

This chapter examines how Labatt survived prohibition. It concentrates largely on the entrepreneurial efforts of Labatt's hard-nosed general manager Edmund Burke – and for good reason. During prohibition, the firm was Burke's fiefdom as the board turned a blind eye to morally ambiguous activities. That Labatt family members did not want to know what was really going on was reflected in the fact that the number of board meetings dropped from twelve a year to just one or two a year between 1921 and 1927. Given the lack of corporate governance, Burke was free to identify and then exploit those opportunities that benefited him as much as the firm.

Edmund Burke: Bootlegger as Entrepreneur

Born in 1863 in the Irish county of Tipperary – known as "Tipple-rary" to its cold-water critics – not far from where John Kinder Labatt hailed, Edmund Burke as an entrepreneur was nothing like John or Hugh Labatt. A Roman Catholic, Burke received a brief legal training before immigrating to the United States in the early 1880s.[7] He had an extensive knowledge of the liquor trade in both Canada and the United States, having cut his teeth selling tobacco and whisky south of the border before joining George J. Foy Limited, a wholesale liquor and tobacco firm in Toronto, just after the turn of the century. By the time the Labatts met Burke in 1908, he had already gained a reputation as a rough-and-tumble "problem solver." Skeptical by nature, he was extremely intelligent and quick on

Figure 6.1 Edmund Burke, c. 1925. As general manager of Labatt during prohibition, Burke was responsible for saving the company from certain bankruptcy.

his feet. He wasn't a tall man, but he projected the confidence of one. At work, he was always impeccably dressed, usually in pinstriped suits and often with a flower in his lapel (see figure 6.1). He wore tan spats and colourful ties. He had sharp features, hard eyes, and what hair he had was already snowy white. Always quick with a joke, he had an oversized personality and an easy charm about him. While usually genial, his Irish temper often got the better of him when he was irritated. There was a kind of Dr Jekyll and Mr Hyde in Edmund Burke. According to one employee, Burke "could cut one down to size in very few words."[8] Even into his fifties, he kept himself in excellent physical condition and was willing to use brute force when provoked.[9] The fiery Irishman came to the attention of Labatt's board of directors through the company's Toronto office, which was in the J.J. Foy Building. When the Foy company fell victim to prohibition, John Labatt II immediately offered him the position of "manager, for a period of one year."[10] Reflecting the importance that Labatt placed on the hiring, Burke was offered a salary of $4,500

Figure 6.2 Portrait of Catherine Constance Scatcherd, c. 1915. Born in 1867, Catherine was the eldest and more capable of John Labatt II's children. In 1894, she married John Allan Dunbar Scatcherd. As a member of the Labatt board, she supported Burke's initiatives during prohibition.

for the year – a huge sum at the time, and more than the combined pay of John and Hugh Labatt.[11]

Burke quickly gained the respect of those at Labatt, including Catherine Scatcherd, who joined the board of directors in March 1919. Catherine was elected to replace her cousin Lieut.-Col. Robert Labatt, who died on 6 February 1919 of war-related injuries.[12] Also gone was William T. Whitehead, who resigned from the board in the last few months of the war. His sound counsel would be missed. Alexander Marshall Graydon, a London lawyer who had married Catherine's younger sister Ismena, replaced Whitehead in 1914 and, along with Hume Cronyn, provided reliable legal advice to the other members of the board when the situation demanded.

In many ways, Catherine Scatchard and Edmund Burke were much alike. Both had a tremendous zest for life, although Catherine still had not fully recovered from the death of her father or her son John, who died on the front lines in Europe at the tail end of the war. To be sure, Catherine Scatcherd had none of Burke's rough edges. Like her brothers, she was gracious and gentle. And if she had some element of Burke's volatile Irish temperament, she never displayed it in public. Yet, like Burke, she refused to be dictated to by social norms surrounding alcohol. Both she and Burke were seemingly immune to the disapproving stares and judgmental gossip of the moral reformers – this would prove to be a valuable asset to Burke, allowing him to perceive opportunities and risks differently than most others. Burke's experience peddling booze south of the border had taught him to act with a certain degree of amoral toughness.

Like Burke, Catherine Scatcherd had thicker skin than most. At the time she joined the board, few women held such lofty positions in Canadian business, and fewer still were associated with the liquor traffic. While the old Victorian notion of a "separate sphere" for women had all but come to an end with the war, few in Canadian society believed it was "proper" for a woman to be on the boards of liquor companies. First-wave feminists had come crashing out of the home to cut off the head of King Alcohol. Women were supposed to work against the liquor traffic, not for it. "Shame on the women if we don't get prohibition," stated prohibitionist Mrs W.R. Lang in 1919.[13] But Catharine would not be swayed by the judgment of Mrs Lang or her ilk. She savoured the opportunity to promote her sisters' interest on the board, and to defend the old London Brewery from its enemies.[14] When it came to the day-to-day operations of the brewery, she chose to stay out of Burke's way, and subtly suggested to others on the board that they do the same. This left Burke in command and free to exploit those opportunities that he believed were both desirable and feasible.

Opportunity

In January 1920, the Volstead Act, which enforced the Eighteenth Amendment in the United States, went into effect and the nation went dry. Wayne B. Wheeler, the shrewd general counsel of the Anti-Saloon League, had written the first draft of the act. The final version was everything he and the other prohibitionists – like the crusading women who had worked so hard and who had now won the right to vote – had wanted and more. Named after the taciturn congressman from Minnesota who sponsored the act, Andrew John Volstead, the law specified that "no person shall manufacture, sell, barter, transport, import, export, deliver, furnish or possess any intoxicating liquor except as authorized by this act."[15] The act had a much stricter interpretation of what constituted an "intoxicating beverage" than the dry legislation in Canada. As the *New York Daily News* warned its readers on the day that the law went into effect: under the terms of the act, "you cannot manufacture anything above one half of one percent (liquor strength)."[16] Overnight, liquor shops were padlocked and the barrels stopped rolling out of the breweries and distilleries of the nation.

Unlike John and Hugh Labatt, Edmund Burke identified the onset of prohibition in the United States as a tremendous opportunity. He knew the liquor business in the United States. As a liquor salesman during the 1880s and 1890s, he had entered saloons and hotels from Minneapolis to Atlantic City. He drank with saloon owners and barkeepers, and treated the local clientele to rounds of drinks. After joining Labatt just before the First World War, he often told stories of the drinking practices of "'em Yankees." His days in the trade had taught him that Americans drank a great deal – even more than their Canadian counterparts. Given what he had seen south of the border, he believed the heavy drinking would continue despite national prohibition. Given Labatt's proximity to major U.S. markets and that federal law in Canada still allowed the manufacture and export of intoxicating beverages, Burke perceived an opportunity – a defining characteristic of successful entrepreneurship.[17] He was confident that, if he could get Labatt's products to the shores of the Great Lakes, there would be a ready clientele waiting for them on the other side of the border.

Burke understood the risks and rewards involved in bootlegging. Many did. After all, it was often written about in the popular press. For example, a few months after the onset of national prohibition in the United States, a budding young writer published an exposé article in the *Toronto Star Weekly* on the money to be made from bootlegging. "Fortunes are being made by the bootleggers," Ernest Hemingway wrote, "who have the liquor shipped to their carefully established residences at Windsor and nearby towns, and then run it across the river to the States."[18] Hemingway reported that a case of whisky that cost $18 in Ontario was being sold by bootleggers for $120 in the border towns of Michigan. But even more money was being made further west. A man living in a small town in Iowa, for instance, paid $250 a case for Canadian whisky. Strong ale, on the other hand, sold regularly for between $2.25 and $3.25 for a case of twenty-four pints. From the sale of one case of bootlegged whisky, a small-time smuggler could earn enough to buy twelve more. Big-time bootleggers, like "The Whisky King" Rocco Perri, dealt with much larger volumes and earned much greater fortunes.

A Calabrian who had come to Canada in his teens, Rocco made connections with the Society of the Black Hand (an underground organization of mostly Italian-American criminals and thugs) and then wooed his future partner in crime, Bessie Starkman, away from her husband and children. Before prohibition, Rocco and Bessie ran prostitutes out of the saloon they owned in Hamilton. But when prohibition hit, the two started "short-circuiting" alcohol back into Ontario. The most common way they did this was to put their booze on to boats, claiming to authorities that it was being exported out of Ontario, only to have it return and sold illegally in the province. They made enough money from this to buy a massive house on Bay Street in Hamilton. But the real money came after the United States went dry in 1920. By 1923, The Whisky King and his wife were grossing $1 million a month from their illicit operations.[19] Prohibition was the greatest thing that ever happened to the goons.

Given the huge profits that could be made, adventurous Canadians, from all walks of life, turned to bootlegging. At a time of mass unemployment, many smugglers were attracted to the trade by the possibility of earning a better living than that provided by sporadic wages or the dole. Contraband Canadian liquor was brought into the United States by every conceivable means. Women would walk across the international border with liquor bottles hidden under their skirts, in their purses, or in baby carriages. Men hid their hooch in lunch boxes, suitcases, or the lining of their coats. Larger loads were shipped in coffins or in boxes deceivingly labelled as "tulips," "bibles," and "Christmas trees." One farmer-cum-bootlegger carefully poked tiny holes in all of his eggs, drained them, filled them with liquor, sealed them back up, and then drove the truckload over the border. Almost 75 per cent of the bootlegged booze went through the Windsor-Detroit Funnel. When the Detroit River froze in the winter, Windsor men skated across the ice to Detroit pushing loaded dories fitted with metal runners.[20] So much bootlegging was going on that in 1921 the head of the U.S. Customs Service informed Congress that the "quantities [of liquor] pouring in from Canada now constitutes a flood."[21]

While the potential payoff was enormous, the legal risks were relatively small. In the eyes of the law, bootlegging was a "summary offence" punishable by a fine or a few months in jail. In addition, there was very little police presence along the border, so there was little likelihood of being caught. The Canadian federal agency that was given the enormous task of patrolling the roads and waterways during prohibition, the Canadian Customs Preventative Service Fleet was tiny and ineffective.[22] On the opposite side of the border, U.S. forces were equally inadequate. The Detroit police force, for example, had one boat to carry out its anti-bootlegging operations, while the police at Rouses Point in northern New York had to hire taxis to carry out their patrols.[23] It wasn't until the last half of the decade that the authorities on both sides of the border beefed up their forces to the point that they were a serious threat to bootleggers.

Until then, the greatest threat to the bootlegger had come from other bootleggers. The underground economy in alcohol had more than its fair share of dirty dealings. Hijackings and murders were all too common. In 1922, the brother-in-law of Sam and Harry Bronfman, Paul Matoff, died from a shotgun blast in Saskatchewan. Prohibition made the Bronfmans incredibly rich and helped launch a Canadian distilling dynasty.[24] But the road to riches was splattered with blood. In Ontario, Jimmy Loria, a member of the Sicilian mob and an enemy of Rocco Perri, was assassinated during the "deadly summer of 1922."[25] Perri believed that Loria was responsible for killing one of his associates and was determined to exact some revenge. On the night of 17 May 1922, after accepting a drive from what he thought was a group of friends, Loria got out of the car to relieve himself by the side of the road. One of Rocco's men came up behind and shot him in the back of the head.[26] The bullet severed his spinal cord and lodged in the roof of his mouth. He was dead before he hit the ground. The killings continued thereafter. Off the coast of Victoria, B.C., in September 1924, three Americans hijacked a small boat, the *Beryl G*, murdered the captain and his son, dumped the bodies overboard, and made off with the contraband liquor. After a sensational trial, two of the culprits were executed in Vancouver and the third was sentenced to life in prison.[27] When stories like this came to light, many Canadians began to reappraise their being in the business of bootlegging. But not Burke.

Edmund Burke had dealt with thugs before, first as a liquor salesman and then during his days as debt collector for George J. Foy Limited. He was willing to deal with these types again in order to steer the old London Brewery through prohibition. Indeed, some of these marginal figures were now among his friends. He trusted them not to do him harm, or to rat him out to the authorities. As a result, he had a different perception of risk than most mainstream Canadians, and certainly a different perception than John and Hugh Labatt. His network of marginal types constituted a valuable resource that could be used for profit in the underground economy. Among them were many of the suppliers of hard alcohol.

Supplies and Storage

At its most basic level, bootlegging is about getting an illegal product from the manufacturer to the consumer. This requires a secure and stable network of suppliers and distributors as well as the apparatus to bypass the law. When it came to supplies, Burke determined that to maximize his profits it was essential, alongside full-strength beer, to have hard liquor to sell to those customers who often preferred to deal with a single trusted bootlegger. Spirits commanded a higher price and took up less cargo room, so there was more money to be made from each shipment. Why risk smuggling a case of beer when a case of whisky brought much higher profits? Still, strong beer would be sold, particularly in southwestern Ontario where the population was both concentrated and large, and the cost of transportation from London relatively low.

The strong beer came from Labatt's own brew kettles. Under Burke's command, the composition of the brewery's output shifted away from the production of near beer to strong beer with 9 per cent proof alcohol. This caught the eye of Hume Cronyn, who urged John Sackville Labatt to keep the company's business above board. "The John Labatt Company has always prided itself on its honourable record," Hume wrote. "I must therefore, as a Director, emphatically protest against any infringement of the law of the land and ask you – as the President and the officer in immediate control – to see to it that we obey both the spirit and the letter of the law."[28] Hume Cronyn had conveniently forgotten about Labatt's amoral practices during the Scott Act period and the fact that John S. Labatt was not actually in charge. As a consequence, his counsel fell on deaf ears. By Christmas 1923, the sale of strong beer accounted for 89 per cent of Labatt's total beer sales. Sales remained at about that level until the noble experiment in Ontario came to an end in 1927.[29]

While most of Labatt's strong beer flowed south of the border, some pooled in the province and was sold in contravention of the Ontario Temperance Act. As more than one of Labatt's employees later confessed, full-strength beer was delivered by truck to various small stores and post offices across the province, where it was sold surreptitiously out the back door.[30] In London, strong beer was often slyly put into temperance cases and sold over the counter to "trusted" customers.[31] Asked about this practice when testifying before the Royal Commission on Customs and Excise, which had been struck on 17 November 1926 to investigate charges of widespread corruption among Canadian customs officials, Labatt's John Aitken admitted that he sold strong beer "to my friends in London."[32]

Sensing that Aitken was being less than fully forthcoming, the commission's chief counsel, Newton Wesley Rowell, asked: "Would you sell to anyone who came along?" "Not unless I knew them," Aitken replied. "You wouldn't discriminate against anyone?" Rowell asked, as he continued questioning Aitken. "Not unless I thought he was a [temperance] spotter," responded Aitken. "So you'd sell to him if he looked alright?" inquired Rowell. "If he was a friend of mine," answered Aitken. Rowell paused for a moment and then sardonically stated: "You appear to have a host of friends in London, judging from sales."[33]

All of the hard liquor being bootlegged by every operator in Ontario was coming from these same distilleries. Prohibition had hit the distilling industry as hard as it had the brewing industry. Only the most innovative enterprises survived. Principal among them was the Canadian Industrial Alcohol Company, which in 1918 purchased the H. Corby Distillery Company near Belleville and hired an ex-hotel owner, Henry Hatch, to manage sales. After the onset of national prohibition in the United States, Hatch connected with scofflaws south of the border and organized his own rum-running fleet, which was so large that it was dubbed "Hatch's Navy." At the same time, he sold his whisky to other Canadian bootleggers, like Rocco Perri. By 1923, Perri had built up a fleet of fifty ships to carry his Corby whisky to the United States.[34] In 1924 – right in the midst of prohibition, when so many other distilleries were closing their doors – the Corby plant underwent a massive expansion that made it one of the largest in the world.[35] Corby Distillery had plenty of whisky to sell to the likes of Burke, who started stockpiling it at Labatt's London-based brewery.

With cases of whisky being brought in from Belleville to supplement Labatt's full-strength beer, Burke had all the products he needed to gain a foothold in the American market. What he needed next was a new system of distribution. In late 1921, Burke began leasing warehouses in strategic locations in the southwest corner of Ontario – places like St Thomas on the way to Port Stanley, St Catharines on the way to Crystal Beach and Niagara, and Chatham on the way to Windsor.[36] He also purchased larger warehouses on the docks at Sarnia and Ford City.[37] These were all convenient locations for smuggling booze across the forty-ninth parallel. Now the question for Burke was how to get the alcohol from the plants to the storage facilities and from there across the forty-ninth parallel – without being caught by the authorities.

Transportation

Burke faced a number of challenges when it came to getting his products to market during prohibition. Initially, the railway companies refused to handle full-strength beer or hard liquor, viewing it as a violation of the spirit of the law. In addition, the Ontario government of Ernest Charles Drury had put in place legislation to prevent the use of provincial highways for transporting intoxicating liquor. The Act respecting the Transportation of Intoxicating Liquors was designed to put a stranglehold on brewers like Labatt, who were still suffering from the restraints of prohibition. To get around this, at least initially while the bootlegging business got underway, Burke had his customers pick up product from the plant. As a number of employees later recalled, customers showed up at the brewery in London in high-powered cars – "whisky six" Studebakers and Reo "speed riders" – to collect their liquor. These cars were often stripped of their interior upholstery to create great load capacity.[38] With lookouts stationed on the roof of the brewery watching for the police, the bootleggers loaded up the back of their cars with bottles of Labatt's full-strength beer and whisky, and then covered up their cargo with old hop sacks. The fact that Labatt's employees did not lend a helping hand allowed Burke to brazenly state later that the company's hands were clean when it came to crimes of concealment. "The fact that Labatt beer was found in a camouflaged car is no evidence that Labatt's committed a crime of camouflage," he told the Royal Commission on Customs and Excise.[39] Once the signal was given that the coast was clear, the rum-runners made a break for it.

Burke quickly realized that this "pick-by-customer" practice was a relatively inefficient form of distribution. He would need to move more product more quickly, and over longer distances, to make the real money he was after. In the summer of 1922, he decided to test the law prohibiting the use of provincial highways for the transportation of intoxicating beverages. The former law student in him felt that the Carriage of Liquor Act was ultra vires, that is, beyond the jurisdiction of the provincial government. But thinking so was academic. What mattered in business was what could be accomplished in practice.

In the early morning of 16 May 1922, Burke watched as five of his men loaded up one of the company's trucks with thirty cartons of full-strength beer. Burke then went into the office, picked up the phone, called the province's licence inspector, J.E. Keenleyside, and informed him that one of Labatt's trucks would soon be carrying liquor on a public highway. Keenleyside quickly mobilized his forces and was waiting for the vehicle as it made its way down Talbot Street, just a few miles north of the Labatt's London Brewery. The beer was seized and Labatt was charged with breaking the law.[40] The case went to court on 9 July 1922, and having heard from both the prosecution and the defence, the judge ruled that the Province had no power to interfere with shipments of liquor, inasmuch as liquor was a commodity of the export trade. The Ontario legislation, the judge concluded, had no authority to intervene with foreign commerce.[41] The charges against Labatt were dismissed. The ruling was a victory not only for Labatt but also for all of those engaged in the illicit liquor trade. Having removed the legislative roadblock, Burke immediately put to use his powers of persuasion to convince the board of directors to build up Labatt's fleet of trucks.[42] By 1925, the company had twenty-eight two-and-a-half-ton trucks.[43]

Having secured transportation to the shores of the Great Lakes, Burke now had to contend with getting his booze across the international boundary. In 1923, he acquired three large fishing boats: the *Agnes W*, the *Cisco*, and the *Brown Brothers*. The *Agnes W* was a typical gasoline-powered fish tug with a covered-in deck that did the regular run from Port Stanley to the Cleveland area across Lake Erie. The *Cisco* and the *Brown Brothers* were steam-powered boats and much larger than the *Agnes W*. They made the longest voyages, setting off from various points on the Canadian side of the border from Port Stanley to the St Clair River and servicing the lucrative Michigan and Ohio bootleg market.[44]

By the summer of 1924, Burke was also shipping booze to the United States by train. With the railway companies now in desperate need of revenue, they took active part in the bootlegging business. By rerouting and relabelling freight cars along the way, the railway companies were able to ship Labatt's booze to the United States under the guise of other commodities. In 1924, sixty-five carloads of export-strength beer were transported by rail to the United States.[45]

There was nothing illegal about exporting intoxicating beverages to foreign places – even if, as in the case of the United States, the country had imposed prohibition – so long as the right paperwork had been filled out. Until it became a source of national embarrassment in the late 1920s, the Canadian government did not care about the export trade in liquor so long as it was getting its share of the revenue stream from taxes. What the government did not want, however, was for the booze to be short-circuited back into dry provinces. To prevent this, the federal government stationed customs officials at the docks and warehouses. Before Burke's boats were loaded up with cartons of beer and whisky, a B-13 form

Figure 6.3 During prohibition, Labatt used unmarked and covered trucks like this one in an attempt to not draw attention to itself. c. 1925.

had to be stamped by customs officials. The form required the name of the boat, a description of the cargo, the name of the purchaser, and the destination. No self-respecting bootlegger would give accurate information. Fake names and destinations were used. Boats that could barely make it across the Great Lakes were said to be heading to Cuba, Haiti, or Bermuda. To turn a blind eye, customs officials were bought off, wholesale. Burke had set up a "snake fund" for exactly this purpose.[46] For enough money, some customs officials would stamp a stack of blank B-13s that Burke or one of his men, like Lou McCaughey, a former policeman from London who had been brought in to supervise the export business at Ford City, would fill out later.[47] When the *Globe* learned about Burke's corruption of public officials, its response was swift and scornful. "This frank avowal of a slush fund and its disgraceful use may well arouse the indignation of the people of Ontario. It is an affront to the public, and a serious reflection on the Government."[48] Burke was unmoved.

Once aboard ship, the booze was wrapped and sewn in sacking material, so that in the event of a run-in with the U.S. Coast Guard, the load could be dumped overboard and retrieved later with grappling hooks.[49] On more than one occasion, Labatt's boats had to make a run for it. As the decade wore on, U.S. officials increasingly dedicated more resources to patrolling the Great Lakes in an attempt to plug the leaks. The danger of trade on the lakes was compounded by the emergence of individuals who had been squeezed out of the lucrative bootlegging trade by the likes of Labatt and were now desperately seeking to reverse their fortunes by hijacking illegal shipments of booze in transit. Many were well armed and fights sometimes broke out.[50] It was not unusual for Labatt's boats to return from a voyage "riddled and splintered with bullet holes," as one Labatt employee later recalled, "as they were chased ... in American waters by rum runners or the U.S. Coast Guard."[51]

The Cartel

The final years of prohibition witnessed the formation of a cartel of Ontario liquor traffickers. Burke had shown his social skills before when interacting with suppliers and distributors as well as marginal types down on the docks. He also demonstrated that he was capable of transforming his social competence into social capital by creating a culture of silence at Labatt and among those in the supply chain. But now he aimed to use his talents to bring together the small group of men who remained in the beer business.

He was motivated by the price-cutting that had returned to the brewing industry. Prices were falling fast. Between 1921 and 1925, the price of a case of beer in Ontario fell from $4.00 to $2.15, which had a negative effect on profits.[52]

Those at the old Carling brewery, which had been taken over by the rum-running syndicate of Low, Leon, and Burns in 1924, were engaged in some of the most predatory pricing practices. The de facto head of the organization was the flamboyant and ever-dapper Harry Low. Having started off work life as an auto mechanic, Low was one of the first in the Windsor area to start smuggling booze across the Detroit River. The bootlegging business made Low and his partners a fortune. In 1925, Low paid $120,000 cash for an English-style mansion in the heart of an exclusive Windsor-area neighbourhood, and then paid an additional $10,000 to have gold-tipped imitation icicles hung from the great hall's ceiling and stained glass installed in all of the windows. For a few years, Carling's exports of lager handsomely augmented the huge profits that Low made from liquor sales to such underworld gangs as the Purple Gang in Detroit and Al Capone's mob in Chicago.[53] An avid sportsman, Low was competitive by nature. Nevertheless, he was willing to co-operate with his rivals when it made financial sense. Approached by Burke in 1924 with a proposal to organize the traffic of Ontario breweries for the double purpose of regulating prices and meeting outside competition, Low welcomed him with open arms. Price-fixing had been a standard practice in the industry since the late 1800s. Prohibition simply changed the circumstances.

In 1924, Labatt, Carling, and nine other Ontario brewers entered into a trust agreement that set sales quotas and prices in the trade along the whole length of the international border from Port Stanley on Lake Erie to Sarnia on Lake Huron. The group was as thick as thieves. The price of a case of twenty-four pints was set at $3.25. Two years later, again on the initiative of Edmund Burke, the agreement became a formal cartel through the formation of the Bermuda Export Company (BEC). This time, the intention was to fix prices for export beer and for selling through a small number of trusted agents selected by each of the eleven breweries. By funnelling their beer through agencies, the brewers could claim ignorance about where the beer ended up and who was drinking it. "The agent has the right to sell to whom they like," Burke told Newton Wesley Rowell at the Royal Commission on Customs and Excise. "We don't know the name of a single customer."[54] If the rest of the members of his cartel knew, they weren't talking. They all lived by Burke's philosophy that "one of the essentials of the modern way of exporting is that you must not know too much or ask too much."[55]

The operations of the BEC enlarged the cartel's area of trade across the Great Lakes basin from the Quebec border in the east to Lake Huron in the west. Labatt and the other breweries shipped their liquor to BEC's docks at Windsor. The BEC then delivered the liquor to the U.S. purchasers, who paid cash in advance of delivery. The BEC's export business, as a customs investigation later learned, was "extensive and profitable."[56] The proceeds of the cross-border sales were split, with the BEC taking a quarter of the revenue. The remainder was remitted directly to the breweries.[57] With profits from the BEC pouring in, Labatt's bottom line swelled to over $117,000 in 1927.

Conclusion

By the time prohibition came to an end, only fourteen of the brewers that were in existence in Ontario at the beginning of prohibition were still in operation.[58] The doors of thirty-five Ontario breweries had gone dark. Some, like Labatt's cross-town rival, Carling Breweries Limited, had reopened under new ownership. But most did not. The personal fortunes of many brewers were lost and legacies disappeared. Most of those brewers who had found some way to survive the noble experiment were so weakened by the experience that they became vulnerable to takeover by one of the handful of healthier competitors.

Labatt owed its own survival to Edmund Burke. At the dawn of prohibition, Labatt was a second-tier brewer, with declining market share and shrinking profits. The firm's sales were restricted to Ontario. But when the sun had set on prohibition in Ontario, Labatt was one of the biggest and most profitable brewers in Canada. Burke proved to be a worldly-wise hired manager who moved the company away from the staid ways of family management. He seized opportunities that accompanied prohibition, developing an intricate system of alliances in the underground economy with friends and foes alike. Ontario's puritanism had closed the domestic door and obliged the company to become devious.

Prohibition straddled two chapters in the company's history, one with John and Hugh Labatt in charge and the other with Burke at the helm. So how was it that Edmund Burke managed to grow the firm while John and Hugh Labatt did not? In part, the answer lies in the respective abilities as entrepreneurs. A defining characteristic of entrepreneurship is the ability to identify and exploit opportunities. John and Hugh Labatt were unwilling and unable to see and seize the opportunity that prohibition presented, partly because neither thought bootlegging to be desirable or feasible and partly because, in their minds, there was no positive correlation between their efforts and the success of the firm. Having become accustomed to the good life, they moved in high social circles, often among people who frowned upon the liquor traffic, even those traffickers who did it legitimately. And even if they had the will, they certainly did not have the social skills or personal connections necessary to survive in the underground economy.

Burke was different. For one thing, he believed that success or failure related to his own skill and effort.[59] This internal locus of control, as scholars of entrepreneurship call it, motivated him, at the outset, to ask the board for a share in the profits. Then it became about making the money. In addition, he was not governed by the social norms of mainstream society. To him, there was nothing immoral about the production and consumption of intoxicating beverages. Alcohol consumption was a harmless pastime and not something that could easily be legislated out of existence. People were going to drink; it was just a matter of where they would get their booze. He turned out to be right, of course: during the noble experiment, millions of otherwise law-abiding citizens defied the government commandment, "Thou shalt not drink." The bootlegger was simply meeting this demand. Despite the marginal nature of bootlegging, Burke exhibited many of the skills associated with conventional entrepreneurs. However, what set him apart from his above-board counterparts, those "heroes we cannot do without,"[60] was that he did all of this while simultaneously circumventing the legal framework developed to discourage the profitable practice of bootlegging.

"A Still Wetter Oasis"

Kidnapping, Public Drinking, and the Corporate Quest for Legitimacy, 1929–39

In April 1938, Labatt's new general manager, Hugh Mackenzie, summoned the gentlemen that made up Labatt's sales force to the company's head office in London, Ontario. Having joined the company eight years before, Mackenzie had climbed up the rungs of the corporate ladder and now, at the age of thirty-seven, was the firm's top supervisor. The appointment reflected the shareholders' desire for the firm to break with its bootlegging past, particularly after the kidnapping of John S. Labatt in 1934 by a gang of thugs with ties to those in Labatt's old "export business." Mackenzie was principled and possessed none of the moral ambiguity of his predecessor, Edmund Burke. At the sales meeting, he congratulated Labatt's salesmen for a banner year. Sales had hit an all-time high, beer was the nation's alcoholic beverage of choice, and almost one in three beers sold in Ontario was made by Labatt. As a result, Labatt's bottom line had swelled. By 1939, Labatt was, in the words of the outspoken president of its chief rival, Edward Plunket Taylor of Brewing Corporation of Canada, "filthy rich."[1]

The challenge during the dirty thirties was not just to make money during the economic depression but also to refashion the identity of the firm and the image of the product it produced; that is, to create what historian Roland Marchand terms "a corporate soul."[2] During the 1930s, top corporate managers heeded the clarion call of outside "image makers" and began to take institutional advertising and public relations seriously.[3] By 1939, the task of creating a good image was an important component of corporate strategy, a duty included in the job descriptions of high-level executives.[4] For those at Labatt, the mission was to transform the image of the brewery from a soulless bootlegger to a soulful good neighbour, while at the same time persuading the public to re-imagine beer in positive terms.

For decades, it will be recalled, the prohibitionists had effectively painted all intoxicating beverages with the same brush. Beer was one of the "three poisons," just as likely as hard liquor or wine to cause personal damage and social decay. This image would have to be overcome if Labatt was to achieve its goal of attaining good-neighbour status. The mission, therefore, was to maintain the gains that Burke had made during prohibition but to do so in a non-Burkean way – only then would the firm gain the respect of the public at large and a privileged place for its product in government legislation.

The Great Depression and the Brewing Industry

In 1929, the international monetary system began to crumble and European currencies plummeted. In the United States, Wall Street crashed, which triggered an implosion of financial markets and a downturn in economic activity. As a trading nation, Canada was soon pulled into international economic crisis. The downturn in the business cycle was not, in itself, unusual; the Canadian economy was often characterized by short, severe contractions in economic activity. Canada's staple-based economy had been down before and had always bounced back. But this time was different. What appeared to be a regionally based agricultural slump – a phenomenon that Prime Minister William Lyon Mackenzie King initially dismissed as a measure of "temporary seasonal slackness" – proved to be a major economic collapse. The provinces, which were responsible for roads, health, education, and the relief of the unemployed, were confronted with dwindling revenues and skyrocketing expenditures. Some provinces teetered on the brink of bankruptcy; Alberta, in fact, went under. As the downturn accelerated, Mackenzie King remained firm: "You're not getting a nickel from me," he cold-heartedly told the provinces that were clamouring for more federal funds to help them pay for relief. Voters found King's comments so callous that they replaced him in 1930. The new Conservative prime minister, a millionaire businessman turned politician by the name of Richard Bedford Bennett, promised jobs for everyone "willing to work" and wagered his political fortunes on the self-correcting mechanism of the price system. It turned out to be a bad bet.

Over the next few years, the economy slid inexorably downward in what seemed an endless decline. The heavy investment of the 1920s and the resultant excess supply of the 1930s caused an almost complete collapse in capital investment. By 1933, gross domestic investment fell to just 11 per cent of what it had been in the heady days of the late 1920s. Almost every sector of the Canadian economy felt the effects of the Great Depression – finance, commerce, agriculture, and manufacturing. While no industry was left untouched, some were hit harder than others. In the west, farmers watched as the price of wheat declined from $1 to thirty-four cents per bushel. The onset of the Great Depression crippled the farm, and the drought that followed in 1930 finished it off. Likewise, the pulp and paper industry was decimated by the economic crisis; its biggest firms fell like dominoes, one after another, into receivership. Similarly, the once mighty iron and steel industry was hammered by the hard times. Between 1929 and 1933, the industry's output fell by 75 per cent and the workforce was cut in half.[5] During the same period, Canada's manufacturing workforce shrank by 29 per cent and output declined by 50 per cent.[6] Across the country, incomes dropped precipitously. Again, it was the western provinces that were hardest hit. Per capita income fell by 59 per cent in Manitoba, 61 per cent in Alberta, and 71 per cent in Saskatchewan. By 1932, one in four Canadians was out of work. The descent into the Depression left industrialists, traders, bankers, and farmers seemingly helpless in the face of falling prices and saw ever-lengthening lines of men and women waiting desperately for work or relief payments.

The combination of declining real incomes and rising unemployment brought on by the Great Depression initially wreaked the same havoc on the Canadian brewing industry as it did elsewhere.[7] With tighter government controls on exports, shipments of Canadian beer to the United States fell from an all-time high of 170,000 barrels in 1927 to just 1,018 barrels in 1932.[8] At home, beer consumption fell from an average of 6.1 gallons per Canadian per annum in 1929 to 3.7 gallons in 1933.[9] Consumption fell further and faster in some provinces than in others. For example, in Saskatchewan, where the farmer's buying power was substantially curtailed and unemployment reached new heights, consumption of beer fell by 60 per cent between 1929 and 1930. In an effort to protect its own brewers from bankruptcy, the Saskatchewan government took steps to shut out beer that was made outside the province.[10] Other provinces soon followed suit, implementing tariffs on out-of-province beer. This marked the beginning of the balkanization of the Canadian brewing industry and would have long-lasting effects. Between 1929 and 1933, the Canadian brewing industry's output fell by more than half.[11] By the dark winter of 1932–33, most breweries were operating at a fraction of their capacity, and consequently, the workforce shrank by almost 20 per cent.[12]

Mirroring what was taking place across the brewing industry, Labatt saw its sales cut in half between 1930 and 1933. During the same period, its profits fell

Table 7.1

Beer sales, brewing and bottling costs, taxes and licensing fees, and net profit at Labatt, 1929–38

Year	Sales	Cost of brewing and bottling	Taxes and licences	Net profit
1929	$2,811,242	$737,369	$534,842	$669,518
1930	$3,372,794	$768,669	$578,765	$725,651
1931	$2,912,970	$745,836	$531,013	$603,913
1932	$2,363,854	$668,134	$495,390	$297,841
1933	$2,079,098	$558,823	$456,012	$292,116
1934	$3,014,714	$944,929	$575,355	$495,044
1935	$4,727,119	$1,684,969	$611,597	$1,116,692
1936	$5,775,297	$1,918,201	$836,182	$1,301,948
1937	$7,138,007	$2,883,609	$1,164,535	$1,443,041
1938	$7,893,962	$3,200,543	$1,292,996	$1,187,630

Source: John Labatt Ltd, *Balance Sheets*, 1929–38.

from roughly $725,000 to $292,000 (see table 7.1).[13] Pressured by the union, Labatt's management attempted to keep as many of its 194 employees on the payroll as possible.[14] To do so, the brewery reduced the working hours of all its employees. In 1931, no one on the factory floor worked more than three days a week.[15] When new employees were taken on, they were only hired on a part-time, seasonal basis. As the economy got progressively worse, the company began cutting the wages of its salaried employees.[16] The union reluctantly accepted the reduced salaries to insure at least some take-home pay at a time when unemployment insurance did not exist and the man was usually the only breadwinner in the family.

Despite the decline in financial health, Labatt was still in an enviable state relative to most in the industry. In part, this was because the market that Labatt serviced was not as hard hit as other markets across Canada. The Ontario economy was more diversified and less dependent on exports than economies to the west and east. Per capita incomes did not fall quite as far as they did elsewhere in Canada, so Ontarians had a bit more money to spend on luxury items like beer. Much as Ontario fared slightly better than other provinces during the Depression, the city of London weathered the economic storm better than most other urban centres.[17] The population of London actually increased by 6,000 during the first few years of the Great Depression as people from across Canada came to London looking for work. This was good news for Labatt, which continued to sell most of its brands – Crystal Lager, Extra Stock Ale, XXX Stout, and its signature India Pale Ale – in and around the Forest City. Most other brewers were not so lucky.

Many breweries folded during the first few years of the Great Depression.[18] Burke's former partner in the export trade, Harry Low, was among those liquor men whose money and luck ran out.[19] No longer able to ship his booze to the United States, Low saw his brewery's profits turn into losses, causing the value of Carling's stock to plummet from a high of $36 a share in 1927 to just $3 a share in August 1930. One worried investor wrote to the *Financial Post* seeking guidance: "Would you advise me to sell my stock, or is there any future prospect of appreciation?"[20] The *Post* told the investor to hold tight. It was poor advice. Within two months, Carling's stock dropped to $1.50 a share.[21] Attempting to salvage what they could, on 30 November 1930, Low and his partners sold their controlling interest in the Carling brewery to a twenty-nine-year-old business visionary by the name of Edward Plunket Taylor. Over the next three decades, Taylor was the source of what Austrian economist Joseph Schumpeter called "creative destruction," ultimately transforming the Canadian brewing industry into a stable oligopoly.[22]

E.P. Taylor's "Grand Design"

Born in 1901, Edward Plunket Taylor was a disrupter. In his prime, no other individual in the history of Canadian brewing was as good at perceiving opportunities and creating the organizations to pursue them. While his parents were financially secure, they were not rich. His father was an investment banker. And his grandfather owned the Brading Brewery, a small Ottawa beer maker that had survived prohibition by selling ale in Quebec.[23] E.P. Taylor started his first business at the age of twelve. At eighteen, he invented a toaster that browned bread on both sides. The royalties from the sale of his invention made him enough money to pay for his education at McGill University. After graduating in 1922 with a bachelor degree in science, Taylor was elected to the board of his grandfather's brewery.

Seeing an opportunity where others saw only chaos, Taylor began buying up floundering breweries during the Depression with the goal of "bringing about in Ontario a similar situation to that which exists in the Province of Quebec, where the industry is controlled by virtually two companies [Molson and National Breweries]."[24] In 1928, there were thirty-seven breweries operating in Ontario with combined assets of $24 million. In Quebec, the industry was far more concentrated so the brewers there had lower operating costs and higher net sales than their counterparts in Ontario. Taylor sought to consolidate the industry in Canada's most populated province.

A few months before acquiring Carling in 1930, Taylor took over Kuntz Brewery in Waterloo. It had survived prohibition by selling full-strength beer to the self-proclaimed "King of the Bootleggers," Rocco Perri. But when the cross-border trade in alcohol began to dry up in the late 1920s, Perri diversified into gambling, prostitution, and – at the behest of his wife, Bessie Starkman – narcotics. Having lost its biggest customer and burdened by overcapacity, Kuntz was ripe for takeover. In the years that followed, Taylor purchased the British American Brewery in Windsor, the Taylor & Bate Brewery in St Catharines, the Dominion Brewery Company in Toronto, and the Grant's Spring Brewery and Regal Brewing Company in Hamilton.[25] In total, his holding company, Brewing Corporation of Canada Ltd, acquired seventeen Ontario-based breweries during the Great Depression.[26] By 1939, Taylor controlled a third of the provincial market.[27] A bottom-feeder, Taylor purchased all of these breweries at rock-bottom prices.[28] Taylor's strategy was to achieve economies of scale and scope by closing down unprofitable plants in order to concentrate production in more efficient and strategically located ones.[29] In theory, this would lead to cost reductions and higher profits.[30] Taylor had wanted to acquire Labatt but knew that his normal tactics would not work on a profitable firm whose shares were closely held.[31] Instead, he decided to dominate the central, most populated region of Ontario, thereby relegating Labatt to the status of a single-unit company confined to a distant southwest corner of the province.

If those at Labatt were worried about Taylor's actions, they were not voicing their concern around the boardroom table. Prior to 1934, there was no mention of Taylor's "grand design" to dominate the Ontario beer market. Nor was there any enthusiasm in the boardroom for beating Taylor at his own game, that is, seeking out and acquiring those breweries that were underperforming and rationalizing their operations.[32] When management was approached by an unnamed "outside party" in the summer of 1932 with a proposal for Labatt to purchase a number of smaller breweries in the province, the board of directors decided that "no action should be taken."[33] Nor was the board interested in maintaining its place in the market that Burke had created for the firm south of the border. This was not the case at the Canadian distillery Seagram, which fashioned a bold new strategy after prohibition came to an end in the United States.[34] Rather than retreat behind the national line, Seagram embarked on an American invasion by purchasing a number of distilleries in the United States in order to make its "blended whisky." In light of public opinion polls in the late 1930s showing that about one-third of Americans favoured a return to prohibition, Seagram's shrewdly marketed its blended product as a more moderate and better-tasting whisky than single malts.[35] Likewise, Hiram Walker, maker of Canadian Club Whisky, decided to remain in the United States after prohibition came to an end and built the largest distillery in the world in Illinois. Labatt chose to take a much more cautious approach to growth, thereby missing a once-in-a-generation opportunity to gain a legitimate presence in the United States.

During the dirty thirties, Labatt made the strategic decision to focus on bringing down unit costs and expanding its market in Canada's industrial heartland, rather than taking out the competition elsewhere in Canada or taking on the competition in the United States. "Our general feeling towards our competitors," stated one senior executive at Labatt, "may be summed up in the phrase, 'live and let live.'"[36] The decision reflected a desire to return to a state of normalcy after the bootlegging days of prohibition. The conservative, risk-averse culture of the pre-prohibition years returned to the firm.

New Personnel

With Labatt now in the top ranks of Canadian brewers and with the profits rolling in, the board demanded a more legitimate approach to business than was exhibited during prohibition. The Labatt family board members, who finally started showing up again at the brewery for regular meetings after the noble experiment, were embarrassed by Burke thumbing his nose at Newton Wesley Rowell and the Royal Commissioners. They sought to clean house, to get rid of all the marginal types that were involved in the export business by bringing in new personnel – professional men, who were specialists in their field; ethical men, who would put a new face on the corporation; men, it was hoped, who would allow them and the public to forget the firm's bootlegging past. One of these men was Hugh Mackenzie.

If the company was to effectively manage its costs during the Depression, the board felt that a more scientific and exact method of accounting was necessary.

For years, Francis W. Raymond and John Labatt II had kept a very close eye on the books. One of the principal reasons for the survival of the old London Brewery during the late nineteenth century was that business decisions were always based on a thorough analysis of costs and prices. Since the 1870s, Raymond had diligently prepared the financial information that John Labatt used to run the company. But shortly after John Labatt's death in 1915, Raymond left the company and, at the same time, the nature of the international profession of accounting changed.[37]

During the First World War, governments used accountants to investigate costs in an effort to prevent profiteering.[38] Concurrently, wartime contractors relied on costing techniques to set prices and calculate profit surpluses.[39] After the First World War, businesses expanded their internal accounting departments and the number of internal (cost) accountants rose. This in turn led to more responsibilities for a firm's chief accountant, and those accountants working at breweries were no exception.[40] For example, at Guinness, Walter Phillips, the chief accountant between 1919 and 1938, was not only doing the accounting but also managing risks, interacting with external financiers, and advising top management on corporate strategy.[41] During the first few years of the Great Depression, Phillips spent much of his time managing costs in an effort to maintain profits in the face of declining sales.

In 1930, Labatt's board of directors hired Hugh Mackenzie to oversee the firm's accounting practices and financial reporting. Born in 1901, Mackenzie grew up in a household that did not want for money. His father, Michael, earned a good living as a professor of mathematics at the University of Toronto; when not teaching, he earned even more doing actuarial work for companies in the insurance industry. Having attended a succession of private schools, Hugh Mackenzie entered the Royal Military College of Canada (RMC) near Kingston, Ontario, at the age of seventeen. At RMC, he studied applied mathematics, engineering, geography, and history. Mackenzie was sharp. Upon graduating in 1921, he was awarded the Governor General's medal together with the rank of Battalion Sergeant Major for achieving the highest all-around standing in his class.[42] He was also athletic. Having played football at university, he continued to pursue his passion after his school days were done. In the early 1920s, he played in a number of games for the Toronto Argonauts as replacement for the experienced "Shrimp" Cochran, who was then, according to historian Albert Tucker, the best quarterback in Canada. Football, however, was an amateur sport at the time and could not provide a satisfying career for an ambitious young man like Mackenzie. He decided to prepare himself for a more stable life as a chartered accountant.[43]

Mackenzie chose a good time to enter the field of accounting. The profession was rapidly expanding after the First World War, and he easily found work at Clarkson, Gordon in Toronto.[44] Mackenzie was trained there as a chartered accountant and soon caught the eye of one of the firm's senior partners, Colonel Lockhart Gordon. A close friend of Major-General Sydney C. Mewburn – who had returned to the Labatt board of directors when prohibition came to an end in Ontario in 1927 – Gordon knew that Labatt was looking for "a first-class qualified accountant."[45] The Royal Commission on Customs and Excise had, not surprisingly, declared Labatt's bookkeeping methods to be "elementary and deficient." Mackenzie had worked for the commission and had a solid understanding of the financial workings of firms in the Canadian brewing industry – although he knew next to nothing about the science of brewing. Almost immediately after joining Labatt, Mackenzie started recording all of the costs of brewing and bottling as a percentage of sales. He also began tracking monthly changes in Labatt's market share. Mackenzie believed that this information was necessary if the company was to achieve its two strategic objectives: expand the firm's sales in Ontario and improve operating efficiency. Mackenzie was well suited for the job of comptroller, and although he had been hired for the specific purpose of overseeing the daily accounting operations of the business, his role at the brewery quickly evolved to encompass much more.

Many at the firm took an immediate liking to Mackenzie. He was bright, physically fit, confident, and respectful of others. Major-General Mewburn liked the

Figure 7.1 *Opposite* Labatt's workforce doubled in size during the Great Depression. By 1938, there were 401 employees working at Labatt, thirty of which were women. Most of the women worked as office staff. For example, Phyllis Copper was personal secretary to John and Hugh. She almost didn't join the company because the minister at her United Church objected to her working for liquor men. Just before she started work at the brewery, John S. Labatt stated that "the burden of hospital expenses is ... a serious load for the individual to carry, and bills resulting from sickness may oftentimes take most of an individual's savings." As a result, the board of directors agreed on a plan for group life insurance and hospital benefits through the Aetna Insurance Company and a pension plan for its employees through the Annuities Department of the federal government in Ottawa. The health plan gave all employees, including the cooper featured here repairing a keg at the Labatt brewery in 1935, three dollars a day while they were in hospital and provided them with an additional fifteen dollars to cover the cost of an operation if it was needed. The pension plan provided for a degree of financial security after retirement. For every dollar paid by the employee into the pension plan, the company contributed a similar amount, up to three per cent of the employee's annual earnings.

fact that he was a graduate of the RMC. And virtually everyone was impressed with Mackenzie's athletic accomplishments. Mackenzie had an easy charm about him. In addition, he had a progressive view on how the firm should function. In his opinion, the relationship between management and labour should not be antagonistic. Rather, it should be based on reciprocity and mutual respect, with management acting as the linchpin between labour and capital to "create a harmonious [business] setting."[46] Although he was ideologically committed to free enterprise, stating that the capitalist system was "in the national interest,"[47] he believed that for it to work, the interests of capital had to be balanced against those of labour.[48] The hiring of Mackenzie demonstrated that the board was eager to resurrect its image as a good law-abiding corporate citizen.

But not everybody was enamoured with the new comptroller. Edmund Burke had been running things his way for more than a decade. In 1930, Burke turned sixty-seven years old. Despite his advanced age, he was not looking to retire any time soon. He was proud of his past accomplishments and felt that his methods of running the brewery were battle-tested. Also, Burke had never liked being told what to do, least of all by a newcomer like Mackenzie. The two butted heads almost immediately. Mackenzie felt that Burke had passed his best-before date. He didn't like Burke's contempt for authority, his shady dealings, or his sense of entitlement at the firm. As his responsibilities at the brewery grew, Mackenzie became conscious of the fact that he was Burke's logical successor. Increasingly, the board invited him, and not Burke, to attend meetings. Mackenzie was never shy about expressing an opinion on corporate strategy.[49] Privately, he was telling the members of the Labatt family that the time for a change had come: in order to continue to grow and prosper as a legitimate business, the firm would have to implement a more modern and systematic approach to management. Burke's way of operating at the margins and playing fast and loose with the rules was a business method of a bygone era. In the post-prohibition environment, neither the government nor the public at large had any appetite for shifty business practices.

For his part, Burke was standing firm. Although he had amassed a small fortune from the export business, he did not want to start anew at some other company or join the burgeoning ranks of the unemployed. Few did. "In the thirties you clung to your job," stated Canadian author Pierre Berton, "as a drunk clings to a lamp post."[50] During the Depression, Canadians tolerated all sorts of poor working conditions in order to keep a roof over their heads. But for Burke, money was not the motivator; it was the excitement of being in the beer business and the prestige of being in charge of one of Canada's oldest surviving breweries.

Although the board reduced his remuneration in 1932 in a timid effort to push him out, Burke went about his business as usual.[51] This was fortunate for the firm because his "old school ways" proved useful when the issue of public drinking returned to centre stage in 1934.

The Return of Public Drinking

While prohibition had come to an end in 1927, drinking full-strength beer in public places was still illegal in Ontario during the first few years of the Great Depression. Between 1927 and 1934, the Ontario government only allowed the public consumption of "Fergie's Foam," which contained 2.2 per cent alcohol by volume, in tightly regulated "beverage rooms" across the province. But in light of the continuing economic crisis and the government's ever-growing need for revenue, the idea of returning to a world that allowed public drinking of full-strength beer began to be seriously considered in the provincial capital.

Eager to have their voice heard, the Ontario brewers revived the old Moderation League, which had been used seven years earlier to bring an end to prohibition. The Moderation League was the obedient servant of the liquor traffic. The brewers had long argued that beer was a temperance drink and that its consumption should be promoted, not prohibited, because it was a healthy alternative to hard liquor. But now, during the Great Depression, the Moderation League added another dimension to its argument: more beer consumption, not less, was the way to end Ontario's economic woes.[52]

The brewers knew that it never hurt to have friends in high places. The Moderation League began courting as many politicians as possible. Somewhat surprisingly, it found an ally in the new leader of the Liberal Party of Ontario. A larger-than-life personality, Mitchell F. Hepburn had voted for "Dry Drury" and the United Farmers of Ontario in the 1919 election, before returning to his Liberal roots five years later.[53] After inheriting a small fortune in 1922, Hepburn decided to follow in his father's footsteps and leave farming for a life in politics. In 1926, he was elected by the people of Elgin West to represent them in the House of Commons in Ottawa. Despite being one of the best speakers on the Hill, Hepburn was unable to gain the confidence of the prime minister.[54] Mackenzie King disapproved of Hepburn's fondness for women and alcohol.[55] While prohibition was in full force in Ontario, Hepburn often made the short trip over the Chaudière Bridge to tipple in Hull, where drinking was still legal. Hepburn made no secret of his fondness for drink: "I have a little Scotch in me," he would often say, flash-ing a rogue's smile, "sometimes more, sometimes less."[56] His penchant for the good life on the Quebec side of the Ottawa River disgusted the prime minister. Realizing that there was little chance that King would ever have him in his Cab-inet, Hepburn left federal politics in 1929 to run for the leadership of the Ontario Liberal Party.

The Ontario Liberals had languished in opposition for a quarter of a century, having been alienated from the federal party and the bagmen who financed it. In the previous 1929 provincial election, under the leadership of W.E.N. Sinclair, a fanatical prohibitionist, the Liberals were reduced to a rural single-interest rump, harshly – but not inaccurately – described by one observer as "a haven for every quack and crack in the country." The terminal illness of the provincial party was due to a lack of leadership and the fervent determination of many Liberals to keep beating the prohibition drum.[57] But at the leadership convention in 1929, Hepburn made it clear that he wanted to distance himself from the past position of the Grits. As far as he was concerned, the people had spoken. There would be no winding back the clock to drier times. Prohibition should not be a "political question" – by which he meant that being dry should not define what it meant to be Liberal.[58] "I maintain that it is unfair and absurd to talk as if all Liberals are prohibitionists and all Conservatives are opposite," Hepburn stated.[59] His position resonated with enough moderate Liberals to get him elected as the leader of the provincial party.

While in opposition between 1930 and 1934, Mitch Hepburn adopted the well-worn tactics of the office seeker. Practicing the politics of deceit by embracing populist rhetoric, he portrayed himself as a friend of both the unemployed and the overtaxed, while attacking the "elites" and the so-called extravagances of George Henry's Tory government. For example, during the Stratford furniture strike in 1933, Hepburn declared that his sympathies lay "with those people who are the victims of circumstances beyond their control, and not with the manu-facturers who are increasing prices and cutting wages at the same time."[60] Al-though Hepburn had promised to keep the liquor question out of politics by not talking about it in public, in private he was telling his friends that prohibition was "a lost cause."[61] If the Tories chose to run in the next election on a platform that endorsed the sale of full-strength beer and wine in restaurants and hotels, he said privately in the spring of 1932, the best Liberal strategy would be "to accept any change in the Liquor Control Act and insist on fighting the issues of taxation and hydro." When they dined at the Château Laurier late in 1932, Hepburn assured

Harry Pritchard of the Moderation League that he would not oppose the Tory's "beer by the glass" legislation. "As long as I am leader of the Liberals," Hepburn stated, "it will never be a prohibitionist party."[62]

With the government's debt at an all-time high due to the costs of the Depression, Premier George S. Henry decided to act as the beer lobby advocated. On 21 March 1934, Attorney General William Price rose in the House and asked leave from the Speaker to give the first reading to an Act to Amend the Liquor Control Act. Price had long been a friend of those at Labatt and sympathetic to the concerns of those in the brewing community. The publisher of the *Globe*, W.G. Jaffray, had criticized him for that, as well as his close association with the brewers' stalking horse, the Moderation League. "Colonel Price is the camel on which the Moderation League hopes to ride to a still wetter oasis," asserted the *Globe*.[63] To be proclaimed after the election, the Conservative government's new liquor act would permit the sale of full-strength beer and wine in hotel dining rooms, restaurants, and clubs.[64]

Despite a near revolt by the dry wing of the Liberal party, Hepburn did not oppose the bill. Behind closed doors, he demanded party unity, and eventually his caucus emerged in unanimous support of the principle that prohibition was a personal moral issue rather than a collective political one.[65] With the bill passed in the House, the only thing left for the Conservative government to do was to call an election, which George Henry set for 19 June 1934. In the months leading up to the vote, the brewers of the province poured thousands of dollars into the Conservative Party's war chest. According to Albert Tucker, Labatt donated $25,000 to the Conservative campaign.[66] Despite Hepburn's assurances that he was a friend of the brewing community, Labatt and the rest of the forces for "moderation" chose to back the party with the wettest track record.

On the morning of 29 June 1934, Edmund Burke woke up to the news that Hepburn's Liberals had won the election. "Conservatives are swept from power; eight cabinet ministers are beaten in landslide; Hepburn is new premier," the headline in the *London Free Press* read.[67] Hepburn had made short work of the stuffy and unpopular Conservative premier. The Liberals had taken sixty-five of ninety seats and over 50 per cent of the popular vote. Hepburn's populist rhetoric resonated with the people of Ontario, who were looking for a political solution to the economic depression.

In the weeks that followed the election, Burke set his sights on establishing a relationship with the man who now ran the province and in whose hands the amendment to the Liquor Act now resided. On 6 July 1934, Burke called James

Millman into his office and asked to be introduced to the new premier. Millman had recently left his job selling Mason and Risch pianos, which proved too tough a task in the midst of the Depression.[68] Expenditures on such luxury items were often the first to be cut by families struggling to make ends meet. Beer, on the other hand, provided Canadians with a relatively cheap means of escape from the hardships of the dirty thirties. Although the consumption of beer fell during the Depression, the decline was small in comparison to the fall in the consumption of (more expensive) wine and hard liquor.

Realizing that the brewing industry was faring better than most other industries, Millman joined Labatt to sell suds in the rich agricultural region between London and Windsor. Millman had connections to the Ontario Liberal Party.[69] He was a friend of Joe McManus, a regional campaign manager for the Liberals during the 1934 election, and had even socialized with Hepburn on a few occasions. In early July, Millman went to a dinner party in London that was attended by the premier. As the event approached its end, Millman invited Hepburn back to Edmund Burke's house for a nightcap. Hepburn and Burke hit it off immediately. "Boy did he [Burke] ever entertain Mitch!" Millman later recalled.[70] Thereafter, Burke socialized with the premier on a number of occasions, taking him and his Cabinet out for dinner when he visited Toronto, having him up to his summer estate on Lake Nipissing, throwing garden parties for him at his home in Lambeth, and visiting Hepburn at his onion farm in St Thomas.[71]

What direct effect Burke's friendship had on Hepburn's public policy is impossible to say for certain. But during his tenure, Hepburn did nothing to impair the liquor traffic in Ontario. Following his first Cabinet meeting on 11 July 1934, Hepburn immediately proclaimed Henry's liquor act into law, and within the fortnight, beer was being sold at ten cents a glass in the newly licensed beverage rooms that were popping up across the province. For the first time in seventeen years, Ontarians could legally drink full-strength beer in public.

While public drinking had finally returned to Ontario, the experience for those who imbibed was profoundly different than what it had been before the onset of the noble experiment. Gone was the 24/7 working-class saloon with its intermingling of the sexes and carnival-like setting. The post-prohibition beer parlour was a heavily regulated, sedate place where patrons sat down and drank their beer.[72] The architecture of these austere beverage rooms was designed to facilitate orderly behaviour and surveillance.[73] There were no games or gambling; no quarrelling or use of profane language; no singing and no dancing – except on special occasions; and certainly no drunken bears. Women who wanted a night of drinking were obliged to sit in areas designated for "Ladies and Escorts." These segregated spaces usually had their own separate entrances and washrooms. Unescorted men could not be served in the Ladies and Escorts side of the beverage room. Thus were women sheltered from the advances of single men and free to enjoy a relaxing and respectable drinking experience. Furthermore, women were prohibited from serving alcohol. Despite the fact that Canadians would now have to drink in a tightly regulated environment and follow a carefully constructed code of conduct, beer by the glass was back. And this was good for Labatt.

Virtually everybody knew that the new liquor law would have a positive effect on beer sales. But few predicted the magnitude of the boom. So great was the thirst for full-strength beer by the glass in London that the kegs went dry before the first day of drinking in public was done.[74] During the first three weeks of August 1934, beer sales in Ontario increased by 120 per cent over the same period in the previous year. The change in legislation helped Labatt post a profit of over $500,000 in 1934. With Labatt controlling roughly 16 per cent of the Ontario market, Mackenzie advised the board to further expand the plant.[75] Mackenzie took some comfort in the fact that Labatt had come through the worst years of the Great Depression. While other Canadian businesses continued to struggle, Labatt was doing remarkably well. It did not go unnoticed.

The Kidnapping of John S. Labatt

On the morning of 14 August 1934, John Sackville Labatt climbed into his high-powered luxury car and drove out of the family's cottage compound at Brights Grove, on the pristine shores of Lake Huron. Running late for a morning meeting in London with his brother Hugh and Major-General Sydney Mewburn, he decided to take a shortcut down a secluded stretch of gravel road to make up some time. As he sped along at about fifty miles an hour, he glanced in his rear-view mirror and noticed that a car was gaining on him. Labatt slowed down to let the other car overtake him, and was somewhat relieved when the Hudson four-door sedan with an American licence plate passed him and disappeared around the bend. But just a few miles down the road, Labatt's pulse began to race again when the same car came back at him. Fearing a collision, John Labatt pulled over to the side of the road and stopped. The other car kept coming until it was within a few feet and then braked abruptly. Dust still in the air, the doors of the black sedan flew open and three men leaped out. Brandishing guns, the bandits ran toward Labatt. "Stick 'em up quick – this is a kidnapping," the gang's leader, Michael McCardell, shouted.[76]

Kidnapping was all too common during the darkest days of the Great Depression. Despite Prime Minister R.B. Bennett's 1930 election promise that there would be jobs for every Canadian who wanted to work, the unemployment rate remained disturbingly high. Desperate and out of work, some people turned to crime. Kidnappers targeted those who could command a king's ransom, and few had prospered more than the beer barons who had survived prohibition. Before the kidnapping of John S. Labatt, two other London liquor men were abducted. One of them was Sam Low, the brother and business lieutenant of dashing rum-runner Harry Low. On that occasion, the kidnappers pocketed the ransom of $35,000 and Low was returned in one piece.[77] In 1932, the shadow of gangland again fell on Ontario. This time, Charles Burns, the former president of Carling Brewery, was taken. Having negotiated his own release, Burns calmly walked into the bank and withdrew $30,000 from his account. He then stuffed the cash into an ordinary brown paper bag, walked across the road, and handed it to his kidnappers.[78] Prohibition had created a subculture in North America characterized by a thirst for easy money and contempt for the law. Many kept to a life of crime after the noble experiment came to an end. The men who kidnapped John S. Labatt were very much a part of the underworld.[79] Despite the attempts of brewers to legitimize their businesses in the post-prohibition period, there were those of "illegitimate means" who were not willing to let the beer barons escape their bootlegging past.

In 1934, John S. Labatt was one of the wealthiest brewers in Canada.[80] At a time when many across the nation could not even afford the gas to run their cars, John Sackville was chauffeured around in a stately black limousine. At age fifty-four, his hair had turned slightly grey. He wore fancy three-piece suits and was often in the company of his dog. The fact that he lived in a large home overlooking Victoria Park in London seemed to confirm the rumours that Labatt was sitting on a mountain of money made from his brewery's bootlegging days.

Michael McCardell had spent time bootlegging booze through the Windsor-Detroit funnel. In fact, he knew some of the men that worked for Labatt down on the Windsor docks. He had heard the stories of how well the brewery was doing and was eager to get his hands on John Labatt's cash. Having pulled Labatt from his car, McCardell ordered him to write a note to his brother. "Dear Hugh," John wrote, "do as these men have instructed you ... and don't go to the police."

Figure 7.2 John Sackville Labatt during happier times. During the early 1930s, he was often seen around London, Ontario, accompanied by his dog. Always well dressed in public, he gave the impression of a man with deep pockets.

On the other side of the paper, McCardell wrote: "We are holding your brother for $150,000 ransom. Go to Toronto immediately and register at the Royal York Hotel ... You will know me as three-fingered Abe"[81] (McCardell had lost an index finger in a shootout with Detroit police). Grabbing the note, McCardell's accomplice, Russell Knowles, jumped into Labatt's car and headed south to London. Once there, he parked the car with the note inside so that it could easily be found. The other kidnappers headed north with Labatt, to a cottage in Bracebridge.

Back in London, John Labatt's car had been found and Major-General Mewburn had taken control. During his years in the military and in public service, Mewburn had established connections with a number of powerful people in the provincial capital. One of the first telephone calls he made was to his friend Major-General Victor Williams, who was the commissioner of the Ontario Provincial Police. Williams was eternally grateful to Mewburn for helping secure his release from a German prison at the end of the First World War. He agreed to help in any way he could to find John S. Labatt.

Williams immediately took command of the entire operation in co-operation with Brigadier-General D.C. Draper, chief of the Toronto City Police.[82] When Hugh Labatt's limousine arrived in Toronto late in the afternoon on 14 August, Draper and four senior detectives from the Ontario Provincial Police, the Toronto Police Task Force, and the Royal Canadian Mounted Police were waiting for him. Mewburn also called the provincial attorney general, Arthur Roebuck, who promised him that "every available resource in the hands of the Provincial Police will be thrown into the task of apprehending the culprits and solving the mystery."[83]

While Hugh Labatt was meeting with the detectives, an anonymous phone call was made to the *London Free Press*. The caller was phoning to break the news of the kidnapping. Recognizing the significance of the story, the editors stopped the presses. When the evening edition of the 14 August *London Free Press* hit the streets, the front-page headline was so large that the victim's first name had to been truncated to a single letter. "J. LABATT KIDNAPPED" read the black-and-white banner.[84] The *Press*'s report destroyed any hope of maintaining a news blackout. Within hours, reporters from all over North America descended on London and Toronto to cover the sensational crime. The kidnapping of John Labatt was now front-page news across Canada and the United States. "London Millionaire Abducted and Gangsters Ask $150,000" read a headline on the front page of the *Globe*.[85] The electronic billboard on top of the *New York Times* building in Times Square flashed a bulletin about the Labatt kidnapping in five-foot-high letters. Many newspapers speculated that nefarious and sophisticated forces were at work. The *Toronto Star*, for example, believed "the theory that a Detroit gang, possibly the famous Purple Gang, staged the kidnapping."[86] The *Star* also noted the significance of the event, stating that it was the "first kidnapping for ransom of a man of large means in Canada."[87] The *London Free Press*, which ran another front-page editorial on 15 August, noted that the kidnapping indicated that "a new era of crime in Canada has commenced ... the introduction into the country of the 'snatch-racket' so common in the U.S."[88] Many were terrified by the prospect. Even William Lyon Mackenzie King had nightmares of his own abduction, which he attributed to "kidnapping talk of Labatt."[89] The fear of more American gangland activity in Canada prompted Premier Mitch Hepburn to cancel all police leave until Labatt's kidnappers were caught. He assured the populace that he would not tolerate an "Americanized Ontario."

The combination of newspaper headlines and a tightening of the police dragnet caused Labatt's kidnappers to panic. In a desperate attempt to salvage the situation, McCardell told Labatt he would let him go if he promised to pay $25,000 after he was released. John Labatt agreed.[90] At 12:30 a.m. on Friday, 17 August, the kidnappers dropped off Labatt at the corner of Vaughan Road and St Clair Avenue in Toronto, just a few miles northwest of the Royal York Hotel, where Hugh Labatt was stationed. Thirty minutes later, he walked past the legions of policemen and journalists in the hotel lobby and paused at the reception desk. "I am John Labatt," he informed the night clerk. "Where is my brother's room?"

Ironically, the kidnapping had a positive effect on business at the brewery. At a time when beer advertising was forbidden in Ontario, the news of John Labatt's kidnapping brought attention to the firm and its beverages. "Your name is in all mouths," Frances Biddulph wrote to John S. Labatt shortly after the kidnapping.[91] When the kidnapping of John Labatt became front-page news, beer parlour patrons began asking for his beer by name. In Canada's biggest beer-drinking centre, Toronto, Labatt was the largest single seller among bottled beers in the months following the kidnapping.[92] By the end of September, Labatt's share of the Ontario beer market had increased by almost 2 per cent from a month earlier.[93] By that time, two of the kidnappers had surrendered and a sensational trial followed in January 1935. Coverage of the jury trial kept Labatt's name in the press over the next two years. With the plant "running beyond capacity," those at the London Brewery now made one in five beers consumed in the province.[94] It was a different story at the Brewing Corporation of Canada, which was running at a quarter of its capacity, making it impossible for E.P. Taylor to achieve scale economies.[95] Business was so bad at the Carling Brewery in London that Taylor decided to close it down in 1936. In a perverse way, the kidnapping of John S. Labatt was a testament to the success and resiliency of the only remaining London-based brewery.

The Departure of Edmund Burke

Three days after the kidnapping, John Labatt was back among family and friends. Brief though it was, the experience had changed him forever. A quiet and diffident man before the kidnapping, Labatt became even more reclusive in the years that followed. He rarely set foot in the United States, fearing that the kidnappers or their accomplices would seek revenge. Whenever the Labatt family left town, John S. Labatt had trusted employees stay with him at his house on Central Avenue. He also hired an ex-military officer to be his bodyguard. And his office at the brewery became something of a fortress.

In the aftermath of the kidnapping, the principals at the brewery were determined to remove any residue of the firm's bootlegging past. Edmund Burke was suddenly back in the crosshairs. No one disputed that Burke had nothing to do with the kidnapping. But it was during his watch that the firm had become connected with those in the underworld. One of the men that Burke had brought in to help with the bootlegging, Louis McCaughey, was identified by Michael McCardell at his trial as the kidnappers' inside man. When this came to light in 1935, McCaughey's employment at the brewery was immediately terminated.[96] Burke had saved the old London Brewery from certain bankruptcy during prohibition. But in its aftermath, a higher ethical standard was demanded. The board was eager to make a clean break with the past. Throughout the autumn of 1935, executives met with Burke to see what it would take to get him out. According to Burke, it would require three months' severance pay and a retirement allowance of $5,000 per year for life.[97] The board wanted him out at any price, and on 9 December 1935, Burke tendered his resignation as general manager. He spent the rest of his days in the company of his long-time girlfriend, Hattie, and tending the exotic animals in his personal zoo.[98]

Even before Burke was out the door, the board of directors had increased the responsibilities of the company's clean-cut comptroller, Hugh Mackenzie. In June

1935, Mackenzie took on the additional role of sales manager. Mackenzie's assigned task was to restructure the way the firm promoted and sold its products.[99] He had orders to clean house, if necessary, and bring in those people who would be "the pride of the brewery." Mackenzie set out to find individuals "of character" who could enthusiastically promote Labatt's beer in hotels, restaurants, legion halls, trade-union clubs, and taverns. He wanted men who were gregarious and congenial by nature, men who were able to talk smoothly to whomever they met. He wanted men who had an ability to tell a good tale or two, a passion for sports, and a willingness to spend long hours in conversation with tavern-keepers and their customers.[100] He didn't want saints, but he didn't want the likes of Louis McCaughey either. He was looking for men who knew whose side they were on, ethical men who were willing to do an honest day's work. In short, Mackenzie wanted more men like J.R. "Doc" McLachrie, who joined Labatt to sell ale to the thirsty steelworkers of Hamilton.[101]

At a time when beer drinking helped define working-class masculinity, "Doc" McLachrie promoted Labatt's products in Hamilton by using all of the means that Mackenzie had put at his disposal.[102] Mackenzie knew that Ontario's new Liquor Control Board would not approve of direct commissions, so he developed a system of bonus incentives instead.[103] Salesmen then competed to be assigned to the biggest and most prosperous urban centres, such as Toronto or Hamilton, where taverns sold relatively large quantities of beer. Motivated by the potential of a hefty bonus, McLachrie drew down heavily on his expense account to treat customers in order to promote sales and brand loyalty. Six days a week, McLachrie did the rounds, showing up at one of the various beer parlours at noon when they opened. He would remain there, treating and entertaining the crowd, until he sensed that his work was done and then he would move on to the next watering hole. He did the rounds until ten or eleven at night. McLachrie succeeded in Hamilton by devoting time and energy to pushing Labatt's products and by maintaining a personal presence in the community. On his day off, McLachrie often attended leisure events, like picnics and baseball games in Hamilton, to generate good will. During the Great Depression, when amateur sports provided a cheap and popular form of entertainment, Mackenzie gave Labatt's money to local soccer, bowling, softball, and hockey teams. At a time when there were tight restrictions on how brewers could promote their products, the sponsoring of local sports teams served as an effective form of indirect advertising.

Product Advertising

In the immediate aftermath of prohibition, brewers like Labatt found it much more difficult than before to advertise their products. In Ontario, direct advertising was prohibited: beer advertisements in newspapers and magazines and on the radio were forbidden by law. Brewers could still give away promotional material at their retail outlets, but the principal means by which they had previously promoted their products were no longer allowed. Within this tightly regulated environment, a few innovative brewers exploited the loopholes in the law. Labatt was one of them. During the 1930s, Labatt began placing advertisements in magazines like *Canadian Homes and Gardens* and *New Liberty* that were published in Quebec, which had relatively liberal liquor advertising laws, but distributed across the nation. Later in the decade, Labatt also began advertising on the radio in Buffalo, knowing full well that many Ontarians listened to broadcasts originating in the United States.

The ads of the period were imbued with emotional and cultural meaning. The ad men at Labatt sought to get Canadians to re-image beer as wholesome and "Canadian." In 1936, Mackenzie approached J. Walter Thompson Co., then the largest advertising agency in the world, at its new Toronto office. Its top brass appointed Mark Napier, a marketing mastermind with an uncanny sense for the cultural logic of the age, to handle the Labatt account. Determined to whitewash the company's bootlegging past, Napier set out to show that Labatt had been instrumental to the development of the nation. In a series of advertisements that appeared in the national monthly *Canadian Homes and Gardens*, Napier highlighted Labatt's long and influential past. "It really all began 70 years ago," read the text of one advertisement in 1937 under the tag line "Then As Now." At a time when Canadians were searching for uniquely Canadian ideas, events, experiences, and commodities – the makers of a national identity – Napier served up Labatt's product as an age-old piece of Canadiana. In other advertisements, Napier linked the evolution of the firm to the watershed moments in Canadian history, like Confederation and the Boer War, "when soldiers knew good ale." By coupling the history of the firm with the key political and economic events in the development of the nation, Napier sought to stake out a place for Labatt products in the hearts and minds of Canadians and raise Labatt to the rank of a good corporate citizen.

Other advertisements tied Labatt's beer to the land. The land held a special place in the hearts and minds of Canadians during the interwar period. It was considered a sanctuary from the dangers of the modern urban world – labour unrest,

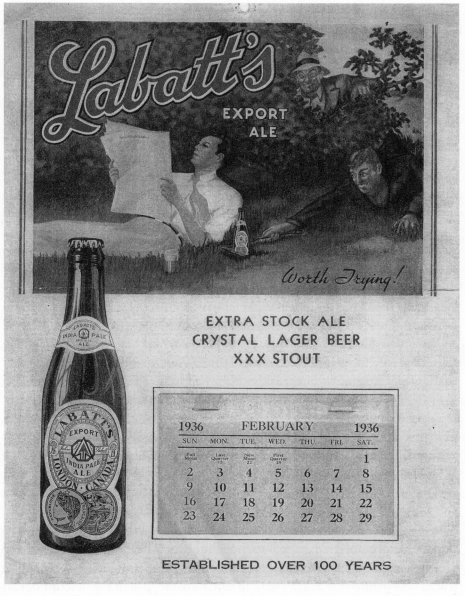

Figure 7.3 A Labatt calendar featuring a middle-class male enjoying a beer in the park where even the hobos are not threatening, 1936. Parks and other outdoor spaces held a special place in Canadian culture during the interwar period. By situating the beer drinker in these outdoor settings, Labatt sought to sanitize its product from the perceived problems of the city and to get Canadians to re-imagine beer as healthy and wholesome.

white slavery, crime – and its products were seen as "natural" and "pure." This back-to-the-land anti-modernism was evident in a variety of cultural manifestations of the period, from the paintings of the Group of Seven[104] to the writings of Harold Adams Innis[105] to the quest for a rustic fisherfolk in Nova Scotia[106] to the creation of summer camps and national parks.[107] Labatt linked its products to the land by placing beer drinking in a country setting (see figure 7.3) and almost never in an urban working-class saloon. By linking beer, brewing, and beer drinking to rural folk – who were virtually always white and middle class – and country places, Labatt's ad men aimed to sanitize their product from the perceived problems of the city and make it more appealing to mainstream Canadians.

To further capture the public's attention, Mackenzie decided to modernize the firm's fleet of ageing trucks. Labatt's trucks were virtually always on the roads of Ontario, in big cities and small towns. Mackenzie believed they could be used as an effective form of advertising. The existing fleet, which had served the company so reliably during prohibition, needed replacement. Many of the trucks were ones Burke had used to export his booze, and were thus a constant reminder to Ontarians of the firm's bootlegging past. Mackenzie wanted all that they stood for to disappear. The question was how to design the new trucks to be both functional and attention grabbing. Mackenzie found an answer in the pages of *Esquire* magazine. The December 1934 issue featured the new automobile designs of Alexis de Sakhnoffsky. Russian by birth, Sakhnoffsky had studied automotive engineering in Switzerland before becoming a designer of flamboyant European sports cars. In 1929, he immigrated to the United States to work for the Hayes Body Corporation. At a time when the North American automotive industry was searching for a way to build faster cars without increasing the size of the engine or reducing the weight of the vehicle, Sakhnoffsky proposed tailoring the body of the car to be streamlined and aerodynamic. Mackenzie was amazed by what he saw in *Esquire* and approached Sakhnoffsky in 1935 to design a streamlined truck for Labatt.

In 1936, the first four "streamliners" were delivered to Labatt, each with conventional tractors powered by six-cylinder motors. The next four trucks had cab-over-engine tractors to make the combined unit a streamlined whole.[108] The trucks were painted fire-engine red and had the name "Labatt's" – in script similar to the signature of John Labatt II – in gold-leaf lettering on the side.[109] The trucks sent the message that the Labatt brewery was at once a historic company, dedicated to quality and tradition, and a modern one, intent on harnessing the positive powers of science and technology to produce its products and get them to market. At a time when many of the other vehicles on the road were dilapidated and rundown, Labatt's shiny new state-of-the-art streamliners were eye-catching and conveyed an optimistic message of progress and the return to prosperity. They were also a material expression of Labatt's desire to move on from its amoral past.

"Let's Teach Temperance": Distancing Itself from the Drunk Driving Problem

In the early-morning hours of Christmas Day 1936, James Sloan was driving back to his home on Golfview Avenue in the Beaches area of Toronto after a late night of drinking with friends. As he passed through the downtown core, he lost control of his car and went careening across the intersection of Jarvis and Fleet streets. Impaired by alcohol, he was unable to avoid a sixty-five-year-old man who had woken up early on Christmas morning to walk his dog. The man and his dog were killed instantly. The police found three Christmas cards in the dead man's pocket, from Mildred, Bill, and Joan. Sloan was charged with drunk driving and manslaughter.[110] Sadly, it wasn't the only incident of drunk driving that Christmas season. In total, there were more than one hundred motor accidents in the city of Toronto, most of them attributable to alcohol. As a result, the *Globe and Mail* pronounced it "the blackest Christmas in the history of the city."[111]

The events of that tragic day mobilized wets and drys alike. The drys saw "Black Christmas" as evidence of the dangers of John Barleycorn. "If we released a bunch of maniacs from 999 Queen St West [the Provincial Lunatic Asylum]," proclaimed Dr A.J. Irwin of the Ontario Temperance Union on 26 December, "we would probably not have had more serious results than we had yesterday."[112] According to Irwin, brewers like Labatt had done their "utmost for some years to create the psychology out of which such tragedies arise."[113] There was no question that Canadians were drinking more beer in 1936 than they had just a few years before. Per capita consumption had finally returned to pre-Depression levels. In 1936, each Canadian consumed, on average, almost 6 gallons of beer.[114] Those in Ontario were consuming more than the national average and about as much beer as was being consumed in Quebec.[115] According to Irwin, the increased consumption was a result of the Moderation League's tactics that led to government policies that made it easier to get a drink. And now, Irwin concluded, "even the holy Nativity must be celebrated with longer hours of selling liquor."[116]

Since Premier Hepburn had re-established public drinking in the province, the brewers and the Moderation League had kept an eye on the retail sector, watching for any actions that might place the whole industry in a negative light and create "an unfavourable attitude on the part of the public."[117] Hugh Mackenzie was particularly worried about barrooms openly supplying hard liquor to customers, serving minors, and enabling drunkenness.[118] The brewers also kept a vigilant eye on the media. The Moderation League's executive secretary, H.S. Pritchard, was quick to write a protest to any editor whenever an anti-beer article appeared in the press.[119]

A few days after Irwin's appeal appeared in the press, John R. Cartwright, an up-and-coming Bay Street lawyer and political adviser to Hepburn, wrote to Hugh Labatt, who had finally found his feet as a brewery executive, warning him that the premier did not want "to be embarrassed on the question of his administration of the [liquor] trade."[120] The government's warning was passed on to Mackenzie. To defend their product, their industry, and the right of the people to drink publicly, the brewery scion and the general manager knew that they and their allies needed to get out in front of this issue, promoting moderation and responsible drinking. In a letter dated 6 January 1937, Hugh Labatt appealed to the president of the Moderation League, Col. Richard Haliburton Greer, "to put the industry on a higher plane and in a proper light, which might help to safeguard the future of the business."[121] Greer, a Toronto lawyer who in 1926 had successfully defended Ben Kerr and kept Canada's "most daring" rum-runner out of jail,[122] was a close ally. "We suggest a publicity campaign," concluded Labatt.[123]

Over the next two years, the beer lobby ran ads in the press to get people to drink moderately and responsibly and maintain the legislative gains that had been made since 1927 and to shift the ownership of the drinking and driving problem onto the drinker. The product was *not* the problem, Labatt and its allies maintained. The problem was the irresponsible way that beer was being consumed. Responsible individuals knew how to control themselves. "Government control," the brewers insisted in one piece of cause advertising, "cannot be effective without *self*-control."[124] And self-control was learned behaviour. In another widely circulating advertisement entitled "Let's Teach Temperance," the brewers argued that temperance education meant "teaching people to use any of nature's gifts temperately."[125] Such an education, said the brewers, was best received in the barrooms of the nation where "*public opinion* discourages excess."[126]

The emphasis on public drinking was a new twist on an old argument. Only by drinking publicly, the brewers suggested in their defence of the status quo, would Canadians learn the rituals and habits of drinking responsibly and thereby become good citizens. Drinking, like eating and smoking, was a social custom –

Figure 7.4 The brewers' moderation advertising appeared in the national press for a two-year period between 1937 and 1938. In this ad, advocating the A.B.C. of true temperance, the brewers stated that the "right method" of "combatting excess must be to continue to make it lawful for people to obtain a mild, healthy beverage." A return to prohibition, they warned, would be a return to crime and irresponsible behaviour. Brewers like Labatt seemed to be ignoring their past with statements like the following, which appeared in the ad above: "What happens ... when the legal door closes, the bootlegger's door opens."

determined by the cultural norms and ideals of a society. Prohibition had deprived a whole generation of the opportunity to learn moderation. "And now the present propaganda against the beverage rooms," the brewers warned, "if successful, would defeat the object of true temperance."[127]

Moderation was the key. It was a "Canadian way of life," the brewers maintained, a means of reconciling the tension between self-indulgence and social well-being, between the pursuit of pleasure and deferred gratification. As the brewers saw it, wisdom through the ages had shown that the lasting enjoyment of the pleasures of life depended on moderation, an ethos and approach to drinking that had been largely absent during the age of excess that prompted prohibition in Canada. The ideal Canadian citizen, as Ontario's brewers lectured in their "Dialogue on Moderation," understood his or her obligations to community and

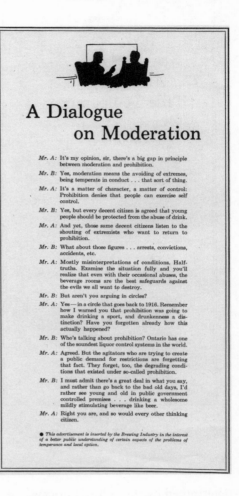

Figure 7.5 This cause advertisement regarding the public good to be derived from moderate drinking called on individuals to show self-control. The brewers were attempting to shift ownership of the drinking and driving issue to the consumer and away from themselves as producers of an intoxicating substance.

country, and reflected this by "avoiding of extremes, by being temperate in conduct."[128] Moderation was a call to drink less of a "good thing" – i.e., beer.[129] The individual who acted immoderately and irresponsibly was the one to blame for the tragic events of Black Christmas, not the brewers and, certainly, not beer.

In 1939, the research department at J. Walter Thomson Co. undertook a readership survey of the brewers' educational campaign, "to know rather than guess whether the advertising was being read, and ... whether on the whole it appeared to carry conviction." In total, the researchers interviewed 1,767 men and women from a cross-section of society – rich and poor, rural and urban, wet and dry. The pollsters determined that roughly three-quarters of those who had read the brewers' ads to promote moderate drinking "thought them convincing."[130]

The brewers' moderation campaign thus played a part in constituting what historian Dan Malleck has termed the "citizen-drinker" – "one who indulges, but responsibly, within the constraints imposed by the state and in a way that does not upset the existing social order."[131] Labatt's own consumer surveys found that in 1939 Canadians were drinking temperately and responsibly.[132] At about the same time, Professor Jackson stated: "The habits of drinking are very much more moderated in this Dominion than in either of the two great Anglo-Saxon countries [Britain and the United States]."[133] Canada had become a nation of moderate beer drinkers. But perhaps most importantly for Labatt and those in the brewing community at large, the propaganda campaign satisfied the Ontario government, and thus public drinking remained.

Conclusion

Few Canadian companies did as well as Labatt during the Great Depression. The company's strategy of promoting its products in the more heavily populated cities of southwestern Ontario along with its continued efforts to improve operating efficiency had positive financial results. Beer's relative affordability during the Great Depression and the friendly treatment that it received from legislators helped propel consumption to new heights. Across the nation, Canadians were drinking more beer than ever before. Per capita beer consumption increased by 50 per cent since the turn of the century, while consumption of hard liquor was cut in half.[134] By responding to the public and political pressure in a way that sought to reconcile their business interests with the public's demands, Labatt and its allies helped brew a nation of beer drinkers. As domestic demand for beer increased, Labatt strategically expanded its plant, doubling its size during the dirty thirties. Still, there was no "soulless" attempt to conquer the competition as E.P. Taylor was doing. Those at Labatt felt there was enough beer money to go around. Demand for beer was growing, and Labatt was content with the same portion of a larger market. With its shares still tightly held by members of the family, Labatt could get away with its live-and-let-live philosophy. In the fall of 1938, as war clouds again began to gather over Europe, Labatt was one of the biggest and richest breweries in Canada.

In its corporate quest for legitimacy, Labatt manufactured a new image and a new corporate "soul." Determined to move beyond its bootlegging past, it got rid of those who had worked for Burke in the export business. Eventually even Burke was shoved out. To replace these amoral men, Labatt hired ethical individuals who possessed specialized training in their respective fields of business, men who were quick on their feet and appreciated the importance of public relations. Labatt put its image-building tactics to good use during the decade in an effort to get the public to re-image beer in more favourable terms as well as to educate the public about the dangers of irresponsible drinking practices. As a result, the firm emerged from the Depression equipped with a new personality: no longer a soulless profit-hungry bootlegger but a soulful good neighbour; a maker of wholesome, natural, Canadian drinks; a corporation that seemingly – given its response to Black Christmas – had a social conscience. This newly fashioned corporate image allowed the firm to compete advantageously as the Great Depression reached its end. The question now was if and how it would withstand the pressures of war.

"To Ensure the Continued Life of the Industry"

The Public Relations Campaign of Labatt and Its Allies during the Second World War

In the summer of 1941, Matthew H. Halton, a war correspondent, arrived in Solum, an Egyptian village near the Mediterranean Sea, just east of the border with Libya. The British army there was under heavy attack by the Afrika Korps under General Erwin Rommel, the fabled "Desert Fox." As the German shells rained down on Solum, Halton fearlessly recorded the fighting and dying in the searing sands of North Africa. The fact that "one brigade with a few guns" ultimately held off the German assault left Halton "shaking with pride." When the fighting was done, a charming young British lieutenant approached Halton and offered him a drink. But Halton knew that, in the desert, it was an unforgivable sin to accept water or other drinks from people, and so he replied, "No, thanks." The lieutenant, however, insisted. "Save your protest and drink the beer," he commanded. "It's Canadian."[1]

Versions of the story appeared in various Canadian newspapers during the Second World War. There was nothing factually wrong with the reporting. Nevertheless, the facts were presented in a way to portray the brewing industry in the most positive light. At a time when moral reformers were attempting to use the war as a lever to lift the lid off the tomb of prohibition, Halton's article and others like it were designed to highlight the brewers' contribution to the war effort: they demonstrated that beer was necessary for promoting camaraderie and good health while at the same time maintaining civilian morale at home. These "news items" were part of a public relations campaign undertaken by Labatt and its allies to keep Canada wet during the Second World War.

This chapter examines the unfolding of the public relations campaign of the Ontario brewers. By casting light on the cultural basis, organizational structure and rationale, and day-to-day practices of the Public Relations Committee of the Ontario Brewers (PRCOB), it aims to add to our understanding of what historians Robert Jackall and Janice Hirota term "the ethos advocacy."[2] At times in the life cycle of a firm, it is essential to defend the whole industry in order to survive. Such was the case for those at Labatt during the Second World War.

The Origins of the PRCOB

Prohibitionism had never fully faded from the collective consciousness, although for most Canadians, it had lost its lustre in light of the failed noble experiment. According to the Ontario brewers' internal polls, in 1940 only 6 per cent of the province's population desired a return to a bone-dry state.[3] But the same survey showed that 19 per cent of the population believed that it would be better to prohibit the sale of beer, wine, and spirits during the war.[4] What was worse for Labatt and its allies, there seemed to be growing support for stricter laws on the production and consumption of all types of liquor. The leaders of the prohibition movement had begun tapping into this sentiment. And while the ultimate objective of the drys remained full-fledged prohibition, they were now more willing to wage a piecemeal campaign. Across the nation, they lobbied for the closing of beverage rooms, the elimination of wet canteens, voluntary abstinence, and restrictions on beer production. Those at John Labatt Limited worried that "the public, in its present emotional state, might favour some form of anti-liquor legislation."[5] Even more worrying were the rumours that "the majority of the Members of the Federal Cabinet were inclined to favour Prohibition."[6]

On 20 January 1941, the elite of the Canadian brewing industry met at the Royal York Hotel in Toronto to consider tactics to keep the nation wet while at war. John S. Labatt, Hugh Labatt, Hugh Mackenzie, and Larry C. Bonnycastle travelled from the Labatt brewery in London, Ontario. Waiting for them in Toronto was D.C. Betts, vice-president of Canadian Breweries Ltd. Making the trip from Montreal was Norman Dawes, president of National Breweries; George Pierce, owner of the infamous 400 Club; and H. William Molson, president of Molson's Brewery Limited. Never short of an opinion on what needed to be done, Dawes proposed creating a new lobbying body to be named the Brewers' Industrial Foundation of Canada. As he conceived it, the foundation would have "a broad membership, which would stress the national aspect of its operation and would have a strong influence on Provincial and Federal governments as well as the public itself."[7] He felt that the brewers could best protect their interests by undertaking "educational work amongst the public, propaganda work amongst the influential, and active anti-prohibition work everywhere."[8]

While all agreed on the need for such an organization, the Ontario and Quebec brewers were at odds when it came to the foundation's strategy and structure. The Ontario brewers believed it was essential to have an outside, independent organization to act as an executive front for the foundation. "If domination and direction appears to come largely from Montreal," Labatt general manager Hugh Mackenzie maintained, "it would be very difficult to attract the other Ontario brewers into the organization."[9] Dawes, on the other hand, was against handing over "complete directional and financial control to an outsider."[10] In addition, Dawes felt that it was more important to create an organization that was national in scope; the Ontario brewers believed that such a far-reaching public relations effort should come later. "We are convinced that each province must look after its own problems," stated Hugh Mackenzie, "and that the nation-wide organization should come into being after the individual provinces have developed their own plans."[11] Given the structure of the Canadian brewing industry (which, unlike in the United States, was devoid of truly national brewers) and given the distinctive nature of provincial drinking cultures, Mackenzie was of the opinion that it was "wiser to develop a public relations campaign within the Province of Ontario and directed by the brewers of Ontario."[12] The other Ontario brewers agreed.

Having made the decision to go it alone, the Ontario brewers contracted the advertising firm of Lord & Thomas to help them structure and orchestrate the public relations campaign in the province. Lord & Thomas was chosen because of its recent success at the art of public relations south of the border. At the time, public relations expertise was much more developed in the United States than in Canada. Indeed, by the end of the New Deal era, public relations was a permanent fixture in American corporate life.[13] For example, in 1939, General Motors had budgeted $2 million for public relations and had employed over fifty people to "sell" itself and the capitalist system to the American people. During the Second World War, public relations played a critical role in uniting Americans behind the war and simultaneously refurbishing the image of American business and free enterprise – an image that had been tarnished during the Great Depression.[14] Every medium was exploited, including lectures, surveys, exhibits that travelled from town to town, advertisements, and sponsorships of radio programs.[15] Public relations advisers were seeking to make the large corporation the symbol of progress and the stage on which individual initiative and the aspirations of the human spirit could play out. Against this, the public relations experts contrasted the "New Dealers," "bureaucratic planners," "radicals," "collectivists," and "socialists" who wanted to rob Americans of the fifth freedom – "the freedom of enterprise."[16]

Lord & Thomas were very much a part of the American public relations experience. Under the leadership of Don Francisco, the firm had handled a public relations campaign for chain stores in California, which were facing higher taxes: their approach was to influence the culture around the issue by reaching out to consumers who would be adversely affected by the higher prices resulting from the tax hikes. Lord & Thomas also oversaw a campaign designed to get Californians to "re-imagine" the chain store as the agent of lower prices and mass consumerism. The brewers believed that Lord & Thomas's "progressive approach" was ideally suited to assisting them in defending their commercial interests in Ontario. By bringing more "modern" methods of shaping consumer perceptions to the situation in Canada, Lord & Thomas would help the brewers improve their image with the public.

At its first formal meeting with the brewers, Lord & Thomas suggested establishing a new body to be called the Public Relations Committee of the Ontario Brewers. It would be made up of four units: the Plan Board, which would be the "heart," or command centre, of the public relations program; the Coordinating Unit, which would act as liaison between the various provincial brewing public relations organizations and "through which would pass all the operations of the [Ontario] programme"; a Mechanical Department, which would engage in clipping services and library work to procure pro-beer propaganda; and a Distributing Department, which would disseminate pro-wet and anti-dry information. The Plan Board was made up of G.F. Mills, J.W. Spitzer, and A.F. Blake of Lord & Thomas, and Larry Bonneycastle of John Labatt Limited. Reporting directly to the Plan Board was a handful of fieldworkers assigned the task of building bridges to the community at large. Miss Jane Alexander, for example, was to work with "influential women and organized women's groups." For her services, she was given a retainer of $50 a month plus $60 a week. James Cowan was paid $415 a month to organize conventions and special events "in specific communities ... where action is urgently required." In total, the PRCOB employed twenty-four people during its first year of operation.[17]

Although the PRCOB's immediate goal was to improve the brewers' image with the public, its ultimate objective was to "ensure the continued life of the industry" by defending the established drinking culture and the existing system of liquor legislation in Ontario.[18] The liquor regime that emerged in Ontario after prohibition, which had come to an end in 1927, gave the state a monopoly on the wholesale purchase and retail sale of alcoholic beverages. The state, through its regulatory agency, the Liquor Control Board of Ontario, also had the responsibility of controlling those spaces where public drinking was taking place. Canadians had long been more willing than their neighbours south of the border to accept a large government presence in their economic lives. The system benefited the brewers over the distillers because only beer and wine could be consumed in the province's public beverage rooms.[19] In part, this accounted for a shift in consumer behaviour during the interwar period. By 1939, each Ontarian was consuming on average 7.38 gallons of beer and only .37 gallons of hard liquor per annum.[20]

To achieve its goal of defending the status quo, those at PRCOB felt that it would be advantageous to build a broad-based coalition of pro-beer advocates. The first group identified as a potential ally was the military. A recent Canadian survey conducted by Lord & Thomas indicated that "the soldiers are likely to be more anti-dry than any other classification."[21] The report also put the veterans of the First World War in the same camp. In addition, the PRCOB believed that labour would "be tremendously displeasured by any changes to the existing system [of liquor legislation]," and thus it too would be an ally. Long gone was the prim, tee-totalling working-class masculinity of the pre-prohibition years. By the time of the Second World War, those of the working class were ready to defend publicly the right to drink responsibly and moderately, seeing beer drinking as a small reward for their breadwinning.[22] The PRCOB immediately targeted these groups by contacting their chief representatives – a technique that had long been used in the United States. South of the border, public relations practitioners often oriented themselves toward "opinion leaders" with the expectation that they would then spread the desired messages through their own networks of communication.[23] As the profession of public relations got its hesitant start in the late 1930s and early 1940s, the same modern methods were utilized by the PRCOB. For example, in September 1941, the PRCOB contacted Tom Moore and Aaron Roland Mosher, who directed the two largest unions in Canada, with the view of "developing a general picture of the labour situation and at the same time opening the way for distribution, through them, of material."[24]

The PRCOB identified the Canadian press as the final group whose service was deemed absolutely essential to the brewers' lobbying efforts.[25] Those at PRCOB recognized that any public relations campaign "must have the support of at least a portion of the newspapers in the province." They also knew that it would be difficult to get such support unless "the newspapers receive some consideration for any favourable publicity they give the brewing industry."[26] Even before the war, circulation growth had become the yardstick by which newspapers measured their success, and advertising dollars became the means to that end.[27] The Great Depression, however, had taken a heavy toll on the daily and weekly newspapers of the nation. The reduced revenues from advertising led to decreased circulation and many bankruptcies. Those newspapers that managed to survive the Depression limped into the war. The brewing industry, on the other hand, had fared remarkably well during the 1930s. The brewers had the money that the newspaper owners and editors sorely needed. "Publishers are human," noted a PRCOB memo, "and therefore an industry which represents large space purchases is much more likely to get the co-operation of the press when publicity of a controversial nature is desired."[28] The PRCOB decided that "the best way to do this [gain favour from the press] was to authorize an institutional campaign." The campaign would "in no way touch on the point at issue between the dry organizations and the industry" but rather would "aim at creating good will both with newspaper editors and with the public at large."[29]

During the winter of 1941, Larry Bonneycastle wrote to Hugh Mackenzie to report that the PRCOB had begun calling on the editors of weekly and daily newspapers to determine whether they were friends or foes of the brewing industry.[30] The brewers needed a way of influencing the public. By the summer of that year, the PRCOB had contacted forty-seven editors and had compiled a detailed list of their personality, views, and opinions. The PRCOB knew, for example, that Rupert Davies, publisher of the Kingston *Whig Standard*, was "violently opposed" to the liquor interests and that "advertising dollars alone would not convince him of the worthiness of the brewers' cause."[31] Similarly, they were aware that the editor of the Acton *Free Press*, A.C. Dill, was no friend of the liquor traffic. "He has no sympathy whatever with the wets," noted PRCOB's Frank Mills, "and would refuse advertising."[32]

But the industry did have its supporters. For example, Col. R.F. Parkinson, managing director of the Ottawa *Journal*, "would accept brewery advertising and ... will put the campaign over, if all stick together."[33] Likewise, W.C. Scott, editor of the *London Ledger*, a newspaper with a circulation of 8,000 in the rural areas surrounding London, Ontario, was squarely in the wet column. Speaking on behalf of his stakeholders, Scott told Henry Janes, a fieldworker at the PRCOB, that "if we can help bury the prohibition movement, we will."[34]

But just as important to the PRCOB was determining which newspaper editors had not yet made up their mind on the liquor question. When Henry Janes first

Table 8.1

Beer sales, production volume, brewing and bottling costs, taxes, and net profit at Labatt, 1939–45

Year	Sales	No. of barrels brewed	Cost of brewing and bottling	Taxes*	Net profit
1939	$8,226,038	378,000	$3,023,904	$1,192,000	$1,733,000
1940	$10,898,350	479,000	$4,604,910	$1,647,000	$1,950,000
1941	$14,439,268	589,000	$6,024,110	$2,029,000	$2,864,000
1942	$17,132,209	612,000	$7,591,638	$2,366,000	$3,089,000
1943	$16,840,730	558,000	$8,041,674	$2,210,575	$2,792,000
1944	$17,363,836	564,000	$8,080,549	$2,208,098	$3,295,000
1945	$17,916,149	603,000	$8,568,424	$2,375,000	$3,347,744

*The taxes in this column include the Dominion sales tax, provincial sales, and other taxes, as well as the cost of licences and permits. The excise tax on malt is included in the cost of brewing.
Source: John Labatt Ltd, *Balance Sheets*, 1939–45.

interviewed W.G. Elliot, editor of the *Woodstock-Ingersoll Daily Sentinel Review*, he was unable to ascertain "his personal views as to liquor or beer." In his report, Janes noted that Elliot was a "bonafide newspaper man of about 52, who smoked a pipe." He was "approachable, well-informed, very conservative minded … but would give careful attention to both sides of the question before he makes up his mind." Following up a few days later, Frank Mills found out that Elliot's principal criticism of the liquor traffic was that the brewers were profiting too much from the war. "You have only to see Labatt's trucks rolling through here day and night to realize this," Elliot told Mills.[35] Nevertheless, Elliot felt that "prohibition was *not* a practical issue," so the PRCOB counted him among those who "are likely to be influenced."[36]

When interviewed by the PRCOB, the editor of *The Farmers' Advocate*, W.H. Porter, also noted the omnipresence of the Labatt's trucks as evidence of the size and prosperity of the brewing industry. Both Porter and Elliot were observant men. Labatt's production had increased by over 50 per cent since the beginning of the war (see table 8.1). And so had profits, despite the fact that the federal government had hit the industry with a succession of new wartime taxes.[37] Asked whether the breweries provided a good market for too-abundant grain crops,

Porter stated that the "farmers can make more profit feeding their barley to hogs than selling it to the brewers." In his final analysis, Mills stated that he "suspects that *The Farmers' Advocate* will listen to both sides of the question." Nevertheless, the PRCOB put Porter in the category of "unlikely to be influenced."[38]

By the end of January 1942, the PRCOB had interviewed 155 newspaper editors and publishers and determined that the "general opinion was inclined to be favourable to the present liquor control system." Only 29 per cent of those interviewed by the PRCOB completely disapproved of the existing liquor laws, whereas 31 per cent completely approved and 40 per cent generally approved. In regard to co-operating with the brewing industry in its public relations campaign, the PRCOB determined that 74 per cent of all editors were inclined to accept the brewers' advertising, assuming that it did not contravene the law. Perhaps more importantly, approximately 40 per cent of all editors stated that their news columns would be available for publicity releases.[39] A separate report noted that this was "a considerable improvement over the situation even a year ago."[40]

Defending the Right to Supply Beer to the Troops Overseas

Much of the early activity of the PRCOB was dedicated to defending the brewers' right to supply beer to the troops overseas. In January 1941, Canadian brewers had been asked to supply the British Navy, Army, and Air Force Institutes, which operated the wet canteens for Commonwealth forces in all fighting theatres. Canadian brewers were already distributing beer to canteens on airfields and army bases across the nation, where there was a preference for bottled beer.[41] Close to a million men and women had enlisted in the Canadian military, and to this group was added the young men from other countries who were in Canada to receive their flying training under the British Commonwealth Air Training Plan. Despite the growing demand for beer on the home front, the Canadian brewers responded to the British order. Within weeks, 400,000 dozen quarts were shipped in the first allotment for the British government.

The fact that Canadian beer was being exported to troops overseas enraged many temperance advocates. Dry critics like Rev. C.W. DeMille of the Canada Temperance Federation argued that beer was detrimental to the war effort. Shortly after the outbreak of hostilities, DeMille stated that Britain had three enemies: "Germany, Italy and Drink. And the greatest of these is Drink."[42] The statement was a variation of a famous First World War quote by the prominent British Chancellor of the Exchequer, David Lloyd George.[43] The fact that DeMille chose to employ words from his teetotalling predecessor demonstrated that Labatt and its allies were fighting history as much as present circumstances: the issues of a generation earlier persisted and remained culturally relevant. As Lloyd George had done in 1915, DeMille argued that the consumption of beer resulted in "the lowering of efficiency in both the armed forces and war industries through the narcotic influence of alcohol."[44] In addition, it depressed the level of national morale "through debauchery of both civilians and enlisted persons."[45] DeMille called on the federal government "to stop the scandal of having ships loaded with Canadian liquor while quantities of war supplies so desperately needed at the front lie on railway lines."[46] Others, like Rev. A.E. Runnells of Trinity United Church, argued that government's liberal liquor laws were undermining the war effort by creating "puffy beer drinkers."[47] Mrs Edgar D. Hardy, president of the National Council of Women of Canada, agreed, and her organization demanded that the federal government prohibit the use of shipping space for transporting beer to the troops in the Middle East.[48]

Labatt, however, was eager to see these shipments continue, not because they were of great benefit to the firm's bottom line, but because of their value in the public relations war. The PRCOB wanted the public to perceive the shipments as a valuable contribution to the war effort and therefore as serving a public good. Shortly after Canadian beer began arriving in the Middle East, the PRCOB began exploiting the Canadian-beer-in-Egypt story for all it was worth. "Arrangements have been made for publicity and pictures of the arrival of the beer in Egypt to be released," Larry Bonneycastle wrote in a PRCOB memorandum.[49] The pictures that appeared in the press challenged the prohibitionists' image of the fighting men. The men looked healthy, happy, and well nourished – nothing like the depressed beer-bloated soldier that the prohibitionists had depicted.

Shortly after, Matthew Halton's article, "They Drank Canadian Beer at Solum," appeared in various Canadian newspapers. After the story's initial publication, the PRCOB had it reworked slightly to incorporate a few "facts" of its own. Internally, the story was marked as "propaganda release." But when it was sent to the editors and publishers, it was marked as a "news item." In the reprinted versions of the story, the PRCOB reached back in history to justify sending Canadian beer to the troops. At a time when pro-British sentiment was high, the PRCOB emphasized the British-ness of beer drinking and Canada's imperial connection. "The

"What about beer in wartime?"

"You might as well say, 'What about beer any time'?"

"Oh no! I quite approve of beer in general . . . but when people have to do without tea and coffee . . ."

"All the more reason why they should NOT have to do without beer! Look, my friend — people are asked to cut down on the consumption of tea and coffee to save *shipping* space. But Canadian ales and beers are brewed in Canada from Canadian malt and Canadian hops. The tax on these products is an important source of income for the government . . ."

"Alright! Alright! I get your point of view, but . . ."

"But nothing! Not only is brewing not harmful but it has actually proved beneficial to the war effort."

"How on earth do you make that out?"

"Ever heard of morale? See here — when a man has worked long hours at the pitch of concentration a munitions plant demands, he is apt to be all keyed up . . . unable to relax . . . that's where a wholesome glass of ale can do most good . . ."

"Interesting theory, but can you prove it?"

"Sure! The record of England in the last war proves it. When they cut down on the supply of beer they had strikes . . . slow downs . . . trouble in munitions plants. When they restored beer, munitions productions went up and up. Even a dyed-in-the-wool temperance man like Lloyd George classified brewing as an *essential industry*."

John Labatt Limited

Brewers Since 1832

LONDON · CANADA

importance of beer as a beverage for the troops," read one news item, "was recognized by Lord Allenby commanding the British fighting forces in the Near East during the last war, whose brilliant campaign brought such a large section within the sphere of the British." A separate PRCOB news item informed the reader that: "One of Lord Allenby's first actions was to order large quantities of beer to be shipped to his troops in Palestine." The article then went on to emphasize the essential role that beer had played in maintaining the physical strength and mental health of the military. "Exposed to the burning heat of the semi-tropical terrain over which they were forced to fight, it was noticed that there was an appreciable lowering of physical resistance and morale owing to the trying climatic conditions. But not long after the arrival of the first shipments of beer there was a noticeable improvement in the general condition of the troops." And then, in a final appeal to the audience, the article ended with the lessons of history: "Profiting from this experience, beer is now being made a regular part of the rations of the armies in the East and in North Africa." Versions of this story continued to be printed in the press during the war.[50]

What, if any, role these PRCOB news items played in swaying public opinion is difficult to determine. The universe of public relations does not readily submit to easy measurements of cause and effect, especially when the product to be measured is as diffused as attitudes about the moral economy of beer drinking in wartime. The fact that the brewers continued to disseminate the "They Drank Canadian Beer at Solum" story indicates that those at the PRCOB, at least, believed that the item was having a positive effect. Perhaps more importantly, when it came time for the federal government to weigh in on the issue, the brewing industry's position prevailed. When the subject became a matter of debate in the House of Commons in the summer of 1942, the minister of finance, James Lorimer Ilsley, stated that he saw nothing wrong with shipping beer to the troops

Figure 8.1 *Opposite* This "What about beer in wartime?" advertisement was sponsored by John Labatt Ltd in 1942. It was part of the Canadian brewers' efforts to get the public to think of beer as an "essential" wartime good. Here, an older man, wise with age and the experience of prohibition, "educates" his younger counterpart about the need for beer in war. "Ever hear of morale?" the older man asks. "See here – when a man has worked long hours at the pitch of concentration for a munitions plant demands, he is apt to be all keyed up ... unable to relax ... that's where a wholesome glass of ale can do most good." The brewers also emphasized the fact that, unlike tea and coffee, beer was "brewed in Canada from Canadian malt and Canadian hops" and the tax on these products was "an important source of income for the government."

overseas. To deny beer to those who were putting their lives on the line for freedom in the scorching-hot theatres of the Far East was a position that Ilsley considered "wholly reprehensible."[51] The export of beer to the troops overseas
continued for the duration of the war.

Defending the Domestic Status Quo

On 3 July 1942, DeMille's Canada Temperance Federation (CTF) took out a full-
page ad in the *Toronto Star*, one of Canada's most widely circulated newspapers.
The propaganda piece called on the federal government of William Lyon Mackenzie King to adopt legislation to curb the consumption of intoxicating beverages
on the home front during the war. The CTF made no distinction between beer
and hard liquor: both were the cause of "poverty, crime, accidents and loss of
time." The CTF listed ten "facts," which were aimed at convincing the public and
the government that liquor "menaces our war effort." Among them was the claim
that "scientific tests have repeatedly shown that alcohol's narcotic effect on workers is to decrease their efficiency" and thereby diminish the industrial prowess
and military might of the nation. The ad also noted that the liquor traffic was
profiting more than most from the war: "While the nation faces a crisis, liquor
traffic thrives and its promoters are enriched." In its final appeal, the CTF asked
rhetorically: "Do you not think it is inconsistent for a government to ask God's
blessing on their war effort and then for that Government to protect a traffic that
is doing so much to undermine the moral and religious life of the nation and to
thwart the nation's effort on behalf of the victory prayed for?"[52]

The CTF advertisement caught the eye of Prime Minister William Lyon
Mackenzie King, and on 14 September 1942, members of the CTF were invited to
his residence on the corner of Laurier Avenue and Chapel Street in Ottawa. A
life-long teetotaller, Mackenzie King was sympathetic to the prohibitionist cause.
In fact, he had contempt for anyone who made a living from the making or selling
of booze. On more than one occasion, he stated that the liquor interests were the
"most corrupt force in the country."[53] During the meeting, the prohibitionists
pointed to a "disturbing trend" in wartime consumption.[54] Beer consumption
was up, way up, they noted, since the beginning of the war. Nationwide, each
Canadian was now consuming on average 8.7 gallons of beer per year. That was
an increase of almost 50 per cent since 1939.[55] In Great Britain, per capita beer
consumption had also increased, but only by 14 per cent between 1939 and 1942.[56]

The increase in Canadian consumption meant that the brewers were selling more beer and making more money. At Labatt, profits had increased by almost 80 per cent since the hostilities began. Mackenzie King was moved by the statistical evidence, and vexed by the amount of money the brewers were making. "The brewers have profited more than anyone out of the war," Mackenzie King wrote in his diary; "Indeed, the liquor interests and the newspapers have been the real profiteers."[57] The prime minister concluded that something had to be done to control consumption and curb the excessive profits and undue influence of the liquor traffic. Just a few hours after meeting with the temperance delegation, Mackenzie King instructed his wartime Cabinet to "press on in the matter of curtailing the liquor traffic."[58] He also told the Cabinet that in due course he would make a broadcast on the subject in relation to Canada's war effort.[59]

When news of the prime minister's plan reached the PRCOB, it immediately began a grassroots lobbying campaign to prevent the plan from becoming a reality. The PRCOB contacted Frank Mathers of the Western Canada Brewers' Association to advise labour groups in the west of what was pending and to persuade them to protest. In Ontario, contacts established early in 1942 with organized labour were immediately utilized. The PRCOB dispatched a fieldworker to Sarnia and Windsor to work in those all-important labour communities, and later turned their attention to St Catharines, Niagara Falls, and Welland. On 18 November 1942, an appointment was arranged with Percy Bengough, acting president of the Trades and Labor Congress of Canada, to enlist his support. Two other fieldworkers reached out to the veterans' organization for the "purpose of procuring protest against any reductions in the sale of beer."[60]

By the end of the month, the PRCOB could report that "the contact with Messrs Mathers and Chiswick was productive and numerous wires to the Prime Minister from labour groups as far west as the Rocky mountains [have been sent] protesting any reduction in sales of beer and ale." In Ontario, wires of protest were sent to the prime minister from the Trades and Labor Councils of Essex County, Woodstock, Brantford, and the Frontier District group, which covered the Niagara Peninsula. The interview with Percy Bengough had also gone according to plan. Bengough followed through on his promise to wire the prime minister reiterating the view of the Trades and Labor Congress of Canada that it was "unalterably opposed to any change in the laws affecting the sale of alcoholic beverages." Bengough also wired various members of Mackenzie King's wartime Cabinet and endorsed the protests across the country against any reduction in the manufacture of beer or ale. Finally, the PRCOB efforts to mobilize the veterans of the nation had resulted in wires sent to the prime minister and his Cabinet from the Canadian Pensioners' Association, the Army and Navy Veterans in Canada, and the Ontario Command of the Canadian Legion.[61]

When it came time for the members of Mackenzie King's wartime Cabinet to voice their opinions on the matters, most felt that beer drinking was a highly valued activity among industrial workers, veterans, and military men of the nation and that "it would be a mistake to go too far in the matter of beer."[62] When the prime minister floated the idea of reducing beer production by 20 per cent, the Cabinet baulked. Mackenzie King spent the afternoon of 19 November 1942 attempting to convince his Cabinet of the merit of his measure. But he could not rally any support. "I get no help from anyone [in the Cabinet]," Mackenzie King lamented, "not even [from] Ralston who is a strong Baptist, teetotaller, etc."[63] Mackenzie King was astonished "how [the] standards of men get undermined through influences around him." The resistance in Cabinet forced Mackenzie King to water down his liquor legislation.

When the federal government announced its Wartime Alcoholic Beverages Order (WABO) on 16 December 1942, the legislation privileged the production and consumption of beer. While the Order-in-Council restricted the annual volume of beer sold by each brewery to not more than 90 per cent of its sales in the previous year, it restricted the production of wine and spirits to 80 per cent and 70 per cent, respectively, of the previous year's production.[64] But the brewers did not get special treatment when it came to advertising. Mackenzie King felt that advertising was "clearly not necessary to promote sales, nor is it justifiable if sales and consumption are to be curtailed."[65] Thus advertising by distillers, vintners, and brewers was prohibited under the new law.

Those at the PRCOB believed that the ban on advertising meant that the brewing industry's public relations campaign would be "severely compromised." They decided that the first step in ending the curtailment of production was to repeal the section of the Order that prohibited advertising. In January 1941, the members of the PRCOB attended a meeting of Canadian publishers to discuss "the ways and means of persuading authorities to amend the government's prohibition on advertising." The decision was made for the publishers to personally pressure Members of Cabinet and the House of Commons. It was further decided that they should stress the fact that the newspaper industry's entire existence depended on its ability to attract advertising dollars. The effort paid dividends in March 1942, when the government amended the WABO to permit brewers to advertise so long as it was devoted to the war effort.

Figure 8.2 During the Second World War, Labatt's brands were Crystal Lager, Extra Stock Ale, XXX Stout, and the brew that still made up the bulk of the company's sales, its award-winning India Pale Ale. On the neck of three of the four bottles is a picture of the iconic Labatt Streamliner and the words "courtesy service," a reference to the company's popular Highway Courtesy Program. Launched in 1929, in a further effort to get the public to re-imagine the brewery as a "soulful good neighbour," the road-side assistance program saw Labatt's drivers help other motorists in need.

Within this new advertising environment, the PRCOB proposed embarking on a propaganda campaign to get Canadians to image beer as a "nutritious" item and therefore essential to waging an effective war at home and abroad. Shortly after its January meeting with the nation's publishers, the PRCOB decided on a "public service" advertising campaign to indirectly link beer to nutrition.

During the war, nutrition emerged as a national priority, not just for the armed forces but also for those on the home front, in particular war industry workers. In 1941, leading nutritional experts warned that upwards of 60 per cent of Canadians were suffering from some form of vitamin and mineral deficiency. Soon thereafter, figures were released showing an alarming rate of medical rejections by the Canadian military. The federal government responded by launching its

first-ever national nutrition-education program.[66] Starting with the creation of
a federal Nutrition Division in 1941 and the inauguration of the Canada Nutrition
Program the following year, Canadians were inundated with nutrition advice
during the war years. A proper diet, they were told, would go a long way toward
maximizing energy, strength, efficiency, and, above all, productivity. At the heart
of this campaign was Canada's Official Food Rules – the precursor to Canada's
Food Guide – which listed the six food groups needed to maintain a healthy diet:
milk, cereals and breads, fruits, vegetables, eggs, and, finally, "meat, fish, etc." The
slogan of the Food Rules reminded Canadians that the goal was straightforward:
"Eat right, feel right – Canada needs you strong!" Or as one headline in *Saturday
Night* put it, more bluntly: "Canada's Faulty Diet is Adolf Hitler's Ally."[67]

In Britain, where there was more freedom when it came to product advertising,
the brewers themselves stressed the potential health benefits to be derived from
drinking beer during the war.[68] In 1942, Ireland's Guinness, for example, ran a
"backs-to-the-wall" advertising campaign. Under the tagline "What the Situation
Demands" was an image of a seemingly random set of objects. Below the image
was a list that described the wartime purpose of each item: "Wheel, for putting
shoulder to; socks, for pulling up; stone, for not leaving unturned; brass tacks,
for getting down to; trump card, for playing; bold face, for putting on it; belt, for
tightening; Guinness for strength."[69] Throughout the war, Guinness continued
to emphasize that its beer was helping to maintain the health of the nation's population. In the United States, brewers like Anheuser-Busch informed the public
that they were helping "to guard your well being" by producing products rich in
essential vitamins. In the United States and Britain, the governments decided that
beer was a valuable beverage for military and civilian health and morale.[70]

The PRCOB was profoundly aware of the developments taking place in
Britain and the United States. Those engaged in clipping services had filled
dozens of file folders with newspaper and magazine articles summarizing the
U.K. and U.S. brewers' efforts to emphasize the nutritional aspects of beer. In
Canada, the PRCOB also argued that there was "an obvious and direct link between this industry and nutrition since beer is a continuing item in the diets
of millions of Canadians and is particularly important to workers in heavy industry – key men in the industrial war effort located in plants on which much
official nutrition effort has been concentrated."[71] In the early years of the war,
the brewers had distributed a pamphlet entitled "Beer, the drink of the Moderate" to thousands of Canadians, informing them about the food value of beer
and its nutritional effects: "Three quarts of a pint of mild ale is equal in food

value to 4.7 ounces of potatoes, 1.8 ounces of bread, 6.4 ounces of milk, 1½ eggs, 3.7 ounces of lean beef and 8.8 ounces of cod-fish." The problem for the beer lobby was that it could no longer make such claims after the federal government's ban on advertising came into effect. In response, the PRCOB embarked on a program of public service advertising.

The brewing industry's "Nutrition for Victory" ads were published in every daily across Ontario, including those traditionally of a prohibitionist bent – such as the St Catharines *Standard* and the *Toronto Star*. Only 25 out of the 275 weeklies in circulation declined to run the PRCOB's ads.[72] Appropriating the words of one of its harshest critics, the Ontario brewers stated in their ads: "Health is a vital dynamic thing contributing to Victory … a proper diet … a matter of national concern." The quote was correctly attributed to William Lyon Mackenzie King.

The ad, and many others like it, touched on wartime notions of femininity. While an unprecedented number of women entered the workforce during the Second World War, women were still expected to be good mothers. "MOTHERS! YOU CAN HELP!" proclaimed one of the PRCOB's ads. "Family health is in your hands," the ad continued. Tapping into the same deep social assumptions regarding a woman's place in wartime society, another PRCOB ad stated: "That's why it is every Canadian woman's duty to know and apply the basic rules of Nutrition." The imagery also reflected and reinforced the underlying cultural logic regarding gender roles. In the corner of the ads was an image of an ideal Canadian family – healthy, wealthy, and happy. A fit-looking boy and girl stood on either side of their mother as their father looked over their shoulders. The ad placed the woman at the centre of the nuclear family, bestowing on her the responsibility for building "stamina … resistance … vitality … by serving the proper food." The ads stressed the importance of nutrition and suggested that the brewers were interested in improving the diets of the Canadian people. All the ads were clearly marked as being "sponsored by the Brewing Industry of Ontario in the interests of nutrition and health as an aid to victory."

In the bottom right-hand corner of all the ads was an invitation to Canadians to mail in for a free fifteen-page booklet, entitled "Nutrition for Victory: Eat to Work to Win." The booklet consisted of a three-page overview on the health elements in food; a two-page list of the basic foods necessary for a healthy diet – as guided by Canada's Official Food Rules; and six pages of breakfast, lunch, and dinner menus. "All the careful, time-taking planning has been done for you," the brewers proudly informed Canadians, "The Brewing Industry (Ontario), recognizing the vital need of a popular knowledge of nutrition among Canadians

... prepares this booklet as a contribution to this important work." With the booklet in hand, all one needed to do was pick one breakfast, one lunch, and one dinner from the twenty-one days of menus that the brewers had provided. For instance, one could choose a breakfast of chilled black currant juice, a foamy omelette, toasted whole-wheat or vitamin-rich bread, jam or jelly, and a beverage made with milk; a lunch of lima beans with bacon or sausage garnish, bread, raw carrot straws, cupcakes, and a beverage made with milk; and a dinner of veal chops, baked potatoes, baked squash, spice cake with applesauce, and a "beverage of choice."[73]

In the month that followed the release of the first ads, the PRCOB received requests for more than 3,000 of the 30,000 booklets it had printed. A PRCOB report on "response to the nutrition campaign" noted that the requests came from high school administrators who were seeking to use the booklet in their health classes, from nuns who were seeking to teach nutrition in school, from army officers who were seeking to educate the military on the value of eating well, and corporate executives who were seeking to keep their employees strong.[74] The $60,000 campaign had a positive effect on the relationship between brewers and publishers. There was now a "ready willingness on the part of publishers to view the industry as one engaged in a legitimate business," noted an internal PRCOB report, "and operating within the law."[75] The same report also noted the goodwill it was generating among the public.

The nutrition-for-victory campaign was aimed not simply at influencing the public by disseminating information regarding a "public good" but also at getting a toehold with the publishers by convincing them that the brewing industry was wholesome enough to deal with. The campaign represented a covert public service style of advertising. Instead of advertising a product, the brewers advertised their "wholesomeness" and "patriotism," while at the same time presenting themselves as objective, impartial "experts" in nutrition.

Fanning the Flames of Discontent

On 11 March 1943, approximately 300 people filled to capacity the Army and Navy Veterans' Hall in Kitchener to endorse a resolution protesting against the "prohibition conditions which are accumulating as the result of the unnecessary and unjustified withholding from the consumers the quantity of beer required for their normal and reasonable use."[76] In other cities, the beer shortage brought an outcry from workers, who threatened to boycott the sale of victory bonds if they did not get more of their favourite beverage. "No Beer – No Bonds" was their battle cry. Across the nation, wartime workers and veterans signed petitions to register their disapproval of the beer restrictions. In March 1943, the president of the Canadian Legion, L.M. Heard, wrote to the prime minister informing him that the beer shortages were "lowering the morale of the troops" and leading good men "to sneak up back alleys looking for entertainment that should be provided in the open."[77] Like many other beer-thirsty Canadians, Heard urged Mackenzie King "to institute such action as will relieve this situation."[78] In the months after the temperance measures were announced, Mackenzie King and many rank-and-file Liberals were flooded with angry protests from citizens all blaming official-dom for the beer shortage.[79]

Those at the PRCOB were profoundly aware of the protests taking place across the nation – and on more than one occasion lent their support to the malcontents. But the beer lobby appreciated that the aid had to be given in such a way as to go unnoticed by the prime minister. Such was the case in February 1943 when James Cook approached Hugh Labatt with an offer to help mobilize protesters at the Toronto Shipbuilding Company where he worked. "I am in a position," Cook wrote to Labatt, "to supply you with a strong petition of thousands of names and addresses of war workers against the restrictions on beer and the early closing of hotels."[80] Not wanting to get directly involved, Hugh Labatt forwarded the letter to James Cowan at the PRCOB. "If you would investigate this man and see if he can be of use," Labatt wrote to Cowan, "we would appreciate it."[81] Labatt was quick to add, however, that any relationship that developed between the PRCOB and Cook would have to be kept secret. "Of course, if his idea is carried out," Hugh Labatt warned, "neither the name of John Labatt Limited nor the brewing industry can appear on the petition."[82] The petition was subsequently signed by over a thousand workers at the Toronto plant and sent to Ottawa. In the final years of the war, the PRCOB became very adroit at stoking the fires of political protest but without getting caught holding the poker in their hands.

Based on the number of political protests, no other shortage brought more of an uproar during the war than the scarcity of beer. Canadians proved willing to put up with a dearth of other items, but the inability to get a glass of beer after finishing a day's work was something that wartime workers and military men could not stomach. Their protests, which were consistently supported and often encouraged by the PRCOB, were many and often. And their message was always the same: "We want more beer." When responding to the public outcry, provincial

FAMOUS SIGNALS OF THE
ROYAL CANADIAN NAVY, No. 1

"SHIP WARHEADS and be in all respects ready for action"

These words, flashed through the ether, marked the end of peacetime service for the Royal Canadian Navy. From the moment when grim-faced men aboard six Canadian destroyers removed the practice heads—substituting explosive-laden warheads—on their torpedoes, the Navy has been on guard, day and night.

In three-and-a-half years, it has grown from an active force with less than 2,000 men to over 55,000. Canadian-built corvettes are playing an increasingly important role in the most important of all battles — the battle of the North Atlantic.

Yes, Canada has a navy of which Canadians are justly proud . . . a navy which your regular purchase of War Savings Certificates will help to ensure does not wait in vain for more ships to guard those precious convoys!

THIS IS ONE IN A SERIES OF ADVERTISEMENTS CONTRIBUTED BY

John Labatt Limited

GOT A SMOKE FRIEND ?

CANADA   ENGLAND

Have you ever been without a cigarette when you wanted one badly? Canadian soldiers overseas find themselves without smokes frequently. One of them writes, "I wish to thank you all deeply for your cigarettes. They are very hard to get over here, and we sometimes have to go days without a smoke." Don't leave any of our men in that state any longer. $1.00 sends 400 cigarettes overseas. Send TODAY as much as you can spare to:

THE OVERSEAS LEAGUE TOBACCO FUND
51 KING STREET EAST, TORONTO

Figure 8.3 "Ship warheads" advertisement, 1942. After war broke out in 1939, Labatt included patriotic messages in support of the war effort in much of its advertising space.

politicians blamed Ottawa for the shortage.[83] Meanwhile in Ottawa, a fiery debate erupted about what exactly should be done given the growing unrest. Pressure was mounting to find a solution, making more than one politician feel uncomfortable. On 3 April 1943, *Maclean's* magazine reported that some members of Parliament were "loathe to go home at Easter recess without more beer for thirsty war workers."[84]

In May 1943, the Liberal government of Mackenzie King responded to the beer shortage by introducing coupon rationing. But the rationing of beer created just as many problems as it solved. In the press, Mackenzie King's handling of the beer question was increasingly criticized. A PRCOB analysis of newspaper "editorials," "columns," and "news items" indicated that between February and May 1943, there were twenty-five clippings that were "favourable" and fourteen that were "unfavourable" to the brewing industry.[85] This was a marked improvement, the PRCOB noted, over the coverage in the past. As in the United States, advertising functions in Canada were changing as market research started to become a more important element in public relations strategies.[86] By 1943, the PRCOB was no longer just shaping and placing news items, it was also monitoring press coverage, collecting data, and quantifying it for the brewing industry.

In the year that followed, the government's restrictions became the subject of an increasingly intense political controversy. During the same period, the PRCOB's press analysis became more complex. By 1944, the PRCOB was monitoring all press publicity. Previously, when the same dispatch appeared in more than one newspaper, only the insertion in one paper was reported; thus, the PRCOB did not have a complete appraisal of the total publicity given to alcoholic beverages in the press of the province. In February 1944, the new methodology was employed for the first time and indicated "a continuation of the favourable trend in public opinion, relative particularly to malt beverages [beer]." Of the total 399 beer news and editorial items that appeared in the press in February 1944, 278 (or 70 per cent) were deemed to be "favourable" to the brewing industry. In comparison, of the 384 press items that related to distilled beverages, only 129 (or 33 per cent) were judged to be "favourable" to the distillers of the nation. Finally, of the 299 news items that related to the Women's Christian Temperance Union and other temperance federations, none were assessed to be "favourable" to the prohibitionist cause.[87]

The shifting cultural landscape emboldened provincial politicians who had long seen beer as a valuable source of tax revenue. Having recently consulted with the PRCOB, Ontario premier George Drew wrote a personal letter to the prime minister on 10 March 1944 requesting a federal-provincial conference on the problems of beer distribution. Drew's Progressive Conservatives had been elected in the summer of 1943 in part by promising voters that they would do a better job of pressuring Ottawa to end the "system of chaos" created by the WABO. Drew maintained that the federal government's beer restrictions created an artificial and unnecessary shortage, and therefore, the limits needed to be removed to increase the supply of beer to meet the demand.

With a by-election in Ontario looming and a federal election roughly a year away, Mackenzie King decided to avoid the publicity (and possible embarrassment) that would accompany a beer conference. He moved quickly to lift the beer restrictions (the restrictions on spirits and wine would remain), giving complete control over the sale and distribution of beer back to the provinces. He realized the political advantages of depositing the baby on someone else's doorstep. On 13 March 1944, the prime minister stood in the House of Commons and declared that restricting the supply of beer "is not sufficiently important to the war effort to justify the risk of continuous misunderstanding and friction between the Federal and Provincial Governments."[88] Always sensitive to the prevailing political wind, Mackenzie King had reversed course.

Conclusion

As the Second World War neared its end, the *Toronto Star* reported that "anti-prohibition sentiment" was at an all-time high.[89] In a subsequent survey conducted by the Canadian Institute of Public Opinion, Canadians were asked: "What do you think is the best way to bring about the temperate use of alcoholic beverages in this country?" Out of those polled, only 19 per cent answered that the solution lay in prohibition.[90] A few years later, a PRCOB report marked "strictly confidential" noted that "the prohibition objective has, by and large, been abandoned." Having noted that the most important battles had been fought and won during the Second World War, the report concluded that from a public relations standpoint, "it may neither be practical nor desirable in the future to counter dry propaganda."[91] Most Canadians were now inclined to see brewing as a "legitimate business." The PRCOB was successful in attaining a favourable mention by the media and manufacturing a flattering image for the brewing industry.

The ethos of advocacy took on an altruistic tone during the war. On the surface, the PRCOB's advertisements were dedicated to promoting a public good – camaraderie, high morale, and nutrition and health as aids to victory. The PRCOB's language and imagery was devoid of any overt product promotion. But below the surface, the public relations campaign was rooted in a desire to maintain the gains that the brewing industry had made since the end of prohibition. Judged by the statistical results, the PRCOB accomplished its task. Although there was a slight falling off in 1943, the production of beer increased throughout the war. Between 1939 and 1945, the total number of barrels of beer brewed increased by 144 per cent, from 2.5 million to 5.3 million. In comparison, the volume of beer produced during the seven-year period leading up to the Second World War rose by only 41 per cent.[92] The surge in demand led to an increase in per capita consumption in Canada of almost 70 per cent during the war.[93] In Ontario, per capita beer consumption remained above the national average, increasing from 7.38 gallons in 1939 to 11.38 gallons in 1945.[94] Export to the troops overseas continued, beverage rooms remained open, and not a single Ontario brewer went out of business. At John Labatt Limited, record profits were earned.[95]

By securing support from a large portion of the press and then disseminating pro-beer propaganda, the PRCOB helped sway public opinion in the brewing industry's favour. During the campaign, Labatt kept a very low public profile. More often than not, those at the old London Brewery were willing to have others fight by proxy. They remained behind the scenes, orchestrating the overall public relations campaign through the PRCOB, which provided the structural means for promoting Labatt's commercial interests. In its advocacy ads, editorials, and news items, the PRCOB used morally loaded messages to project the impression that brewing and beer drinking were essential to the war effort. It tapped into the underlying cultural logic of the age to sell beer drinking as beneficial to the nation at war. While maintaining an image of acting on behalf of a public good, the PRCOB aimed to influence public sentiment on the meaningfulness of beer during wartime and to generate an unprecedented level of goodwill toward those engaged in the business of brewing.

Fast Following into the "Big Three"

Labatt and the Emergence of a National Brewing
Oligopoly, 1945–62

Nine years after the Second World War had come to an end, Jake Moore, Labatt's director of finance and a rising star at the brewery, addressed a group of security analysts. While the subject of his talk was the "outlook for the brewing industry," Moore could not resist reflecting on past developments. The most obvious change in the industry since the end of the Second World War was the fact of fewer independent breweries in operation. In 1945, the Canadian brewing industry was made up of sixty-one breweries (twenty-eight in the west, twenty-nine in Ontario and Quebec, and four in the Maritimes); together they brewed 159 brands. Ontario and Quebec were home to the nation's largest breweries – Labatt, Canadian Breweries Limited (CBL), Molson, and National Breweries. This region was the heartland of the Canadian brewing industry and the Canadian economy more generally, and its captains of industry had long looked to the "hinterland" for growth opportunities. Nevertheless, in 1945, not a single brewery was truly national. The biggest breweries were regional concerns, catering almost exclusively to beer drinkers in their home provinces. But by 1954, many of these smaller, regionally oriented breweries were in the hands of the nation's biggest breweries. In 1954, Labatt along with CBL and Molson dominated the domestic market, producing over 80 per cent of all beer sold in Canada. These breweries constituted a national brewing oligopoly that was referred to as the Big Three. Striking a Darwinian chord, Moore stated that the breweries that had disappeared were those of a weaker nature, unable to adapt to the changes taking place in the institutional and technological environment. And while Moore lamented the disappearance of the nation's smaller breweries because "they provided us all with a basic popular support for the industry that the larger breweries find difficult to duplicate," he was quick to note "the portents are for a continuation of the process of concentration or amalgamation."[1]

Time would prove him right. By 1962, the Big Three produced almost 95 per cent of the beer sold in Canada. Nearly all of the sixty-one breweries that were in operation in 1945 were still producing beer, but now most of them were owned by CBL, Molson, or Labatt. The Big Three had a physical presence in every region across the land, except for the Maritimes and Northern Ontario, and their brands dominated the marketplace.[2] Over a fifteen-year period, the market structure of the Canadian brewing industry was transformed from a relatively large group of regional brewers catering to local drinking preferences into a stable national oligopoly.

On the surface, the transformation of Canadian brewing mirrored changes taking place elsewhere in the industry. The period 1945 to 1975 witnessed the consolidation of the brewing industry in the Netherlands, Belgium, France, Italy, West Germany, Australia, New Zealand, the United Kingdom, and the United States. To be sure, the degree of concentration differed from nation to nation.[3] In West Germany, the level of concentration was relatively low, while in the United Kingdom it was moderate, and in France, the Netherlands, Belgium, and the United States, it was high.[4] In Canada, the level of concentration was also high. But the post-war consolidation of the Canadian brewing industry started earlier and went further more quickly than in any other country. One of the questions this chapter seeks to answer is why. In addition, this chapter examines the factors that led to the emergence of a national brewing oligopoly in Canada and how Jake Moore and the other decision-makers at Labatt fast followed into the Big Three.

Going Public

On Sunday, 28 May 1944, Labatt's shareholders met at the Tamahaac Club, a members-only social club in the lush green woods of Ancaster, Ontario. They gathered to discuss the current state of affairs and to consider making an unprecedented change to the financial structure of the family-owned firm. As the war approached its end, the brewery faced a major challenge: the firm's financial structure threatened to limit the company's ability to expand in the future. For close to a century, Labatt had benefited from a corporate structure that prevented outsiders from interfering in the affairs of the firm.[5] But now the shareholders were considering transforming the privately owned brewery into a public corporation. Carried out correctly, the change would safeguard the interests of the Labatt family shareholders and raise the financial capital needed for post-war expansion. With the ever-aggressive E.P. Taylor signalling that he would soon be taking his "merger for monopoly" strategy national, Labatt had to react or be forced out of the market in just a few years. The Labatt family members unanimously agreed that the time had come to sell a substantial part of their holdings in the company to the public.

Following the meeting, company chairman Major-General Sydney Mewburn asked Colonel Lockhart Gordon, a partner at the accounting firm of Clarkson, Gordon and Company, to examine how the corporate restructuring might best be accomplished. Colonel Gordon subsequently delegated the task to his son. Having joined his father's firm in 1927, Walter Gordon had quickly distinguished himself as a creative financial thinker. During the Second World War, he had worked at the Ministry of Finance and had played a role in crafting the innovative policies that helped the federal government pay for the war and, subsequently, maintain the wartime prosperity into the peace.[6] He displayed the same inventiveness at war's end while working on the Labatt's reorganization.

Less than two weeks after the invasion of Normandy by the Allied forces and just as William Lyon Mackenzie King began remodelling the federal government for the post-war peace, Gordon wrote to Mewburn assuring him that the time was right for the financial restructuring. Investor confidence was up, Canadians were generally optimistic about the future, and the economy was showing no signs of cooling off. The pretty economic picture led Gordon to conclude "market conditions are ideal for a public issue at the present time."[7] The shareholders at Labatt agreed, and the only question was the form the restructuring would take.

Gordon believed that the shareholders had three options. First, Labatt could merge with another prominent Canadian brewer. If they chose this route, Gordon stated that the best bet was to merge with Montreal-based Molson. As Canada's oldest continuous brewery, Molson had performed well during the war. By 1944, Molson was manufacturing over 650,000 barrels of beer a year and, together with National Breweries, controlled over 97 per cent of the lucrative Quebec market. Like Labatt, Molson was eager to expand to meet the anticipated post-war demand for beer. Having recently purchased a large piece of land to the west of its existing brewery on Notre Dame Street, Molson drew up plans for an expansion that would see its output increase by more than 300 per cent over the next eight years.[8] Like those at Labatt, the owners of Molson believed that it would be easier to expand once the basic character of the firm was changed from a closed, private limited-liability firm into an agile, publicly traded company with deep pockets. Gordon suspected that the family shareholders of Molson "must be facing substantially the same problems which face the shareholders of John Labatt Limited."[9] He proposed that "the two families combine a percentage of their shares in a holding company, which would then purchase the stock from each family by selling its own shares to the public through underwriters."[10] The main advantage of this approach, Gordon stated, was that it would create "a wider market and the possibility that a better price would be obtained for the shares."[11] The only problem was that the Labatt family would almost certainly lose control of the brewery that had carried the family name since 1847.[12] This proved unacceptable to the Labatt family members who had a share in the brewery.

A second option was to sell a block of the shares to management at the firm. Hugh Mackenzie had not been shy about letting the family know that he wanted a piece of the brewery. "I … need not say," he wrote to John Sackville Labatt on 2 June 1944, "how much I would like to feel that I had a financial interest in the company."[13] He believed that John Labatt Limited was entering a period of transition "from an owner-plus-employed-management type of company to an owner-management-type."[14] The difference in the two kinds of companies lay in the amount of power assigned to management. Mackenzie maintained that with management as part of the ownership, everyone – labour, shareholders, and customers – would benefit and the desired capital for expansion would be raised. Mackenzie's plan was to form a holding company that would allow Labatt's senior managers to purchase 20 per cent of the family's stock at a price of $250 per share. He proposed to raise the necessary capital, in part, by transferring the company's reserve fund to a surplus account so that a special dividend could be paid in the total amount of $4.5 million.[15] Unfortunately for Mackenzie, the family felt that the plan was equivalent to a "gift" to management of 20 per cent of the shares in return for an "extraordinary payment" from past and future profits.[16] The proposal was rejected, leaving Mackenzie without a financial stake in the company that he had help shepherd through the Great Depression and the Second World War. Just as the family declined to welcome even a minority interest by another prominent brewing company, so, too, they resisted any attempt by management to own part of the firm.

The final option was to sell the shares to the public through underwriters. This plan, according to Gordon, had a couple of advantages. First, a market of Labatt stock would be created, allowing for additional shares to be sold in the future.

Second, Gordon estimated that the principal shareholders would receive $350,000 in cash, which would free them "from the worry with respect to the succession of duties upon his or her death."[17] After some discussion and debate, the Labatt family shareholders opted to sell the shares through underwriters on the stock exchange. In June 1945, the existing shares were split ten for one, which increased the total number of shares to 1,000,000. Twenty per cent of the shares were sold to the public for $20 a share, raising $4 million for the brewery's modernization and expansion.[18] The corporate restructuring demanded the public distribution of the company's first annual report in December 1945, in which John S. Labatt acknowledged the contribution of both the new and the old shareholders "who risked capital in order to provide the plant and equipment necessary to produce the commodity which the Company sells."[19]

While the first public issue created a market for the shares together with 2,300 new stockholders, the control of the company remained firmly in the family's hands. The family not only controlled 80 per cent of the issued shares but also these shares were locked into a voting trust that prevented individual family members from disposing of their shares without the consent of 66 per cent of the trust's membership. On 5 November 1945, John S. Labatt told family members that one of the primary reasons for creating a voting trust was to "enable us to continue to meet as a family and discuss the affairs of the Company between ourselves as we have always done in the past without outside interference."[20] Labatt's board of directors continued to be composed entirely of members of the family, whose power of appointment was absolute, while Mackenzie, Moore, and the other men around the brewery in the grey-flannel suits guided the strategic direction of the firm.[21] The corporate restructuring gave the London-based brewery access to the capital it needed to spread its wings across the nation and marked the beginning of the modern Labatt corporation.[22] Nevertheless, the company would have to get off the mark fast if it was to compete: E.P. Taylor's CBL was already out of the gate.

First Mover

CBL was the first brewer to become truly national. Since 1930, Taylor had been acquiring breweries in Ontario and rationalizing their operations. The smaller plants that he acquired were shut down, with no regard given to their brands. But the brands of larger breweries, such as O'Keefe and Carling, which had appreciable market share, were maintained even after the plants associated with their names had been closed. This "merger for monopoly" strategy met with mixed results prior to the war. To be sure, Taylor was successful at reducing the level of competition and gaining a 30 per cent share of the Ontario market. But his plants were often burdened by excess capacity. Writing to Norman Dawes, president of National Breweries, Taylor characterized the position of his brewery in 1939 as being at a competitive disadvantage to Labatt – a brewer that he described as "embarrassingly profitable and engaged in lavish expenditures on its customers."[23] But in the years that followed, CBL profited from the wartime demand for beer and rising prices, and Taylor began to talk about geographic expansion. "There are too many breweries in all of the provinces," he stated toward the end of the Second World War, "and there is a golden opportunity to sell our products in the entire country."

Taylor was bullish on the industry's post-war prospects. He had witnessed the remarkable speed with which Canadian industry had converted to war production. And as the end of the war approached, he became increasingly convinced that Canadian industry would show equal speed in converting back to peacetime production. In Taylor's optimistic view, the post-war period would not witness an economic slump as there had been following the First World War; rather, the economy would take off into a period of unprecedented growth. In 1945, he formed Argus Corporation – a conglomerate with a clutch of companies – to cash in on the post-war demand for consumer goods. He believed the good economic times would increase the demand for beer, soaking up CBL's excess capacity and then some.

Taylor was prescient. The immediate post-war period witnessed a huge increase in the demand for beer. For the first time in Canadian history, a large majority of the population had the disposable income necessary to participate in consumer pleasures. Across the nation, Canadians were drinking more beer than ever before. Between 1944 and 1952, per capita consumption increased from 8.99 to 13.72 gallons per annum. In the years that followed, per capita consumption remained stable at approximately 13.50 gallons per annum.[24] Ontarians and Quebecers continued to be the heaviest beer drinkers, but by 1950, western Canadians were catching up. Taylor's positive perception of things to come, combined with his proclivity for risk-taking, sent him searching for existing breweries that would help him expand production to meet the post-war demand.

In the final months of the war, CBL assumed control of the Bixel Brewing and Malting Company of Brantford and the historic Walkerville Brewery in Windsor,

Table 9.1

Market share (%) held by breweries selling in Ontario, 1944–62

Year	Labatt	CBL	Molson	National	Others	Total
1944	30.6	31.0	7.2	15.8	15.4	100.0
1945	25.3	40.7	5.9	16.5	11.6	100.0
1946	24.7	41.9	5.5	16.2	11.7	100.0
1947	23.1	46.8	5.3	14.0	10.8	100.0
1948	20.6	50.0	6.0	12.8	10.6	100.0
1949	18.9	55.6	6.7	10.3	8.5	100.0
1950	18.4	56.9	7.6	9.3	7.8	100.0
1951	21.6	55.3	7.6	8.3	7.2	100.0
1952	23.1	54.2	7.9	7.6	7.2	100.0
1953	22.3	51.5	8.7	10.2	7.3	100.0
1954	22.3	56.9	8.5	5.9	6.4	100.0
1955	22.4	64.4	8.9	-	4.3	100.0
1956	22.0	63.4	10.1	-	4.5	100.0
1957	20.9	63.1	11.6	-	4.4	100.0
1958	20.7	60.9	13.7	-	4.7	100.0
1959	21.8	n/a	n/a	-	n/a	n/a
1960	23.3	56.6	15.0	-	5.1	100.0
1961	23.1	56.6	15.2	-	5.1	100.0
1962	23.5	55.3	16.5	-	4.7	100.0

Sources: John Labatt Limited, *Report to the Directors*, (1962); Jones, "Competition in the Canadian Brewing Industry," 129.

Ontario. It also acquired Capital Breweries in Ottawa. This final acquisition was the most important because it solidified CBL's position in Eastern Ontario and helped to accelerate the firm's push into Quebec. CBL's acquisitions at the end of the war strengthened its overall position relative to others in competing for a slice of the lucrative Ontario market (see table 9.1).[25]

With his goal of creating a regional brewing giant accomplished, Taylor set his sights on conquering the national marketplace. "Having been successful in Ontario," he stated, "we have now raised our sights and plan to repeat the process … so that we can become a truly national concern."[26] In 1952, Taylor acquired control of the company that had been the source of his initial inspiration. National Breweries had been losing market share since the end of the war. Between 1947 and 1951, its share of the Quebec market declined from 50.3 per cent to 39.8 per cent and annual production fell from 1.5 million to 1 million barrels. The decline was due in large part to failure on the part of management to recognize the shift in consumer tastes. Beer drinkers in Quebec were moving away from heavy and hoppy ales such as National's principal brand, Dawes Black Horse. In an attempt to save the firm, a retrenchment program was inaugurated. Norman Dawes wanted Hugh Mackenzie as his white knight, taking over the top job at his firm. Dawes had worked closely with Mackenzie on public relation matters during the war. He had great respect for Mackenzie, whom he considered not only a talented business executive but also a virtuous beer man. True to character, the ever-loyal Mackenzie would not be enticed into leaving Labatt. With too many plants and too many brands, National Breweries had to bear the unrelenting costs of over-capacity. Once a vibrant presence in Quebec, National Breweries was suddenly vulnerable to a takeover.

After Norman Dawes rejected his merger offer, Taylor purchased enough stock to gain control of the company. By purchasing National, CBL became Canada's biggest brewer in terms of capacity and sales. Taylor subsequently renamed the firm Dow Brewery Limited after the company's best-selling brand. Dow would join O'Keefe and Carling as brands that CBL would produce, market, and distribute on a national scale in the years to come.

After acquiring National Breweries, Taylor turned his attention to gaining a foothold in the west. The western economy was booming, especially after the discovery of large reserves of oil beneath the wheat fields of Leduc, Alberta. And although sales in Manitoba, Saskatchewan, Alberta, and British Columbia combined to total only a quarter of the domestic beer market, Taylor was convinced that the west would soon experience "a growing population" and with it an increasing appetite for beer.[27]

In theory, Taylor could have produced his flagship brands in central Canada and shipped them westward, as had been done south of the border. The American shipping brewers had gained a national presence at the end of the nineteenth century by utilizing the railroads, refrigeration, advertising, and, above all, economies of scale.[28] But such an approach was practically impossible in Canada. This was in part because, as Taylor noted in a confidential memo, "the immense distance in Canada means it is not practical for breweries in the east to ship to the west and compete with western breweries."[29] Ontario-based brewers had been attempting to gain a share of the western beer market since the late 1800s. But as Labatt and Carling discovered, western Canadians were generally unwilling to pay the premium for their beer. As in the United States at the end of the nineteenth century, smaller brewers were able to outperform their larger counterparts based on price and taste, especially given the consumers' preferences for draught beer.[30]

As a result, Taylor determined that the proper course of action was "to purchase two or three prosperous western concerns."[31] "It is our plan," Taylor boldly stated, "to build up in the four western provinces a strong and robust brewing consolidation in the same manner that Canadian Breweries Limited was put together and developed in eastern Canada."[32] To that end, in 1953, CBL acquired Western Canada Breweries Limited, a regional holding company that owned Vancouver Breweries and Drewry's Breweries in Manitoba and Saskatchewan. The following year, CBL purchased Grant's Brewery in Manitoba, and the year after that, it acquired Red Deer Brewing Company in Alberta.

CBL's aggressive external growth strategy was made possible by a relatively permissive policy toward mergers on the part of the federal government. Generally speaking, Canadians have been sympathetic to the concentration of corporate power. And while laws have been passed to prevent combines and promote competition, the courts have more often than not interpreted these laws in favour of big business.[33] In 1952, Canada's anti-trust legislation was seemingly strengthened when the federal government revised the Combines Investigation Act. The act gave the courts the first real possibility of discouraging any merger that "operated, or is likely to operate, to the detriment, or against, the interest of the public." At the time, no one knew how the act would be interpreted. It wasn't until the 1959 trial of CBL for contravening the merger section of the act that an answer emerged.

The government's charge was that over the course of thirty years, CBL purchased or otherwise gained control of thirty-seven breweries in Ontario. These mergers, according to the prosecution, operated to "the detriment or against the interest of the public." But the court disagreed. In his ruling, Justice McRuer of the Supreme Court of Ontario stated that there was no evidence to show that the public interest had been "detrimentally affected" by the activities of CBL. Furthermore, in the judge's opinion, it was not an offence "for one corporation to acquire the business of another because it wishes to extinguish a competitor." Following the ruling, the *Globe and Mail* reported that it was "No Crime to Be Big."[34] A few days later, the *Financial Post* jubilantly echoed the sentiment with a headline that read: "Bigness isn't necessarily Badness."[35] The court's decision represented a green light to the Big Three and, as a result, the post-war acquisitions continued unabated.

After the trial, CBL picked up where it had left off. In 1961, it acquired three more breweries in Alberta, increasing its manufacturing capacity by more than 500,000 barrels a year (see table 9.2). Finally, in 1962, CBL acquired the Bennett Brewing Company in St John's, Newfoundland. By the end of the period under review, CBL controlled breweries stretching from the Atlantic to the Pacific.

Fast Follower

While CBL was the first Canadian brewer to go national, the innovative corporation soon had competition on the national scene. At Labatt, there was a sense that it needed to copy CBL's strategy or perish. As early as 1945, executives at Labatt began to reflect on what was needed to succeed in the post-war world. "We must remain in business," Mackenzie stated, "and to remain in business we must make sales and profits in new places as well as old."[36] The strategists at Labatt further concluded that in order to survive, the brewery would have to expand its capacity to meet the surging post-war demand for its products. All of this meant that Labatt would have to jettison what Mackenzie once termed Labatt's live-and-let-live philosophy and acquire a number of existing breweries across the nation. "We have always grown with Ontario," Hugh Labatt stated, following Mackenzie's lead, "and now we are planning to grow with Canada as a whole."[37] Building on the momentum of recent years, the brewery focused on becoming national in scope, selling its beer from coast-to-coast.

First, Labatt moved into Quebec. In 1950, Quebecers consumed over 50 million gallons of beer. The province had the most liberal liquor laws and market research showed that Quebecers knew and liked Labatt's products. But as was the case in Ontario, Labatt could not produce enough beer to meet the post-war demand. And even if more beer could be produced at the London plant, there was no way to compete from a distance with the large local firms that supplied Quebecers with almost all of their beer.

Then in the summer of 1951, an opportunity emerged to break into the tightly held Quebec beer market: Frontenac Breweries of Montreal was put up for sale. It was just the opportunity those at Labatt had been waiting for. "Its purchase will allow us easy entry into the Quebec market," Mackenzie told the board of directors, "and will also give added relief to London since the present Quebec volume now produced here will be transferred to the Quebec plant."[38]

Hugh Mackenzie immediately assigned John Cronyn the task of appraising the value of the Montreal brewery. The son of Verschoyle Cronyn, a First World War flying ace who had joined Labatt's board of directors shortly after the war was over, John Cronyn had graduated from the University of Toronto with a degree in chemical engineering. Upon graduation, he began to search for work. Just at that time, Cronyn's great-uncles, John and Hugh Labatt, were anxiously looking for young members of the family to join them at the brewery. Hiring Cronyn seemed so sensible to them that they hired him without consulting management. This infuriated Hugh Mackenzie. Usually calm in command, Mackenzie wrote an angry letter to the board of directors demanding a statement on the company's hiring policy. It wasn't that Cronyn was unfit for employment. Indeed, in many ways he was just the type of individual that Mackenzie was looking to hire. (Since the end of the Second World War, Mackenzie had been hiring men who were enthusiastic and university educated – men like William Shortreed who had gone to Duke University and then graduated with a law degree from the University of Toronto. Mackenzie put Shortreed in charge of the firm's marketing, sales, and public relations.[39]) But to Mackenzie, the hiring of Cronyn smacked of nepotism and undermined the authority of management. "Under the circumstances it would be an advantage, from an operational point of view and to hold the esprit de corps at its present level," Mackenzie indignantly wrote, "to be able to advise the executives and department heads of the Company that the policy of the Directors is to bring additional members of the family into the Company only under exceptional circumstances and when the employment of the individual appears desirable from a management point of view."[40] Never comfortable with confrontation, the Labatt bothers backed down, and the board resolved that John Cronyn would stay but that in the future, management would have the final say on all appointments.

The appointment of Cronyn was one of John Sackville Labatt's last acts. In 1950, he retired as president due to ill health. While he remained on the board of directors, his brother Hugh assumed the role of the newly combined offices of president and chairman.[41] Cronyn proved to be a valuable addition to the firm. He was the first to admit that his university training did not fully equip him for success in the business of brewing, so in 1949, he enrolled at the United States Brewers Academy in New York. When he returned to Labatt with his brew-

Figure 9.1 Brewery workers in London, Ontario, pack Labatt's India Pale Ale into the new easy-to-carry cases, c. 1955.

master's diploma, he was made production manager in charge of brewing, bottling, and transportation.

Given his understanding of the latest brewing techniques and technologies, Cronyn was deemed the best man to assess the value of Frontenac Breweries. After touring the plant and examining the equipment, he determined the brewery was worth roughly $3.4 million. While the figure represented a substantial capital expenditure, Mackenzie felt it was justified because it was the quickest way to gain a foothold in Quebec. The board of directors decided to make an offer equal to Cronyn's appraised value.[42] Wanting to get the best possible price for his brewery, Norman Dawes informed E.P. Taylor of Labatt's bid. Never one for half measures, Taylor offered to pay 110 per cent of the highest price specified in any bona fide offer up to a maximum of $4.25 million.[43] The offer was too rich for Labatt's blood, and Frontenac joined the long list of breweries acquired by Taylor.

Despite being outbid, the brain trust at Labatt was still eager to gain a slice of the lucrative Quebec market. To that end, in March 1952, the board authorized the purchase of twenty-six acres of land in the Montreal suburb of Ville LaSalle.[44] Labatt planned to build a $5 million state-of-the-art brewery on the site, with an initial annual capacity of 230,000 barrels.[45] Management believed that such a large and expensive plant was justified because of the size of the market. "The market that can be supplied from Montreal is 41.5% of our total market," management reported, "and to attempt to sell to them from London at an uneconomic distance makes difficult, if not impossible, the obtaining of a reasonable profit from such sales."[46] Labatt planned to use the Montreal facility to produce all their beer for the Quebec market as well as for thirsty beer drinkers on the east coast.[47]

Labatt's Western Expansion

In 1952, Labatt followed CBL into the west by purchasing one of western Canada's largest independent brewers: Shea's Winnipeg Brewery. Its origins lay in the Old Winnipeg Brewery, which was built in the brothel district of Colony Creek by Celestin Thomas in 1873, before Winnipeg won its city charter. A change in the company's capital structure in 1926 placed a percentage of voting stock in public hands, and by 1946, more than 50 per cent of the shares were owned by two Winnipeg hospitals. In 1952, the hospital boards indicated their intention to sell their shares in the brewery in order to raise funds for their health care facilities.

The story of the Labatt's takeover of Shea's is significant because it gives further insights into the institutional barriers that brewers in Canada faced in their quest to go national. The first barrier related to distribution. In the west, brewers were allowed to own hotels, which gave them an exclusive channel for funnelling their beer to consumers. For example, in Manitoba, virtually all of the hotels were "tied" to either Shea's or CBL. Almost 90 per cent of the draft beer and approximately 57 per cent of the bottled beer was sold in the hotels that Shea's and CBL owned. Various provincial governments in the west passed laws in the 1950s requiring the brewers to sell their hotel holdings. But the brewers often found ways around these laws. For example, when E.P. Taylor heard about the government's plans to cut the ties between the brewers and the hotels, he decided to sell the company that held CBL's hotels, Reliance Securities Ltd, to a friendly buyer. "If we have to get out of the hotel business," Taylor stated, "we must have Reliance in friendly hands in order to retain the gallonage of these hotels." With that goal

Figure 9.2 Labatt's Winnipeg brewery, c. 1956. During the 1950s, Labatt went on a spending spree in its quest to become a truly national brewer. Due to the system of interprovincial trade barriers, Canadian brewers were forced to have a physical presence in any province where they wanted to sell their beer. In 1952, Labatt purchased Shea's Winnipeg Brewery in Manitoba.

in mind, Reliance was sold to Alex Campbell, former vice-president of finance at Taylor's Western Breweries Ltd. Campbell agreed not to transfer his shares in the company to anyone deemed by Taylor to be "unfriendly."[48] The move allowed CBL to sidestep the government's legislation and maintain its market share in Manitoba. Thus, in 1953, when Labatt was seeking to enter the Manitoba market, CBL and Shea's controlled the principal mode of distribution. If Labatt wanted to get its beer into the hands of consumers, it would have to purchase Shea's.

The second barrier was the tariff on out-of-the-province beer.[49] In 1928, as part of the recurring oscillation in federal and provincial jurisdiction, the federal government of William Lyon Mackenzie King gave the provinces the right to regulate

the local trade in liquor. In the period that followed, provincial governments instituted tariffs and imposed import quotas that limited out-of-province beer or
stopped it altogether. The tariffs were often substantial. In Manitoba and Alberta,
for example, a charge of five cents per bottle was imposed on out-of-province beer.
For large central Canadian brewers like Labatt, who were seeking to expand their
market share after the war, this increased the price of their brands by approximately 30 per cent over local brands.[50] In Saskatchewan and British Columbia,
imported brands were priced at a premium and exclusively available in govern-
ment-owned and -controlled liquor stores.[51]

The third barrier to the large central Canadian brewers shipping their beer to
distant markets was the system of sales quotas in the western provinces. Following
prohibition, production became concentrated in the hands of a few relatively
large western breweries (e.g., Sick's, Lucky Lager, Drewry's, and Shea's). Having
cornered their regional markets, the large brewers often agreed not to compete
with one another for market share. In Manitoba, such an agreement split the market more or less down the middle, with 60 per cent of sales going to Shea's and
40 per cent allocated to Drewry's. The quota agreements were attached to the firm.
Thus, when CBL acquired Drewry's in 1955 it instantly gained 40 per cent of the
Manitoba market.

For these three reasons, Hugh Mackenzie met with representatives from the
Winnipeg brokerage house of Osler, Hammond and Nanton in March 1953. The
broker represented the two Winnipeg hospitals that were seeking to sell their
shares. Mackenzie was interested but determined not to overpay, so he assigned
Jake Moore the task of determining the fair market value.[52] A thirty-eight-year-
old chartered accountant, Moore had joined Labatt in February 1953 as treasurer
and director of finance.[53] Born in 1915 into one of London's pre-eminent business
families, Moore had grown up aware that social connections mattered in London.
Through his grandmother, he was descended from the influential McClary family,
founders of one of Canada's largest appliance companies.[54] Even before the First
World War, McClary – unlike the nation's breweries – was manufacturing and
selling its products from coast to coast, with branches in Vancouver, Winnipeg,
Toronto, Montreal, and St Johns.[55] Moore came from money. In his youth, he attended Ridley College, a private school in the Niagara region, where he became
friends with Alex Graydon, the grandson of John Labatt. In 1934, Moore began
his university studies at the Royal Military College in Kingston and, after his graduation, went to work as an accountant at Clarkson, Gordon and Company. Graydon and Moore remained close during the war. When Graydon was appointed

Table 9.2

Brewery acquisitions in Western Canada, 1955–61

Brewery	Province	Annual capacity, in 1961 (barrels)	Acquiring company and year
The Drewry's Limited	Manitoba	200,000	CBL (1953)
Kiewel Brewing Company	Manitoba	60,000	CBL-Labatt (1953)
Pelissier's Brewery Ltd	Manitoba	40,000	CBL-Labatt (1953)
Shea's Winnipeg Brewery	Manitoba	200,000	Labatt (1953)
Drewry's Ltd (Saskatoon)	Saskatchewan	90,000	CBL (1955)
Drewry's Regina Ltd	Saskatchewan	85,000	CBL (1955)
Grant's Brewery Ltd	Manitoba	50,000	CBL (1955)
Red Deer Brewing Co. Ltd	Alberta	100,000	CBL (1955)
Vancouver Breweries Ltd	British Columbia	390,000	CBL (1955)
Lucky Lager Brewing (N.W.)	British Columbia	230,000	Labatt (1958)
Lucky Lager Brewing (Victoria)	British Columbia	100,000	Labatt (1958)
Sick's Capilano Brewery	British Columbia	150,000	Molson (1958)
Sick's Edmonton Brewery	Alberta	140,000	Molson (1958)
Sick's Lethbridge Brewery	Alberta	225,000	Molson (1958)
Sick's Prince Albert Brewery	Saskatchewan	175,000	Molson (1958)
Sick's Regina Brewery Ltd	Saskatchewan	150,000	Molson (1958)
Saskatoon Brewing Company	Saskatchewan	100,000	Labatt (1960)
Fort Garry Brewery Ltd	Manitoba	60,000	Molson (1960)
Big Horn Brewery Co. Ltd	Alberta	50,000	CBL (1961)
Bohemian Maid Co. Ltd	Alberta	110,000	CBL (1961)
Calgary Brewing & Malting	Alberta	250,000	CBL (1961)

Source: Roseman, "The Canadian Brewing Industry: The Effects of Mergers and Provincial Regulation on Economic Conduct and Performance," 233.

to Labatt's board of directors in September 1952, following the death of John S. Labatt from a heart attack earlier that year, he recommended recruiting his old friend. Moore accepted, moved to London, and quickly proved to be an asset to his new employer. In addition to being a natural with numbers and brilliant at interpreting a balance sheet, he was a strategically minded risk-taker.

Having visited the Winnipeg brewery and examined the company's books, Moore recommended buying Shea's brewery. The Winnipeg brewery, he reported, had a capacity of 185,000 barrels annually, which made it bigger than the Labatt's plant in Toronto and almost as big as the planned Montreal brewery. It also owned more than fifty hotels and a controlling interest in two smaller Manitoba breweries.[56] Based on earnings, Moore concluded that $9 million was "a fair and proper price" for the western firm.[57] An offer at that price was made, and when it was accepted, Labatt became the biggest brewer by volume in Manitoba.

By the summer of 1956, Labatt had plants operating in Ontario, Manitoba, and Quebec, and centralized management from London became increasingly difficult. Again following the lead of CBL, Labatt began to decentralize its operations. Like E.P Taylor, Jake Moore was of the opinion that national breweries should be operated on "as decentralized a basis as possible so that decisions can be made at the level closest to the scene of action."[58] The move made sense, given the different provincial liquor regulations. Separate operating divisions were created for each province where the company had a physical presence. Each operating division was given responsibility for all company activities in their respective areas. At the same time, a head office was set up in London to serve in an advisory capacity to the heads of the operating divisions. Relieved of all the detailed supervision of the day-to-day activities in the three operating divisions, executives in London could concentrate all of their efforts on directing the overall operations and formulating corporate strategy.[59]

For Jake Moore, who had become general manager of Labatt in 1956 after Hugh Mackenzie was forced out by the board for being too "progressive" on labour issues and unionism, the next strategic step was to break into British Columbia. While the B.C. beer market was a third of the size of the Quebec market and a quarter of the size of the Ontario market, it was still larger than the Manitoba and Saskatchewan markets combined. In 1957, annual per capita beer consumption in B.C. was 13.28 gallons.[60] According to Labatt's research, beer sales in B.C. would increase 50 per cent over the next ten years.[61] During the summer of 1957, Moore spent a good deal of time in B.C. in order to gain a greater appreciation of the business of brewing on the west coast. On one visit, he joined George

Figure 9.3 In 1958, Labatt acquired Lucky Lager brewery and its brands, based in Victoria, British Columbia, giving the company a strong foothold west of the Rockies.

Norgan, president and largest shareholder of Lucky Lager Breweries, for dinner. Lucky Lager was the name given to the old Coast Breweries Limited, which had been formed in 1928 through the amalgamation of the four oldest breweries in British Columbia: Victoria Phoenix Brewing Company, Westminster Brewery, Silver Spring Brewery, and Rainier Brewing Company of Canada (see figure 9.3). While Norgan claimed that Lucky Lager was currently "doing a fine business," he was looking to sell his 25 per cent stake in the brewery because he felt the company could not survive the "invasion of the big breweries with the tremendous power to advertise through mighty journals that we couldn't touch."[62] To determine the value of Norgan's shares, Jake Moore turned to Ron Woodman. Woodman had served with the Royal Canadian Air Force during the Second World War and then had attended the University of British Columbia on a government grant. After graduating from Harvard with an MBA in 1952, he joined the Labatt's management team.[63] Given Woodman's education and experience on the west coast,

Figure 9.4 In 1962, Labatt purchased the Bavarian Brewery in St John's, Newfoundland, featured here, giving the company a presence from coast to coast.

Moore believed he was the right man to determine the value of the Lucky Lager Breweries and, more generally, to assess the timeliness of the company's further expansion. In his final report, Woodman argued that Labatt should move now in order to counter the progress of E.P. Taylor's Western Canada Breweries.[64] Moore was confident in Woodman's assessment and recommended the purchase of Lucky Lager to the board on 25 November 1957.[65]

However, the board was somewhat divided over the issue of further expansion. The conservative culture at Labatt ran deep. Richard Ivey, who had joined the board in 1948 when Sydney Mewburn retired at the age of eight-five, was of the opinion that Labatt should hold off on any further acquisitions "until such time as the Company's earning has shown improvement."[66] The first member from outside the family to sit on the board, Ivey normally got his way. For example, when Jake Moore expressed an interest in becoming the first non-family president of the corporation following Hugh Labatt's death of a heart attack in 1956, Ivey rejected the notion and, instead, orchestrated the appointment of another Labatt family member, W.H.R. Jarvis. Stern, taciturn, calculating, and at times ruthless, the sixty-one-year-old Ivey believed that Labatt's entire effort should be spent on strengthening its presence in Quebec, where the company was having problems supporting a province-wide distribution organization on low volumes.[67] He also felt that the shareholders were entitled to greater dividends.[68] But the rest of the board was in a more expansionist mood. Capturing the sentiment of the majority, Jack P. Labatt, who had just joined the board of directors, stated that the brewery of his great-grandfather needed to "go ahead to become truly national."[69] As a result, Labatt began buying Lucky Lager shares, beginning with Norgan's 25 per cent stake. By the end of June 1958, Jake Moore could report that "Labatt had acquired eighty-four per cent of Lucky's shares."[70] The acquisition gave Labatt a base in British Columbia capable of producing its provincial quota of 40 per cent as well as the iconic regional brand in Lucky Lager.[71]

Before the decade was out, Labatt had taken control of the Saskatoon Brewing Company in Saskatchewan and had begun construction on a new brewery in Edmonton, Alberta. When Labatt purchased the Bavarian Brewery in St John's, Newfoundland, in 1962, it too could claim to be a "truly national concern." As Jake Moore, who in 1958 had become the first non-family president of Labatt, stated in October 1962: "the acquisition gives the Company production facilities from the Atlantic to the Pacific and puts us in a position to compete in the total Canadian market."[72]

Always a "fast follower," Molson soon undertook its own national expansion. Like Labatt, it employed both a brownfield and greenfield approach, acquiring existing breweries as well as building new ones. Molson's first move came in 1955 when the oldest continuous brewery in Canada struck back at the Ontario brewers that had invaded its home territory by building a 300,000-barrel brewery on Fleet Street, right in CBL's backyard. In 1958, Molson went west, purchasing the prairie powerhouse Sick's Brewery (see table 9.2). Sick's was the maker of such popular prairie brands as Bohemian and Old Style Pilsner. Molson would continue to manufacture these brands alongside its own. In 1962, Molson again quickly followed the actions of Labatt and CBL by purchasing Newfoundland Brewery Ltd, an established brewery in St John's, Newfoundland.

By 1962, three breweries were national in scope. Indeed, only two areas in Canada did not possess a plant that was manufacturing the national brands of the Big Three: Northern Ontario, which was dominated by six small local brewers, and the Maritimes, which was controlled by Oland and Son and Moosehead Breweries. With only a few exceptions, the main route to geographic expansion and market consolidation in Canada after the war was by the acquisition of small- and medium-size firms.

The Nature of Competition

One of the defining features of the Canadian brewing industry after the war was the virtual non-existence of price competition. This was because the price of beer was fixed by the various provincial liquor control boards. To be sure, the liquor authorities often acted on the brewers' advice – raising the spectre of "regulatory capture."[73] For example, in Nova Scotia, New Brunswick, and British Columbia, the liquor authorities arrived at the fixed retail price by merely adding a markup after the beer was purchased from the brewers. In Quebec, the Quebec Brewers' Association, the Tavern Keepers' Association, and the Licensed Grocers' Section of the Retail Merchants Association fixed the price of beer jointly. In Ontario, the Liquor Control Board fixed the price at which beer was sold in government stores and public drinking places. Until 1956, Manitoba fixed prices in a manner similar to Nova Scotia, New Brunswick, and British Colombia; after that, the government set the fixed price after negotiating with local brewers.

With the price of beer fixed, competition took the form of advertising races, and "the brewery with the largest advertising budget," as the Big Three acknowledged, "being the brewery to gain."[74] Jake Moore made a similar observation in 1954 when he stated that "the heavier expenditures for sales promotions permit the larger brewery to gain increasing public acceptance at the expense of its lesser known rival."[75] By 1956, Labatt was spending $900,000 on advertising. While a huge sum relative to those breweries outside of the Big Three, it was small compared to the amount being spent by CBL and Molson, which was $4.5 million and $2 million, respectively.[76]

To make matters worse, CBL and Molson were proving craftier when it came to how they advertised their products. Every Canadian brewer faced a number of hurdles when it came to promoting their brands in the post-war period. In the aftermath of prohibition, provincial governments had placed tight restrictions on liquor advertising in an attempt to curb consumption. There was no uniform national advertising code to which beer advertising had to adhere. Instead, all liquor advertisements had to conform to provincial liquor control board standards, which could range from controls on the size and content of the advertisement to outright bans.[77] When television hit the Canadian scene in the late 1940s, the federal government prohibited brewers from running TV commercials. And even after these regulations were relaxed in 1955, the commercials could not feature a person drinking, or a beer bottle, or a glass of beer. However, a beer's disembodied label could be featured, so long as it was entirely separate from the action in the commercial.

Despite the tight government restrictions on advertising, loopholes existed and were exploited, first, by CBL, then by Molson, and then by Labatt. Because they were based in central Canada, the Big Three promoted their brands in magazines like *Maclean's* and *Saturday Night* that were published in Quebec – where the restrictions on beer advertising were relatively slack – but sold across the country. This type of advertising had a national impact, so Canadian consumers were aware of the brands of the Big Three before a national beer market existed. In part to capitalize on this brand recognition, the Big Three expanded outside of central Canada after the war. In addition, the Big Three had the financial means and tactical motivation to run print and radio ads in the United States – where brewers had freer range to advertise their products – knowing full well that they would be seen by a large Canadian audience. The actions of the Big Three frustrated regulatory bodies who complained that they could control only the forms and context of advertising generated within particular provinces, while the newsstands and airwaves were full of material sent in from the United States.[78]

When it came to advertising on television stations in Canada after the regulations were relaxed in 1955 (and before 1963), the brewers were restricted to only twelve seconds of "hard-sell" advertising, when the product could be identified by brand name.[79] The other forty-eight seconds of the then-standard sixty-second spot were filled with a "soft sell." The Big Three brewers spent thousands of dollars to craft commercials that put this "fill-time" to effective use. For instance, in 1956, CBL spent over $800,000 on television commercials, while Labatt and Molson spent close to $300,000 each.[80] Conversely, those brewers outside of the Big Three did not spend a single dollar to promote their products on television that year.

The Big Three used the fill-time to associate their brands with the "good life." The ads constructed a "desirable lifestyle" in relation to contemporary social conditions, including shifts and tensions in the broader gender order. Television commercials often showed fit, happy, handsome, white, heterosexual people engaged in a range of pleasurable pursuits. In addition, the Big Three sponsored sporting events on television. For example, in 1957, Molson began sponsoring *Hockey Night in Canada,* which was Canada's most popular televised sports program. In 1960, Labatt became the official sponsor of the Canadian Football League.

While these national forms of advertising were far more expensive than local or regional methods of promotion, they were also superior in promoting brand loyalty. Smaller brewers could not compete. Since the circulation of national media was much wider than their market, smaller brewers found it impossible to use national advertising economically. When asked why his firm did not advertise in periodicals or other media that was circulated on a national basis, the vice-president of Oland and Son – brewer of the popular east-coast beer Alexander Keith's IPA – Victor Oland stated: "We did for a while ... for almost a year, but then we figured that only 8 per cent of the people lived in the Maritimes who were in a position to buy our beer, which meant that immediately 92 cents of the dollar was lost." Lacking the financial resources of the Big Three, Oland resorted to local advertising and promotion in 1957 when he attempted to break into Quebec. Unfortunately for Oland and Son, its expenditure of $103,000 on advertising was minuscule compared to the amount being spent by the Big Three. The east-coast brewer gained just 0.3 per cent of the Quebec market.

By 1962, the brands of the Big Three dominated the Canadian market. In every province outside of Atlantic Canada, the best-selling brands were those owned by CBL, Molson, and Labatt. In Quebec, Molson Export, Dow Ale, and Labatt 50 were the top-selling brands. In Ontario, Carling Black Label, O'Keefe's Old Vienna, Molson Canadian, and Labatt Pilsener were the most popular brands with drinkers. In Manitoba and British Columbia, one in three beer drinkers drank Labatt Pilsener, making it the best-selling brand in those two provinces. In Saskatchewan, the best-selling brand was Molson Old Style Pilsener and Bohemian – which were both formerly Sick's Brewery products.[81] The production and promotion of nation brands played a critical role in the rise of the Big Three and the demise of local brewers.

In 1956, Labatt was brewing five brands of beer: Crystal Lager, Extra Stock Ale, Pilsener, IPA, and 50. The last of these was a recent addition to the Labatt's line of products and was designed to tap into the growing demand for lighter beers. The market research conducted by Joe D. Varnell, who reported to Hugh Mackenzie on all marketing matters, indicated a nationwide trend for milder-tasting beers. Eager to offer something new that consumers would like, Mackenzie instructed Tom Morgan, Labatt's brewmaster, to make a lighter IPA. To do this,

Morgan adjusted the hop content of Labatt's IPA to make a slightly smoother, less bitter-tasting ale. Varnell suggested that the new beer be labelled Anniversary Ale, in recognition of the fiftieth anniversary of John and Hugh Labatt's first formal association with the company in 1900.[82] The beer was soon nicknamed "Fifty" in English Canada and "Cinquante" in Quebec. Advertisements that appeared in the national press billed "50" as "the lightest and smoothest of all ales."[83]

Labatt's marketing masterminds targeted Labatt 50 at a specific market segment. Product differentiation and market segregation were celebrated marketing strategies during the 1950s.[84] The belief was that the market could be divided into smaller, homogeneous markets that differed in product preference. Under Alfred Sloan, General Motors had done this by offering "a car for every purse and purpose," from Chevrolet to Cadillac.[85] Following GM's lead, Labatt began differentiating its products from one another in the 1950s, giving each an identity that was designed to appeal to a specific target audience. Labatt 50, for example, was aimed at "smart young moderns," while its Pilsener was for more mature, wealthier beer drinkers, be they men or women. Like many print ads for alcohol during the 1950s, those promoting 50 and Pilsener depicted mixed-gender socializing in suburban settings.[86]

But this was not always the case. Labatt's IPA, for example, was targeted specifically at men. "What you like in an ale and what a woman likes are not necessarily the same," one ad proclaimed, "so if you are looking for a man's drink with plenty of old-time flavour – hearty, zestful and satisfying – switch now to Labatt's India Pale Ale." The IPA ads that appeared in the press appealed to post-war ideals of masculinity. The drinker of Labatt's IPA was portrayed as a James Dean–type figure – a macho, rugged, no-nonsense individual; a man who knew what he wanted. He was strong and robust: the Canadian equivalent of the Marlboro Man. At a time when Hollywood movies such as *The Searchers, Shane, Rio Bravo*, and *Rebel Without a Cause* were capturing the imaginations of North American audiences, Labatt's ads for IPA were aimed at appealing to male fantasies and desires. No longer were the brewers' advertisements just about the merits of a product or about price. They were aimed at enhancing the product's aura and associating the brand with a lifestyle.[87] For a certain segment of the population, drinking Labatt's IPA reinforced their sense of self, or who they wanted to be. In Ontario, that segment proved to be quite large: Labatt's IPA outsold all other Labatt's brands combined during the 1950s.

Figure 9.5 This 1958 advertisement for Labatt 50 was aimed at "young smart moderns."

Barriers to Entry

The enormous outlays needed to market national brands were an important deterrent to potential Canadian entrants into the domestic brewing industry. But south of the border, a number of firms had both the capital and the expertise to take on Canada's Big Three on their home ground. Indeed, the biggest American brewers – Anheuser-Busch, Schlitz, Pabst, and Ballantine – were far larger than the biggest Canadian breweries in terms of production capacity and sales. Furthermore, since Canadians often saw American magazines and television commercials, an awareness of American brands existed in Canada. Yet these brewers were unsuccessful in gaining a presence in Canada during the postwar boom. Why?

The short answer is because the Big Three brewers were successful in raising artificially high entry barriers. After the Second World War, the nation's brewers – through their lobbying agency the Brewers Association of Canada – successfully pressured the federal and provincial governments to protect them from foreign competition. The federal government responded to the brewers' pressure tactics by increasing the tariff on imported beer to a minimum of 12.5 per cent per gallon.[88] In addition to having to pay the federal tariff, foreign brewers seeking to sell their products in Canada had to hurdle three non-tariff barriers used by provincial authorities to discourage the domestic consumption of non-Canadian beer: listing practices, distribution requirements, and discriminatory markup policies. Each province had its own unique distribution system, with its own distinct policies and practices. These added to the foreign brewers' cost of doing business in Canada and thereby further protected domestic brewers from competition. Liquor control boards routinely imposed conditions on the supply of imported beer. For example, sales quotas and performance standards had to be continuously met. Distribution systems often restricted the sale of imported beer to provincially run liquor board outlets, where foreign brewers were forced to pay extra fees and meet additional requirements.[89]

In 1956, Goebel Brewing Company of Detroit, Pabst of Milwaukee, Ballantine of New Jersey, Anheuser-Busch of St Louis, and Schlitz Brewing Company of Milwaukee sought permission from the LCBO to sell their beer in Ontario. The LCBO referred the American brewers to the Brewers Warehousing Company Limited, which agreed to distribute their products provided that the American brewers agreed to market their beer in standard cartons and stubby bottles and to pay a service charge of $1.25 plus a deposit of sixty cents per case of twenty-four bottles.

Figure 9.6 Brewers' Retail displayed all the ales, lagers, porters, and stouts available for sale in Ontario, c. 1963. The take-home price of a six-pack was $1.28. Notice that there is not a single foreign brand, and that the Big Three offered free home delivery for all their beers.

All of the American brewers wanted to use non-returnable bottles or cans and asked that this be taken into account in the price structure as far as the deposit was concerned. Their request was denied. Despite representations by the United States Brewers Foundation and the United States Embassy, Brewers Warehousing remained firm: the American brewers would have to meet its requirements. Goebel proposed a solution: the deposit could be charged when the bottles were purchased, refunded when they were returned, and the store would discard the bottles. But again Brewers Warehousing was not open to a "departure from established standards."[90] The U.S. brewers' attempt to break into the Canadian market was thwarted by the system of distribution.

During the 1950s, only one Maritime firm attempted to enter the highly competitive central Canadian market. Oland and Son was the owner of the historic Alexander Keith's brewery in Halifax. In 1956, Oland still held 67.5 per cent of the market share in Nova Scotia. But this was down from the 73.3 per cent of three years earlier. Oland's losses had come at the hands of the Big Three: by 1956, they controlled 32.5 per cent of the Nova Scotia market. With its share of the market declining at home, Oland decided to expand into the Ontario and Quebec market to take advantage of the large number of Maritimers in the army and civil service.[91] That year, it asked Brewers Warehousing to distribute its products. Since Oland was a Canadian company, Brewers Warehousing only charged seventy-five cents to cover the cost of handling a case of its beer. While the fee was less than that charged the American brewers, it was more than twice the amount being paid by the Big Three. When asked at the trial of CBL if he thought Oland and Son had been treated fairly by Brewers Warehousing, Victor Oland stated that it had not, and in retaliation, he "went back to Nova Scotia and I was instrumental in having a further barrier against their goods [the brands of the Big Three] coming into the province."[92]

Conclusion

If there is any consensus in the literature regarding the causes of consolidation in the brewing industry, it is that the factors are complex, often differing from time to time and place to place. In Canada, a mixture of entrepreneurial and institutional factors determined the pace, direction, and form of consolidation. The post-war consolidation of the Canadian brewing industry started early and went further faster than in other developed economies as a consequence of E.P. Taylor accomplishing his objective in Ontario. Once the war had come to an end and his breweries were producing at near capacity, Taylor was in a position to expand across the nation. His intuition and ambition, combined with the imperialist outlook of central Canada's commercial elite, led him to look to the "periphery" for opportunities for growth. His pioneering vision had a profound effect on the structure of the industry. Labatt's success came from being a fast follower.

In terms of the form of consolidation, institutional factors played a decisive role. The nature of the regulatory regime forced the Big Three to embrace a policy of external growth. Interprovincial trade barriers, provincial jurisdiction over the retail sale and distribution of alcoholic beverages, local sensitivities, and a permissive policy toward takeovers combined to make the acquisition of small- and medium-sized firms the main route toward market consolidation in Canada. To become truly national concerns, the Big Three had to have a physical presence in each of the regions. The end result was that the Canadian brewing industry took on a multi-plant form during the period under review.

These post-war acquisitions completely changed the market structure of the Canadian brewing industry: advertising and sales promotion became the form of competition. At a time when the price of beer was fixed by the various provincial liquor control boards, advertising became essential for a brewer's survival. The Big Three's success lay in the fact that each was able to produce a small number of standard brands, which appealed to a large segment of the beer-drinking population, and to market them with sophisticated and expensive advertising campaigns. The result was the gradual extinction of local styles and the homogenization of the survivors into similar-tasting pale ales, lagers, and ales. The comparative advantage of Labatt and the rest of the Big Three was directly related to the size of their promotional expenditures and the use of national media, as well as their ability to control the channels of distribution.

PART THREE

**Multinationals
and
Globalization**

Le Défi américain, 1962–67

The 1960s witnessed the perfection of the multinational enterprise (MNE), as expansion abroad became a strategy of growth for an increasing number of firms. In many ways, the MNE was the epitome of post-war economic dynamism: flexible, efficient, and – in the minds of its critics – imperialistic. The MNE often evolved naturally out of the domestically successful industrial corporation. Having relentlessly expanded the output of its standard production line and incrementally introduced new types of products at home, the post-war industrial enterprise invested in new geographical markets beyond the national boundary in order to grow.[1] "In going abroad," stated the economist Charles Kindleberger, "they grew abroad."[2]

Americans led the world in the creation of MNES. Their enormous corporations combined superb technology with vast capital resources, an all-out commitment to research and development, and the best modern managerial techniques. These were the industrial enterprises that economist John Kenneth Galbraith described as being almost beyond control.[3] They had conquered the market and, some suggested, had even overpowered the state. Sometimes they had also won over the host nation's entrepreneurial class. According to social scientist Kari Levitt and a number of other economic nationalists, in Canada, there was a willingness on the part of the corporate elite to become a partner of the U.S.-based MNE.[4] Together, Levitt maintained, they fashioned a new order for holding the Canadian economy in thrall, narrowing its range of opportunities, and eliminating its power of choice. Canada succumbed to a "silent surrender."[5] But it was not just Canada that had to confront the enormous power of America's corporations. According to French author Jean-Jacques Servan-Schreiber, the whole world would have to come to terms with *le défi américain*.[6]

Breweries were slower to evolve into MNEs. Consumer taste, entrenched regional brands, barriers to trade, and convoluted distribution systems made brewing a form of static warfare: gains for those with international aspirations came only slowly. Until the end of the Second World War, the only international brewer was Ireland's Guinness, which, in reaction to falling sales at home and increased protectionism following the First World War, introduced advertising in Great Britain and established a brewery in London.[7] The seeding of brand-driven taste would help open the door to globalization. After 1945, two other brewers that dominated their small home markets – Holland's Heineken and Denmark's Carlsberg – set out to turn their beers into global brands. In most countries, however, brewing remained a local enterprise. "It has not been the nature of the beer business," one American brewing executive stated in 1964, "to know what is going on abroad."[8] Beer came from Milwaukee and that was all there was to brewing. But as the decade evolved, an increasing number of breweries started to look for international opportunities for growth. Among them was Schlitz – the maker of "the beer that made Milwaukee famous" – and its target was Labatt. The 1960s would be a time when Labatt sought to resist the "American Challenge" and remain in control of its own destiny.

Prey

On 29 October 1962, Jake Moore presented the first in a series of talks entitled "Know Your Company." The lecture was part of a broader program designed to educate the company's 2,400 Canadian employees about the historic brewery. "A real understanding of your company will not only help you in your day-to-day work in that it will put your own job in better perspective," Moore stated, "but it will also put the Company in a better perspective both in the industry of which it is a member and in the municipal, provincial and national economies."[9] Proud of what the company had already accomplished, Moore noted that Labatt was enjoying a period of sustained growth and prosperity. Labatt manufactured two flagship brands – 50 and Pilsener – and eight regional brands at its ten different breweries across Canada.[10] For years, the company had been living within its means and, of the Big Three, had shown the greatest percentage of profit growth in the past five years.[11] In 1962, Labatt sold almost 2 million barrels of beer, which was almost double the amount that it had sold just five years before. This translated into a 20 per cent share of the Canadian beer market and profits of $4.4 million on sales of close to $100 million.

Labatt had also recently gained a foothold in the United States by acquiring a controlling interest in General Brewing Corporation, the maker of Lucky Lager beer in the United States.[12] With a plant capacity of approximately 3 million barrels and sales of 2.2 million barrels in 1962, General Brewing Corporation was the biggest brewery in California and the twelfth largest in the United States. General Brewing operated four plants to serve its principal markets in San Francisco, Los Angeles, Washington State, Salt Lake City, and Vancouver. Labatt purchased its initial stake in the western brewery in 1958 because it was interested primarily in the B.C. market.[13] But by the 1960s, executives at Labatt were growing increasingly interested in the potential for growth south of the border. In particular, they were bullish about the money to be made in the Golden State. "I am sure that you appreciate that this [California] is a large market," Jake Moore had told a group of security analysts in Montreal several months before the "Know Your Company" lecture series got underway, "and that the factors affecting its growth are very similar to those affecting the Canadian market."[14] California was the fastest growing state in the union, with a population as large as the whole of Canada. In 1961, annual per capita beer consumption averaged just over 15 gallons per Californian, which was 2 gallons more than the average Canadian was consuming.[15] While Lucky Lager was experiencing a profit squeeze due to price reductions for beer in California and higher-than-expected expenses, Moore was optimistic about the company's long-term prospects. At the dawning of the age of Aquarius, Labatt was a dominant player in both the Canadian and Californian beer market.

Also, Labatt had finally begun to diversify into related fields of production. Its expansion into the biotech field in 1961 stemmed from the problem of disposing of its waste products, particularly spent grains and brewer's yeast. The search for a better and more profitable means of disposal led the company into the animal feed business and to an association with Philips-Duphar, a large pharmaceutical company from Holland. To fully develop this part of the business, Labatt created a new biotechnology division with John Cronyn as vice-president. "It is our hope this Division will grow to equal the stature, size and profit of our brewing operations and it could even surpass it," Moore stated in 1962. And then, sounding a nationalistic chord, he added that he was "confident that it will provide employment for Canadians and products for Canadians which are currently imported."[16] As innocent as the statement was at the time, it captured the emerging tension at

Figure 10.1 This billboard ad was part of Schlitz's "real gusto in a great light beer" campaign, c. 1961. The campaign helped to propel Schlitz to the top ranks of American brewers.

Labatt. The 1960s would see the forces of internationalism come face-to-face with those of Canadian economic nationalism.

While Labatt was one of the most profitable breweries in Canada, it was also the most vulnerable to a takeover. A stock split of three for one in 1961 had multiplied the number of public shares to 4,327,095 and diluted the Labatt family holdings to just under 40 per cent.[17] Nevertheless, as Moore stated in December 1961, "it is still the heirs of this man [John Labatt] who today are the majority shareholders with approximately 35% interest."[18] But unlike at Molson and Canadian Breweries Ltd, the board of directors and management at Labatt's did not hold a large block of shares. Furthermore, with the exception of Jack Labatt, there was no longer an executive at Labatt who bore the family name of the founding father. This was significant because it has generally been the case in the evolution of multinationals in the alcoholic beverage industry that having ownership concentrated in the hands of a small number of shareholders, in particular families, has helped in the growth and survival of firms.[19] Labatt was a prime target for takeover.

Predator

Among the ranks of giant American brewers, Schlitz was the first to openly express an interest in purchasing a controlling interest in Labatt. One of America's oldest breweries, Schlitz could trace its roots to 1849 when August Krug, a German immigrant, opened an eponymous saloon and brewery in Milwaukee. When Krug died without successors in 1856, his widow, Anna Marie Uihlein, married the brewery's bookkeeper, Joseph Schlitz, who changed the name of the brewery to his own and ran it until he drowned in a shipwreck off the coast of England in 1875. Like Krug, Schlitz died without heirs, so the brewery passed into the hands of his step-nephews: Alfred, August, Charles, and Edward Uihlein. Under the guidance of the Uihlein brothers, Schlitz expanded into Chicago in the 1870s and then used the city's railway hub to fan out across the American Midwest. The Uihleins had spent a small fortune acquiring prime real estate and building saloons in the Midwest that only served Schlitz's beer. These real estate holdings helped the Milwaukee-based brewery survive national prohibition: many of the best locations were sold off in the 1920s to oil companies for gas stations. With the return of legalized beer sales in 1933, Joseph Schlitz Brewing Company embarked on an ambitious program of modernization and geographic expansion. At times, the expansion was accomplished by acquiring existing breweries: for example, in 1949, Schlitz entered the New York market by purchasing the Erhart brewery in Brooklyn. Entry by acquisition secured Schlitz's access to distribution channels used by local brewers, providing some protection from retaliatory pricing; however, to capitalize on its scale and expertise in processing, advertising, and distribution, the Milwaukee-based brewer was also willing to build new breweries when existing ones were not available for purchase.[20] By the 1950s, as a result of its post-war expansion, Schlitz was vying with Anheuser-Busch for top spot in the American brewing industry, and the Uihleins, who controlled 93 per cent of Schlitz's shares, were one of the richest families in America.

In 1961, Robert Uihlein Jr became the president of Schlitz. The grandson of August Uihlein, he had long assumed that he would enter the family business. "My father was a strong willed Germanic type," Robert Uihlein once told a reporter, "who insisted at an early age that I go with Schlitz."[21] Having graduated from Harvard with a bachelor's degree in 1938, Uihlein attended the University of Wisconsin Law School. After completing his law degree, he followed the family tradition of attending the United States Brewers Academy in New York to improve his knowledge of the science of brewing. His first full-time job came in 1942 when he joined Schlitz's sales department. For the next eighteen months, he was on the road almost constantly. In 1944, he became the Milwaukee sales manager, and then moved into plant management as the assistant to his uncle, Erwin C. Uihlein.[22] In 1959, he was made executive vice-president. With Schlitz experiencing declining sales, due in part to a lackluster advertising campaign for its principal brand, the board of directors chose forty-five-year-old Robert Uihlein to turn things around.

As president and chief executive officer, Robert Uihlein Jr demanded excellence from those around him. He was competitive by nature – although he had been barred from varsity competition in college sports because of hearing loss in one ear. At six feet, four inches tall with broad shoulders and chiselled Germanic looks, Uihlein was an imposing figure. He was confident, charming, tactical in business, and willing to take risks. Pictures of him with the grin of a cat that got the cream often graced the pages of the Milwaukee *Journal* and the *Sentinel*. He was widely respected by the citizens of "Brew City."

Uihlein wasn't afraid of having smart, independently minded people around him. One of his first acts as president was to hire a group of "genius I-Q types," many of whom were put to work in the marketing department.[23] One of them, Fred R. Haviland, had experience in brewing, having worked on advertising campaigns for Anheuser-Busch. Haviland understood the power of having the right messaging. "You imbibe the image along with the brew," he once insightfully stated.[24] In 1961, he suggested that Schlitz promote its flagship brew by using the slogan, "real gusto in a great light beer." The advertising campaign that followed struck a chord with the American public and helped increase Schlitz's sales by 19 per cent during Robert Uihlein's first year as president. By 1963, Schlitz had annual profits of well over $9 million on sales of $255 million. That year also saw Schlitz set a new record in production.[25] Reflecting on the company's year-end result, Uihlein told the press that "sales of our brands – Schlitz, Old Milwaukee and Burgermeister – continue to climb as the company's momentum accelerated in 1963."[26] The problem for Schlitz, and indeed all those engaged in the business of brewing in the United States, was that the growth in beer consumption was starting to slow. Facing limited growth potential at home and eager to surpass Anheuser-Busch as the nation's number-one brewer, Schlitz decided to expand by seeking out markets beyond the national boundary.

In the fall of 1963, Schlitz International was created with a mandate to "make Schlitz an international brand around the world."[27] To oversee the operation,

Uihlein appointed a Canadian, James Duncan Blyth. A chartered accountant by training, Blyth had been vice-president of finance at CBL before joining Schlitz and had helped implement many of the innovative strategies for Carling's international expansion. In the late 1950s and early 1960s, E.P. Taylor had licensed the production of Carling Black Label in the United States and Great Britain. Fuelled by the memorable ad slogan "Hey Mabel, Black Label," the rapid ascendency of Black Label propelled Taylor's Brewing Corporation of America into the top echelons of the U.S. brewing industry.[28] Blyth had been part of Taylor's inner circle when formulating Carling's growth strategy. When he came to Schlitz, Blyth brought with him the experience of developing an international brand as well as an intimate knowledge of Canadian brewing.

Blyth knew that there was money to be made in Canada. With those born just after the Second World War coming of drinking age soon, the future looked bright to those in the business of brewing. The industry's sales in 1964 were 10.86 million barrels, up from 9.43 million just four years earlier. Beer was by far Canada's most popular alcoholic beverage. In 1964, the average Canadian drank 14 gallons of beer and only a half-gallon of wine and a gallon of spirits.[29] It was also getting even easier to buy a beer. Except in the Maritimes, Canadians could get their favourite brand delivered right to the door. And when out on the town, they could purchase beer in beverage rooms, taverns, restaurants, bars, cocktail lounges, cabarets, private clubs, dining cars on trains, and a number of other licensed establishments.[30] For the Big Three the escalating demand for beer resulted in a steady flow of healthy profits. And even though thirty-five cents on every consumer dollar spent on beer went to the government, the Big Three were still making, on average, 5.2 per cent in net profits.[31] For those brewers interested in international expansion, Canada was a highly prized destination.

But Blyth knew that it was next to impossible for foreign brewers like Schlitz to gain a significant slice of the Canadian market via exports. The tariff and non-tariff barriers made it uneconomical for foreign brewers – even those like Schlitz who had plants close to the Canadian border – to ship their beer to Canada.[32] One way to hurdle the tariff wall and gain access to the lucrative beer market was to acquire an existing Canadian brewery. In her classic study, *Multinational Enterprise*, economist Mira Wilkins noted that American firms often found it impossible to obtain effective market penetration with exports from the home front, so they set up manufacturing facilities abroad.[33] This had long been the case in Canada. Since implementation of the National Policy in 1879, American companies had been setting up branch plants north of the forty-ninth parallel to avoid paying the federal tax on imports. But for brewers like Schlitz, having one branch plant in Canada would not be enough due to the interprovincial tariffs on out-of-province beer. If Schlitz wanted to capture a large share on the Canadian market, then it needed plants in every province – and the quickest way accomplish this was to acquire an existing Canadian brewery. Of the Big Three, Blyth told Uihlein, Labatt was the most susceptible to a takeover.

In November 1963, Robert Uihlein Jr instructed Blyth to approach those at John Labatt Limited with a proposal to acquire a controlling interest in the firm. A few weeks later, Blyth met with John Cronyn and Jack Labatt in London. At the meeting, Cronyn stated that he was not necessarily opposed to an investment by Schlitz, as long as it represented less than a 35 per cent stake. Jack Labatt, however, was of a different opinion. Labatt had met the Uihleins in Milwaukee a few weeks earlier and had very much liked the encounter. He respected the family's accomplishments and had a particular admiration for Robert Uihlein Jr. In many ways the two men were cut from the same cloth. Sons of brewer barons, both had gone to expensive private schools in their youth. Later in life, they had both proved to be irrepressible risk-takers. Jack Labatt, for example, had lied about his age during the Second World War in order to see action, and had then taken up sailing and flying after the war. Both were university educated and had entered the business of brewing at a young age. And both had attended the Brewers Academy in New York in order to become certified brewmasters. That was just what real beer men did. Both were graced with good looks and a zest for life. Despite the gap in ages (Robert Uihlein was twelve years older than Jack Labatt), the two men understood and liked each other.[34]

Jack Labatt believed that a takeover by Schlitz would be good for the old London Brewery – in part, because it would return Labatt to being a brewery run by brewers, not accountants like Jake Moore. Jack and Jake had been at odds for some time. Moore thought that Jack was arrogant, undisciplined, and, at times, unprofessional. "He doesn't shine his shoes and his suits are never pressed," Moore once complained to Jack's brother, Arthur. Jack Labatt, on the other hand, thought that Jake Moore was a gruff, power-hungry bean-counter. Jack believed that a Schlitz takeover would re-establish the authority of the board directors over the affairs of the firm – something that been lost, he lamented, under Moore's management.[35] In Jack's opinion, the firm would benefit from "a shareholder group to redirect management from time to time."[36] But beyond what was good for the brewery, a takeover would be good for the family members who still owned shares in the firm. An investment by Schlitz would see an exchange of shares for cash.

This would allow Jack Labatt to diversify his financial holdings along with those of his mother, his aunt Angela – the widow of Hugh Labatt – and the other members of the family.[37] For these reasons, he worked behind the scenes to persuade his family members to support Schlitz's takeover of Labatt.

His efforts had their desired effect. Most family members agreed to sell their shares to Schlitz. Having being assured by Jack Labatt of enough family support to justify an offer, on 2 February 1964, Schlitz formally announced its intention to purchase 35 per cent of the issued shares of John Labatt Limited. The American brewer planned to purchase 750,000 shares from the family and 750,000 on the open market and offered $23 per share, which represented a premium of about 20 per cent over the quoted stock-market price just a few months before.[38] The bid represented the first attempt by American interests to buy into a major Canadian brewery, and at a time when Canadian economic nationalism was on the rise, it did not go unnoticed.

The Politics of a Takeover

On 20 February 1964, the leader of the New Democratic Party, Tommy Douglas, rose in the House of Commons and began to hammer the Liberal federal government of Lester B. Pearson on its inability to protect Labatt from falling into the hands of American capitalists. Douglas called the governing party to do more to "prevent the Schlitz brewery of Milwaukee from absorbing the John Labatt brewery of Canada."[39] But it wasn't just nationalist-socialists like Douglas who were opposed to the takeover. At the opposite end of the political spectrum, the former Conservative prime minister and now leader of the official opposition, John Diefenbaker, also lectured the Liberals on their handling of the foreign investment question and, more specifically, the takeover of Labatt by Schlitz. While the left and right in Canada were divided on many things, they agreed about the threat posed to Canadian independence by American corporate imperialism.

Both Diefenbaker and Douglas were particularly critical of the actions of the minister of finance, Walter Gordon. In many ways, Gordon was an unlikely figure to be a target of the nationalists' criticism, given that much of his public life had been dedicated to the foreign investment question. In his 1961 book, *Troubled Canada*, he had written about the dangers of losing control of Canadian companies. "Foreign ownership inhibits the development and training of large corps of experienced Canadian entrepreneurs, business managers, promoters and finan-

ciers," Gordon wrote.[40] Economists like Mel Watkins and Abraham Rotstein gave
academic credence to his stance.[41] Public opinion polls suggested that about half
of the population agreed with Gordon that Canada had enough foreign investment. In 1962, Gordon ran for public office and was elected to represent the people of Toronto-Davenport in the federal House of Commons. He was re-elected
the following year when Lester B. Pearson won a minority government on a platform of promising that, if elected, they would begin their term with "60 Days of
Decisions," which would include introducing a new Canadian flag, reforming
health care, and implementing a public pension plan. Having helped Pearson become the leader of the Liberal Party several years earlier, Gordon was rewarded
with a Cabinet position.[42] Pearson was not a devout economic nationalist. Indeed,
he had little interest in the foreign investment question and, more generally, in
economic matters. Nevertheless, he respected Gordon's opinions and felt he owed
his old friend for "all that he had done for the party."[43] Pearson gave Gordon the
finance portfolio.

On 13 June 1963, Walter Gordon introduced his first budget. Consistent with his
ideological bent, the budget included measures directed toward reducing foreign
investment in Canada. Among the nationalistic measures was a punitive 30 per
cent takeover tax on sales of shares in listed Canadian companies to non-resident
individuals as well as corporations, and a withholding tax on dividends to non-
residents. Gordon's boldness may have been in keeping with the Liberal "60 Days
of Decision" election theme, but the euphoria did not last long. The budget was
prepared too hastily and political opposition to it was intense. Furthermore, as the
civil servants had privately warned, implementation difficulties came to the surface.[44] Within a matter of weeks, Pearson's minority government withdrew the
contentious nationalistic provisions. Gordon's bright career never quite recovered
from the episode. Writing in the old *Toronto Telegram* a few days after the watered-
down budget finally cleared the Commons, columnist Doug Fisher presciently
anticipated his political obituary. To Fisher, Gordon was an example of political
puffery, a man whose reputation had been inflated by his party and its newspaper
supporters who presented him as a "symbol of the all-wise."

After the ill-fated budget of 1963, Gordon – according to his biographer Stephen
Azzi – "ceased to be a crusader against foreign investment, becoming instead a defensive figure, carefully trying to rebuild his position for some future battle."[45] For
the remainder of his term as finance minister (until 1965), he pragmatically attempted to balance domestic and international forces.[46] When asked in February
1964 what he planned to do, if anything, to prevent the takeover of Labatt by U.S.

interests, Gordon responded, "there is no legislation that would prevent that kind of transaction taking place."[47] Apart from a withholding tax on dividends to the United States, there was nothing to be done. Diefenbaker berated Gordon for so quickly conceding defeat. Having declared that the Conservative Party believed "in the Canadianization of industry,"[48] Diefenbaker accused Gordon of being the handmaiden of U.S. public policy-makers. "I know that Dillon and Hodges [U.S. secretary of the treasury and secretary of commerce, respectively] are not officially members of the cabinet of Canada," Diefenbaker polemically professed in the House of Commons, "but what did they say to him [Gordon] when he made the pilgrimage to Washington recently?" In Diefenbaker's mind, Gordon had become the Trojan Horse of American capitalism. Diefenbaker's hyperbole aside, there was little economic nationalism left in the policies of the Liberal government.

Internal Divisions

With the Liberal government unwilling to protect the iconic Canadian brewery from a hostile American takeover, divisions started to appear among the ranks of the board of directors at Labatt. Jack Labatt and Richard Ivey fully supported the Schlitz takeover, and they put pressure on the other members of the board to accept the deal. But most on the board did not share their enthusiasm. Jack Labatt's cousin and fellow board member Alex Graydon, for example, was passionately opposed to the deal, stating that if the members of the family needed cash then other means could be found that would not involve losing control of the brewery that had been in family hands since 1847.[49] In addition, Graydon and the majority of others on the board took very seriously the reports that a takeover of Labatt by an American firm would lead to public resentment and a subsequent decrease in sales. Many also resented the fact that the old London Brewery could so easily fall into American hands.[50] The most recent addition to Labatt's board of directors, John Allyn Taylor, was one of the people who felt this way. Born in 1907, Taylor had received a BA from the University of Manitoba before moving to London in 1935 to join the company that would eventually become Canada Trust. He quickly became attached to his adopted city and managed to work his way into the tightly knit social circles of the London establishment. Taylor was impressed with the post-war growth and expansion of Labatt.[51] The quality of the brewery's management was excellent, he stated, but it would certainly be threatened by the proposed change in ownership, which would also "have an adverse effect on the value of the

Figure 10.2 Jack Labatt (left) with John Henderson "Jake" Moore during less contentious times, 1958.

shares in the hands of the remaining shareholders."[52] Thus, he maintained, the Schlitz offer should be rejected.

Taylor's statements strengthened the position of Jake Moore, who was facing the first serious challenge to his leadership.[53] Moore had not been consulted in the weeks leading up to the offer. Indeed, he had only become aware of it two days before it was presented to the Labatt family. Moore did not share Jack Labatt's fondness for Schlitz's owner. When he visited the Uihleins in Milwaukee with his wife, Woody, Moore was taken aback by the family's brashness.[54] This disturbed Woody in particular, who warned her husband that the character of Labatt would certainly change if people like the Uihleins gained control.[55] Since assuming the presidency, Moore had worked hard to create a corporate culture that empowered the individual but tied them to a common cause. In his 1962 "Know Your Company" address, he stressed how deeply rooted Labatt was in the economic life of the Canadian people. He worried that this would be lost if the Schlitz deal went through. Hence, Moore sought an offer from a friendly Canadian buyer – a white knight, in the parlance of corporate finance.

On 3 February 1964, Moore received a tentative counter-offer by telephone from E.P. Taylor.[56] But the offer was quickly withdrawn after lawyers informed Taylor that CBL's acquisition of Labatt could be successfully challenged under the Combines Investigations Act.[57] Two days later, Moore contacted David B. Weldon, the head of Midland Securities. Weldon had a reputation for providing wise counsel to many in the Canadian establishment, and he advised Moore to contact Peter Thomson, a partner in the Montreal brokerage firm of Nesbitt, Thomson Limited. Thomson was also president of Power Corporation – a one-time hydro-electric utility company that in the post-war period had been transformed into a huge investment vehicle for Canadian stocks. Those at Power Corp. thought Labatt would make a good investment. But like Schlitz, Power Corp. wanted a controlling interest in the London-based brewery. Thomson stipulated that any public offering for Labatt shares had to be contingent on a firm promise of 750,000 shares from the family.[58]

The problem for Power Corp. was that Richard Ivey and Jack Labatt had tied a majority of the family holdings to a deadline of 7 February for acceptance of the Schlitz offer. The board did not have the time required to carefully consider a different deal. At a late-night meeting on the day before the deadline, Labatt's board of eight directors was forced to report that it was "unable to find an acceptable Canadian alternative to the offer of Jos. Schlitz Brewing Company of Milwaukee to purchase effective control of John Labatt Limited."[59] Dismayed, Moore sent telegrams to the managers of the company's provincial division, instructing them that the control of the company would soon pass to "new hands but the present management methods will continue."[60] To senior executives, he wrote individual letters guaranteeing their positions and salaries for three years whatever the outcome, while all employees were assured in a general statement that the board would continue to protect their jobs and interests.[61] Over the course of the following week, the public submitted 2.5 million shares. Of these, Schlitz purchased 950,000 shares, bringing its total investment in Labatt of 1.7 million shares to 39 per cent.[62] The price paid for a controlling share in the iconic Canadian company was $39 million.

American Justice

The takeover of Labatt and the passing of Canada's third-largest brewery into American hands seemed complete, when suddenly the U.S. Justice Department in Washington issued a restraining order against Schlitz. All of its newly acquired Labatt shares were placed in escrow until the government had prepared a charge of potential monopoly under the Clayton Antitrust Act as modified by the Celler-Kefauver Anti-Merger Act. The legislation prohibited any corporation from acquiring any part of the share capital of another corporation "where the effect of such acquisition may be substantially to lessen competition, or to tend to create a monopoly." While modern conglomerates, with their immense size and concentrated power, had become acceptable in the United States, anti-trust action remained a possibility when the growth of a corporation threatened competition.[63]

The Justice Department, under Robert Kennedy, was receptive to evidence of any tendency toward monopoly. The government had already successfully sued Pabst for its acquisition of the Milwaukee-based brewery Blatz. It also brought an anti-trust suit against Falstaff for purchasing the Narragansett Brewing Company of Rhode Island, and Rheingold for buying the Jacob Ruppert's Knickerbocker Brewing Company in New York City.[64] Due to prohibition, the U.S. brewing industry had lagged behind other industries in terms of concentration. But after the Second World War, a national brewing oligopoly emerged as big brewers like Schlitz redoubled their efforts to attract new consumers and aggressively pursued dominance in distribution and advertising.[65] Robert Uihlein Jr was the first to admit that his company had played a leading role in the industry's concentration. "We expanded not merely by gobbling up ... some of the ... surviving U.S. brewers," he boasted, "but by selling against them more strongly on national, regional and local levels."[66] The consolidation of the American brewing industry had reached new heights in the late 1950s and early 1960s. By 1963, the top ten U.S. brewing companies controlled 55 per cent of the American market, and Schlitz – as the nation's second-largest brewer – produced 8.4 per cent of all beer sold.

On the west coast, Schlitz had set its sights on taking control of the California market. It already had two breweries in operation in the Golden State, having purchased the Burgermeister Brewing Company of San Francisco in 1961.[67] If it were to acquire Labatt, it would also have a dominant interest in General Brewing Corporation. The presence of General Brewing among Labatt's holdings was a red flag to the U.S. Anti-Trust Division as it seemed to suggest that Schlitz was intent upon removing the competition. Determined to prevent that from happening, the government sued Schlitz. The case was placed before the District Court in San Francisco. Lawyers from Schlitz immediately asked that the company be allowed to place two representatives on the Labatt board, where they could influence decisions on the disposition of General Brewing. The request was denied. Practically speaking, it did not matter: Jack Labatt and Richard Ivey were conducting themselves on the Labatt board as though Schlitz were the major shareholder, pressuring the other members to endorse the sale of General Brewing with the argument that once the subsidiary was sold, the case against Schlitz would collapse.[68] "Basically a sale of General Brewing at this time would eliminate the anti-trust problem with regard to ownership by Schlitz," Richard Ivey stated in a letter to the other board members.

Ivey was of the opinion that there was no reason to keep General Brewing. After all, General Brewing was not growing. In 1963, Labatt assigned Ron Woodman the task of turning things around. As Labatt's regional general manager, Woodman had been responsible for overseeing the expansion and growth of the brewery in western Canada. The board felt he would have similar success south of the border and named him president of General Brewing. Upon arrival in California, Woodman immediately initiated a review of operations and presented his findings to the board on 21 October 1963. The major problem at General Brewing, he reported, was that productivity remained low while overhead was high. The California brewery also suffered from not having a full line of products to offer distributors. In 1963, "premium brands" (i.e., a beer made from a better recipe, using good grains, and stored in cold storage facilities to allow for a more consistent brew) made up 38 per cent of the beer market in California, compared to 12 per cent three years before. Woodman believed that if Labatt wanted to make any "substantial headway in the market," it must be able to give the distributors "a complete line of products including a cheap beer, a regional beer, a premium beer and an imported beer and/or ale."[69] The board agreed and gave Woodman the authority to enter into a licensing agreement to brew Labatt's brands south of the border.

But the move did not stop the losses. In the fall of 1964, executives had come to a different explanation for General Brewing's sagging sales: the company was "spending less money than its competitors on advertising."[70] Management at General Brewing asked Labatt's board for more money. Ivey demanded that the board reject the request. "Apart from the fact that I do not think that the present proposal is workable," Ivey stated, "in my view the discrepancy between the available market and the productive capacity of General Brewing is so wide that the only practical approach would be to cut back and curtail costs wherever possible." Ivey believed that General Brewing needed to be sold. But if a reasonable offer could not be obtained for the brewery, then "serious consideration should be given to the minimizing of the risk with regard to the California operations."[71] The issue continued to divide the board and consumed valuable time and energy.[72]

Feeling caught in the middle and wanting to know his options, Moore contacted Fredrick Ackerman, a veteran of American business.[73] Ackerman had been one of the founders of Greyhound Corporation – the great intercity bus company. In 1964, he was serving on the boards of both Greyhound and General Brewing. When Moore invited him to join the Labatt board, Ackerman reciprocated by making Moore a member of the board of directors at Greyhound. And the two men became good friends. Through Ackerman, Moore met the head of the Democratic Party in New York, who in turn introduced Moore to the lawyers at Simpson Thacher & Bartlett, a firm specializing in anti-trust matters. The Manhattan-based lawyers agreed to prepare a brief for Moore on the role of Labatt's board of directors while the Schlitz case was in the courts. One of the firm's young up-and-coming junior partners, William Manning, prepared the final report. In Manning's legal opinion, it was unlikely that the Justice Department would lose the case. "The government should prevail," Manning confidently stated.[74] In the meantime, however, the board of directors at Labatt must "continue to manage its affairs in the interests of all of its shareholders, including Jos. Schlitz Brewing Company, irrespective of the effects of any actions taken by them."[75] Moore interpreted this to mean that he did not need to collaborate with lawyers and executives at Schlitz. Indeed, he could actively work against Schlitz as long as his actions were deemed to be in the interests of the majority of Labatt's shareholders.[76]

It was welcome news because Moore had already begun to move in that direction. Feeling that he had the support of a majority of Labatt's board of directors and the Canadian public at large, Moore instructed General Brewing to bring its own civil action against Schlitz for attempting "to monopolize the production and sale of beer in the State of California and the West."[77] He also asked for a court decision forcing Schlitz "to divest itself of all stock of John Labatt Limited." Jack Labatt was outraged by the action and charged Moore with "suing our largest shareholder."[78] Richard Ivey was also infuriated, and at the end of 1965, after seventeen years on the board, he resigned in protest.[79] Moore was living dangerously. He was walking the high wire without a safety net. If the case went Schlitz's way, then Moore would be done. But there was no turning back now.

"Restored to Canadian Hands"

On 24 March 1966, after more than two years of waiting anxiously, Moore received word that the federal district court in San Francisco had finally made its ruling on the fate of Labatt. After weighing all the evidence, Judge Stanley A. Weigel ruled that the acquisition of Labatt would make Schlitz the biggest brewer in California, by virtue of Labatt's ownership of General Brewing, as well as the largest in United States, and that was something the court couldn't allow. Judge Weigel agreed with the U.S. Justice Department that the takeover was a violation of Section 7 of the Clayton Antitrust Act. Schlitz's team of high-paid corporate lawyers immediately challenged the court's verdict on the grounds it did not take into account the fact that, once General Brewing was sold, Schlitz would be free to pursue its real objective of developing a substantial investment in the Canadian brewing industry.[80] It took almost another full year for the U.S. Supreme Court to review the lower court's decision and rule that there were no grounds for an appeal. By upholding the lower court's judgment, the Supreme Court indicated that it was set on curbing the process of mergers and acquisitions in the U.S. brewing industry, which had seen the number of breweries in operation decline from 307 to 144 between 1952 and 1965.[81] The court gave Schlitz ninety days to divest itself of all the shares it held in Labatt.

Uihlein had remained confident that he would eventually get his hands on Labatt and, consequently, did not have a plan for selling the stock. This gave Moore a golden opportunity. Like Mackenzie before him, Moore wanted to own a piece of the brewery. He was aware that among the elite in London, those who owned businesses – especially old, successful ones like John Labatt Limited – were held in much higher regard than "mere" managers. Always an ambitious man who associated material wealth with personal success, Moore was determined to buy a controlling interest in the firm that he had presided over as president since 1958. But to do so, he would need a great deal of money – much more than he had. So he set about putting together a group of Canadian investors.

To help in that task, Moore contacted Tony Griffin, president of Triarch Corporation in Toronto. Triarch was a small merchant bank founded in 1953 by Sir Siegmund Warburg, a scion of one of the great German-Jewish banking dynasties.[82] Since Triarch was not solely committed to the public issue of shares and debentures, it had more flexibility than larger investment houses when it came to financing big transactions. "We are specialists in this kind of thing," Griffin confidently stated.[83] Griffin proposed that Moore form a holding company

Figure 10.3 In 1965, Labatt made its beer available in cans for the first time. Brewers like Labatt were motivated to use cans because they were lighter, cheaper, and easier to stack and ship than bottles. Also, many consumers liked the fact that buying beer in cans, rather than bottles, did not require a deposit. The first cans, like those above for Labatt's Pilsener and IPA, were flat-topped and made of heavy-gauged steel. To open these cans, a hole had to be punched in the top with the sharp end of a church key opener. Becoming popular in the 1960s, beer cans were an icon of mass production.

to purchase Schlitz's shares in Labatt.[84] Moore immediately acted on the advice, establishing Jonlab and then inviting a select group of Labatt's senior managers and a small number of friends to buy in. Among them were three Labatt vice-presidents – John Cronyn, D.E. Weldon, and William Carson – as well as the great-grandson of John Kinder Labatt, Allan Scatcherd Jarvis. Moore also invited two senior members of the Progressive Conservative Party, Edwin Goodman and Earnest Jackson, to invest.[85] Having rounded up over thirty investors, Jonlab still only had enough funds to purchase about 25 per cent of Schlitz's shares. Others with even deeper pockets would have to be found.

One of the first people Moore then contacted was J. Grant Glassco, president of Brazilian Light and Power Company (BLPC). Glassco was another Clarkson, Gordon partner and a close friend of Walter Gordon. Moore felt that Glassco would like the idea of being a white knight of Canadian capitalism.[86] He was right. Glassco was sitting on a mountain of cash, which he had acquired from the recent sale of BLPC's telephone utility to the Brazilian government. Glassco committed $10 million, along with a loan from the Bank of Commerce to purchase 1 million of the 1,700,000 shares. The purchase was the first investment in a Canadian company by BLPC, and it was to have a profound effect on the evolution of John Labatt Limited and the career of Jake Moore.[87] With roughly two-thirds of the shares in BLPC's hands, Jonlab went ahead and purchased 400,000 shares, and then Investors Mutual of Canada acquired the remaining stock.

A few days after the deal was done, Jake Moore announced the news to the press. "One of the major current preoccupations of Canadians and a topic which we hear a good deal about almost every day," he stated on 23 February 1967, "involves retaining or regaining control of Canadian companies by Canadians and Canadian capital. As president of a major Canadian company which has gone through this kind of exercise," he continued, "I want to announce that the 39% interest in John Labatt Limited which was held by Jos. Schlitz Brewing Co. since February 1964 will be restored to Canadian hands ... [and] we shall again be an all Canadian company."[88]

Conclusion

For Moore and the men around him, the years leading up to the "Summer of Love" were a challenging period. "It has not been an easy or happy time," Moore admitted. "I guess I have had to run through all the emotions and frustrations in the book while this has been going on."[89] Moore could take some comfort in the fact that, despite all of the internal wrangling, Labatt continued to grow. Between 1961 and 1967, net earnings had increased by well over 50 per cent. During the same period, annual production had almost doubled from 1,700,000 to 3,200,000 barrels of beer. And although Labatt was still the smallest of the Big Three, the company's share of the domestic market had increased from 20 per cent in 1961 to 27 per cent in 1967. Much of the gain had come in Quebec, where Labatt now controlled almost 30 per cent of the market and 50 was the best-selling brand of beer.

The attempted takeover by Schlitz had caused divisions at the top of Labatt brewery. Having fully supported Uihlein's Canadian invasion, Jack Labatt now found himself without allies and with a clear signal that he was no longer welcome at the boardroom table. Feeling the pressure to depart, he resigned from the board of directors in 1967. This left a cabal of executives who were loyal to Jake Moore and supported virtually every strategic move that he made. As Jake Moore came more and more to perceive himself as the white knight of Canadian capitalism, the firm that he led increasingly focused on building enterprises and brands within Canada.

Moore and the men around him had succeeded in maintaining the momentum of the post-war period. Far from being the willing partners of the U.S. MNE, as Kari Levitt and other nationalists have maintained, a majority of executives at Labatt fought hard to keep American capitalism at bay. Without any support from the Canadian state, Moore and the executives around him orchestrated a complex and multi-pronged strategy to keep Labatt Canadian. Ironically, they were helped by a system of American justice that was set on curbing the power of major corporations. Ultimately, the takeover was thwarted by a combination of American anti-trust policies and a particular grouping of Canadian business interests.

The Quest for Popular Brands, 1959–82

In 1959, Labatt's marketing managers met at Oakwood, Ontario, to discuss the subject of brands. Those at the conference had the foresight to realize that in the future a handful of popular national brands would dominate the marketplace and that huge savings could be achieved by promoting a single brand with a cohesive identity and advertising theme across the nation.[1] The task at hand would not be without its challenges, however. The nature of the nation was such that regional, religious, linguistic, and ethnic diversity frequently prevented a brand from easily gaining national popularity.[2] The period under review was particularly difficult for those brand managers who were seeking to standardize their message due to the large number of immigrants arriving from Europe. Between 1951 and 1971, the foreign-born in Canada increased twentyfold. This phenomenon triggered a debate over what was, and was not, "Canadian" and made it difficult for the image-makers to develop truly national brands that appealed to Canadians from coast to coast.[3]

For those Canadian firms in the alcoholic beverage industry, the task of developing successful national brands was made doubly difficult because of the regulatory environment that balkanized the Canadian brewing industry. Prior to the rise of national breweries in the 1950s, there was little incentive to develop national brands. Only after the Big Three gained a physical presence in each of the provinces and secured the means of distribution did Canadian brewers attempt to create and promote national brands. But even then, the process was not without its challenges, as the introduction to this book made clear.

This chapter examines the difficulties that Labatt experienced in creating Canada's first truly national beer brand: Labatt Blue. It also examines the logic behind the Labatt decision first to make American-styled beer and then to license the right to brew the "real thing." In short, it considers the factors that led to the Americanization of Canadian beer.

The "National Lager Problem"

On 1 June 1967, Labatt's director of marketing, Paul J. Henderson, wrote to his boss, Peter Hardy, who at the time was president of Labatt Breweries of Canada Ltd. Henderson was exasperated that Labatt's flagship lager, Pilsener, was not selling well in Ontario. "For a long time," Henderson stated, "we have all been aware that Ontario's progress … cannot be secure or soundly based until we have a stronger national lager brand." All the more frustrating for Henderson and his fellow executives was the fact that they had been trying to solve the "national lager problem" for more than five years.

At the time, a truly national beer brand still did not exist in Canada. The closest thing to one was CBL's Carling Black Label. Since the 1930s, CBL had promoted Black Label as its flagship lager. But the brand lacked popularity in many parts of Canada. While highly favoured in Ontario and having some strength in Manitoba and British Columbia, Black Label was not – as one rising star in the company, Peter Widdrington, noted in 1965 – "a serious contender in any other market."[4] Six years earlier, Molson had launched two new brands, Golden Ale and Canadian Lager, but neither brand had a significant share of the national market until the 1970s.[5] The diverse nature of the nation prevented a brand from easily gaining national popularity.[6] Added to this, the Canadian beer market was almost perfectly divided into ale drinkers and lager drinkers.

In the west, there was a well-established tradition of brewing and drinking Pilsner. A pale, golden lager, Pilsner (or Pilsener) was first brewed in Pilsen, a city in Western Bohemia in the Czech Republic. When it first appeared, Pilsner revolutionized the brewing world due to its seductive glow and its crisp, mild, and refreshing flavour. The custom of brewing Pilsner was first brought to Western Canada by German and American immigrants during the last half of the nineteenth century. One such brewer, Fritz Sick, had emigrated from Freiburg, Germany, to Trail, British Columbia, in the 1890s. After a couple of short-lived business ventures, Sick moved his family to Alberta and opened the Lethbridge Brewing and Malting Company. Soon after, he began making Old Style Pilsner beer. The brew was an overnight success. Over the next few decades it gained so much in popularity that when Labatt began construction on its state-of-the-art brewery in Edmonton in 1964, Old Style Pilsner had a tight grip on the Alberta market. In addition to dominating the Alberta market, Sick's Old Style Pilsner shared a top spot with Carling Pilsener and Lucky Lager in British Columbia.[7] In Saskatchewan, where lager sales constituted 97 per cent of the beer market, Sick's Bohemian, a Pilsner, was the best-selling beer. In 1962, Labatt's Pilsener only had 8 per cent of the Saskatchewan market, making it the fifth best-selling beer in the province, behind Old Vienna (with 9 per cent market share), Black Label (with 10 per cent), Molson Pilsener (with 22 per cent), and Sick's Bohemian (with 46 per cent).[8] In Manitoba, where there was also a vibrant tradition of brewing and drinking Pilsner, Labatt's Pilsener was the best-selling brand, with a 35 per cent market share.

Unlike in the west, in Ontario, Quebec, and the Maritimes, the brewing industry had been controlled by a group of brewers who were, for the most part, of British descent. Men like John Kinder Labatt, John Molson, Thomas Carling, Eugene O'Keefe, John Sleeman, William Dow, and Alexander Keith had established breweries to produce British-styled ales, porters, and stouts. Thus, the western thirst for Pilsner/lager did not exist to the same extent in the east. That is not to say that lager drinking did not take place. It did, and in some places – as Labatt's market research showed in 1960[9] – lager's popularity was rapidly growing. While only 5 per cent of Quebecers and 20 per cent of Maritimers stated in 1965 that they drank lager on a regular basis, in Ontario the number of regular lager drinkers was close to 35 per cent.[10]

Relative to elsewhere in Canada, the Ontario beer market was huge. In 1962, annual per capita consumption in Ontario was 18.25 gallons. That same year, those in the four western provinces drank, on average, about 30 per cent less than their Ontario counterparts. On the east coast, per capita beer consumption was even lower. For instance, in 1962, each New Brunswicker drank on average just 7.5 gallons of beer per year. In part, the lower-level beer consumption was a result of the lingering shadow of prohibition. Before the 1960s, the Maritime provinces had the most restrictive liquor laws in the country.[11] But it was not just that each Ontarian was drinking more; it was also that there were more of them. Total beer consumption in Ontario in 1962 equalled 11.5 million gallons. Ontarians were consuming more beer than all of the other provinces (excluding Quebec) and territories combined.[12] To put it in slightly different terms, Ontario beer consumption represented 62 per cent of total Canadian consumption. Having a significant slice of the Ontario beer market was therefore critical to the growth and survival of Canadian brewers in the post-war period.

The problem for Labatt was that its flagship lager, Pilsener, had never captured the imagination of beer drinkers in Ontario, where a third of the nation's lager drinkers lived in 1962. Since Pilsener's earliest days, it had held only a small share of the Ontario market, accounting for between 6 and 12 per cent of lager sales (see table 11.1). Carling Black Label and Old Vienna had maintained a strong grip on the Ontario lager market until 1963 when Molson Canadian challenged the duopoly through aggressive direct sales and a stepped-up advertising campaign.[13] To the extent that Labatt's Pilsener was being consumed at all, Labatt's market research showed, it was downed by a relatively small group of people outside the beer-drinking mainstream.[14] Labatt's Pilsener drinkers were typically better-educated men and women. "There is clear cut evidence," Paul J. Henderson noted in the winter of 1964, "that Pilsener does much better among certain socio-economic groups – i.e. white collar consumers, in better districts; and not as well among blue collar groups."[15] The brand was also more popular with recent immigrants, particularly those of European descent. On 29 October 1964, P.J. Henderson wrote to his colleague, B.G. Elliot, lamenting the fact that "Pilsener seems to have got itself into a rather restricted area – i.e. new Canadians and Europeans, not unqualified good things in other studies."[16] Henderson could not hold back his disappointment. "Obviously, this is not a satisfactory state of affairs," he stated. "A main lager brand should have a broad appeal," he continued, "especially to the big volume drinker."[17]

So what was the cause of the problem? Why was Labatt's Pilsener having such a difficult time capturing a significant share of the national lager market? When the problem was first identified in 1962, more than one Labatt executive thought that perhaps the product itself was to blame. Under the heading, "hypothesis which may account for the problem," P.J. Henderson wrote that, "the product itself is not sufficiently acceptable to consumer tastes in the problem markets."[18] The proposition was disturbing, but, as Henderson himself insisted, it had to be explored. Immediately, blind taste tests were performed to compare Labatt's Pilsener to its key competitors. The taste tests revealed that there was little difference between Labatt's Pilsener and the other lagers on the market.[19] Since the mid-1950s, the Big Three had been producing blander beers in an effort to appeal to as many beer drinkers as possible. At this point, there was very little in the way of substance to distinguish between the brands of the Big Three. "In brewing today

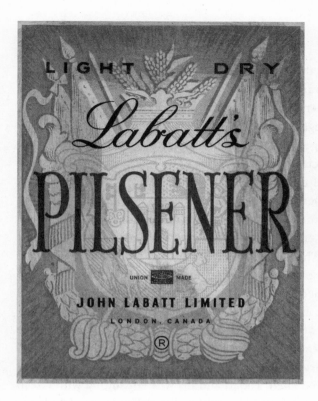

Figure 11.1 Labatt's Pilsener label, 1961. The arms of the city of Pilsen, in the background, added to the brand's derivative and distinctively European identity.

all brands of any one type are fairly close," stated Labatt quality control manager John Compton in 1963, "and it is the finer points we are working on."[20] Public opinion surveys undertaken by Labatt's marketing managers further confirmed the extent of the homogenization. In 1964, over 80 per cent of those Canadians polled stated that "the mass of brands are much alike."[21] When it came to Labatt's flagship lager, blind taste tests showed "no significant difference in preference between Pilsener, on the one hand, and Canadian, Black Label, and Old Vienna, on the other."[22] When P.J. Henderson, N.E. Hardy, J. Burke-Gaffney, C.A. Stock, D.G. McGill, and T.M. Kirkwood met in Toronto on 5 July 1965 to further discuss the national lager problem they took some comfort in the fact that the evidence showed that the product itself was not the problem. "Any marketing failures of the brand," Labatt's marketing managers declared, "can *not* be charged to the product."[23] Rather, they concluded, "Pilsener has an image problem."[24]

But what was wrong with Pilsener's image? Senior management struggled to come up with an answer to this question for a number of years. Ultimately, they determined that part of the problem was that the brand was considered too European and, therefore, "not basically Canadian."[25] At a time when the government, the popular media, and the public at large was preoccupied with protecting the

"Canadian way of life" from the threat of newcomers,[26] Pilsenser's popularity was being undermined by the brand's association with a number of countries in central Europe. In 1964, Labatt's marketing men conducted a survey of beer drinkers in the Welland-Windsor region of Ontario. This study, and a subsequent one undertaken in Canada's largest city, Toronto, in 1965, concluded that "users and non-users very heavily associate Pilsener with Europe."[27] In May 1967, C.A. Stock summarized the findings of the market research that Labatt had done over the previous four year by stating: "Its name [Pilsener] has strong European connotations, especially with Germany, Austria and Czechoslovakia."[28]

Ironically, Labatt's marketing managers had emphasized Pilsener's central European heritage since the brand's introduction in 1951. Ads had played up the fact that the beer was based on a central European recipe that had been brought back to Canada after the Second World War by Hugh Labatt. "Only Labatt's Pilsener Lager Beer has the exciting flavour," one ad proclaimed, "because only Labatt's possess the secret of the original lager recipe from Pilsen, birthplace of lager beer." The company also emphasized that Pilsener was made from European yeast and hops imported from the Pils region of Czechoslovakia. Early promotional pictures showed Hugh Labatt and his wife consulting with Czech brewers in Prague. In 1961, the Labatt's Pilsener label was changed to include the arms of the city of Pilsen (see figure 11.1). At the same time, Labatt began using a foil label for the first time, in part because "women are particularly attracted by the gay, colourful sparkle and charm of foil labels."[29] The ads for Pilsener featured middle-class couples in formal attire (and certainly not jeans and T-shirts), enjoying their lager in a cocktail lounge rather than a working-class beer parlour (see figure 11.2).[30] Until the end of the 1960s, the people pictured in Labatt's lager ads were middle-aged or older. Government regulations on beer advertisements kept alive the tradition of romance and glamour in the scenes depicted.[31]

In a further attempt to appeal to recent immigrants, Labatt began running a few ads in German. The ads declared that Labatt's Pilsener was "good in taste" and "should be your beer." "Gut Im Geschmack," read one advertisement in a Toronto newspaper, "Labatt Pilsener, Soll Dein Bier Sein."[32] The European bond was further forged with Labatt's use of "Mr Pilsener," a jovial, white-haired, Alpine figure, who was often decked out in lederhosen and a Tyrolean hat. Mr Pilsener started to appear in ads during the 1950s. The diminutive European character also appeared on beer serving trays, bottle openers, postcards, and, for a period in the early 1960s, on every cap, bottle, and case of Labatt's Pilsener (see figure 11.3).

Figure 11.2 Labatt's Pilsener advertisement, 1960.

Figure 11.3 Postcard of Labatt bottling plant with the jolly Mr Pilsener looking on, c. 1965.

The marketing managers at Labatt concluded that it all added up to a derivative and decidedly European brand identity at a time when the symbols of national identity were being reformulated and modernized.[33]

Creating a "Canadian" Brand

In the mid-1960s, marketing executives at Labatt began making changes to the firm's flagship lager brand to make it appear less "ethnic" and more "Canadian." One of the first changes was to replace the city of Pilsen's coat-of-arms on the label with a coat-of-arms featuring a maple leaf, a long-time symbol of national identity (see figure 11.4). Since Confederation, the maple leaf had appeared on coins, flags, and military adornments. (In 1867, Alexander Muir had composed "The Maple Leaf Forever," which in the years following had become English Canada's de facto national anthem.) At the same time, the name "Labatt's" became more prominent on the label and the word "Pilsener" – which 87 per cent of those surveyed in Toronto associated with a country other than Canada[34] – became less so. In an effort to remind consumers of Labatt's continued commitment to quality and tradition – elements that modern marketing experts assert are central to a brand's authenticity[35] – the label also featured an image of the four gold medallions that the company had won at international brewing competitions since the 1870s. "The new label," one internal report noted, "gives the impression of a Canadian beer, and expresses the vigor and energy of people on the move."[36] Finally, Mr Pilsener vanished once and for all from the company's merchandise and promotional campaigns.

At the same time, Labatt's marketing managers decided to emphasize the colour blue more fully on the label. Internal research showed that blue projected "relaxation," "smoothness," "coolness," "balance of product," and "quality."[37] In addition, the image-makers at Labatt had Louis Cheskin's groundbreaking 1951 study, *Colour for Profit*, which suggested that blue was the "preferred colour of men."[38] But beyond its universal psychological appeal, the utilization of blue would allow Labatt to avoid the politics of "red and white" in Canada. During the 1960s, "British" versus "Canadian" symbolism was highly contested, particularly in Ontario. The adoption in 1965 of the new Canadian flag – a red field with a white square in the centre in the middle of which was a maple leaf – led to Ontario's adoption of a modified Red Ensign as its provincial flag. Labatt's use of the colour blue sidestepped both forms of "nationalism."

Figure 11.4 Labatt's Blue label, 1968.

Other aesthetic aspects of the brand took much more time to change. Senior management struggled for years with what to do about the brand's name. In April 1963, B.G. Elliot, Labatt's executive assistant to the vice-president and general manager, stated that the name "Pilsener" should be abandoned because it was not resonating with beer drinkers in Ontario. Elliot's report, "Recommendations for a Brand Name," contained a long list of possible appellations to replace "Pilsener." Some were quickly struck off the list as antagonistic to certain segments of the population. For example, the brand name "Friar's" was rejected because it might offend Roman Catholics, who were "an important part of our market."[39] Likewise, the name "Mohawk" was crossed off the list because it had "bad connotations" and "only a very tenuous association with beer."[40] On the other hand, "North Star" was thought to be a good moniker because it was a "Canadian term" that was "well known" and "nationally popular."[41] The name "Viking" was also in the running because it "was strong in masculinity and adventurous quality." Finally, the appellation "Grand National" was seriously considered because it "expresses high quality with reference to achievement ... and [is] extremely well suited for bilingual use."[42]

None of these brand names were adopted at the time, however, due to an internal dispute over the appropriate approach to marketing and which market(s) should be privileged. Some executives felt that a regional approach to marketing beer was best. For example, Tom Cadham, head of Labatt's Saskatchewan Division, thought a regionally oriented advertising campaign might best serve the company. "Where there has been tremendous success in several provinces for the product [Pilsener]," Cadham asked, "should any change from the present proven successful approach be made?"[43] In holding to his position, when P.J. Henderson asked the heads of the various operating divisions to suggest a new name for Pilsener, Cadham refused to participate. This infuriated Henderson. "I am mystified by the form of your division's response to our solicitation," Henderson angrily wrote to Cadham in December 1966. "We have on a number of occasions attempted to explain that we are undertaking the exploration only of a beer brand designation other than Pilsener ... If your division chooses not to play a part by throwing the names you like into the pot, Tom, I guess this is your prerogative."[44]

Unlike Cadham, Henderson was confident that the national lager problem could only be solved by a "national approach" to marketing. He was not alone. He had the support of all of those at Labatt's head office in London, none of whom went on the record as advocating a different approach. Seemingly everyone in London agreed with Labatt vice-president J.R. Robertson, who had previously stated that the trend in Canada was "towards larger marketing areas, not smaller."[45] This kind of language around standardizing the image of brands reflected the trend of corporate mass advertising more generally during the period. There was a constant tension between regional managers who thought they "knew their markets" and the centralized professional public relations technocrats, like Robertson, who were perturbed by the messiness/untidiness of mixed messages/brands.[46] Robertson was not even willing to concede that Quebec, which was in the midst of the Quiet Revolution, represented a special case. "If any region warranted regional brands because it is a different cultural area with a different language," Robertson stated, "that region is Quebec. But even here, brewers have seen fit to promote brands that are national in the context in which Ale is national." Thus, in regard to the national lager problem, Robertson recommended that, "every effort should be made to achieve the same image and to direct the same appeal to different parts of the country."[47]

Robertson was not naive, however. He was the first to admit that "no brand can be all things to all people – so some penalty must be paid in certain areas."[48] The question was which areas should be privileged and which should pay the penalty when it came to rebranding Labatt's lager. Increasingly, Labatt's executives were of the opinion that the Ontario market should be privileged. To be sure, it would be nice to maintain – or even better, increase – market share in the west.

But the litmus test was now Ontario. Any changes would be judged, first and foremost, on their effects on market share in Canada's most populated province. "This Pilsener matter," wrote Labatt executive vice-president N.E. Hardy to P.J. Henderson, "must be primarily the responsibility of the Ontario division. But since there are national considerations and because head office research facilities are probably involved, I am asking you to give the utmost assistance to the Ontario division by coordinating this important project and assigning to it your department's top priority."[49]

In the west, however, beer drinkers had started referring to Pilsener as Blue because of the predominance of the colour on the label.[50] But executives at Labatt's head office did not have enough faith in their western base to label the brand with that name – at least, initially. Instead, Labatt's marketing managers decided that perhaps the new brand name should contain the word "blue." Shortly after, senior executives were sent a list of 160 names and asked to "circle those which they believed to have good potential as brand names for Labatt's lager beer." The long list included: Blue Grade, Blue Bonnet, Blue Twin, Blue Wave, National Blue, Blue Star, Blue 'n' Gold, Blue Extra, Blue Eagle, Northern Blue, Blue #1, London Blue, Blue North, Blue Keg, Blue Shield, Cool Blue, and Happy Blue. The name that emerged as the top pick was Blue Star. In the months following, the consultants, Ben Crow & Associates, conducted a market survey to measure the acceptability of Blue Star as a replacement name for Labatt's Pilsener. They found that the appellation fared rather badly against "Pilsener" in key Ontario markets. In addition, some senior executives thought the name change might bewilder regular beer drinkers. "By changing across the country to Blue Star, those who know the brand as Labatt's Pilsener will be confused," N.E. Hardy stated, "and those who know it as Labatt's Blue will be confused, and everyone will be confused as to the logical nickname, Blue, Star, B.S. etc."[51] And thus it was rejected.

On 1 June 1967, N.E. Hardy wrote to P.J. Henderson stating that it was important that "faster progress be made" in resolving the national lager problem. "For a long time we have all been aware that Ontario's progress," Henderson stated, "dependent largely on the performance of '50' Ale, cannot be secure or soundly based until we have a stronger national lager brand in that market and one that is able to compete effectively in the key lager markets which Pilsener does not do."[52] In late 1967, it finally dawned on executives at Labatt that perhaps the answer had been staring them in the face for some time. "Is it not possible," P.J. Henderson wrote, "that the solution to our national lager problem lies solely in the word Blue." Part of the attraction of the name "Blue," was that – in the words of

Figure 11.5 Labatt's Blue advertisement, 1972.

one senior executive – "by itself, it is bilingual."[53] While the Quebec lager market
was small, executives at Labatt were still determined to create a brand that would
appeal to beer drinkers in both English and French Canada. In the months that
followed, Labatt began testing the brand name Blue in smaller Ontario markets.
The tests went well. In July 1968, the wording "Call for a Labatt Blue" was added
to the Ontario label and a Blue advertising theme was launched across the
province.[54] At the same time, the phrase "the great beer Westerners call Blue" was
added to the label in the west.[55]

   In 1968, Arthur Lenox, a long-time Labatt executive and former editor of the
company's magazine, *The Spearhead*, contacted the advertising firm J. Walter
Thompson to see if it could produce an attention-grabbing television commercial
for Blue. Colour television had only recently hit the Canadian scene, and executives at Labatt believed that Blue would be a natural attention-getter on the screen
if it were associated with the right jingle and moving images.[56] J. Walter Thompson promised that it would come up with something interesting and assigned the
task to one of its young executives, Bob Byron. Having taken a short retreat to

Table 11.1

Labatt's Blue market share (%) of beer sales, provincially and nationally

	ON	MB	SK	AB	BC	Canada
1960	6.90	n/a	n/a	n/a	n/a	n/a
1965	10.20	37.15	10.40	12.10	7.00	6.55
1968	11.48	37.42	n/a	14.97	10.00	6.57
1970	16.75	42.50	29.00	23.35	14.00	13.11
1975	15.50	38.25	22.18	n/a	32.25	15.12
1980	23.64	25.68	14.50	18.37	34.18	16.06
1985	25.73	18.62	12.55	11.25	21.00	15.23

Sources: *Minutes*, 5 September 1975, and from the *Labatt Collection*: "Labatt's Blue 1988 Marketing Plan," Box A08-053-711; "Labatt's Prairie Region 1988 Marketing Plan," Box A08-053-711; C.A. Stock to E.G. Bradley (15 August 1975), Box A08-039-228; "Saskatchewan Benchmark Study" (1 November 1970), Box A08-053-603; "Ontario Lager Benchmark Study" (17 July 1970), Box A08-053-603; "British Columbia Benchmark Study" (1 December 1970), Box A08-053-603; "Quebec Benchmark Study" (24 November 1970), Box A08-053-603; "1983 Spring Tracking Study – Summary of Brands by Province," Box A08-053-318; "Pilsener Share of Market Trends – 1959–1967," Box A08-058-713; Brand Designation Committee, "A Working Paper – Problem Definition" (March 1970), Box A08-053-603; "Marketing Priorities F81 and Beyond," Box A08-053-598.

reflect on the challenge, Byron returned with an idea for an ad campaign with three key elements: a blue balloon – as a symbol of escape – light music, and the refrain, "When you're smiling, the whole world smiles with you."

By the late 1960s, those in the automobile, tobacco, and alcoholic beverage industries were marketing to what the *Wall Street Journal* in 1967 termed the "Mustang generation" – young educated men and women who supposedly lived in pads (apartments) and spent much of their money on socializing and consumer goods.[57] At a time when popular culture was very youth-oriented, the people in Labatt's Blue ads were visibly younger than those featured in previous advertisements for Pilsener. These youthful people were also situated in more casual settings. The Blue ads of the late 1960s and early 1970s depicted relaxed, mixed-gender socializing, with hints of the "swinging" singles lifestyles (see figure 11.5). The focus on youth would pay dividends when the minimum drinking age was lowered from twenty-one to eighteen or nineteen in all of the provinces and territories between 1970 and 1972.

The rebranding of Labatt's Pilsener as Labatt's Blue and the subsequent ad campaigns had positive results. To keep market dislocations to a minimum, Labatt phased out Pilsener slowly in markets where the brand was strong and phased in Blue more quickly where Pilsener was weak. Beer drinkers in the west still recognized Blue as the lager that they had come to prefer. In each of the western provinces, Blue's market share increased significantly after the rebranding. In Alberta, Blue's share of the market increased from 14.97 per cent to 23.35 per cent between 1968 and 1970 (see table 11.1). In British Columbia, Blue's market share doubled between 1968 and 1972, from 10 per cent to 20 per cent. Gains were also experienced in Manitoba, where Blue's popularity increased by 5 per cent between 1968 and 1970. By the summer of 1971, Blue was the best-selling beer brand in the west.

In Ontario, beer drinkers saw Blue as a new, modern, Canadian-made lager that was "brewed for people born in Canada."[58] By February 1970, Labatt Blue's share of the all-important Ontario market increased to 16.75 per cent, up from 11.48 per cent of two years earlier.[59] Labatt's gains had come at the expense of its competitors, with 17 per cent of Molson Canadian drinkers, 13 per cent of Old Vienna drinkers, and 12 per cent of Black Label drinkers switching to Blue.[60] Even more encouraging for those at Labatt was that younger drinkers were starting to swap their regular brands for Blue. In November 1971, 30 per cent of those between twenty-one and twenty-four years of age stated that they drank Blue on a regular basis.[61] As the baby boomers came of drinking age and per capita consumption continued to increase during the early 1970s, Labatt Blue benefited from having a modern brand image and a catchy, bilingual name that resonated with the young adults of the nation.

By 1975, Blue was the best-selling lager brand in the nation. Five years later, it had the distinction of being Canada's most popular beer and – as a Labatt report noted – was "the single largest marginal profit contributor that this company has."[62] But what pleased executives at Labatt most was that the rebranding of Pilsener as Blue had helped propel the company to the top spot in the Canadian brewing industry. In 1975, Labatt controlled 38.2 per cent of the national market.[63] The rise from third place, which Labatt had held in 1959, to first place was due in large part to the rising popularity of Blue and the applied marketing knowledge and innovative strategies of its managers.

Building and managing Blue was a time-consuming and complex exercise that required a deep knowledge on the part of Labatt's marketing managers of market tastes, consumer fantasies and needs, and societal and cultural trends. The exercise was rarely coherent and straightforward. More often than not, it was marked by trepidation, anxiety, uncertainty, inconsistency, infighting, and debate. And while the process was ultimately successful, it took a heavy toll on Labatt's executives. Few, if any, felt like going through such a protracted and expensive exercise again. As a result, Labatt's brand managers increasingly looked south of the border for inspiration.

Creating Derivative Brands

On 31 January 1977, C.A. Stock wrote to his colleague at the Labatt Brewery in London, Ontario, stating that "it seems very possible that the times are right for a reduced calorie beer."[64] Stock's comments reflected the fact that beer drinkers in Canada were beginning to look for something unique to drink, something different from the similar-tasting brands of the Big Three. But instead of creating a new distinctive-tasting brew, those at Labatt decided to make a version of a mass-produced American beer.

South of the border, beer drinkers had become enamoured with "light" beer, particularly Miller Lite, whose introduction to the American public in 1975 helped propel Miller Brewery Co. of Milwaukee from fifth to second place in the U.S. brewing industry. Before Miller Lite's stunning success, U.S. brewers had experimented unprofitably with low-calorie beers. The first light brew, Gablinger's Diet Beer, was a complete flop. Introduced to the dieting public in 1967, the beer was the invention of biochemist James Owandes, who discovered a way to isolate an enzyme that could break down high-calorie starches and make them easier for the brewer's yeast to consume. The result was a lighter-bodied, lower-calorie brew with 4.6 per cent alcohol by volume. That same year, Meister Brau of Chicago developed the new product and launched it to the local market as Meister Brau Lite. Like Gablinger's, it was a failure, primarily because it lacked flavour and was marketed to women and the diet-minded – two groups that didn't drink much beer. Meister Brau became so disenchanted with its product that it sold the trade name, "Lite," to Miller Brewing Co. in 1972. The problem that the first light-beer brewers could not overcome was that reducing the amount of malt in order to cut calories (and, subsequently, lower the alcohol content) resulted in beer that tasted, as one industry insider at the time put it, "like dishwater."[65]

Unlike its predecessors, Miller Lite tasted more like regular beer. Miller had managed to develop a new process using starch-removing enzymes that kept calories at the diet level (about 96 calories per 12-ounce U.S. bottle, compared with 150 calories for regular brews) while maintaining both the taste and the approximate alcohol content (3.6 to 4.2 per cent alcohol versus 4.8 per cent for standard U.S. beer). This allowed the company to market the product not simply as a beverage for the diet conscious but also as a tasty, low-starch beer that enabled beer drinkers to consume more without feeling bloated.

Miller promoted the product with one of the most innovative advertising campaigns in the history of brewing. When reviewing Meister Brau Lite's history, Miller discovered that the brand sold well in the blue-collar town of Anderson, Indiana. This suggested that light beer could appeal to regular beer drinkers. Instead of pitching it as a diet beer, Miller decided to promote it as a great-tasting premium brew that was "less filling." As the memorable inaugural campaign put it, Miller Lite was: "Everything you wanted in a beer ... And less." The pitch was perfect for the 1970s when consumers were becoming more health conscious. In its commercials, Miller used legendary sports figures like Matt Snell, Billy Martin, John Madden, and Bubba Smith, who joked about their playing days and argued about the merits of drinking Miller Lite. Some insisted it "tastes great," while others argued it was "less filling." Miller sold more than 5 million barrels of Lite in the first year. Company sales rose 43 per cent in 1976, while other U.S. brands experienced marginal increases or outright losses.[66] Miller's competitors quickly took note, and by 1978, there were more than twenty brands of light beer on the U.S. market.[67]

Canadians got their first taste of American-styled light beers in 1973 when Labatt began test marketing Cool Spring Lager in British Columbia and Alberta, before taking it to Ontario two years later. Cool Spring had 3.9 per cent alcohol by volume and about 10 per cent fewer calories than regular-strength beer. Compared to the Miller Lite campaign, however, Cool Spring's promotional efforts were hopelessly unimaginative. "Who's going to drink it?" ask one ad, followed by the passive proposition, "Maybe it's for you." It turned out to be for very few.

The problem for Canadian brewers was that, unlike their American counterparts, they could not label their brands as "light." Under the terms of the federal government's Food and Drugs Act, to be labelled as "light," beer had to contain between 1.2 and 2.5 per cent alcohol by volume. The federal regulations were drafted to ensure that light beer would be significantly different from traditional brews and that all the brands would use similar formulas. The regulations baffled

Figure 11.6 Labatt was the first brewer to introduce a "light" beer to the Canadian market when it launched Special Lite in 1977. The time and effort it took to solve the "national lager problem" led those at Labatt to become derivative when it came to creating brand identities.

those at Labatt. "As it now stands," stated Labatt's young director of corporate affairs, Hugh Segal, in 1977, "we can't advertise or label Labatt's Cool Spring brand as a light beer because it, like the other three low alcohol beers on the market, contains 3.9% alcohol by volume, and 2.5% alcohol is the limit." Nor could low-alcohol beers be promoted as low-calorie alternatives, because they contained more than the permissible 50 per cent of the calories of regular beer. Hugh Segal and others at Labatt believed the laws were unfair and out of step with the times. So Labatt decided to take the government to court.

Before the court ruled, Labatt brazenly introduced Special Lite to beer drinkers in Ontario and British Columbia in December 1977. Unlike its U.S. rivals, Special Lite's brewing process did not use enzymes, but a natural yeast action.[68] The resulting brew contained 99 calories and 4.0 per cent alcohol by volume. Unfortunately for Labatt, the federal government took issue with the use of the word "Lite" and ordered Labatt to halt production after only one day.[69] "The whole situation is a little bewildering," stated the president of Labatt's Ontario breweries, Bruce Elliot, on 2 January 1978. "It was our understanding that the Health and Welfare Ministry was keen on the beer industry introducing a good-tasting but lighter alternative to regular beer. Now that we have, we find that we have to contend with roadblocks."[70]

As Labatt and the federal government fought it out in the courts, Molson launched Molson Light. In the commercials that appeared during the 1978 NHL playoffs – a year that saw the Montreal Canadiens beat the Boston Bruins four games to two in the Stanley Cup final – Canadians were informed that Molson Light was a golden lager with 4.5 per cent alcohol by volume. "You've got to have heart," Molson Light commercial watchers were directed before being asked: "Had one yet?" That same year, Carling O'Keefe introduced Highlight to beer drinkers in B.C., Saskatchewan, Manitoba, and Ontario. The brand was promoted as "the light beer that you have been waiting for." Unfortunately for Carling O'Keefe, Miller Brewing Co. took issue with the brand's name and filed suit in federal court against the Canadian brewer for trademark infringement. Carling O'Keefe vowed that it was not trying to capitalize on Miller High Life's success south of the border. Indeed, the Canadian brewer insisted that any American association would be detrimental to the brewer because Canadians believed that U.S. beers were too watery. It was a weak argument, and in September 1978, Carling O'Keefe changed the brand's name to Trilight and relaunched the beer using the same label and packaging.

With all the big brewers having a reduced-calorie, low-alcohol beer on the market by the summer of 1978, they all had something to lose if the federal government got its way in court and they weren't allowed to use the word "light." "If the government wins the case," stated Donald Thompson, communications director for Molson's Ontario breweries, "the light [beer] market is dead."[71] Fortunately for the brewers, in December 1979, the Supreme Court of Canada ruled six-to-three in favour of Labatt and found that all of the Food and Drugs Act's regulations concerning the brewing of beer were invalid. Besides wiping out the regulations, the court struck down Section 6 of the act in its application to beer. That section of the act stated that "where a standard has been prescribed for a food, no person shall label, package, sell or advertise any article in such a manner that it is likely to be mistaken for such food, unless the article complies with the prescribed standard." It also ruled that the federal Cabinet had no authority to prescribe standards of composition, strength, potency, purity, quality or other property of any article of food, drug, cosmetic or device insofar as beer was concerned. The ruling meant that light beer was here to stay. And while many Canadians didn't like this first batch of light brews, the foundation had been laid for a revolution in Canadian brewing.

Immediately following the ruling, Labatt decided to introduce its light beer to Quebecers. Executives at Labatt were bullish on the Quebec market because, as C.A. Stock put it, Quebecers were more "Americanized" than any other Canadians as "they have been heavily exposed to U.S. TV commercials for light beers."[72] But Quebecers were as unreceptive to Labatt's light beers as other Canadians. Many Canadians considered Special Lite to be "funny tasting" and "too light."[73] Additionally, executives concluded that the brand had an image problem in that it appealed "disproportionately to women and white-collar drinkers."[74] The brand was dumped in favoured of a lighter version of the firm's flagship brand, Blue. Nevertheless, the early experiment in making a light beer revealed that executives at Labatt were increasingly looking to the United States for guidance.

The Licensing of American Brands

By the end of the 1970s, Canadian beer drinkers were becoming somewhat tired of the traditional brands being mass-produced by the Big Three. Increasingly, they were looking for something new and exciting to drink. Many Canadians were well aware of the popular American beer brands. Brewers like Anheuser-Busch, Miller, and Coors had been spending millions of dollars a year on attention-grabbing advertising campaigns to promote their flagship brews. Often these beer commercials aired during major sporting events, like the Super Bowl.

After almost a decade of unsuccessfully attempting to persuade Canadians to purchase domestic imitations of American beers, the Big Three opted instead to produce the "real stuff" under licence. Labatt set its sights on making a deal with the maker of the "King of Beers," Anheuser-Busch. In 1980, Anheuser-Busch was harbouring as-yet-unannounced international ambitions. While the American beer giant was the undisputed brewing leader in the United States with 32 per

Figure 11.7 Peter Widdrington (left) and August Anheuser Busch III at the signing of the 1980 licensing agreement that permitted Labatt to brew and market Budweiser in Canada.

cent of the market, growth had become stagnant by 1980. Executives at Anheuser-Busch decided that in order to grow in the future, it would have to tap into external markets.[75] With that goal in mind, they determined that Budweiser had the best chance of becoming a global brand. For Anheuser-Busch, a licensing agreement with Labatt had the advantage of circumventing international trade barriers. Foreign beers that were brewed in Canada under licence were not subject to either the federal tariff or the discriminatory markups that other imported beers faced at the provincial government outlets. Furthermore, a licensing agreement with Labatt would substantially reduce transportation costs and allow Anheuser-Busch to more effectively get its product to market by utilizing Labatt's tightly held channels of distribution. It also insured that its brews were available at the largest retail outlet for beer in Ontario, Brewer's Retail/The Beer Store, and other leading outlets across the land.

At Labatt there was a sense that the brewing industry was moving in a new direction, that in the future there would be a homogenization of tastes and a globalization of brands.[76] "We predict that the brewing industry will one day be dominated by a few huge breweries and a handful of global brands," stated Don McDougall, president in 1980, "and think being ahead of everyone else might be a good idea."[77] Having joined Labatt shortly after receiving an MBA from the University of Western Ontario in 1961, McDougall quickly moved up the company ranks. Between 1973 and 1980, he held the position of senior vice-president and president and was a driving force behind the licensing agreement with Anheuser-Busch. McDougall was representative of most Canadian business executives at the dawn of the 1980s. Smart and forward-thinking, he was also inward-looking and skeptical about the ability of Canadian corporations to compete on the global stage. It never crossed McDougall's mind to license Labatt's flagship brands to other breweries around the world. Like many Canadian businessmen, McDougall failed to believe in the superiority of his firm's products and to look beyond the national boundary for opportunities for growth. "We believe that Budweiser will be a successful major brand for the company," stated McDougall, "to supplement the sales of its national brands: Blue, 50, and Lite."[78]

Having signed a ninety-nine-year licence to brew Budweiser in Canada, in the summer of 1980, Labatt rolled out the product in Alberta and Saskatchewan, a region where there had been a long tradition of brewing and drinking American-style lagers.[79] It wasn't until the following year that Labatt made Bud available to beer drinkers in Ontario, Quebec, and British Columbia. By 1982, Budweiser had captured roughly 7 per cent of the Canadian beer market.[80] Executives at Labatt were thrilled. "Bud's success in this large section of the industry's market has been nothing short of phenomenal," stated Sid Oland, who had succeeded Don McDougall as president of Labatt Brewing Company in 1980.[81] A fifth-generation brewer from the Maritimes, Oland had been around brewing all of his life. After graduating from Dalhousie University and Harvard Business School, he joined his family's brewing company, Oland and Son, in 1960. He had witnessed a number of profound changes in the way the industry operated while working at the family firm on the east coast. After joining Labatt in 1972, he had seen the further consolidation of the industry, the employment of women as sales agents, and the introduction of light beer. But nothing compared to the rapid rise of Bud, in his mind. "Frankly, I have never seen a new brand come into such large portions of the Canadian market with such velocity," Sid Oland marvelled, "and retain the ground it initially won."[82] With the licensing of Bud, the Americanization of Canadian brewing was underway. At a time when the global brewing market was starting to send the message that national distinctiveness sells well on world markets, Canadian brewers surrendered to foreign brands.

The other big Canadian brewers immediately took notice. For Carling O'Keefe, licensing the right to brew and market an American beer in Canada held out the

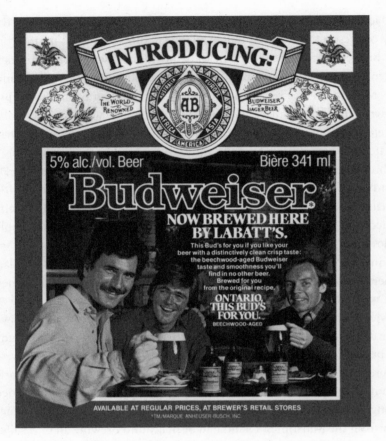

Figure 11.8 In 1980, after reaching an agreement with Anheuser-Busch to brew the "King of Beers" north of the border, Labatt launched Budweiser in Canada with a major advertising campaign.

possibility of reversing its fortunes. Once the industry leader, Carling O'Keefe had suffered during the 1970s from not having a national brand.[83] Executives hoped that licensing the right to manufacture a well-known American beer would give them a brand that they could promote from sea to sea. The decision was made that Miller High Life would be Carling O'Keefe's Bud. Carling launched Miller during the summer of 1983 and quickly gained a significant slice of the Canadian market. Two years later, Molson signed an agreement to brew Coors and Coors Light under licence in Canada. With each of the Big Three brewing a popular American beer, market share remained more or less the same as when the licensing started.

On 4 May 1982, Sid Oland was scheduled to appear on the CBC's current affairs program *The Journal* to answer questions about Labatt's decision to brew Bud in Canada. *The Journal*'s host, Barbara Frum, had a reputation for asking uncomfortable questions, so those at Labatt thought it best to prepare Oland for the interview. Executives anticipated that one of the questions Oland would be asked was whether Budweiser's sales had cut into the sales of Labatt's regular brands. "I can't get into the nitty-gritty of the numbers because that kind of information belongs to either insiders in the Company or the shareholders," Oland was prepared to answer. "But I can say that our major, mainline brands – 50 and Blue – have been impacted far less than the mainline brands of our competition."[84] The answer was true enough at the time. But within a year, a different picture had emerged. In British Columbia, where the market share of Labatt's flagship lager had fallen to 18 per cent by the spring of 1983, Budweiser was eating into Blue's share of the market. "Most of Budweiser users were previously Blue users," one internal report noted.[85] Likewise in Quebec, where Labatt 50 had a 19 per cent share of the market in 1983, there was evidence that "Budweiser should be considered as a threat to 50 since a good portion of Budweiser's users come from 50."[86]

In the short term, Labatt benefited from the production of Budweiser. But in the long run, the move served to cannibalize the sale of its own brands. To make matters worse, the brewing of American brands would ultimately serve to undermine the firm's international competitiveness. By the early 1980s, the signs were already pointing to the globalization of the brewing industry. But no one at John Labatt thought to ask: what products would the old London Brewery have to offer the world if its beer was American?

The Life and Death of the Stubby

At the same time that Labatt was licensing the right to brew American brands in Canada, it was making its own bottles look more American. During the 1960s and 1970s, the "stubby" bottle was ubiquitous in Canada. As the only acceptable container for beer, it filled fridges from coast to coast. The stubby was born in typical Canadian fashion. Brought into this world by committee, it was the offspring of practical concerns and the pursuit of profit. Well into the 1950s, Canadian brewers used a wide variety of beer bottles. Most were heavy, bulky, non-standard twelve-ounce "pint" and twenty-two-ounce "quart" beer bottles. Their long necks made

Figure 11.9 Labatt's regional beer brands, c. 1977. These brands, most of which were acquired during Labatt's geographic expansion during the 1950s and 1960s, were sold in smaller regional markets alongside Labatt's "national" brands, 50 and Blue. All Canadian beer was packaged in "stubby bottles" during the period 1961 to 1984.

them hard to store and added to the brewers' transportation costs. In addition, being made of green glass (for ale) or clear glass (for lager) meant that the hops in the beer were not protected from the damaging effects of ultraviolet rays, which could result in the beer spoiling and giving it a "skunky" taste.

The brewers wanted to solve these problems, and in 1958, the Dominion Brewers' Association set up a committee to study whether or not Canadians would be better served by inventing a new type of bottle. The objective was to create a universal container that would be used by every brewery for every type of beer. After three years of design meetings, market research, and overcoming bureaucratic red tape, the new bottle was introduced on 1 May 1961 for a six-month trial in two selected markets: Peterborough, Ontario, and Rouyn, Quebec. Soon after it was released nationally. Known originally as the "amber compact," because of its colour and size, the new bottle had a neck that was three inches shorter than the bottles previously used. Its truncated neck and wide body made it look stout or squat, which ultimately led to it being nicknamed "the stubby." While the public generally received the stubby favourably, not all Canadians took to it right away. Some people complained that it resembled a medicine bottle. Hotel waiters claimed that it was far harder to open than the traditional long-necked bottle. To remedy these problems, the bottle's original cone-shaped top was altered to the more familiar round shoulders.[87]

Despite some initial ambivalence on the part of the public, the Big Three liked the new bottle immediately for what it did for their bottom lines. "The standardization of bottles," Labatt's Paul Henderson stated in 1963, "has resulted in very significant savings."[88] While it held that same twelve ounces of beer, the stubby was lighter and stronger and much easier to store in cartons than the previous bottles. A twenty-four-bottle case of stubbies weighed five pounds less than a case of traditional long-necked bottles.[89] This translated into savings in numerous areas: in the bottle plant because of increased line speeds; in transportation because of weight reductions; in capital investment because less warehouse space was needed; and in materials because of reduced glass expenditures.[90] During the 1960s, the mass-produced brands of the Big Three began to look and taste increasingly similar.

At the beginning of the 1980s, the stubby's existence was in jeopardy as Labatt and the rest of the Big Three lobbied provincial governments to ease bottling regulations so that they could sell their beer in tall American-style bottles. The Canadian brewing industry's decision to reject the stubby in favour of taller bottles was strategic – albeit short-sighted – in that it served to strip Canadian beer of some of its Canadian-ness. The packaging switch was an attempt to set one brand apart from another by bottling in a distinctive package with new labelling and promotional support. But as with most competitive moves, once one company starts shifting its brands into new bottles, other companies quickly follow. The new bottles were designed to produce a significant shift in market share. But the cost was high. In 1984, Labatt wrote off $19.7 million in inventory of stubby bottles, spent approximately $40 million buying new glass, paid higher distribution costs because of the different bottle sizes, and spent many more millions to inform Canadians of the change.[91]

Dismissing the Microbrewery Revolution

By 1985, it was becoming clear that the go-go 1980s was shaping up to be a decade of revolutionary change. The brewing industry had been highly consolidated since the emergence of a Canadian brewing oligopoly during the 1950s and 1960s. For almost forty years, the Big Three had controlled nearly all the production of beer from coast to coast. In 1985, Labatt, Molson, and Carling O'Keefe produced roughly 97 per cent of the beer sold in Canada.[92] This virtual monopoly on sales, along with the fact that the flagship brands of the Big Three tasted more or less the same, gave birth to a microbrewery revolution. For the first time in decades, new breweries started to appear on the Canadian landscape in the aftermath of what was termed the "Real Ale" movement in Britain. In 1971, British drinkers began to mobilize against the bland, standardized products of mass production in support of beer conditioned in casks with no additives or preservatives. One of the people inspired by the Real Ale movement was Frank Appleton, a college-trained microbiologist who had worked for almost a decade at Carling O'Keefe before quitting and moving to the wilds of the Kootenays to start a new life as a homesteader and freelance writer.

In 1978, *Harrowsmith Magazine* published Appleton's article, "The Underground Brewmaster," in which he railed against big beer. "Like tasteless white bread and the universal cardboard hamburger," Appleton wrote, "the new beer [of the Big Three] is produced for the tasteless common denominator. It must not offend anyone, anywhere. Corporate beer is not too heavy, not too bitter, not too alcoholic, not too malty, not too gassy or yeasty."[93] Appleton's article was a call to arms for would-be craft brewers. He advised people to start brewing their own beer: not only was it much cheaper than the beer that Canadians were pur-

The Group of 50.

The Few.
The Proud. The 50.

Figure 11.10 As Canada became more racially diverse during the 1990s, Labatt's advertising moved away from suggesting an answer to the thorny question of "Who are we?" Taking its lead from such former artistic greats as Northrop Frye and the Group of Seven, Labatt returned to the safer approach of associating its product with the land. They tried to shift our attention from a historical quest for identity (Who are we?) to a spatial quest (Where is here?).

chasing at government-regulated outlets but also "if you did it right, you could make a better more satisfying drink than what the big guys produced."[94] The article caught the eye of John Mitchel, another ex-pat from England, who was running the Troller Pub in Horseshoe Bay, West Vancouver. Mitchel decided he wanted to build a brewery to supply his pub with real ale like he had tasted in England. Having read "The Underground Brewmaster," he knew he needed to conscript Frank Appleton to help him out. In 1982, Appleton and Mitchel built Canada's first craft brewery, Horseshoe Bay Brewery, in an empty 770-square-foot boat shop at Sewell's Marina in Vancouver. Over the next year, a handful of brew pubs opened across Western Canada, and in 1984, Vancouver's Granville Island Brewery became the country's first free-standing microbrewery. Other microbreweries soon followed, especially in those areas where there were a large number of ex-pats from Britain "thirsting for a good old pint."[95]

Initially, those at Labatt had little to say about the microbrewery revolution. In fact, they didn't even seem to comprehend that the revolution was against them. In June 1984, J.R. McLeod wrote to Labatt's vice-president of corporate development and public affairs, R.A. Binnendyk, stating that he had received a number of inquiries from liquor commission officials asking whether Labatt supported or opposed brew pubs. McLeod admitted he didn't know what to say and asked Binnendyk for "any thoughts which would clarify our attitude."[96] After some reflection, Binnendyk decided that Labatt's public stance should be that "we welcome" the brew pubs. "We usually cannot win a public debate against the small guy," R.A. Binnendyk stated on 9 July 1984, since "in most cases we end up with egg on our face."[97] Binnendyk suggested that Labatt "should appear to be welcoming people who might enhance the intrigue of the industry."[98] But behind the scenes, the company began vigorously lobbying various provincial governments to force the new brew pubs to carry its packaged beer – a further sign that those at Labatt misunderstood the meaning and significance of the craft brewing revolution.

Conclusion

The making of the Labatt's Blue brand was a complex process that consumed an enormous amount of resources. As a result, such a bold and innovative project was never undertaken again. The marketing decisions that Labatt made after solving the national lager problem did little to strengthen the competitive advantages of the firm. Unable to break with the traditional view of their industry as an oligopolistic battle for market share, Labatt chose to copy American-style beers and promote and package them in an American way. When that failed, they decided to brew the "real stuff" under licence. The myopic move served to cannibalize the sales of Labatt's own brands and helped Americanize the Canadian brewing industry. When the brewing industry became truly global after 1990, Canadian brewers no longer had unique, distinctively Canadian brands to offer the world.

One might argue that Labatt was just responding to a consumer demand – that Canadians wanted American-style beers and Labatt sensibly supplied them. To a certain degree, the assertion has an element of truth. In the 1980s, a thirst for distinctive-tasting beers existed. The lack of ingenuity on the part of Labatt and the rest of the Big Three gave rise to the craft brewing revolution. But Labatt's management failed to recognize the shift in North American consumer preferences – i.e., the rejection of homogenized product lines and the return to something more artisanal. Traditional brand loyalties were sagging in the age of heightened consumer preference. But one must remember that during the 1980s, the Big Three brewers controlled over 96 per cent of the market. What did they have to gain by brewing popular American brands under licence? The answer is: a slightly larger share of the domestic market. And that is the point. Labatt was representative of the Canadian corporate condition: an inability on the part of all but the most dynamic of Canadian corporations to look beyond the national boundary for opportunities for growth.

Less Beer, More Wine, and Other "Sexy" Things

Labatt's Diversification Drive, 1967–90

During the 1960s and 1970s, businesses around the Western world embraced diversification as a strategy for growth and survival.[1] Without entirely abandoning their old product lines, adventurous enterprises embarked upon the production of new commodities, thereby expanding their "basic areas" of manufacturing. As early as 1955, business theorist Peter Drucker began arguing that good executives could master certain general principles of management that were applicable in almost any business setting. Drucker's book, *The Practice of Management*, became standard reading for a whole generation of corporate executives and led to the widespread belief in "general management skills."[2] Given the currency of Drucker's ideas, it was not a great leap for many in the world of big business to conclude that "professional managers" could use their skills to leverage competencies across a multitude of businesses.[3] By 1969, over 90 per cent of the Fortune 500 companies were diversified to some extent and the drive for growth through diversification, in the words of one famous observer, "had almost become a mania."[4] This became the age of the giant protean corporation.

The diversification drive was in part a response to the rapidly changing macroeconomic environment. After the Second World War, many traditional industries experienced slower rates of growth as demographic shifts and technological innovations affected product markets. At the same time, intensified R&D and rising consumer incomes stimulated the production of new goods and services. The oil shocks of the 1970s and the subsequent stagflation further fostered diversification. Given the shifting socio-economic environment, many old industries, faced with diminished returns from mature product lines and plateauing demand, chose to diversify into related and unrelated areas of production. A large firm with many products in many markets was, in theory, less dependent on individual markets or technologies and was therefore less vulnerable to any single set of unfavourable circumstances.[5] Diversification was also, theoretically, a wise strategy for growth because it increased a firm's market power,[6] debt capacity,[7] economies of scale and scope,[8] and synergies between business units,[9] and internalized controls and costs. Diversification could thus be rewarding, but it took substantial resources and continual commitment. The timing and type of diversification was also crucial in determining its success or failure.

Diversification had long been a part of the brewing industry. During the nineteenth century, brewers diversified into real estate, purchasing pubs or taverns in order to have an exclusive outlet for their beer. To survive prohibition, North American brewers diversified into making near beer, soft drinks, ice cream, malt extract, cheese, maple syrup, and even ceramic tiles. But despite these early diversifications, very few brewers were significantly diversified prior to the 1960s. That changed, however, in the decades that followed.[10] Flush with cash from their beer sales, a number of breweries diversified into the production or distribution of other intoxicating beverages. For example, Heineken moved into the distribution of wines and spirits in the 1970s when it acquired Bokma Distillery, a producer of one of Holland's most popular gins. Other breweries diversified into foods and non-alcoholic beverages. For example, in 1969, Swedish brewer Pripps bought the seafood company Abba-Fyrtornet AB.[11] In 1978, British brewer Allied Breweries followed a similar strategy; in an attempt to ensure a steady cash flow and spread risk, it acquired J. Lyons & Co., a leading producer of cakes, cookies, and other confectionary foods.[12] The 1970s also witnessed well-established firms operating outside of the industry enter the beer business through the acquisition of existing firms. For example, in 1969, tobacco giant Philip Morris acquired the venerable Milwaukee brewer Miller with the objective of exploiting its core competency of marketing. Like cigarettes, beer was a mass-consumed product that relied heavily on brand advertising. After the acquisition, Philip Morris transferred some of its best marketing people to the brewery; they went to work on creating one of the most successful brands of all time: Miller Lite.

In Canada, a brewing oligopoly emerged earlier than elsewhere in the Western world, so Canadian brewers were among the first to diversify into other industries. The Canadian regulatory and cultural environment further fostered what the editors of *Fortune* magazine termed "the conglomerate commotion" in Canada.[13] Since the National Policy of 1878, Canadian manufacturers had preferred to be the big fish in a relatively small pond. Instead of doing one thing well the world over, most Canadian companies preferred to engage in many types of businesses at home. Since the 1930s, E.P. Taylor had run the Orange Crush soft drink company as an offshoot of his brewery acquisitions. During the Second World War, he had drawn together numerous food processing and retail companies into a holding company known as Canadian Food Products. Between 1945 and 1955, Taylor's Argus Corporation acquired scattered holdings in a range of diverse companies, including Dominion Stores, B.C. Forest Products, Hollinger Mines, Dominion Tar, and Massey-Harris. Virtually no industry was off limits.

Labatt's diversification drive started a little later than Taylor's. On 12 April 1967, Jake Moore told a group of financial analysts that Labatt would be diversifying into "new and exciting industries." The brewery had experimented with diversification before, having expanded into animal feeds and pharmaceuticals in the early 1960s. But these diversifications had not gone well, so Labatt was still predominantly a brewing company in 1967, with more than 85 per cent of its sales and profits coming from beer. "Beer is still king at Labatt's," Moore proclaimed in the heady spring days leading up to Canada's centenary.[14] Moore told those in attendance that day that the brewery was generating a healthy net free cash flow (i.e., the cash being generated from brewing exceeded the capital required for reinvestment, upgrading, and the maintenance of quality brewing facilities), which could be used to finance new business ventures. The stockbrokers liked what they heard – in part, because the market was rewarding high-growth companies with high stock prices. The only question they had for Moore was which businesses Labatt would be buying next.

Beer into Wine

The brokers soon had their answer: Labatt was expanding into wine.

Like brewing, winemaking involved the fermentation of agricultural products into alcohol. In addition, the marketing and distribution of wine occurred within the same regulatory environment as beer.[15] Admittedly, Canada was still a beer-drinking nation: in 1967, annual per capita consumption of beer reached a new all-time high of 18 gallons, whereas annual wine consumption per person was only 0.8 gallons. Still, the consumption of wine was increasing rapidly, having almost doubled since 1950.[16] The diversification into wine was deemed by those at Labatt to be "a matter of logical progression."[17]

The company's initial entry into the wine business came when it purchased the shares of Parkdale Wines. The Parkdale winery had been established in the 1930s as a 250-acre fruit farm on old Highway 8 in Grimsby, Ontario. By the 1960s, the winery was producing sherry, port, vermouth, flavoured wines, Champagne, and red and white table wine. Soon after the acquisition, Labatt renamed the winery Chateau Cartier Wines, after its flagship brand. As the 1960s ended, Chateau Cartier set up a subsidiary, Normandie Wines, to make and distribute wine on the east coast. Despite the concerted efforts of Labatt's management to develop a nationally distributed line of wines, it became apparent in the early 1970s that significant penetration of provincial markets could only be achieved by acquiring a winery with established listings in each of the provinces. Like beer, wine was heavily taxed when it was made outside of the province in which it was sold. The executives at Labatt decided to go the route taken on the way to becoming a national brewer. In 1972, Labatt purchased Casabello Wines Ltd of Penticton, B.C., and then Chateau-Gai Wines of Niagara Falls, Ontario, the latter acquisition signalling the company's commitment to the wine business.

Formed in 1928 by a merger of several small wineries, Chateau-Gai was run from 1936 to 1964 by Alexander Sampson, a one-time newspaperman. By the time of Sampson's death in 1964, the winery had established listings in almost every Canadian province. Following his death, the winery was purchased by a group of investors led by Thomas R. Comery. As the company's president and principal shareholder, Comery needed to be carefully courted. But as Labatt quickly found out, Comery would not be easily wooed. "Comery has been approached on more than one occasion in the past by Labatt concerning the acquisition of control of Chateau-Gai," Labatt's charismatic vice-president of corporate development, Peter Widdrington, told the board of directors in December 1972, "and he has shown little interest in any proposition put forward."[18] Comery's unwillingness to sell frustrated Widdrington, who was used to persuading others to do his bidding. Widdrington wasn't about to give up, however. It wasn't in his nature. He had accomplished almost everything that he had set out to do up until that point. And gaining control of Chateau-Gai was the next objective on his list.

Born and raised in Southern Ontario, Widdrington had attended Pickering College before entering Queen's University. Having received a BA in economics, Widdrington went to Harvard for an MBA. At Harvard, Widdrington met Michael Mackenzie, the eldest son of Hugh Mackenzie, who told him about the business of brewing at Labatt. When Widdrington returned to Canada after graduation, he contacted N.E. Peter Hardy, who had attended Pickering College in the 1930s.

Figure 12.1 Two Chateau-Gai wines, Capistro and Capistro Light.

Having recently been promoted to general manager of Labatt's Ontario Division, Peter Hardy hired Widdrington in the summer of 1955 and sent him to Toronto to work for Cy Wentworth as part of Labatt's sales force. As a twenty-five-year-old salesman, Widdrington toured the legion halls and bars of West Toronto extolling the virtues of Labatt's beer. "When asking someone to try a Labatt brand," he was instructed, "ask them to try it for 30 days. If they will do this for you, you have broken their 'habit ordering' and in all likelihood you have secured a new customer."[19]

Confident, personable, bright, and good-looking, Widdrington rapidly moved up the ranks at Labatt. His qualifications in marketing research, and planning development led to regional appointments, first in Ontario, then in Manitoba,

Figure 12.2 Peter Widdrington, c. 1975.

and subsequently in British Columbia. In 1968, he was sent to California to head
up General Brewing. When General Brewing was sold in 1971, Widdrington returned to London where he was groomed to be president. By then, he was already
a legendary figure in the company. Immensely popular, he regularly played hockey
with the company's employees in London. Widdrington stood in stark contrast
to Jake Moore. A flamboyant dresser with a salesman's flair, Widdrington wore
his blond hair rebelliously long for a Canadian executive. To those at the company,
Widdrington was a boy wonder.

When Comery rejected Labatt's initial takeover offer, Widdrington set in
motion a clever scheme to gain control of the winery. The plan was to approach
the other shareholders with a generous offer to purchase their shares. But before

that was done, Labatt contacted Comery and made the same offer to him, but with the additional sop of a powerful position at Labatt. It was too good an offer for Comery to pass up.[20] The acquisition of Chateau-Gai enabled Labatt to achieve its objective of forming a wine division with national distribution.

While the company's wine sales increased steadily during the first five years, the profit levels originally anticipated were never realized. In 1975, wine sales contributed just $195,000 to Labatt earnings, and declined in real terms thereafter.[21] The poor showing was due to a number of factors. In Quebec, Labatt continued to lose market share because of provincial government favouritism toward local wines.[22] Outside of Quebec, Labatt faced increasing competition from imported foreign wines, which enjoyed certain competitive advantages. For example, foreign vintners were able to manufacture their wines at a much lower cost than their Canadian counterparts, and in some cases their governments subsidized their export sales. By 1980, roughly 50 per cent of all wines sold in Canada were from foreign countries. The situation was made even worse by the fact that the Ontario government continued to require that Ontario vintners manufacture their wines from Ontario-grown grapes (which, at the time, were not as good as the grapes grown in Europe).[23] On the east coast, Normandie Wines had used European grape concentrates in its winemaking process. While deemed superior to the wines made from Ontario-grown grapes, the finished product was not as good as that of European nations. At a time when consumer tastes were becoming more sophisticated, domestically produced wines were shunned by Canadian consumers.

Flour, Pasta, and Candy

Caught up in the diversification mania of 1960s, Labatt's search for synergies saw the brewery diversify into food. Its first move came in 1968 with the purchase of Ogilvie Mills, a major Canadian food company that had been in operation since 1801 when Alexander Ogilvie built a small gristmill at Jacques-Cartier near Quebec City. By the end of the nineteenth century, Alexander's son, William Watson Ogilvie, had turned Ogilvie Mills into a force to be reckoned with in the milling industry. Even Charles A. Pillsbury, the American flour industrialist and co-founder of the firm that bore his name, had to tip his hat to William Watson Ogilvie's accomplishments. "Ogilvie," Pillsbury conceded in 1895, "is the largest individual flour miller in the world." When William Ogilvie died five years later,

Figure 12.3 Labatt's diverse products, c. 1977. Labatt's diversification drive through the 1970s and 1980s brought a variety of products under the corporate umbrella.

the direct association between the family and the firm came to an end. In 1902, Ogilvie's executors sold the company to a Montreal syndicate that changed the firm's name to Ogilvie Flour Mills Limited. During the Laurier boom from 1896 to 1911, the firm grew by manufacturing high-quality flour made from Western Canadian wheat and exporting most of it to Britain.[24] The company survived the Great Depression by adopting modern marketing methods, which included new packaging for its products. At the same time, the company diversified into specialty items. With demand for its products soaring during the Second World War, the company built cereal and feed mills in Montreal. After the war, Ogilvie joined the likes of Labatt, expanding by way of mergers and acquisitions. One of the biggest acquisitions came in 1954 when Ogilvie purchased Lake of the Woods Milling Company – maker of the popular Five Roses Flour brand. Thus, by the mid-1950s, Ogilvie was marketing a complete line of baking flours, cake mixes, and hot cereals. In 1959, Ogilvie's expansion took another large step forward with the acquisition of Catelli Foods of Montreal. Catelli specialized in supplying ready-made pasta to the increasing number of Italians immigrating to Canadian cities. Catelli was itself highly diversified, having expanded into sauces and pickles even before its purchase of Ault Milk Products Ltd and Habitant Soup. By 1967, Ogilvie was a major player in the Canadian food industry.[25]

The decision-makers at Labatt felt that Ogilvie would be a good fit because both companies "were basically converters of agricultural materials into food or beverage products."[26] While studies undertaken on the milling and baking industry in Canada showed that the consumption of flour had levelled off and export markets were uncertain, Ogilvie had an investment portfolio valued at more than $11 million.[27] In addition, its Catelli-Habitant subsidiary was still growing. Jake Moore assured a group of financial analysts that Ogilvie's strong financial position would be good for Labatt because it would provide his brewery with "a financial base from which we could develop."[28] The potential operating efficiencies and financial gains from the merger led Labatt's board of directors to authorize an offer of $60 million for Ogilvie, which would be financed largely by an exchange of equity.[29] By the end of January 1968, Labatt had acquired 97 per cent of Ogilvie's shares. The acquisition of Ogilvie virtually doubled Labatt's gross sales overnight and set John Labatt Limited on a path to becoming a major Canadian corporation.[30]

Labatt took another step along the trail in 1969 when it purchased a controlling interest in Laura Secord of Toronto. Laura Secord had been making candy in Canada since 1913 when Frank O'Connor opened his first sweet shop at 354 Yonge Street in Toronto. The twenty-eight-year-old entrepreneur wanted a clean, wholesome image that would appeal to Canadians. He described his candy factories as "studios," and in another moment of marketing genius, he decided to name his company after Canada's beloved heroine, whose exploits had been drilled into the heads of schoolchildren for generations. A chain of stores quickly followed. By 1950, there were ninety-six shops in Ontario and Quebec, and Laura Secord chocolate was a well-recognized Canadian brand.

But then, in October 1967, the American candy manufacturer and retailer Fanny Farmer acquired control of the iconic Canadian firm. The takeover caused economic nationalists to take note.[31] Economic nationalism had not faded from the Canadian scene following the thwarted takeover of Labatt. If anything, it had only become stronger. Even the once-tarnished Walter Gordon had regained his lustre. In the late 1960s, Gordon was talking tougher than ever about the need to do something to prevent Canadian companies from falling into American hands.

Along with Abraham Rotstein and author Peter C. Newman, Gordon established the Committee for an Independent Canada to promote Canadian economic and cultural independence. After collecting 170,000 signatures, the group presented a petition to Prime Minister Pierre Elliott Trudeau demanding limits to foreign investment and ownership. The unprecedented support for economic nationalism was also reflected in the literature of the period. A number of books, such as Richard Rohmer's best-selling, albeit un-Canadianly dramatic novel *Ultimatum* and Al Purdy's *The New Romans*, warned Canadians of the inherent dangers of American economic imperialism.[32] Some Canadians called on the federal government to "close the 49th parallel" so as to keep American capital out of the Canadian economy.[33] In fact, the government could start right now, many argued, by preventing the takeover of Laura Secord. But it was not to be. "The heart of Laura's story was that she outwitted the Yanks," lamented Scott Young of the *Globe and Mail*, "and now we have let her down ... They are carrying off our heroine."

Amid the rising tide of the "new nationalism" – as the economic nationalism of the 1960s and 1970s was termed – many Canadians saw the takeover of Laura Secord by Fanny Farmer as evidence that Canada was destined to become part of the republic south of the border. But just two years after the takeover, Fanny Farmer wanted out. Wanting in, Labatt paid cash for a 64 per cent share in the candy company that operated studios in Toronto and Montreal and distributed its products through roughly 200 of its own stores and 400 other outlets.[34] When Labatt acquired the historic candy-maker and brought it back to Canada, some hailed the London-based brewer as one of the saviours of Canadian capitalism. This was much to the liking of Jake Moore, who was increasingly making business decisions based on his perception of himself as a guardian of the Canadian economy. The repatriation of Laura Secord served to promote the image of a company that was prepared to assert sovereignty over the Canadian economy.

Unfortunately, the expansion into candy had done nothing to fatten Labatt's bottom line. Despite the introduction of a new line of candy, ice cream, and ready-to-eat puddings, Laura Secord lost over $4 million in 1974. The shortfall at Laura Secord was due, in part, to the high cost of living, which adversely affected candy sales. But the company also suffered from a lack of technical knowledge, leading to a great deal of inefficiency. For example, when Peter Widdrington visited Laura Secord's massive new plant in Scarborough, Ontario, he was shocked at the level of waste. "Here's this huge belt with Turtles moving along it and scads of women on either side of it, packaging the Turtles," Widdrington stated. "The only problem was the belt was moving about three times faster than the women were packing. And at the end of the belt there was a huge pile of Turtles on the floor. It must have been four or five feet high." Widdrington admitted that he did not know much about the candy business, but quickly added, "even I know that's not right."[35] To make matters worse, the retail staff was eating and giving away about 5 per cent of the company's inventory.[36] Ever the optimist, Widdrington refused to state that the move into confectionaries was a failure. Instead, he insisted that it was just one of a number of "false starts."[37]

Bringing Baseball to Toronto

Labatt had been interested in bringing a professional sports team to Canada since the late 1960s. In part, the interest was stimulated by a concern over Labatt's corporate image. A 1970 study by a young, brilliant sociologist named Michael Adams indicated that while many Canadians felt that Labatt was a "good citizen," they did not know that Labatt was owned and operated by Canadians. Many of those interviewed thought Labatt was owned by either Schlitz, Rothmans International PLC, or Pall Mall. According to the report, unlike Molson, which had a very positive association with the Montreal Canadiens, nothing specific came to mind when those interviewed thought of Labatt – "other than the fact that they made good beer." Adams's report confirmed the findings of an earlier study that Labatt was not doing a very good job with Ontario sports fans.[38] In his final report, Adams recommended that Labatt improve its image and its brand sales by "stressing its being a genuine Canadian company" and "associating itself intimately with some sports team."[39]

The idea was not new. Beer promotion through sport had been taking place for years. By sponsoring sports, brewers gained tremendous exposure before, during, and after the event. In addition, it created a positive association between beer drinking and the traits associated with sports: strength, vitality, health, fitness, speed, and endurance. Labatt's own research showed that beer drinkers tended to be sports fans and that "the vast majority of the population relates to sports in one way or the other."[40] Consequently, during the 1960s, Labatt intensified its association with sports. In 1969, after three years of unsuccessful attempts to become part-owners of the Vancouver Canucks of the Western Hockey League, Labatt tried, but failed, to purchase the Oakland Seals of the National Hockey League and move the team to Canada.[41] Unable to acquire a professional hockey team, those at Labatt turned their attention to baseball.

Figure 12.4 This Labatt advertisement from 1977 conveyed the image of a company that was progressive and everywhere. In tapping into the women's liberation movement of the 1970s, it was also one of the few Labatt ads that overwhelmingly featured women. During the 1970s, the lives of (mostly white, middle-class) women were transformed by advances in politics and medicine. Women began to think about careers as well as jobs and were able to consider divorce in a way that would have shocked their grandmothers. The fashions of the age captured the cultural shift, as more women chose to wear pants and not just skirts. In previous Labatt ads, when women were portrayed carrying a case of beer, there was no ambiguity about who it was for: the women's husbands. However, in this ad, there is a new level of ambiguity. The beer might well be for the woman herself, to consume on her own.

Beer had long been associated with the "old ball game." In the 1870s, George Sleeman, owner of Silver Creek Brewery in Guelph, Ontario, built a baseball field behind his brewery and sponsored a team to promote camaraderie and build bonds among his employees. Having pitched for the Guelph Maple Leafs in the 1860s, Sleeman was passionate about baseball. In 1877, he helped establish the International Association, the first serious rival of the National League. In the years following, the National League faced other challenges from upstart baseball leagues, some of which were backed by beer money. For example, when the American Association challenged the National League's monopoly on baseball in 1882, it did so by appealing to blue collars rather than bluenoses. The American Association's three-pronged strategy consisted of lower ticket prices, Sunday games, and alcohol in the stands. The National League scoffed at the new organization, referring to it as the "Beer and Whisky League." In the end, the National League withstood the challenge and absorbed the best players and teams of the American Association, which threw in the towel after the 1891 season. In a sense, however, the American Association had the last laugh – at least in regard to adult beverage concessions. The link between beer and baseball was forever forged.

Labatt was eager to exploit that connection. Executives at Labatt realized that in the years to come gains in brewing industry volume would be slowing down, so earnings growth would have to come from increased market share.[42] One way to achieve that was to breed brand loyalty by associating a sports team with the brewery. The brain trust at Labatt was not interested in baseball per se, but rather saw it as a means to an end. "We view our involvement in baseball," Peter Widdrington explained, "as an extension to our investment in the Ontario beer market, where a 1 percent point increase in market share represents a marginal profit of $1,500,000 at current [1974] prices and industry volume levels."[43] He continued: "Baseball is a great game ... It's fun to watch; it's sexy."[44] Widdrington believed that an association with baseball would improve not only the company's image but also its sales.

Labatt had the support of Toronto mayor David Crombie as well as Paul Godfrey, the powerful chairman of the Metro Council, who were eager to obtain a major baseball franchise to enhance the city's image. Canada's other major metropolis, Montreal, had already acquired a team, the Expos, with the strong financial backing of Charles Bronfman of Seagram Distillers. A team in Toronto would allow the two cities to continue their rivalry on the baseball diamond.[45] In 1974, Metro Council received a report showing that, in comparison to the twenty-four North American cities with major league baseball teams, Toronto ranked fourth in population. The same report showed that there were close to 5 million people within a 160-kilometre radius of the city and that the median household income ranked second among major league baseball cities. If major league baseball came to Toronto, the report predicted, attendance at the Canadian National Exhibition stadium (CNE) would be between 1.5 and 1.7 million in the first year alone. The figures led both the municipal and provincial governments to throw their support behind a deal.[46]

Initially, Labatt directed its efforts toward obtaining an expansion franchise in either the American or National League. Widdrington and those around him felt that baseball fans would identify with the gradual improvement of the team on the field and that any increase in start-up costs of the farm system would be more than offset by a lower initial payroll cost for the major league team. It soon became apparent, however, that expansion of the number of teams was highly unlikely due to the precarious economic situation in Canada and the United States. In the midst of the 1970s recession, very few major league owners supported expansion because certain existing franchises were in financial trouble.[47]

With obtaining an expansion team being out of the question, Labatt turned its attention to acquiring an existing franchise. In January 1975, Peter Widdrington met with Jerold Hoffberger, chairman of Baltimore-based National Brewing Company. Following a path established by brewers-cum-baseball-team-owners like Jacob Ruppert of the New York Yankees and August Busch of the St Louis Cardinals, Hoffberger blended the beer business with baseball ownership. Hoffberger became chairman of the Baltimore Orioles in June 1965 after National Brewery Company purchased a controlling interest from American financier Joseph Iglehart. The following December, the Orioles obtained slugger Frank Robinson from the Cincinnati Reds, which helped propel Baltimore to four pennants in the next six seasons. Hoffberger might have sold the team to Labatt in 1975 but for two issues: the expansion of the CNE in Toronto could not be completed for that year's baseball season and a lame-duck situation in Baltimore would have resulted in substantial operating losses. In addition, there were rumours that the League's board of governors would veto the deal because it would leave the Washington area without a major league baseball team.[48]

Unable to gain control of the Orioles, Labatt attempted to acquire the San Francisco Giants. Soon after the Giants came on the auction block in the summer of 1975, Widdrington met with Charles Rupert, the Giant's executive vice-president. The two men were on the verge of a deal when they hit a stumbling block: the Giants had nineteen years left on their Candlestick Park lease. The two sides could not agree on whether the vendor or the purchaser would be responsible for the liability.[49] Despite the uncertainty surrounding the deal, Widdrington got to work on putting together a partnership back in Canada. In September 1975, he instructed D.J. McDougall, head of Labatt brewery, to contact Montreal business magnate R. Howard Webster. In addition to owning hotels, real estate, and oil companies, Webster controlled Canada's most-read newspaper, the *Globe and Mail*. The two men met for a drink at the Windsor Hotel in Montreal, where McDougall informed Webster that he could buy in to the deal for $4.5 million. In return, he would get a stake equal to that of Labatt – i.e., 45 per cent. Webster asked a few questions and the deal was done.[50] The final 10 per cent in the franchise was offered to Labatt's principal banker, Canadian Imperial Bank of Commerce. The "Labatt group" – as the partnership was called – was prepared to make a total investment of $10 million.[51]

In February 1976, the mayor of San Francisco was able to persuade a few powerful businessmen to keep the team in the "City by the Bay." Fortunately for Labatt, major league baseball was again looking to expand its ranks. The expansion of the American League later that year to include Seattle promoted a similar expansion in the Eastern Division to even out the schedule of games. With the choice between Washington and Toronto, the American League owners voted overwhelmingly on 20 March 1976 to grant a franchise to Toronto. The Labatt group paid US$7 million to acquire Canada's second baseball franchise.[52]

Directors at Labatt selected the name "Blue Jays" from a list of 30,000 entries in a "Name the Team" contest. Having recently renamed their lager Blue, Labatt's executives hoped that fans would nickname the new ball team the "Blues." They were dismayed when fans began referring to the club as the "Jays." They had also hoped that beer would flow freely at the ballpark. While it was still illegal in Ontario to drink outdoors in public spaces, such as parks, beaches, the streets, and in stadiums, Labatt felt that there was a good chance that the law would be amended to allow beer drinking at the Jays games. After all, the last few years had seen a remarkable opening up to alcohol.[53] But Premier Bill Davis would have none of it. He knew that the population was more or less split on the issue of beer and baseball. A 1977 survey of 230 municipalities in Ontario showed that the communities were split down the middle over the issue of selling beer in sports stadiums. Without a clear majority in favour of beer and baseball, Bill Davis was loath to take decisive action on the liquor question.

Thus, when the Toronto Blue Jays took to the field for their first game on 7 April 1977, there was no beer to be had at the ballpark. Davis's advisers worried that he would be booed at the season's opener and suggested that he not attend. He went anyway, and Canadians showed their quintessential politeness by limiting their protests to a chorus of "we want beer."[54] In the years that followed, Jays' fans became increasingly frustrated at the inability to sit back and watch the game with a hot dog and a "cold one." What was even more infuriating to many game-goers was that while they sat in the stands – often in the rain or under the hot summer sun – the well-to-do watched the games from their private boxes where they enjoyed beer, wine, or hard liquor because they were able to get a "special occasion permit" from the Liquor Licence Board. Critics maintained that this was "unfair," "hypocritical," and "a double standard." "Why allow the wealthy to flaunt

Figure 12.5 Labatt's Blue advertisement, c. 1979.

their special status by drinking at ball games in front of the vast majority of us who cannot afford private boxes?" asked one disgruntled fan in a letter to the editor of the *Globe and Mail*.[55]

Both opposition parties saw the political advantages of defending the man in the stand. Ontario Liberal leader Stuart Smith stated that the ordinary working person should be able to drink beer at the stadium if people who can afford to rent private boxes are able to.[56] Those in the New Democratic Party agreed, adding that people did not go to baseball games to get tanked up on beer. They went for the baseball. Beer was simply a mild amenity to help the peanuts go down.[57] The argument in support of beer at the ballpark took a familiar form: People were going to drink. If there was no beer at the ball game, then many people would simply smuggle hard liquor into the stadium in wineskins, flasks, or small bottles. This would create a dangerous environment because the hard liquor drinker was "loud," "rowdy," "aggressive," and "violent." Beer drinkers, on the other hand, were "sedate," "merry," "moderate," and "family-oriented."[58] For five long years, Jays fans had to do without beer at the game. It was only on 7 July 1982 – on the very last day before a three-month recess – that the Ontario government reversed course and introduced its beer-in-the-ballpark legislation.

The dry spell, together with the shrinking Canadian dollar, had hurt the Blue Jays' finances. However, Widdrington continued to put a positive spin on matters, stating that the "yearly losses [at the club] which have flowed through to us have never exceeded $500,000 after tax." He was set on holding on to the ball club, in part because the Jays' worth went well beyond gate receipts and end-of-the-year profitability. As later surveys showed, Labatt's corporate identity was increasingly intertwined with its support for sport and, in particular, its ownership of the Toronto Blue Jays. In addition, few Canadians now questioned the nationality of those who owned the old London Brewery.[59] Even though the club often struggled on the field during the 1970s and early 1980s, Labatt exploited the relationship between beer and baseball in its advertisements (see figure 12.5). Across the nation, Blue Jays fans often showed their support for the team by ordering a Labatt Blue. Even better for those at Labatt, by the late 1980s, the market value of the Blue Jay franchise had increased by roughly 400 per cent since the first season's opening pitch.[60] Of all of the diversifications during this period, the expansion into baseball made the most sense.

The End of the Brascan-Labatt Relationship

With the diversification drive in full swing, the relationship between Labatt and its parent company was forever changed in 1979 when Brascan became the target of a hostile takeover. Being big was never a guarantee of survival, especially if a company's stock was widely held. During the early 1970s, Brascan had sold off a portion of its holding in Brazil and reinvested the proceeds in Canada. Under Jake Moore's leadership, Brascan diversified into hotels, cable television, pineapple plantations, financial services, and resource companies like Great Lakes Power Limited and Western Mines Ltd.[61] Brascan also owned one-third of the shares in John Labatt Limited, which constituted the largest block of shares held by any one investor. This gave Brascan a powerful position on Labatt's board of directors.[62]

Moore had never fully cut himself off from day-to-day operations at the brewery. On occasion, he would drop by the plant in London, making the thirty-minute drive from his finely appointed home on the outskirts of the Forest City. Moore felt that he still knew what was best for Labatt. His voice often dominated around the Labatt's boardroom table, where he continued to sit as chairman. He weighed in on all of the major decisions during the diversification drive. As Albert Tucker notes, Moore's "hands-on approach" brought into question "the meaning of Widdrington's role as chief executive officer at Labatt," and often left Widdrington "wondering how he could be his own man."[63] The tension between the two men reached an apogee in the spring of 1979.[64]

After the sale of its remaining stake in its Brazilian electrical utility in December 1978, Brascan had about $447 million in the bank. Such a large amount of cash on hand made Brascan an attractive target for corporate raiders. Knowing this, executives at Brascan's head office on the forty-eighth floor of Commerce Court West in downtown Toronto frantically searched for a solution that would protect the firm from predators and meet the demands of its 38,000 shareholders for a responsible return on investment.[65] In January 1979, it dawned on Jake Moore that Labatt might be used to protect its parent company. The first step would see Brascan use the mountain of money it had in the bank to purchase all of the shares in Labatt. At that point, Brascan would be Labatt's sole owner. The second step would see Labatt and Brascan engage in a reverse takeover, whereby Labatt would become the principal owner of Brascan. While Labatt would have a controlling interest in Brascan, the power would still lie with Moore because Brascan's management would remain intact and dominant.[66]

On 16 February 1979, Labatt's board members met at the offices of Goodman and Goodman, Barristers and Solicitors in Toronto. At the meeting, a task force was created to consider the merits of a reverse takeover.[67] This possibility infuriated Peter Widdrington, who expressed his profound opposition to any such deal and left the meeting. A number of other Labatt directors followed his lead.[68] When an independent financial adviser informed the board that Labatt's purchase of Brascan shares would "result in the reduction of the Corporation's capacity to borrow for other purposes and in a reduction in the book value of Labatt shares," the deal fell apart.[69]

With the proposed reverse takeover off the table, Brascan went shopping for another money-maker. It did not take long to find one. In May, Brascan made a move to acquire all of the outstanding shares in F.W. Woolworth Company of New York, which at the time was among the largest American chains of retail stores. Woolworth was huge. Even bigger than Brascan – a fact that led one observer to compare the proposed takeover to "Jonah swallowing the whale."[70] To get the deal done, Brascan would have to use all of its cash on hand and borrow another $700 million from the Canadian Imperial Bank of Commerce for a total of roughly $1.2 million.

To make matters even more complicated, while Brascan was trying to gobble up Woolworth's, the Bronfman brothers of Montreal were trying to acquire Brascan. Since January 1979, Peter and Edward Bronfman, through their holding company Edper Investments Limited and in close consultation with Jack Cockwell, their financial counsel, and Trevor Eyton, a Toronto-based corporate lawyer, had been buying up Brascan shares. The Bronfmans were not interested in owning Woolworth. Since Jake Moore would not abandon his plans to acquire the American retailer, the Bronfmans decided to outmanoeuvre him by acquiring 31 per cent of Brascan's shares on the New York Stock Exchange.[71] By early May, the Bronfman brothers had increased their stake in Brascan to 51 per cent, which was enough to enable them to elect the majority of the board's members and appoint the executive personnel. When that happened, the Woolworth purchase was abandoned and Jake Moore resigned as chairman and chief executive officer of Brascan.[72]

At the annual meeting of shareholders in 1979, Peter Bronfman and Trevor Eyton were elected to the Labatt board of directors and the relationship between Labatt's management and the board became much more stable. For Widdrington, the new Brascan ownership allowed him to operate without constant interference from above. To the extent that the new owners interfered at all, it was nearly always to show their support for Labatt's further expansion into diverse industries.

Doubling Down on Diversification

On 27 May 1980, Labatt's top executives met on the outskirts of Goderich, Ontario, at the luxurious Benmiller Inn & Spa. They were there to discuss the future direction of the corporation. Over the preceding decade, Labatt had become significantly less dependent upon its brewing business. In 1980, earnings from non-brewing operations accounted for 47 per cent of total operating earnings – up from 14 per cent ten years earlier. Peter Widdrington was pleased with the transformation and wanted to keep the diversification drive going, even though some theorists were now questioning the wisdom of the strategy. In 1980, Robert Hayes and William Abernathy, for example, wrote a scathing article in

Harvard Business Review entitled "Managing Our Way to Decline," which criticized the myopic management principles that had led to diversification and corporate America's competitive inertia.[73] Haynes and Abernathy had a point. Certainly Labatt's diversifications into candy and wine had not gone well. But Widdrington simply dismissed these early failures as "false starts" and determined to double down on diversification.[74]

Expanding into new areas of production in the United States had a particular appeal to Widdrington. He had spent several years in the Boston area while doing his MBA at Harvard and had subsequently lived and worked in California. He liked the changes that were taking place under President Ronald Reagan, the move away from the social welfare state to an environment that promoted strong property rights and deregulation. He was excited by the prospect of turning John Labatt Limited into a North American beverage and food-processing company. "We are looking at the U.S. for growth and expansion," Widdrington told a group of financial analysts in Toronto in January 1986. "It is very much part of our on-going plan."[75]

With the support of Brascan's board of directors, Widdrington focused the company's ambition in a southward direction. The cabal of senior executives around him constituted an informal planning committee that decided to expand into the U.S. dairy industry, which Widdrington was particularly bullish on. At a time when many observers categorized dairy as a mature, low-profit business, Widdrington saw things differently. "Some of the major national dairies are diversifying or moving out of dairy altogether," Widdrington stated, "and this creates opportunities for some of the regional players."[76]

In 1985, Labatt acquired Johanna Farms of Flemington, New Jersey. Started in 1927 by Max and Julius Piser, Johanna Farms was a dairy farm that processed milk from the owners' cows. In 1955, Eugene Goldman took control of the company and began buying milk from other farmers in the region; over time, the company became a major bottler (back when milk came in glass bottles) before changing to paper and plastic containers. When they were old enough, Eugene Goldman's sons, Peter and Kurt, began working their way up the company's ranks, with Kurt serving as general manager until becoming president in 1976. Under his leadership, the business added yogurt manufacturing and various types of juice products to what had mainly been a milk processing and distributing business. The Goldman brothers felt a strong family attachment to the firm and would only sell to Labatt if they could continue to manage the company. Widdrington agreed. But the Goldmans' had one more condition: Labatt would give financial support for Johanna

Farms' further expansion into beverages and specialty dairy items. Widdrington had no problem with this either. After all, the brewing side of Labatt was still generating a healthy cash flow: in 1985, it generated $80 million in operating profits. With the guarantee from Labatt in place, Johanna Farms' management engineered a buying spree, gobbling up Lehigh Valley Farms in Pennsylvania, Tuscan Dairy Farms in New Jersey, Queens Farms in the New York City area, and Greenspring Dairy in the Baltimore-Washington market. By 1988, Johanna Farms was twice the size it was when it merged with Labatt three years earlier.[77]

In Labatt's packaged-food operations, similar policies were applied to capital investment in plant improvements, product development, distribution, and further acquisitions. Initially, Catelli, which had been acquired as another small subsidiary of Ogilvie in 1968, formed a nucleus for growth in this group. Outside Canada, it had branches in the New England states and the Caribbean. The largest firm in the packaged-food group, however, was Chef Francisco, a processor of frozen entrees, soups, and desserts. Based in Oregon, Chef Francisco expanded its market throughout the western and central United States, and its operation from the supply of foods for airlines and institutions to retail distribution for consumer supermarkets. After 1984, further acquisitions in this group included Omstead Foods, a processor of frozen fish and vegetables; Everfresh Juice, a company that specialized in fruit-based beverages; and Pasquale Food Systems, Inc. of Birmingham, Alabama, which processed fresh pasta dishes for American supermarket delicatessens. Labatt's strategy continued to consist of encouraging the managers of the acquired firms to stay on and call the shots.

Conclusion

By the peak of its diversification diet in the late 1980s, Labatt had gobbled up pasta-maker Catelli, Chateau-Gai Wines, U.S. frozen-food-maker Chef Francisco, Omstead Foods (the world's largest processor of freshwater smelt), juice-maker Everfresh, dairy company Ault Foods, U.S. dairy company Johanna Farms, grain processor Ogilvie (the world largest producer of wheat starch and wheat gluten), The Sports Network (TSN), Discovery Channel, Réseau des Sports (an all-sports French-language channel), Supercorp, BCL Entertainment, and Dome Productions (a television and video post-production facility at the SkyDome). In total, during the late 1970s and 1980s, Labatt spent over $1 billion to acquire more than thirty different businesses.

Unfortunately for Labatt, the diversifications did not bring the riches that Wid-drington had promised, thus demonstrating the folly of management-by-MBA. The wine and juice businesses continued to underperform. Profits only materialized occasionally before both businesses were put on the auction block in the early 1990s.[78] Likewise, the dairy division was a continuous drain on the company's resources. Whereas Labatt's brewing division returned a profit of $218 million in 1993, the dairy division, which had a book value of $140 million, showed no profit at all. Milk and the products made from it could not be marked up with the same ease as beer. Earnings from Labatt's food group were also less than satisfactory. While the food division generated $3.35 billion in sales in 1990, it only produced $90 million in operating profits.[79] Brewing, on the other hand, generated almost $200 million in profits that year.[80] Like a number of Canadian companies, Labatt had diversified beyond what was optimal.

At its bloated heights, John Labatt Limited was an unwieldy combination of assorted assets. There was no discussion of how each business contributed to Labatt's "core competency" – something that C.K. Prahalad and Gary Hamel, in their 1990 prize-winning article in *Harvard Business Review*, claim is critical to a successful corporate strategy.[81] Nor was there any discussion of how Labatt would achieve synergy through its acquisitions. There was little sharing of activities and skills among the various divisions. To make matters worse, the firms that were purchased were often given free rein. Their managers had most of their capital requests satisfied, were subject to minimal performance reviews, and were handsomely rewarded with cash and stock options. What was lacking was any clear understanding of exactly how the acquired firms related to each other and what factors contributed to success.[82] Like the feudal lords that Adam Smith scorned for trading their leadership for a pair of silver buckles, Labatt's executives were myopic in that their decisions were aimed at increasing short-term earnings rather than promoting long-term growth. They were also motivated by ego. Determined to become one of Canada's biggest diversified companies, Labatt missed out on being part of the early phase of the globalization of the brewing industry. The diversification drive consumed so much of Labatt's time and cash that it reduced the company's ability to seize a number of opportunities that might have added to its strength as a beer maker. While beer continued to bring in the money, much of it was wasted on poorly managed enterprises that were unrelated to Labatt's core competency. In the world of big business, there is often a price to be paid for short-sightedness and ego-driven management. Just how great a price Labatt paid would be revealed in the years that followed.

Into the Blue

The Takeover of John Labatt Limited, 1990–95

Just after midnight on 18 May 1995, two men in raincoats, with their collars turned up and their heads hung low, walked into the swank Four Seasons Hotel in Toronto just a few minutes apart. One of the men was Gerry Schwartz, the president and CEO of Onex Corporation, which had been devouring companies like a hungry shark over the last decade. Now the corporate vulture was stalking new prey. The other man was George Taylor, the unassuming CEO of John Labatt Limited. Taylor did not want to be there that night. But he had no choice. Due to a series of dubious decisions and a bit of bad luck, the 148-year-old company that he ran had become a target for takeover. Schwartz wanted to buy the company and sell off everything but the money-spinning brewery. Taylor didn't care for Schwartz and cared even less for his low-ball offer. Just a few years earlier, Taylor could have refused the meeting, but all the structures that had protected the brewery were gone and the winds of globalization were blowing.

The Globalization of the Brewing Industry

Globalization came late to the Canadian brewing industry, as it did to the business of brewing elsewhere. The close cultural tie of beer to the national identity proved hard to abandon. But other industries had set the course by stretching the appeal of their brands. Since the Second Industrial Revolution in the late nineteenth century, many firms – with competitive advantages derived from economies of scale and scope – had established production facilities in foreign markets. Geographic expansion into distant lands provided a way for modern industrial enterprises to exploit their comparative advantages. The automobile industry, for example, had begun to globalize in the earliest days of mass production. By 1928, Ford and General Motors were assembling vehicles in twenty-four countries, including Japan, India, Malaysia, and Brazil. Ten years later, both automakers were operating large-scale "transplant" facilities in Europe. After the Second World War, an increasing number of businesses – a few of them Canadian – embraced a strategy of foreign direct investment as a means of global growth.[1] Many firms were motivated to move across the world due to maturing markets at home. For example, American fast food giant McDonald's went global beginning in the 1970s, erecting its golden arches in places where there was an emerging class of consumers with the money to spend on family entertainment. By the 1990s, Big Macs were being sold in twenty nations around the globe, including Brazil, China, and Russia.[2] The homogenization of pop culture – what sociologist George Ritzer termed the "McDonaldization" of the world – was underway.[3] Firms from around the world became successful challengers to what eminent business historian Alfred Chandler termed "first movers" – those industrial organizations like Ford, GM, RCA, DuPont, and Dow that had established branch plants in distant lands early in the twentieth century.[4] Having relentlessly expanded the output of their standard production line (i.e., increased their scale) and introduced new sorts of products (i.e., increased their scope), post-war industrial firms invested in new products and new geographic markets in order to grow.[5] The global enterprise evolved naturally out of the successful national corporation.

For those firms in the brewing industry, however, globalization did not occur until the end of the twentieth century. Consumer taste, entrenched regional brands, barriers to trade, and convoluted distribution systems made brewing a form of trench warfare: gains for those with global aspirations came only slowly. During the 1980s, a small group of exceptional brewers like Heineken of Holland, Guinness of Ireland, SAB of South Africa, and Kirin of Japan were able to gain a global presence despite the relatively small size of their domestic markets. These forward-looking brewers pushed taste and culture in a new direction and succeeded by developing the corporate strategies, global brands, and market knowledge that allowed them to penetrate foreign markets.[6]

Canadians had witnessed this early global push first-hand when Australia's Elders IXL (pronounced I EXCELL) Limited declared its intention in 1987 to shake up the Canadian brewing industry by purchasing Canada's third-largest brewery, Carling O'Keefe. The forty-five-year-old head of Elders, John D. Elliott, believed that in the future "a handful of international brands will dominate the beer business" and he wanted the firm's flagship brand, Foster's Lager, to be one of them.[7] Foster's Lager gained international popularity following the launch of an advertising campaign that featured Paul Hogan, star of the 1986 sleeper-hit film *Crocodile Dundee*. Elliott planned to use Carling O'Keefe's plants to further "Fosterize" the world. "The takeover [of Carling O'Keefe]," Elliott told the Canadian press, "would allow Elders … to serve America and Asia."[8] With that strategy in mind, Elliott agreed to pay tobacco giant Rothmans $392 million for Carling O'Keefe. When Elders IXL and Molson subsequently became partners in 1989, it reduced the number of big breweries in Canada to two.

By global standards, Canada's biggest breweries were inefficient. The structure of the Canadian beer industry was such that it worked against economies of scale. The system of provincial trade barriers meant the industry's production system was hopelessly fragmented in numerous uncompetitive plants across the country. Provincial rules forced the operation of breweries of suboptimal size. According to a Conference Board of Canada report, the minimum plant size necessary to achieve ideal manufacturing efficiencies produced an annual output of at least 2.2 million hectolitres of beer.[9] Other reports put that figure higher.[10] But by the mid-1980s, only five of Canada's thirty-eight breweries were operating at the 2.2-million-hectolitre capacity (all of them in Ontario), and about half of Canada's production came from suboptimal plants. The same study concluded that beer production per plant in Canada was just over one-quarter the level, on average, of plants in the United States.[11] Canadian breweries were operating at a significant disadvantage relative to the optimal American plants. These findings led the Brewers Association of Canada to conclude that the Free Trade Agreement between Canada and the United States of America (FTA) being negotiated would be the death knell of domestic brewing. It threatened the federal government that if the protective practices were not grandfathered under the new accord, then the brewers of the nation would come out publicly against the entire FTA.[12] The threat worked, and brewing was one of only three industries excluded from the 1988 agreement.[13] However, the protection did not last long. Just two years later, G. Heileman Brewing Company, maker of Lone Star and Rainier beers, petitioned the U.S. government to challenge the Canadian trade barriers in court for violating both the FTA and the General Agreement on Tariffs and Trade (GATT). In October 1990, GATT ruled in favour of Heileman and gave Canada deadlines of March 1992 to resolve the discriminatory price markups and July 1992 for the removal of all other barriers. The ruling meant that Labatt could no longer hide behind the tariff wall, in an artificial environment free of price-based

competition. For the first time, Labatt was forced to compete in an open, integrated, international marketplace. To survive, it would have to have significant
international activity and competitive advantages over foreign firms.

Despite the liberation of markets and the increasing international activity, in
comparison to other industries in 1990, brewing remained relatively unconsoli-
dated and largely local.[14] Parochialism dulled the entrepreneurial verve of most
brewers; they could only think inside of their regional/national boxes. But that
changed during the 1990s, as the industry became more concentrated and truly
global. The industry was propelled toward globalization in part because traditional markets had gone flat. In the main markets of northern Europe, consumption remained static or declined after the mid-1970s, making it difficult for
brewers to raise the price of their brands in established markets. In Belgium, for
example, annual per capita beer consumption declined substantially during the
period, from 130.5 litres to 104.0 litres.[15] As a result, Belgium's biggest brewer,
Interbrew, geared up for a global quest. Facing a similar decline in consumption
at home, Danish brewers Carlsberg and Tuborg established new breweries either
in countries that were large enough to obtain the economies of scale necessary
for profitable production or in developing countries with little or no previous
experience in brewing and with high protective tariffs. The first of these breweries
were established in Africa and Asia, but then Tuborg and Carlsberg began brewing
in England, Sweden, and Germany, sometimes by licensing the right to brew their
flagship brands to native firms. By 1990, more "Danish" beer was brewed abroad
than in domestic plants.[16] Likewise, Holland's Heineken and Ireland's Guinness
had long derived a substantial percentage of their sales from outside of their home
continent.[17] Initially, they did this through exports, then by entering into licensing
agreements, and finally by way of foreign direct investments. By the end of the
1980s, 40 per cent of Guinness's total sales and 25 per cent of Heineken's came
from outside of Europe.

In Canada, the brewers were also running out of domestic customers. After
decades of galloping post-war growth, beer consumption had fallen flat. The first
of the baby boomers were now in their mid-forties and drinking less than when
they were in their twenties and thirties.[18] Research showed that, in part, this was
because some beer drinkers were becoming tired of the bland-tasting, modestly
packaged brands of the Big Three. With tastes becoming more sophisticated,
many boomers switched to drinking wine or spirits, which had a cachet that beer
did not.[19] The executives at Labatt could take some comfort in the fact that
Generation Xers were proving to be a hedonistic lot. They liked their beer as much

as the baby boomers before them, and had a greater propensity to binge drink.[20] In addition, studies indicated that female Gen Xers were far more likely than the women who preceded them to drink beer on a regular basis. The problem was that Gen X was a small cohort, which meant per capita beer consumption began to fall. After hitting a post-war high in 1975 of 87.0 litres per capita annually, beer consumption fell to 77.1 litres per person in 1990. But unlike their European competitors, Canadian brewers had diversified into related and unrelated industries rather than internationalizing their beer operations.

Further fostering globalization was the fact that, while traditional markets were stagnant, emerging markets were rapidly expanding. Between 1975 and 1995, for example, per capita consumption of beer in Mexico increased by 33 per cent.[21] Brazil and China also witnessed a rapid rise in beer consumption. As barriers to international trade were lowered during the last two decades of the twentieth century, brewers from established markets rushed to gain a foothold in the emerging markets of the world.

The 1990s was a decade in which the leading brewers – first movers – in advanced economies launched aggressive global campaigns, resulting in an unprecedented global consolidation. To survive and grow within this environment, firms had to be nimble, developing and redeveloping the strategies and structures necessary to give them advantages vis-à-vis their competitors. If a firm failed to develop these advantages, it often became prey for those leading brewers that were seeking to extend their global reach.

In this predatory global environment, the maxim became "hunt, or be hunted." The increased competition in the global marketplace prompted companies to embrace mergers and acquisitions as a strategy for growth and survival. For Canadian firms, the possibility of being hunted became even more likely with the dismantling of the regulatory regime that had protected them for more than a century. As an early sign that Canada was now "open for business," the Progressive Conservative government of Brian Mulroney replaced the Foreign Investment Review Agency with Investment Canada in 1985. The subsequent ratification of the North American Free Trade Agreement (NAFTA) in 1992 further acknowledged a major shift toward globalization. The Mulroney government never blocked a single takeover under the Investment Canada Act. Nor did its two Liberal successor governments under prime ministers Jean Chrétien and Paul Martin. After decades of government protection, the trade barriers finally came crashing down. There was now – in the words of business historian Michael Bliss – "less place to hide."[22]

For those at John Labatt Limited, the challenge was to do what the Canadian banks had done at the end of the nineteenth century: be "quick to the frontier."[23] They would have to seek out new consumers in emerging markets while gaining market share in those markets that had already been established. If they did not prey upon, they would be preyed upon. There were already clear indications that the brewers that would do best would be those who had been "sticking to the knitting" – to use Tom Peters and Robert Waterman's famous phrase: those producing and distributing beer in their home markets while looking for new opportunities around the world.[24]

"Back to Basics"

In July 1989, as the Rolling Stones tuned up for their *Steel Wheels* tour – being promoted by Labatt's subsidiary Concert Productions International – the consultants at Sherbrooke and Associates put the final touches on a strategic review for John Labatt Limited. The purpose of the review was to assess the company's strategy, management style,- and organizational structure.[25] Other than praising the positive way that the brewery was being run, the report had little good to say about the operations of the firm. It was highly critical of most of its non-brewery operations. As a result of the diversifications of the 1970s and 1980s, John Labatt Limited (JLL) had become an unwieldy assortment of disharmonious parts. It had lost sight of its "knitting." "JLL is in too many weakly related businesses to manage them well given the lack of strong interdependencies across businesses and insufficient management talent," read the report.[26]

The consultants held nothing back. JLL's senior management had asked for a thorough and honest assessment of its operations and those at Sherbrooke and Associates had promised to deliver, even if it meant criticizing those in charge. There was a privileged frat-boy mentality at John Labatt Limited, Sherbrooke and Associates maintained. The constant flow of profits from the brewery had led those at JLL to take an easy-going "non-confrontational management style" that was undermining the overall performance of the corporation. Those at Sherbooke and Associates were flabbergasted to learn that, to make matters worse, "performance reviews had become rituals of reviewing the numbers rather than analysing them."[27] According to the business consultants, JLL's culture of conflict avoidance had "encouraged a kind of pork-barrel decision-making process where each manager refrains from saying anything critical, even if constructive, about

Figure 13.1 In 1989, Labatt sponsored the Rolling Stones' *Steel Wheels* tour and promoted it through its subsidiary Concert Productions International.

another manager's plans or performance in return for such behaviour being reciprocal."[28] As a result, divisions were being inefficiently run, resources were being wasted, and strategic opportunities were being missed.

Sherbrooke and Associates concluded that John Labatt Limited was in too many businesses that were underperforming. The solution to JLL's problems lay in "getting back to basics." Making beer was what Labatt did best, and Sherbooke and Associates recommended it should do that and little else. Virtually all the other businesses should be sold. "The packaged food business should be exited as soon as possible," the business consultants insisted, "the juice business should be fixed and sold, and the grain business should be sold or restructured."[29]

The recommendation was in line with the business philosophy of the age. Whereas the dictum of big business during the 1970s was "diversify, diversify, diversify," during the final two decades of the twentieth century, it was get back to basics.[30] Corporate managers had come to the realization that they could not manage everything and anything, contrary to what management maharishi Peter Drucker had once preached. The cult of the MBA was beginning to be questioned. Instead, managers needed to refocus on activities related to their core business. The new generation of management gurus promised that this business strategy would bring positive results. For example, London Business School professor of business leadership Constantinos Markides stated that by getting back to basics, firms could streamline their operations and improve their competitiveness so that they could be more efficient global competitors.[31] Within this environment, the companies to watch were no longer the large multi-faceted businesses it had celebrated in the 1960s and 1970s but rather those that were highly focused, with a well-defined market niche – companies like IKEA, manufacturer of affordable home furnishings, and Apple Inc., maker of personal computers.

The back-to-basics movement was made even more pressing by the emergence of takeover artists who aimed to acquire and then break up any company with a depressed stock price. During the 1980s and 1990s, buying and selling corporations became a business in its own right, abetted by huge blocks of shares that pension funds and collective investors could trade. The diversification drive of the previous two decades had led to the creation of a number of conglomerates that were so big and unwieldy that the value of the individual units was greater than the value of the corporate whole. Corporate raiders like Henry Kravis, Ronald Perelman, Carl Icahn, T. Boone Pickens, Gerry Schwartz, and Mitt Romney began buying controlling interest in these conglomerates and then breaking them up and selling off the assets at a profit. Investment banking firms like Drexel Burnham Lambert in New York and Gordon Capital Corp. in Toronto set up blind pools of capital for corporate raiders. Fuelled by junk bonds, takeover artists raided corporate North America seemingly at will, and made vast fortunes in the process. In their heyday, they hobnobbed with the junk-bond king Michael R. Milken at his annual "Predators' Ball." The threat of a hostile takeover caused companies to refocus on their core products and competencies and return to a more optimal level of diversification. The trend in business in the late 1980s and early 1990s – in the words of *The Economist* – was toward firms "drawing in their horns, not pushing them out."[32]

When the consultant's report reached the desk of Peter Widdrington, he knew his days were numbered. As the driving force behind Labatt's diversification, Widdrington suspected he would be blamed for the excesses of the 1980s. He was right. Just two months after Sherbrooke and Associates issued its scathing report,

Labatt's Edper-Brascan ownership asked Widdrington to step down as president and chief executive officer of John Labatt Limited. To ensure a smooth transition, the board invited Widdrington to stay on as chairman and gave him the opportunity to recommend his replacement as CEO. It did not take him long to produce a short list of names, which included George Taylor, president of Labatt's food business; Ed Bradley, Widdrington's right-hand man in corporate development and planning; and Sid Oland, president of Labatt Breweries. Being so closely tied to Widdrington and the diversification drive of the 1980s, Bradley was never seriously in contention for the top job. On the other hand, what Taylor had going for him was that he was the antithesis of the easy-going and glamorous Widdrington. Quiet and thoughtful, the father of four was a solid and reliable numbers man. Having begun his career at Labatt's Ontario brewing division in 1960, Taylor had front-line experience on the brewing side of the business. But Taylor had been in charge of a division that had not shown much growth over the last five years. The board of directors decided to appoint Sid Oland as president and CEO of John Labatt Limited.[33]

Oland was a beer guy down to the bottom of his glass. A bear of a man, he had a casual, slightly rumpled look about him, and a restrained demeanour, which led some to mistakenly conclude he was arrogant and sullen.[34] The great-great-grandson of James Oland, who had established a brewery in Dartmouth, Nova Scotia, in 1867, Sid Oland knew the beer business as well as anyone at Labatt. After a classical training at Bishop's College School and Dalhousie University, he headed off to the banks of the Charles River in Boston to get an MBA. After graduating from Harvard, he entered the family business as a sales trainee.[35] When Oland and Son was acquired by Labatt in 1971, he joined the London-based brewery. In 1973, Oland was moved to Labatt head office; a year later, he was appointed general manager of Labatt's Saskatchewan brewery. He held the position on the Prairies until 1976, when he returned to the city of hops and barley to become general manager of Labatt's Ontario breweries.[36] In 1980, he was appointed president of Labatt Brewing Company. During his time as president, from 1980 to 1989, the brewery's gross sales tripled and profits more than quadrupled. In the years after ratification of the FTA, Oland set out to make the brewery a low-cost manufacturer of high-quality mass-produced beer. These accomplishments led the board to conclude that Oland was the right man to return Labatt to its former glory as a focused and profitable beer company.

While Taylor did not get the uppermost post, the analytical accountant was assigned the critical task of selling off Labatt's non-core assets. As the new executive vice-president of John Labatt Limited, Taylor did not waste any time getting down to business. In late 1989, he orchestrated the sale of Labatt's Canadian wine-making operations, Chateau-Gai, and pasta maker Catelli. Financial analysts praised the act. "Wine in Canada is not a growth business," stated Jacques Kavaflan of Midland Doherty in Montreal. "Beer is more profitable, and they've got a leading position in the beer market."[37] Shortly thereafter, Taylor sold Labatt's interest in Zymaize artificial sugar and the firm's maple syrup–making business in Vermont. Then on 14 May 1991, Taylor placed a collection of largely U.S. food holdings on the auction block in the hopes of raising $350 million. Among the businesses up for sale were Chef Francisco's frozen soups, Pasquale's frozen pizza, Omstead Foods, and Oregon Farms grocery products. Labatt's money-losing U.S. juice and milk businesses were not included in the sale because they were deemed "too difficult to sell" at that time. As one analyst succinctly put it: "I'm not sure who would want to buy them."[38] The units on the block together employed 3,500 people and generated sales of about $475 million.[39] Again, market watchers liked the move. "Labatt has to get back to basics," stated Michael Palmer, an analyst with McCarthy Securities Ltd, "and the more moves it makes in that direction the more encouraged we are."[40] Under fifth-generation brewer Sid Oland, Labatt's master plan was now to do what it did best – make and market beer – and to do it in more places around the globe. There would be challenges, of course. Given that Labatt was a latecomer to the global game, growth opportunities would be harder to find. Nevertheless, Oland was convinced that Labatt needed to try.

"Overseas for Opportunities for Growth"

In September 1990, Labatt's new president and CEO addressed the shareholders of John Labatt Limited. "We will continue to look overseas for opportunities for growth," Sid Oland stated.[41] There was a certain irony in a Maritimer telling Central Canadians where the future lay. Of all the markets around the globe, Europe still had the greatest appeal to those at Labatt. Having only recently gained a foothold in the United Kingdom, Oland decided that Labatt should push on to the Continent.[42]

Of the various continental markets, Italy was deemed to be the one that offered the greatest opportunity for Labatt – despite the fact that since the days of the Roman Empire, Italians had been wine drinkers with little appetite for beer. As late as 1957, 70.2 per cent of the middle classes and 83.3 per cent of the lower classes never drank beer.[43] Nevertheless, those at Labatt were encouraged by the fact that major economic and social developments since the 1970s had brought about a shift in drinking habits. Adjustments in working schedules and meal routines had led to a significant increase in beer consumption between 1970 and 1990. By 1990, the per capita consumption of beer in Italy was 25.1 litres per annum. While a drop in the bucket compared to beer consumption in Belgium, Germany, the United Kingdom, Canada, and the United States, it was a remarkable rise from the per capita 11.3 litres consumed by Italians in 1970. And while Italians still loved their wine, the market share for beer had increased almost fivefold between 1970 and 1990, up from 3 per cent to 15 per cent of all alcohol consumed.[44] Those at Labatt saw this as a positive trend that would continue in the future.

The question for those at Labatt was how to break into the Italian market. As in Canada, the brewing industry in Italy had become increasingly concentrated since the end of the Second World War. By 1970, the top four breweries controlled almost 70 per cent of domestic production.[45] These brewers increasingly faced competition from foreign brewers, like Heineken, which had entered the Italian market after the ratification of the Treaty of Rome in 1957. While Heineken's approach was to build a plant in Italy, other brewers opted to sign agreements with Italian brewers to have their beer brewed under licence.[46]

Labatt, however, decided on neither approach and, instead, broke into the Italian market by purchasing a couple of smaller regional breweries. In 1990, Labatt acquired an interest in Italy's number-six brewer, Prinz Brau, a low-end player in the market.[47] Labatt acquired it more for its excess production capacity than for its portfolio of what Sid Oland described as "bargain-basement brands."[48] The second brewer that Labatt purchased was more promising. Founded in 1859 and into its fifth generation of family ownership, Birra Moretti was based in the more efficient and more industrialized northern region of Italy and was the country's seventh-largest brewer. Although heavily in debt, Moretti produced a handful of premium brands that were well known throughout the country to young Italian men who had spent time in the north during their military service. The problem was that these former soldiers, as well as the rest of the Italian population, could not always get Moretti's beer – it was not widely available in other parts of the country. Oland sought to change that by exploiting a great Canadian talent of turning regional brewers into national ones. Labatt paid about $70 million for a controlling interest in the two breweries.

At the time of the acquisitions, Sid Oland told investors that Labatt had made its Italian investment so as to be positioned in continental Europe in time for the economic union of the European Community in 1992.[49] Unstated was Labatt's desire to turn the wine-loving Italians onto beer.[50] "The market will develop and we'll be there," Labatt's Bill Bourne optimistically stated. A cerebral, unassuming marketer who had worked for Carling O'Keefe before joining Labatt in 1989, Bourne was assigned the task of integrating Birra Moretti and Prinz Brau into a single operating unit.[51] Oland's stated goal was to double the Labatt's share of the market from 10 to 20 per cent "over the next few years."[52] It wouldn't be easy. In order to make money in Italy, Labatt would have to cut through the infamous Italian red tape and deal with the Mafia and a price system that heavily taxed beer and not wine.[53]

In the first year following the acquisitions, Labatt concentrated on producing beer and reorganizing the internal structure of its Italian operations. Once that was accomplished in the fall of 1991, the company began work on the public relations and marketing side of the trade. That same year, Labatt introduced John Labatt Classic to the Italian market. The going was tough at first, and did not produce the profits that were initially anticipated. "We were losing a million dollars a month," Bourne recalled.[54] Nevertheless, the growth in sales gave Bourne and his colleagues at Labatt reason for optimism. While the Italian beer industry grew at 6.7 per cent in 1990, the growth of Birra Moretti – as Labatt's Italian operations were named – reached 35 per cent, propelling the company from seventh to fourth place in the Italian brewing industry.

Appointed as general manager for a six-month term, Bourne ended up staying for five years. In those five years, Moretti doubled its production and tripled its revenue, and the company went from losing $1 million a month to making $5 million a year. It was an accomplishment in which Labatt's senior management took a good deal of pride. "We are EBIT+ [earnings positive before interest and taxes] in Italy," George Taylor proudly proclaimed in April 1994.[55] The only problem was that Birra Moretti was a small game. And very few outside observers believed that acquiring Moretti was a big enough move to make Labatt a major player on the world stage. "It is major in the sense that for the first time they're brewing in continental Europe," industry expert Jacques Kavaflan stated, "but I can hardly get excited about it."[56]

On those few occasions when making a blockbuster international acquisition was debated around the boardroom table at Labatt, fear and hesitancy won out over daring and determination. At a time when the industry was witnessing a wave of global mergers and acquisitions, those at Labatt debated buying Australia's Bond Breweries for as much as $1.8 billion.[57] But the size of the deal and

Figure 13.2 Labatt launched John Labatt Classic in 1985 to tap into the small growing segment of beer drinkers looking for more up-scale brands.

the maturity of the market caused those at Labatt to get cold feet. Labatt also half-heartedly went after Spain's largest and fastest growing brewery, Cruz del Campo, maker of the country's most popular Pilsner, Cruzcampo.[58] But again Labatt lost its nerve during the courtship, and the icon of Andalusia went to Guinness for $1.2 billion.[59] With so many big breweries in the global hunt, easy prey was increasingly hard to find. When game was spotted, those who moved fast and fearlessly ended up with the prize.

Unable to clinch a really big deal, Labatt dedicated more capital and resources to its British venture.[60] Its initial foray into Britain had not gone well, in large part because of Labatt's inability to get its product into the hands of consumers. To be sure, the licensing agreement with Greenall Whitley had allowed Labatt to hurdle the tariff moat. But once in Britain, Labatt found it difficult to connect with consumers. Labatt subsequently signed agreements with a number of other local breweries to make its beer under licence. To ensure the quality of its product, Labatt sent a team of technical experts to Britain to keep an eye on the production process.[61] Reports indicated that there was nothing wrong with the way the beer was being produced. Nevertheless, the Brits weren't buying it because of deeply engrained preferences for "their" beer. In 1991, Labatt's Canadian Lager ranked a lowly number nine among lager brands in Britain.

Senior executives determined the tied house system was the cause of the problem.[62] Unlike in Canada, where most beer drinking was done in the home, in the United Kingdom the pub was still the hub of drinking activity. The pub had long been the centre of community engagement.[63] Some pubs, like Ye Olde Trip to Jerusalem in Nottingham, had been serving ale to patrons since the Crusades. But most pubs were tied to the nation's biggest brewers, who demanded that their beer be privileged over that of their competitors. Often the competition's brands – even relatively unpopular ones like Labatt's Canadian Lager – were kept out of tied houses. Thus, the tied house system created a barrier to Labatt's growth in Britain.

Labatt received some promising news in 1989 when the Monopolies and Mergers Commission (MMC) issued a detailed report of its multi-year investigation of competition in the U.K. beer market. During its investigation, the MMC discovered that there was a complex monopoly at work in the United Kingdom that favoured brewers who owned tied houses or who had loan-tied agreements with free houses. The MMC further determined that this restricted the growth of brewers without tied estates. In order to restore a meaningful measure of genuine freedom to the "free trade," the MMC recommended that a ceiling of 2,000 tied on-licensed outlets be placed on any one brewery group.[64] The recommendation was embraced by Margaret Thatcher's government, which had come to power in 1979 on a neo-conservative platform of laissez-faire economics. When the "Iron Lady" walked into her first Cabinet meeting following her election as leader of the Conservative Party, she slammed Friedrich Von Hayek's *The Road to Serfdom* down on the table and declared: "This is what we believe." Hayek had nothing specific to say about the brewing industry, but his book was a warning about state intervention. The only role for government, Hayek maintained, was to promote and protect free market competition. With that goal in mind, in December 1989, Thatcher's government issued the Beer Orders, which forced the "Big Six" brewers

Figure 13.3 Labatt launched a multi-million-dollar advertising campaign in Britain in 1990 for Labatt's Canadian Lager, using the tagline "Malcolm the Mountie always gets his can." British actor and comedian Tony Slattery played Malcolm the Mountie in the first series of TV commercials, singing call-and-response to a self-consciously ersatz, life-size moose puppet. In another promotional spot, Malcolm thwarted a criminal gang by dumping ice cubes in their path. The commercials served to anger Canada's national police force more than win over beer drinkers in Britain, who thought in terms of tins rather than cans. The U.K. beer market proved far different from the cozy Canadian oligopoly to which Labatt was accustomed.

– who controlled over 75 per cent of the U.K. beer market – to sell off a good portion of their pubs.

In theory, this gave Labatt an opportunity to finally gain meaningful ground in the United Kingdom. But in practice, the Big Six were tremendously strategic when it came to disposing of their pubs. The first pubs to go were the least desirable from a purchaser's perspective, often being rundown and in out-of-the-way places.[65] Unwilling to throw good money at bad establishments, Labatt managed to tie itself to only 257 pubs by December 1992, which was well short of its goal of owning "at least six hundred by the end of the year."[66] Labatt's "pub crawl" – as the author Paul Brent termed it – "cobbled together enough of a stake to occupy management's time, but was not enough to really drive sales of Labatt brands in the country."[67] To make matters worse, the recession, price wars, flat industry-wide sales, and big hostile breweries were squeezing sluggish foreign brewers like Labatt. "There is no need to belabour the point that the economic milieu in which we operate is far from robust," stated Sid Oland in September 1992.[68] Times were tough in Britain. By the end of the year, Labatt had only 3 per cent of the U.K. market and was still losing money.[69]

While the beer business was experiencing difficulties overseas, Labatt was still recording healthy profits. So much money was pouring in from domestic operations that the board of directors declared an $860 million special dividend to be distributed to shareholders. This was not the case at many of the companies that Labatt's principal shareholder, Brascan, owned. Nor was it the case at many of the companies owned by Brascan's parent, Edper Enterprises.[70] By the summer of 1992, Edward and Peter Bronfman's Edper empire was in deep trouble from loan losses created by the meltdown in the Canadian commercial property market. During the recession of 1990–91, the Bronfman brothers had witnessed the value of Edper-related stocks fall by fifty to 98 per cent. This caused rumours to swirl on Bay Street that Brascan was trying to sell its 37.3 per cent controlling interest in John Labatt Limited in order to preserve what was left of the Bronfmans' crumbling kingdom. Despite repeated denials by Brascan's top brass, the rumours would not go away – primarily because they were true.[71] The financial press even speculated that Labatt was being "cleaned up in order to make it more attractive to a purchaser like Anheuser-Busch."[72] The press was wrong in terms of the details, but right in terms of the general proposition that Brascan was set on getting out of the beer business.

In the fall of 1992, George Taylor was asked to find a friendly buyer to purchase all of Brascan's shares in John Labatt Limited.[73] For more than a year, Taylor vis-

Table 13.1

World top ten brewing groups by percentage of world beer production, 1990

Rank	Brewery	Production volume (millions of hectolitres)	Percentage of world beer production
1	Anheuser-Busch	104.6	9.1
2	Miller	62.2	5.4
3	Heineken	46.5	4.0
4	Kirin	34.6	3.0
5	Foster's	30.5	2.7
6	Danone	26.0	2.3
7	SAB	25.8	2.2
8	Brahma	25.5	2.2
9	Guinness	24.3	2.1
10	Coors	23.7	2.1
	Total	403.7	35.1

ited brewers around the world to see who would be interested in buying Labatt. In the end, he concluded that Japan's Kirin Brewery was the most likely candidate. Kirin could trace its roots to 1869 when Norwegian-American brewer William Copeland began selling his beer to foreign residents near the port of Yokohama.[74] In 1885, Copeland sold the brewery to a group of investors who renamed the business Japan Brewery. Three years, later Japan Brewery introduced a German-style lager to the market, naming after the mythical dragon-like animal Kirin. The popularity of the beer grew so much that, in 1907, Japan Brewery changed its name to Kirin Brewery.[75] After the Second World War, Kirin diversified into a variety of food- and beverage-related businesses. In 1972, the company went into partnership with Canadian distiller Seagram to produce spirits in Japan (Seagram had grown from its Depression-era bootlegging roots into one of the world's largest distillers under the direction of Edward and Peter Bronfman's uncle, domineering hard-baller Sam Bronfman).[76] By 1990, Kirin was the fourth-largest brewer in the world (see table 13.1). The brewing industry was becoming increasingly concentrated, with the top ten brewers controlling just over 35 per cent of the world's production of beer. For a company like Kirin, which was looking to stretch its global reach, Labatt was attractive because of the constant profits being generated in Canada and its close proximity to the United States.

To virtually everyone involved, it looked as though the Japanese brewer was destined to become the new owner of Labatt. But then, at the eleventh hour, the Bronfmans suddenly pulled the bung on the deal. For the straight-talking, no-nonsense Sid Oland, the Bronfmans' flip-flopping was too much to take: he stepped down as president and CEO in 1992 after just three years. The best of the beer men was gone. The board of directors immediately summoned George Taylor back from England, where he was vacationing with his wife, and thrust him into the top job.[77]

The Bronfmans' decision not to sell Labatt to Kirin upset a large number of investors who were looking to earn a windfall from their shares. When John Tory – a Labatt board member and prominent Toronto corporate lawyer – canvassed Labatt's principal shareholders, he discovered that the big money was generally displeased with the fact that a cloud of uncertainty had lingered over the company for more than two years, depressing the price of the company's shares.[78] Nevertheless, most of the big institutional investors and pension fund managers hung on. In February 1993, they were rewarded for their patience when Edper-Brascan finally sold its interest in Labatt to investment dealers for $993 million. The shares were in turn sold to the public at a huge profit.[79] "Edper's pain is Bay Street'a gain," read one headline.[80]

On the surface, little seemed to change as a result of Edper's departure. Most of Labatt's top management remained in place. For instance, the dynamic Surrey, England, native, Hugo Powell, remained on as president of Labatt Breweries Canada. And despite calls from shareholders to get rid of the Edper loyalists from Labatt's board of directors, Peter Bronfman, Trevor Eyton, and Sam Pollock, Labatt's chairman, stayed on.[81] But below the surface, Edper's divestiture of its stake stripped Labatt of its long-time corporate protector, making the firm vulnerable to a takeover.[82]

Canada's Beer Wars

On 21 March 1993, Labatt's director of business development Glen Cavanagh was leaving his hotel room in Vancouver when he got a phone call from a colleague who told him to turn on his television to the Canadian music awards. Cavanagh was in Vancouver to oversee the production of a commercial to promote a top-secret new product, Labatt's Ice Beer. Cavanagh did as instructed and was horrified to see that Labatt's arch rival, Molson Breweries, had chosen the Junos – as

Canada's music awards were popularly known – to launch their own "ice beer," using the tagline: "Welcome to the Ice Age." It was the same phrase that Cavanagh was going to use to promote Labatt's ice beer. Somehow Molson had found out about Labatt's new brew and had beaten Labatt to the punch. It was a marketer's worst nightmare.[83]

Labatt had been developing ice beer for over ten years, spending $26 million in the process. Admittedly, the product was a bit of a fluke. In the early 1980s, Labatt was conducting R&D on freeze concentration to see if it reduced the volume of beer. The hope was that once the frozen concentrated beer arrived at its distant destination, it could then be mixed with water and brought back to sale strength before being packaged and sold. It didn't work, and Labatt's technical director, Graham Stewart, pulled the plug on the project in 1986. However, the R&D did not go to waste. Those at Labatt thought that the same technology could be used to produce "ice beer." They believed the image of ice would appeal to Canadian drinkers, especially those who were already "icing" their beers by leaving the bottles outside in the snow or in the cold garage – essentially freeze concentrating them at home.

Labatt developed the technology to freeze the beer until ice crystals began to form. What made the ice process work was a series of high-speed wipers and agitators that stopped the beer from freezing solid as the temperature in the brewing tank began to fall. The beer was kept below its freezing point for about twenty minutes and then pumped out for aging. The ice crystals were left behind, and once a day almost two tons of slush was removed from the tank. Labatt's salesmen maintained that the slush contained a number of noxious substances – proteins, polyphenols, and tannins – that gave the beer a bit of a haze and a harsher taste. By "ice brewing" the beer, these unwanted substances were removed, producing a brilliantly clear and crisp lager that was slightly stronger than regular-strength beer.[84]

Labatt Ice was the latest salvo in the beer wars and was supposed to deliver a decisive blow to Molson. Every aspect of Ice had been thoroughly thought through – from where the beer was to be produced to how it was to be presented to the public. In terms of the packaging, the marketing managers at Labatt settled on the trendy colours of black and silver – colours that professional sports teams like Wayne Gretzky's L.A. Kings had recently switched to. The beer bottle was to have an austere glacier-looking logo on the label, which the marketing mavens hoped would appeal to the super-cool party crowd. There was a grunge feel to the brand, which, like the music of Nirvana or Alanis Morissette and the

thrift-store fashion of the age, had a stripped-down element to it. To spearhead
its advertising campaign, Labatt had hired Alexander Godunov, an expatriate
Russian dancer better known to younger drinkers for playing one of the violent
German terrorists who battled John McClane in the 1988 action movie *Die Hard*.
The image-makers at Labatt hoped that Godunov's sculpted-granite features
and "grunting monosyllabic speech" would bring the image-conscious younger
generation flocking to Ice.[85] In the process, Ice would cut into the lead that Molson Canadian enjoyed among the all-important nineteen-to-twenty-four age
group. Finally, Ice – the brand for Gen X – would help carry the burden for Blue
– the baby boomer's beer – which had been doing the heavy lifting for Labatt
for more than two decades.[86]

But all of Labatt's aspirations for the brand were jeopardized by Molson's pre-
emptive strike. Occasionally, as the Juno Awards were handed out – to Celine
Dion for best female vocalist, Leonard Cohen for best male vocalist, and The
Tragically Hip for entertainer of the year – the camera panned the audience.
Sitting in the fourth row was a group of impeccably dressed Molson executives,
looking jubilant over the tremendous coup that they had just pulled off. What
they had not realized was that they had started a quarrel as cantankerous as any
in the history of Canadian brewing.

Marketing warfare was hardly new to the world of Canadian brewing. For
years, the Hatfields and McCoys of the Canadian beer business had been taking
shots at each other in the media and in the courtroom. An early sign that the beer
wars of the last decade of the twentieth century would be as hard fought as those
of the 1980s came in 1990 when Molson took Labatt to court over the brand name
Blue. Molson claimed that Labatt had never registered the name and it, not
Labatt, had used it first to promote one of its beers.[87] That same year, when Molson closed some of its plants, Labatt ran newspaper ads suggesting that Molson
drinkers might find their favourite brands no longer tasted the same. And then
in 1991, Labatt took Molson to court over the use of the brand name Black Label
in Newfoundland because the Bavarian Brewing Company – which Labatt
acquired in 1962 – had registered the name in 1945.[88] The next skirmish occurred
in 1992 when Labatt launched its Genuine Draft. Produced through a distinctive
cold-filtering process that eliminated the need for heat pasteurization, it was the
first draft beer in a bottle from a national Canadian brewer. Labatt shelled out
$20 million to launch the new product, using the taglines: "Canada's original gen-
uine draft" and "the new cold standard."[89] Molson, however, took issue with how
Labatt's Genuine Draft was being marketed, arguing in federal court that it was

Figure 13.4 In 1992, Labatt launched Labatt Genuine Draft.
Produced through a distinctive cold-filtering process that
eliminated the need for heat pasteurization, it was the first
draft beer in a bottle from a national Canadian brewer. This
Labatt Genuine Draft ad tapped into Gen X's propensity for
heavy drinking.

too similar in name, packaging, and advertising to Miller Genuine Draft that it
brewed in Canada under licence.[90] In addition to taking Labatt to court, Molson
launched "La Copycat Contest," which challenged consumers to find three ways
that Labatt used ideas from the "look and feel" of Miller Genuine Draft.[91]

In the early 1990s, Labatt and Molson continued to analyze each other's products. Their employees were sent to stake out beer stores to record what brands
Canadians were buying. Both companies also employed just about any legal
means at their disposal to keep abreast of what the "other guy" was doing. But it

was on the front lines – in the bars and restaurants of the nation – that the greatest skirmishes took place. The shock troops of the beer wars were the jolly, glad-handing individuals known as company reps. "This war is going to be won in the trenches," stated Greg Mackenzie, a Labatt's sales rep who was working in west Toronto as the battle heated up over ice beer.[92] "We have to go out and kick butt."[93] In the pre-prohibition period, beer reps like Mackenzie plied the owners and staff of licensed establishments with free shipments of beer, kickbacks, leasehold im-provements, and merchandise. But during the 1990s, with tighter government regulations, they relied on camaraderie, free T-shirts, and footing the bill for theme nights.[94]

With the domestic beer market still shrinking – as many baby boomers cut back on their drinking, while others began brewing their own beer, and still others switched to drinking craft beer or wine – a blowout between the two major Cana-dian brewers became increasingly inevitable. At the same time, a number of U.S. brewers began "dumping" their beer in Canada.[95] For example, Stroh was selling its Old Milwaukee beer in Canada at 16.3 per cent less than in the United States; Pabst was peddling its brands at a 17.4 per cent discount; and Heileman was of-fering a 33.4 per cent cut rate.[96] In an effort to compete, Labatt introduced its own discount beer, Wildcat Lager, in the summer of 1993. At the same time, it lobbied the government to put a halt to the dumping by American brewers. Labatt got some relief in August 1993 when the Canadian and American governments signed a Memorandum of Understanding on Provincial Beer Marketing Practices. Under the terms of the agreement, U.S. brands could only be sold in Canada at the newly established minimum price. In return, U.S. brewers were granted equal access to points of sale in Canada.

The increased competition put pressure on the flagship brands of the "Big Two," with Blue's share of the market falling to 15 per cent in 1993 from 16 per cent a year earlier.[97] While Blue was still Canada's best-selling beer brand, execu-tives at Labatt worried about its prospects for future growth. In this environment, winning the ice beer wars become even more important. "Ten years ago, you could always count on growth, even if you just retained your share of the market," stated Labatt's spokesman Paul Smith. "Now, the only way to grow is to get a share from the other guy."[98] Those at Labatt concluded that they could not let the launch of Molson Canadian Ice Draft go unanswered.

Two days after the Juno Awards, Cavanagh and a few of his colleagues filed into a conference room for an emergency meeting. It was decided that Labatt would launch its ice beer immediately – two months ahead of schedule and without three of its four ice beer plants in operation. From its only ice beer facility in Montreal, Labatt began pumping out Labatt Ice day and night. The marketing mavens at Labatt decided to promote the product using the phrase: "If it is not ice brewed, it is not ice beer." In promoting the brand in this way, they sought to lay claim to authenticity, a cornerstone of modern marketing.[99] The claim was repeated again and again by Labatt executives after the product's launch. They also offered to open the hallowed ice-beer chamber in Montreal to demonstrate how "true" ice beer was actually made.[100] Molson Canadian Ice Draft, they maintained, was a simply a me-too product, an inauthentic knock-off of Labatt's ice beer, and a poor substitute at best.

Unable to secure a clear victory in the court of public opinion, Labatt subsequently had Molson answer for its actions in the court.[101] "We created and we own the term 'ice brewed' and 'ice brewing' and we took legal steps to make sure that we protect this significant investment," declared Sharon Paul, executive vice-president of public affairs at Labatt.[102] Labatt argued that Molson found out about its revolutionary idea and, lacking the equipment to copy it, hastily brewed up a fake ice beer and then rushed it to market. The court case was potentially worth much more than a 1 or 2 per cent point shift in domestic market share. Those at Labatt had their eye set on getting the court to rule that "ice beer" was an exclusive product and, therefore, could only be made by, or with the authorization of, Labatt.[103] If the court ruled in Labatt's favour, then the Canadian brewer could potentially make millions of dollars from licensing the product to other brewers around the world.

As the case wound its way through the courts, those at Labatt decided it would be advantageous to market its ice beer south of the border through a U.S. brewing company. As the inventor of the product, Labatt felt that it had a good chance of carving out a niche market for it in the United States. Given its decade-long relationship with Anheuser-Busch, Labatt believed that the St Louis–based brewer was the best partner to brew Ice under licence. In the course of negotiations with Anheuser-Busch, Labatt disclosed the marketing research on its new product as well as details about the ice brewing process. Anheuser-Busch and Labatt entered into an agreement regarding the confidentiality and future use of the information that Labatt had disclosed. The negotiations were proceeding well until 4 August 1993, when Anheuser-Busch suddenly informed Labatt that it would make and market its own ice beer. The shock of the announcement was almost as jolting as being upstaged at the Junos. Two months later, Bud Ice Draft started to appear in stores across the United States. Labatt immediately cried foul and took

America's biggest brewer to court. Unfortunately, however, the case did not go Labatt's way. After two days of deliberation that capped a three-week trial, the St Louis jury ruled that the terms "ice beer," "ice brewing," and "ice brewed" were not trademarks but simply generic words for a category of beer. Labatt had lost, and brewers across the continent rushed to get in on the ice beer craze.[104]

In the end, it barely mattered who won the ice beer wars. By 1994, the thirst for ice beer had diminished. Consumers had reached the conclusion that ice beer was not that much different than regular-tasting beer.[105] "With 50 ice beers on the market, people would try one and say, 'Well, these don't taste any different than regular beer. This is kind of a scam,'" Glen Cavanagh later recalled. "And the credibility went down the toilet very quickly."[106] Those at Labatt remained oblivious to the fact that a growing number of beer drinkers were willing to spend a bit more for higher-quality brews. While a small but growing number of craft brewers were offering distinctive-tasting, high-quality beers, those at Labatt were engaging in gimmickry. In the words of one keen observer, the early 1990s constituted a "silly season" in the history of big brewing in Canada.[107] And once the nonsense was over, all Labatt could do was return to promoting its flagging flagship brands.[108]

Failure in Mexico

When George Taylor took over as CEO of Labatt in 1992, he was determined to control more of the North American market. "My primary objective for Labatt at this point in time," Taylor told a group of security analysts on 13 April 1994, "is to build on our core strengths." By that he meant that Labatt should "focus in very tightly on ... expanding in the beer business – especially in North America."[109]

Of the three North American markets, Mexico had the greatest promise for future growth. Whereas the Canadian beer business was a zero-sum game of expensive market share swaps and no growth, the Mexican beer business had been growing at over 5 per cent per annum since 1983.[110] That is not to say that the beer business in Canada was not lucrative. It was. But the market was not growing, and in an increasingly globalized business environment, firms needed to grow in order to survive. Unlike in Canada, in Mexico the biggest beer-drinking group was expanding. In 1992, there were approximately 26.5 million males under the age of twenty-five in Mexico – the equivalent of Canada's total population.

Furthermore, the prime beer-drinking segment of the population – those between the ages of twenty and forty-five – was predicted to grow by 10 million over the next ten years. For those at Labatt, this made "the Mexican alcoholic beverages market extremely attractive from a future growth perspective."[111]

The problem was that the Mexican beer industry was a government-protected duopoly, which made it hard for foreign brewers like Labatt to break into the market. Mexican brewers were sheltered by a tariff of 20 per cent on foreign beer. In addition, Mexico's two biggest brewers, FEMSA and Grupo Modelo, had a stranglehold on the industry by virtue of the "tied account" distribution system. The two companies produced virtually all of the domestic beer consumed in Mexico and controlled a national network of distributors that had the exclusive right to supply restaurants, bars, cantinas, and corner stores. Those at Labatt concluded that they could not just show up and start producing beer in Mexico. It didn't matter how good Labatt's flagship brands were – without a way to get its beer into the hands of consumers, Labatt would fail in Mexico as it had in Chicago a century earlier.[112] In May 1994, Labatt's top brass determined that the only way to crack the Mexican market was to purchase one of the big Mexican breweries. "Only then," noted a strategic report on what was now being referred to at Labatt as "Project Argo," "will a foreign company ... have legs."[113] Like the Argonauts who searched for the Golden Fleece in Greek mythology, Labatt hoped to strike it rich in Mexico.

Of the two mega Mexican breweries, Fomento Económico Mexicano, S.A. de C.V. (FEMSA) held the best chance of giving Labatt its "legs" in Mexico. FEMSA was a large holding company based in Monterrey, Mexico. The company could trace its origins to the Cuauhtémoc Brewery, which was founded in 1890. The Cuauhtémoc Brewery faced a substantial challenge during its early years since beer was not the alcoholic drink of choice for most Mexicans. To make matters worse, foreign brands dominated the limited market for beer.[114] But the brewery overcame these obstacles by pioneering advertising and establishing a network of distributors across Mexico. At the same time, the firm vertically integrated bottling and packaging into its operations. Along with the savings gained from employing unskilled foreign workers, vertical integration allowed the Cuauhtémoc Brewery to substantially reduce its costs.[115] With the growth of the working and middle classes in Mexico over the course of the twentieth century, the thirst for beer increased. Like their American counterparts, Mexicans were overwhelmingly lager drinkers. Having successfully lobbied the government for protection against foreign competition, the brewery promoted a number of lager brands – Carta

Blanca, Tecate, Dos Equis, Sol, and Bohemia – that came to dominate the Mexican beer market in the north and the south. Grupo Modelo's brands – Corona Victoria and Modelo Especial – were popular in central and western Mexico. By 1950, the Cuauhtémoc Brewery was the third-largest enterprise in Mexico, after the state-owned oil and railway companies.[116] During the 1960s and 1970s, the brewery diversified, so that by the 1990s, when Labatt came calling, FEMSA had major interests in the beer, packaging, and soft drink industries.

In 1993, the beer division of FEMSA was the company's largest operation with sales of $1.358 million. The brewer had a 48 per cent share of the Mexican beer market and owned a board portfolio of high-quality brands. FEMSA's largest brewery at the time produced 6 million hectolitres of beer annually (or about 220 million cases), which was triple the amount produced at Labatt. In addition, FEMSA Cerveza had the best national distribution network in Mexico with approximately 240,000 retailers, 256 distributors, and more than 1,000 convenience stores that were tied to the brewery.[117]

A partnership with Labatt was appealing to those at FEMSA. Labatt still had a small American presence and moderate aspirations. Having come to the conclusion that it could not take on the big American brands – Blue could never beat Bud – Labatt dedicated itself to becoming "the number one distributor of specialty beer brands in the United States."[118] Knowing this, those at FEMSA believed that a merger with Labatt would give it access to the American market where its brands, like Tecate, could grow. After all, the Hispanic population in the United States was predicted to increase from 26 million in 1994 to 35 million by 2000 and the per capita income of Hispanics in the United States was three times that of those in Mexico.

With both sides realizing that there were strategic advantages to a partnership, a deal was struck. For $720 million, Labatt bought a 22 per cent stake in FEMSA. The deal increased Labatt's brewing volume by roughly 40 per cent. "Growth in today's global market requires the right partnership," Taylor proudly stated the day after the deal was done on 6 July 1994, "and with this alliance we have clearly positioned ourselves for growth."[119]

Had the timing been right, Taylor might have joined the ranks of Edmund Burke and Jake Moore as a saviour of the venerable Canadian brewery. But the timing could not have been worse. Just a few months after Labatt paid out almost three-quarters of a billion dollars for FEMSA, a currency crisis struck the Latin nation. In December 1994, the peso began a free fall as two political assassinations, a guerrilla insurgency in southern Mexico, and a change of government led for-

Those who like it, like it a lot.

Figure 13.5 In 1971, Labatt purchased the historic Maritime brewery Oland and Son, maker of the popular regional brand Alexander Keith's India Pale Ale. In the 1990s, along with its other flagship brands – 50, Blue, and Blue Light – Labatt promoted this brand nationally, as in this ad.

eign investors to pull their money out of the country. And despite U.S. officials and powerful media outlets like the *New York Times* assuring the public that the currency crisis "does not reflect fundamental flaws in Mexico's newly liberalized economy," the value of the peso continued to drop.[120] By March 1995, the Mexican peso was worth only half of what it was when the financial crisis began.

Labatt had done everything right in the months leading up to the deal with FEMSA, except for one thing. The usually conservative Canadian brewer had not hedged its Mexican purchase against a possible devaluation of the peso. This was in spite of the fact that those at Labatt knew that the Mexican currency was given to significant fluctuations. Before the deal went through, Taylor had written a confidential memo to the individual members of the board stating that one of the "important considerations in this investment is the currency risk of both the

Canadian dollar and the Mexican peso."[121] The problem was that Taylor and his advisers had underestimated the extent of the risk. In their collective estimation, "Mexican inflation would be 5% higher per annum than U.S. inflation and that the peso would be devalued by 5% per annum." Personally, Taylor believed this estimate was "reasonable and hopefully conservative in the long term."[122] It was neither, and as a result, the firm lost heavily.

When the peso hit a new record low on 10 March 1995, Taylor conceded that "there is no question whatsoever that the devaluation is a significant setback for the company."[123] Just nine months after buying its stake in FEMSA, Labatt was forced to write down the carrying value of its holding by $272 million and expected a further $110 million reduction in the investment's carrying value.[124] By June of that year, Labatt's debt-to-equity ratio had risen to 58 per cent.[125] The fizz had gone out of Labatt's Mexican holdings. The market was tremendously bearish about the prospect of Labatt turning a profit in Mexico in the near future. "You can't be positive about it," stated Jacques Kavaflan. "There's not going to be an earnings contribution from Mexico until the end of the century."[126]

Taylor, however, continued to see the glass as half-full. He argued that the FEMSA investment was "a long-term play." While the Mexican investment might be a drain on profits in the short term, he optimistically predicted that Labatt would make money in Mexico over time. But shareholders were skeptical. Many of them wanted Labatt to sell off its stake in FEMSA as well as its investment in the Blue Jays and TSN and return the company to what it was during the 1950s and 1960s – a highly focused, massively profitable *Canadian* brewery. The shareholders' dissatisfaction with the way the company was being run, along with the Mexico mess and the fact that Brascan no longer protected the firm, renewed talk of a takeover.

Takeover

On 25 February 1995, the *Globe and Mail* reported that "takeover rumours continue to bubble around John Labatt Ltd."[127] This time it was Onex Corp. of Toronto that was gearing up to take a run at the company. Onex specialized in purchasing troubled enterprises and then spinning off their non-core assets in order to get them back to basics before selling what remained for a handsome profit.[128] Onex's CEO, Gerry Schwartz, had learned the art of leverage buyouts from takeover wizard

Henry Kravis while working on Wall Street after graduating from Harvard with an MBA. He had also done a few high-yield bond issues with the "Junk Bond King," Mike Milken, before Milken was sent to jail for securities fraud. In 1982, Schwartz married Heather Reisman, the niece of Canada's chief free-trade negotiator, Simon Reisman. Heather Reisman was a force to be reckoned with in her own right, serving as president and CEO of Cott Corporation, a bottler of soft drinks, between 1992 and 1994, before going on to found Chapters/Indigo. In partnership with Schwartz, the two were virtually unstoppable. With their combined wealth mounting, the power couple purchased a rundown house in Toronto's wealthiest neighbourhood, Rosedale, and turned it into a magnificent urban estate. "Fort Schwartz" – as the press dubbed it – was decorated with British sculptures, medieval paintings, and sixteenth-century Chinese pottery, and could comfortably entertain 200 people. In the garage was a fleet of luxury cars that included a Porsche 911 Targa, a Ferrari, a 1957 Ford Thunderbird, and a 1967 Austin-Healey that Schwartz had restored himself.[129]

The flamboyant Schwartz knew a business opportunity when he saw one. Labatt's stock had been in the doldrums for months, beaten down by the devalued peso and a continuing fight with brewer Anheuser-Busch over the rights to the term "ice beer." If Schwartz could get John Labatt Limited at the right price, then Onex would make a barrel-load of money. Schwartz's plan was to purchase Labatt, liquidate the remaining non-beer assets, then privatize the old London Brewery and move it inside the Onex stable. Schwartz knew that such a takeover would require a good deal of cash, so he lined up the deep-pocketed Ontario Teachers' Pension Plan, TD Securities, Gordon Capital, and Argentinian brewer Quilmes Industrial SA as partners. In addition to putting in some cash of its own, Onex would orchestrate the takeover and manage the brewery after the acquisition.[130]

In May 1995, Schwartz contacted Taylor to arrange a meeting to discuss the terms of a peaceful takeover. Taylor, however, was not immediately inclined to meet. In many ways, Taylor was the antithesis of Schwartz. Quiet, calm, and funny, Taylor preferred to spend his weekends on his 70-hectare farm in St Marys, Ontario, far away from the party-going crowd of Toronto's high society. A man who valued understated achievement, he had little time for brash businessmen like Schwartz. Nevertheless, Taylor decided that he owed it to Labatt's anxious shareholders to at least hear what Schwartz was proposing.

The two men and their aides met secretly just after midnight on 18 May at the posh Four Seasons Hotel at the corner of Bay Street and Yorkville Avenue in

Toronto. Schwartz stated that Onex and its partners were going to make an offer amounting to $940 million or $24 a share for Labatt, and he wanted Taylor's public support. Taylor would have none of it. Indeed, he was offended by Schwartz's low-ball offer and was of the opinion that the shareholders should reject it.[131] "If shareholders accept this offer," Taylor warned, "they will forego significant value for their ownership in our premier brewing and broadcast assets."[132] In Taylor's opinion, Schwartz's hostile bid undervalued Labatt's North American brewing assets by as much as $800 million.[133]

Unwilling to surrender the corporation without a fight, Taylor went searching for other suitors. Taylor was helped by the fact that the gale-force winds of globalization were now blowing, filling the sails of a small number of adventurous brewers and pushing them to far-flung places. The Dutch brewer Heineken was one of them. Shortly after the Berlin Wall came down in 1989, Heineken made investments in breweries in Hungary, Poland, and Slovakia.[134] At about the same time, Guinness gained a significant stake in Asia Pacific Breweries of Singapore, which was the brewer of such popular lager brands as Tiger and Anchor.[135] Likewise, Anheuser-Busch appreciated that developing markets were the place to be. Growth markets in the Third World had a much greater co-efficient of expansion. In 1995, Anheuser-Busch acquired an 80 per cent stake in the Wuhan Brewery in China. While the global search for easy prey had hurt Labatt in its quest to acquire a really big international brewery, it had the potential of helping Labatt's shareholders get top dollar for their stock. Predatory brewers from around the globe were always interested in those firms like Labatt that had steady revenue streams. At the end of 1994, Labatt had $268 million in cash or about $3 a share, despite declaring a special dividend and making the FEMSA acquisition. The company's ability to produce surplus cash was one of the main factors attracting prospective buyers. Another factor was the company's portfolio of successful national and regional brands.[136] This was important because brands added value to a firm by sustaining a constant flow of revenue due to the consumer's propensity for long-term brand loyalty.[137] Firms with strong regional or national brands were profoundly attractive to international beer companies because they could upgrade and enhance the marketing of local/regional/national brands while simultaneously introducing their global brands to the market.

This approach was pioneered by Belgium's Interbrew SA, which was formed in 1987 through a merger of Brasseries Artois and Brasseries Piedboeuf. In the spring of 1995, Interbrew entered the chase for Labatt. The Belgium brewer was older than Labatt. Indeed, it was older than any brewer in North America, having

Figure 13.6 This advertisement for Interbrew's flagship brand Stella Artois, a Belgian Pilsner, captures the fact that drinking identities were becoming more fluid and complex by the end of the twentieth century.

its roots in a pub named Den Horen (the Horn) that began operations in the Flemish city of Leuven in 1366.[138] In 1717, Sebastien Artois, a master brewer at the Horn, bought the operation and renamed it Artois. During the nineteenth and twentieth centuries, Artois incorporated many of the latest technical advances in brewing, which helped the brewery become one of the premier establishments in Europe. In 1926, it began brewing Stella Artois, a Pilsner-style beer, for the Christmas season. The brand proved so popular that Artois decided to sell it all year-round. The Piedboeuf brewery, on the other hand, was founded in 1853 in Jupille-sur-Meuse, near Liege in the French-speaking part of Belgium. Its most famous product was the Jupiler brand, which like Stella Artois was a Belgian-style Pilsner.[139] At the time of the merger in 1987, Piedboeuf and Artois were the two biggest breweries in Belgium.[140] In 1989 and 1990, Interbrew used its cash on hand to purchase two other highly regarded Belgian breweries, Hoegaarden and Belle-Vue. It then expanded into such emerging markets as Romania and China.[141] By 1995, the debt-free family-controlled company, whose blue-blood board of directors was made up of barons, counts, and viscounts, was the world's sixth-largest brewer, with sales of more than $2 billion.

When the Belgian brewer signalled that it was interested in buying Labatt, Schwartz suddenly found himself operating in a vacuum. Taylor had instructed everyone at Labatt not to talk to Schwartz. "It was largely a personal thing," Schwartz maintained. "I tried to get three or four people on the Labatt's board to get me together with George Taylor to say, 'let's work together.'" But Schwartz could not get them to meet because Taylor had taken the view that anybody "who talked to Onex was a traitor." As a result, the people Schwartz knew well on the board would not help him.[142]

The board members, however, were willing to talk to those at Interbrew. The Belgian brewer was interested in Labatt for a number of reasons. First, Interbrew saw the merit of the Mexico purchase, especially after the peso had stabilized. Second, Labatt produced a constant stream of revenue from its Canadian operations. In 1994, the old London Brewery increased its domestic sales volume to 8.4 million hectolitres, which generated net sales of $1.245 million. Worldwide, the company produced 12.3 million hectolitres of beer, which made it almost as big as Interbrew. Those at the Belgian brewery were impressed with Labatt's recent cost-cutting measures in marketing, production, distribution, and administration, which had resulted in savings of $120 million over the last three years.[143] Third, purchasing Labatt would give the Belgian brewer a base from which to attack the $30-billion North American beer market, which it had been eyeing for a number of years. At the time, Stella Artois and Jupiler were virtually unknown to North American beer drinkers. And after exhaustive study, Interbrew's executives decided that it was impossible to penetrate the highly competitive North American market through exports alone. For all these reasons, Interbrew offered $28.50 per share – $4.50 more than Onex had offered – for Labatt. At $106 per hectolitre of beer output, the Interbrew's bid was well below the record of around $150 per hectolitre that Britain's Guinness paid when it outmanoeuvred Labatt for Spain's Cruzcampo.[144] However, the price per hectolitre translated into a total purchase price of $2.7 billion for John Labatt Limited. Taylor proved successful in finding a buyer with better bloodlines and a greater appreciation of Labatt's worth than Schwartz's Onex Corp.

When Labatt accepted Interbrew's offer, it did more than bring an end to a month-long business saga: it brought an end to a time when Canadian-owned breweries produced most of the beer that Canadians consumed. "Ale and Farewell," read a headline in the *Wall Street Journal*.[145] The last of the Big Three – a Canadian icon – was gone. The takeover elevated Interbrew to the fourth-largest brewer in the world, and it wasted no time at getting down to the business that should have been done by Labatt so many years before. Despite all the talk at Labatt about getting back to basics, not much de-diversification had taking place at the company since 1992. The Canadian press still correctly referred to Labatt as an "entertainment conglomerate." It still owned the baseball Blue Jays; the Toronto Argonaut football team; Toronto's entertainment palace, the Sky-Dome; TSN; Discovery Channel; and all kinds of other non-beer assets. Interbrew was set on jettisoning everything that could not be stored in a keg. "It's very simple," stated Interbrew's Belgium-based spokesman Gerard Fauchey shortly after the takeover, "We're brewers, not managers of hockey or baseball teams or television stations."[146]

Conclusion

In the end, a combination of structural and firm-specific factors led to the fall of Labatt. Structurally speaking, Labatt's efficiency and overall global competitiveness was undermined by the system of interprovincial trade barriers that forced the company to have a physical presence in each of the provinces in which it sold beer. The regulatory regime in Canada was such that it fragmented the industry along regional lines, leading to cost inefficiencies and suboptimal production levels that hampered the development of large, internationally competitive firms. Safe behind the wall of federal tariffs, Canada's biggest brewers had little incentive to internationalize through foreign direct investment. Rather, they spent millions of dollars a year on national advertising campaigns in an effort to gain a larger share of the domestic market. The doppelganger of federal and provincial legislation protected existing firms and allowed them to survive without developing managerial capabilities, marketing skills, and global brands.

Nevertheless, as early as the 1960s, there was reason to believe the industry was moving in a new direction. Attempted and successful takeovers, licensing agreements, and the growing presence of international brands indicated that globalization of the industry was in the making. And yet, Labatt failed to learn the knack of looking beyond its own backyard: rather than thinking in more expansive terms, it could only think in terms of moving the fence at the expense of its neighbour. Even after the GATT ruling, which brought an end to the state's protectionist policies, Labatt continued to spend millions on domestic advertising in an effort to gain an advantage in the beer wars. Remarkably, the company was still unable to break with the traditional view of their industry as oligopolistic battle for market share.

Time and time again during the 1980s and 1990s, Labatt went in the wrong direction, promoted the wrong products, picked the wrong markets, and squandered precious resources. At home, Labatt leadership continued to be oblivious to the fact that the late twentieth-century beer drinker was no longer the "good old" white boy with a workman's palate. They introduced new low-quality, gimmicky beers that quickly lost their appeal with the beer-drinking public. On the international front, Labatt was too often timid when it came to making new acquisitions, and when it finally did make a major move, it failed to hedge its bet. Once Brascan was gone, the company was walking the high wire without a safety net. Any stumble could prove fatal. On the global stage, firms needed to take calculated risks and then pursue them aggressively. In the last act of its corporate life, Labatt did none of these things. And that is why Labatt's brands don't have a global presence, and why the Belgians don't drink Blue.

Conclusion

In their recent study, *Reimagining Business History*, historians Philip Scranton and Patrick Fridenson encouraged those interested in the commercial past to pursue new methods and areas of inquiry, including the much-neglected field of business failure.[1] The analysis of failure is important, Scranton and Fridenson maintain, because "economic organizations, like all others, cannot ignore their intrinsic fragility."[2] Too often, business historians have overlooked failure in favour of success. As Fridenson notes in an earlier work, the standard narrative in business history progresses from "humble beginnings to flowering success," thus leaving us with a distorted record of our overall commercial past.[3] In seeking a better balance, Fridenson invites historians to "place failure on a common scale with success" by reversing the order of the sequence to follow the much more common progression of "success followed by failure."[4]

Such was the overall evolution at John Labatt Limited, as well as a number of buggy whips along the way. During its formative years, Labatt successfully dealt with the external shocks to its core business, from the advent of the railway to the departure of the military from London to changes in consumer taste to the onset of the Canada Temperance Act. But success was followed by failure, first in the Windy City and then during prohibition. By 1921, Labatt had one foot in the grave before Edmund Burke breathed new life into the old London Brewery. When prohibition finally came to an end, Labatt was in the top tier of Canadian brewers. Having quickly followed Canadian Breweries Ltd's lead, Labatt became one of the Big Three brewers that collectively controlled over 95 per cent of the Canadian beer market by the 1980s. But the strategic choices that senior management made during the 1970s, 1980s, and early 1990s, particularly to diversify, license American brands, and spend millions of dollars in an attempt to gain the upper hand in the domestic beer wars, undermined the international competitiveness of the firm. Labatt paid for these strategic mistakes by losing its autonomy. But that is the way that the Canadian system works.

While Labatt no longer exists as an independent enterprise in the world of brewing, there are lasting and salient lessons from the brewery's rise and fall for those interested in ownership and control, brands and advertising, public affairs, entrepreneurship, and competitiveness in business.

Ownership and Control

Between 1847 and 1995, Labatt was a sequentially family-owned and -controlled firm, a family-owned managerial enterprise, and a widely held public company run by professional managers. What role did these various ownership and control structures play in the evolution of the firm? Initially, John Kinder Labatt determined all of the values that guided the operation over time – a commitment to producing British-styled ales, porters, and stouts; a confidence that the firm's product was as good as any on the market; an aversion to risk and external debt; a commitment to family; an aggressiveness when it came to sales; and conservativeness that led Labatt to move only when pushed. The discrimination that Labatt faced before coming to Canada gave him a powerful sense of family solidarity and discipline, crucial assets for a successful family firm. The brewery also survived the challenges of the early years because John Kinder Labatt carefully formulated a succession plan for future generations. In his final act, he left the business that bore the family name to his third eldest son, thereby ensuring the successful intergenerational transfer of family assets. This too is essential for success as a family enterprise.[5] These decisions were not based on emotion, but rather on sound economic reasoning.

John Labatt II was the most capable of John Kinder Labatt's children. Historian Albert Tucker has argued that more so than any other individual, John Labatt II was responsible for putting Labatt on its modern corporate footing. There is no question that he consolidated the business under his watch. In mid-life, John Labatt II was dynamic and visionary. But success led to arrogance and a number of strategic mistakes and subsequent business failures. Furthermore, he was stuck at times in the cage of tradition, blind to the onset of the managerial revolution and the shift that was taking place in consumer tastes. For too long, he continued to produce ales instead of lagers and to run his business as a form of paternalistic personal capitalism. Thus, I would argue that Tucker overstates his importance. By the time of Labatt's death in 1915, the company had been reduced to a second-tier brewer whose operations were confined to the southwest corner of Ontario.

Over the course of his two marriages, John Labatt II was philoprogenitive – also a critical element in the multi-generational success of family businesses. But John Labatt II was cursed with nine girls and two (surviving) boys – cursed because the most gifted of his children were female at a time when women could not own or manage companies. While there was no infighting or animosity between the brothers, the third generation of Labatt men lacked the initial generation's hunger to succeed. Too long under their father's protective wing, neither John Sackville nor Hugh Labatt had the entrepreneurial talent necessary to grow the firm. Under their watch, the Buddenbrooks effect set in. By 1921, only six years after John Sackville Labatt had taken over as president, the family-owned and -controlled firm was on the brink of bankruptcy and would have gone out of business in 1922 had it not been for the entrepreneurial efforts of the firm's general manager, Edmund Burke.

Burke saved Labatt. As a professional manager, working for a share of the profits, he was given carte blanche to run the business as he saw fit during prohibition. He turned the company into one of the most successful bootleggers in Canadian history. If Burke had been moral in business, there would have been no business for the prohibitionists to get morally exercised about. However, his bootlegging would have been impossible if the firm were not family-owned and -controlled. The nature of Labatt's personal capitalism created a structure that allowed for privacy, secrecy, and clandestine operations. It is unlikely that a group of public shareholders would have turned a blind eye to Burke's bootlegging the same way the Labatt family did during prohibition. Thus, at this point in the firm's evolution, family ownership played a vital part in survival of the business.

That being said, it is just as unlikely that Labatt would have survived the consolidation of the industry after the Second World War had the firm not gone public. Labatt simply did not have the capital depth necessary to follow Canadian Breweries Ltd's lead in expanding across the nation by way of mergers and acquisitions. One might argue that Labatt could have gone public yet retained family control by holding on to a majority of the shares and thus determining the composition of the board. This, according to business historian Teresa da Silva Lopes, is how the most successful companies in the international alcoholic beverage industry are structured. According to Lopes, family ownership and control is an essential determinant of survival. But one must remember that if Labatt had remained a family-controlled public company, it would have fallen into Schlitz's hands in the 1960s. The family shareholders wanted to sell out to Schlitz and their representatives on the board did everything they could to make the takeover happen. Thus, it is not so much the structure of ownership and control as the individual character, motivations, and capabilities of those in charge that determine the success and survival of firms.

State Regulation

Through the years, Labatt had been helped and hurt by the government's actions as the emerging Canadian state calculated the bounds of its fiscal moral economy. Before Confederation in 1867, in the era of Canadian colonies, Labatt felt the first touch of the State – but as the new Canadian nation matured, that touch became firmer and more intrusive. Heavily taxed, Canadian brewers faced tight and, at times, suffocating regulation. While prohibition was (paradoxically) good for Labatt, it was devastatingly Darwinian to the industry as a whole. Prohibition of alcohol did not prevent people from drinking. It simply forced imbibers into back alleys and blind pigs. It created a black market in booze that was impossible to tax and regulate and gave opportunities to those, like Edmund Burke, who operated in the shadows and whose innovative actions were perceived by many as against the public good. As a result, crime increased, revenue from government taxes decreased, people got ill from bad stock, and good people were turned into lawbreakers.

In the aftermath of the noble experiment, provincial governments across the land aided the industry by passing legislation that privileged beer drinking over the consumption of hard liquor. The brewers themselves had been instrumental in bring this situation about. By creating alliances with other moderates in society and elevating beer's status by making its consumption an expression of Canadianness, the brewers kept prohibition in the past. As Labatt worked on transforming its image from a soulless bootlegger to a soulful good neighbour, it simultaneously altered the public's perception of beer from one of the three poisons to a wholesome, Canadian temperance drink. In the process, Labatt helped manufacture a nation of beer drinkers. By the end of the Second World War, Labatt had regained its status as a good corporate citizen, and beer was, by a wide margin, Canada's alcoholic beverage of choice. But Canadians have never been the world's most prolific drinkers. As we have seen, this too was because of the brewers' efforts to teach temperance and responsible drinking practices by way of cause advertising, public relations campaigns, and other tactics. All of these had a normalizing and constituting effect.

In prohibition's wake, the macroeconomic position of Canadian industry, however, was not helped by the fact that provincial governments instituted tariffs and imposed import quotas that limited or altogether stopped out-of-province beer. The brewing industry's productive system became hopelessly fragmented in numerous uncompetitive plants across the country. Thus, Canadian brewing has always faced the congenital Canadian problem of interprovincial trade barriers and their crippling effect on productivity.

Without the scale economies in production and advertising enjoyed by the bigger American brewers operating south of the border, Canadian brewers found themselves at a competitive disadvantage relative to their international counterparts. But fortunately, those self-same government tariff and non-tariff barriers also prevented foreign brewers from entering the Canadian market without the aid of licensing agreements. Canada's biggest brewers were thus able to survive despite not having firm-specific advantages over the international competition. The combination of federal and provincial legislation protected brewers like Labatt and enabled them to survive without developing managerial capabilities, marketing skills, and global brands. Even as late as the 1980s, the federal government of Brian Mulroney recognized "the historical and continuing highly-regulated and trade-restricted domestic market [beer] environment," when it exempted the brewers from the Free Trade Agreement.[6] In a classic example of what economist Dani Rodrik terms "smart globalization," Mulroney's Progressive Conservative government prudently embraced elements of both laissez-faire and *étatisme* to shield Canadian interests, in this case by continuing to protect Canadian brewers until the tariff walls finally came down in the 1990s.[7]

Brands, Advertising, and the National Identity

In consumer-oriented industries with a high level of competition and concentration, like brewing, developing popular brands is essential for the growth and survival of individual firms. A successful brand segments and imperializes the market. Today, the world's biggest brewers own the most popular global brands, many of which still have strong ties to national identities. Think, for instance, of

the American-ness of Bud or the Irish-ness of Guinness. But it has been very difficult for Canadian firms to develop national brands because of the linguistic,
ethnic, religious, and regional diversity of the nation. A few Canadian companies
have managed to navigate this diverse terrain by exploiting the ambiguities and
contradictions within the project of Canadian identity.[8] Others have appropriated
the symbols of national identity to promote their brands.[9] But even this approach
has proven problematic. National symbols have at times divided as much as
united Canadians. They have also been the target of those who have felt alienated
within the Canadian federation. Such was the case in 1992, for example, when
French nationalism was on the rise in Quebec. In an effort to maintain the popularity of its flagship brand Blue in the predominately French-speaking province,
Labatt quietly substituted a wheat shaft for the maple leaf on the beer label. But
the move infuriated English Canadians as much as it placated French Canadians.

Brewers have also found it difficult to create brand images that resonate with
Canadians of various ethnic backgrounds. During the 1980s, for example, Labatt
attempted to imbue Blue with authenticity by featuring "ordinary" hard-working
Canadian men and women in its advertisements. The campaign offended some
Canadians. For example, great Canadian jazz musician Oscar Peterson criticized
the lifestyle commercials of Labatt for "setting the worst example of human relationships for anyone" and urged consumers to boycott Labatt's beer in order to
fight racism. "I don't believe that I'm the only black in this country that owns a
cottage," Peterson stated. "I don't believe that I'm the only black that's gone fishing
with his or her neighbour," he continued. According to Peterson, the "lily-white"
ads convinced ethnic children that Canada's consumer "goodies" were not for
them.[10] To the extent that ethnic minorities appeared at all in beer commercials
prior to the 1990s, they played stereotypical roles. "I have seldom, if ever, seen a
Canadian Indian in a [beer] ad for any reason but pictorial value, and seldom
without a horse," complained Peterson. "I've seldom seen an Eskimo without an
igloo, seldom seen a black not singing or baring his teeth."[11] For too long, Labatt's
advertising focus was on maximizing sales in its traditional markets, and not in
attracting new beer drinkers. This left the door open to foreign up-market brands
and eventually distinctive craft beers. Canadian brewers would struggle for years
with how to include visible minorities in their promotional campaigns in a way
that was neither token nor patronizing.

To be successful, a brand's identity needs to be refashioned from time to time
to meet the evolving demands of the marketplace. When brands are not rejuve-
nated, they lose their popular appeal. Take, for example, Labatt 50, which has seen

its market share decline significantly since the 1980s because there has been little effort on the part of the brand managers at Labatt to keep 50 "forever young."[12] This is not to say that national brands cannot be created and re-energized. But it takes time, insight, and tremendous effort. Building and managing brands is a complex ongoing exercise, requiring marketing managers to have a deep knowledge of consumer behaviours and tastes, demographics, consumer fantasies and needs, and societal and cultural trends. It requires extensive market research and the exchange of innovative knowledge among managers, employees, consultants, clients, and distributors. Building a brand is an analytical process that depends on data-driven decision-making and instinct. Viewed from the outside, branding/rebranding exercises and advertising campaigns often appear to be coherent and straightforward. But in reality, these exercises and campaigns are frequently characterized by trepidation, anxiety, uncertainty, inconsistency, contestation, and debate. One will recall the difficultly that Labatt had in solving the national lager problem and the resources that it took to rebrand Pilsener as Blue. But when done right, creating national brands can be both culturally and financially rewarding.

In the end, it was all too much for Labatt, and the decision-makers decided to take the much-easier route of licensing existing brands. Licensing agreements have often been celebrated by brand managers, business theorists, and business historians as an effective means for firms with global aspirations to break into distant markets by piggybacking on another brewer's brand recognition – especially when the target market is protected by tariffs.[13] The literature also suggests a win-win scenario:[14] the licensor gains access to the market and existing channels of distribution while reducing transportation costs, and the licensee gains a popular international brand to produce and promote within the national boundary.[15] In theory, the licensee's share of the domestic market thus increases. But this is not always the case, as Labatt's experience shows.

To wit, the licensing agreement between Anheuser-Busch and Labatt in 1980 was a case of win-lose, with Budweiser cannibalizing Blue and initiating the Americanization of the Canadian brewing industry. When the brewing industry became truly global after 1990, Canadian brewers no longer had unique, distinctively Canadian brands to offer the world. More recently, AB InBev has been determined to pare down its expenses by shrinking its portfolio of brands.[16] The global giant has focused on its star labels to pitch them more efficiently to a worldwide audience. Most of Labatt's advertising budget now goes into promoting Anheuser-Busch's brands in Canada, which helps explain why Bud is now Canada's best-selling brew.

Strategic Choices, Competitiveness, and Globalization

At the most basic level, all of Labatt's decision-makers described in this book faced the same persistent challenge: to maintain the momentum of the firm during both halcyon days and periods of external shock. But those who made the strategic responses were rarely motivated by the same individual fears, aspirations, and sense of purpose. John Kinder Labatt, for example, was driven to enter the business of brewing out of a longing for home and a fear of going it alone. John Labatt II was often motivated to grow the business because of a need for attention for himself as a brewer and a desire for prestige for the brewery that he owned and controlled. Edmund Burke was enthused by the prospect of easy money and by a sense of excitement; Hugh Mackenzie, by a general sense of honour, duty, and respect for all of those – labour, competitor, government official – who were involved in the business of brewing. While he was at the helm of the firm, Jake Moore's strategic choices were often determined by his somewhat self-aggrandizing belief that he was the white knight of Canadian capitalism, while Peter Widdrington was motivated by the sense of power that came with being a big fish in a small pond.

But these and other individuals captured in the book were also influenced by the spirit of Canadian capitalism. As historian David Landes notes, the mutually reinforcing phenomena of culture and place matter when it comes to the nature of entrepreneurship and the growth and survival of firms.[17] Just as John Labatt II could not let go of his Victorian moral rectitude when he entered the business of brewing in the United States in the 1890s, so too Peter Widdrington could not shake off the inferiority complex that most Canadian business executives displayed during the 1970s and 1980s. The decision-makers at Labatt were too often inoculated by the old Canadian corporate parochialism. The spirit of Canadian capitalism has often been cautious and conservative in nature. In part, this explains why the Canadian state has often played a leading role in economic development of key industries.[18]

This cultural aversion to risk has also led a number of Canadian businesses to "stay at home." Instead of taking on the competition abroad, Canadian business has too often chosen to cater to the local market and diversify into related and unrelated areas of domestic production.[19] More so than elsewhere around the globe, Canadian corporate managers believe that having "all your eggs in one basket" is a dangerous strategy. This mentality emerged out of a conservative corporate culture that stretched back to at least the late nineteenth century. There has long been an unwillingness on the part of Canadian businessmen to believe in the global appeal of their products – beyond natural resources. Only a handful of Canadian companies, like Roots and Canada Goose, have had the courage to strike a distinctively Canadian identity abroad. Canada's biggest brewers did not. Instead, they were too often derivative when it came to formulating corporate strategies, leading many of them to diversify into unrelated businesses within Canada rather than concentrating their efforts on taking their principal business overseas.

Lacking clarity about what sort of company it wanted to be, Labatt diversified into media and entertainment, food businesses, dairy products, fruit juices, chemicals, and retailing, among many other enterprises.[20] Diversification could be rewarding, but it took substantial resources and a good sense of timing. For those firms in the alcoholic beverage industry, diversification generally produced positive results when it related to the firm's core competencies – that is, when there were physical and/or knowledge linkages to the firm's assets that could be easily extrapolated and exploited. For example, when Louis Vuitton Moët Hennessy diversified into perfumes in the 1990s, it allowed the firm to exploit not only its high-end marketing knowledge in terms of the general management of brands and distribution but also its knowledge about specific markets, such as the luxury-hungry Far East.[21] On the other hand, diversification often went wrong when a firm expanded into industries that were unrelated to its core business, and thus when physical and knowledge linkages were absent. Think, for example, of Imperial Tobacco's diversification into frozen food and beer in the 1960s, when cigarettes came under attack for health reasons. However, managing the acquired companies proved difficult, and the profits were minimal. The bloated company then caught the eye of a takeover artist, who purchased the company and broke it up. The tobacco side of the operation was refloated as an independent company on the stock market.[22] Similarly, Labatt's diversifications required a different set of skills from its core competency and thus did not bring the anticipated profits. Like a number of companies, Labatt diversified into alien and treacherous territory. And paid a heavy price. Management made a mistake by diversifying – by doing too many things at once, rather than focusing relentlessly on its core competency.

Whether brewing beer or smelting steel, Canadian business has been inclined to live in a parochial cocoon. But to succeed in business, particularly in today's global environment, firms need to draw on their core competencies and expand their horizons. During the final part of its life, Labatt was emblematic of the Canadian corporate condition: an inability on the part of all but the most dynamic of Canadian corporations to look beyond the national boundary for opportunities for growth. The globalization that was opened up by Canada's embrace of free trade in the late 1980s severely challenged this comfort zone and, in general, exposed Canadian businesses to Darwinian forces they had all too often been avoiding since Confederation. It appears that the business theorists of the post-diversification craze are right: the wisest strategy for business is to "stick to the knitting." Firms should do what they do best and do it the world over.

Notes

Introduction

1 Penrose, *The Theory of the Growth of the Firm*, 137.
2 Boothman, "Strategic Transformations," 291–311.
3 Casson, *The Entrepreneur*.
4 Landes, *Dynasties*, xiv.
5 Chandler, *Scale and Scope*, 268, 339.
6 Chandler, *The Visible Hand*.
7 Chandler, *Scale and Scope*, 262. See also Hannah, "Scale and Scope," 301.
8 Colli, *The History of Family Business*.
9 James, *Family Capitalism*.
10 Casson, "The Economics of the Family Firm," 17.
11 Ibid.
12 Lopes, *Global Brands*, 67–86.
13 Colli, *The History of Family Business*, 65–72.
14 Landes, *Dynasties*, 227.
15 Quoted in *The New York Times* (28 February 2003), W1 and 7.
16 Bygrave and Hoffer, "Theorizing about Entrepreneurship," 14.
17 Hunter, *Molson*.
18 Colli, *The History of Family Business*, 13–14, 67.
19 Casson, "The Economics of the Family Firm," 17.
20 Schumpeter, *The Theory of Economic Development*, 65–8.
21 Belisle, *Retail Nation*.
22 McQueen, *The Eatons*, 34.

23 Ibid., 93–111.
24 Ucbasaran et al., "The Nature of Entrepreneurial Experience," 541–55.
25 Ibid., 146–84.
26 Pitts, *In the Blood*.
27 James, *Family Capitalism*.
28 Sawler, *Last Canadian Beer*, 36–44.
29 Dennis Oland's conviction, however, was overturned by the New Brunswick Court of Appeal in 2016, and a retrial was ordered.
30 Austin, *Alcohol in Western Societies*; Harrison, *Drink and the Victorians*; Barrows, "Parliaments of People"; Roberts, "Taverns and Politics."
31 Heron, *Booze*, 10.
32 Moore, *Bootleggers and Border*, 34–6.
33 Noel, *Canada Dry*; Heron, *Booze*, 53–77, 113–28, 174–85; Cook, *Through Sunshine and Shadow*; Spence, *Prohibition in Canada*; Hallowell, "Prohibition in Ontario, 1919–23"; Chapman, "The Mid-Nineteenth-Century Temperance Movement in New Brunswick and Maine," 43–60; Dick, "From Temperance to Prohibition in 19th Century Nova Scotia," 530–52; R.D. O'Neill, "The Temperance Movement, Prohibition and Scarcity in Ontario, 1900–1916"; Sheehan, "National Pressure Groups and Provincial Curriculum Policy," 73–88; Sturgis, "Beer under Pressure," 83–100.
34 Schrad, *Vodka Politics*, 169–97; Karlsson, *The History of Iceland*, 296; Larsen, *History of Norway*, 521; Okrent, *Last Call*, 117–354.
35 Martel, *Canada the Good*, 5.
36 Campbell, *Sit Down and Drink Your Beer*.
37 Malleck, *Try to Control Yourself*, 8–9.
38 Heron, *Booze*, 379.
39 Bower and Cox, "How Scottish & Newcastle Became the U.K.'s Largest Brewer," 43–68.
40 Forster, *A Conjunction of Interest*, 110–26.
41 Miller, "Air Power is Peace Power," 297–327; Hansen, *Gaining Access*.
42 Marchand, *Creating the Corporate Soul*.
43 Fahey, "Brewers, Publicans and Working-Class Drinkers."
44 Waterhouse, *Lobbying America*, 250.
45 Lopes, *Global Brands*, 1–66, 129–79; Duguid, "Developing the Brand," 405–41; Merrett and Whitwell, "The Empire Strikes Back," 162–90; Wilson, "Selling Beer in Victorian Britain," 103–25; Johansen, "Marketing and Competition in Danish Brewing," 126–38; Weir, "Managing Decline," 139–62.

46 Barwise and Robertson, "Brand Portfolios," 277–85.

47 Saiz and Perez, "Catalonian Trademarks," 255.

48 Aaker, *Building Strong Brands*; Doyle, "Building Successful Brands," 18; Barwise and Robertson, "Brand Portfolios," 277–85; Casson, "Brands," 41–58. Wilkins, "When and Why: Brand Names," 19–20; Jones, "Brands and Marketing," 1–12.

49 Lopes and Casson, "Entrepreneurship and the Development of Global Brands," 661–80.

50 Lopes, "Brands and the Evolution of Multinationals," 1–30; Chernatony and Riley, "Defining 'Brand,'" 417–44; King, *Developing New Brands*.

51 For more on the differences between the tangible and intangible elements of brands, see Chernatony and Riley, "Modeling the Components of the Brand," 1077–90.

52 Lopes, *Global Brands*, 148–79; Casson, "Brands," 41–58.

53 Lopes, *Global Brands*, 6 and 153; Bilkey and Nes, "Country-of-Origin Effects," 89–99; Guy, *When Champagne Became French*, 2; Beverland, "The 'Real Thing,'" 251–8; O'Neill, Houtman, and Aupers, "Advertising Real Beer," 5–15.

54 Peñaloza, "The Commodification of the American West," 82–109; Grayson and Martinec, "Consumer Perceptions of Iconicity and Indexicality," 296–312; Beverland, Lindgreen, and Vink, "Projecting Authenticity through Advertising," 5–15.

55 Cochran, *Pabst*, 129–59; Baron, *Brewed in America*, 257–64; Plavchan, *A History of Anheuser-Busch*, 91–2.

56 For more on the notion of sticky knowledge, see Lopes, *Global Brands*, 7–9.

57 Cochran, *Pabst*, 216.

58 Chandler, *Scale and Scope*, 267; Deconinck and Swinnen, "Tied Houses," 231–6.

59 Hawkins, *A History of Bass Charrington*; Owen, *The Greatest Brewery in the World*.

60 Gourvish and Wilson, *The British Brewing Industry*, 92, 94, 98, 146–7, 273, 438–9; Hannah, *The Rise of the Corporate Economy*, 190; Owen, *The Greatest Brewery in the World*, 5, 164; Gourvish and Wilson, *The British Brewing Industry*, 438–49.

61 Higgins and Verma, "The Business of Protection," 1–19; Duguid, "Developing the Brand," 405–41.

62 Murton, "The Normandy of the New World"; Wagman, "Peace, Order, and Good Banking"; Hammerschmidt "Images of Canadian Advertising."

63 Wagman, "Peace, Order, and Good Banking," 548–56.

64 Ibid., 560.

65 Penfold, "'Eddie Shack Was No Tim Horton,'" 48–66.

66 Rutherford, *The New Icons*, 91–5.

67 McDowall, *Quick to the Frontier*, 83–6.

68 Carstairs, "Roots Nationalism," 235–55.

69 Opp, "Branding 'the Bay/la Baie,'" 223–56. For more on "image worlds," see Nye, *Image Worlds*.

70 *Globe and Mail*, 14 November 1963, 1.

71 Frederick, *Rebels and Colleagues*, 186.

72 Beverland, "The Real Thing,'" 251–8. For more on "inauthentic" brands, see Brown, Kozinets, and Sherry, "Teaching Old Brands New Tricks," 19–33.

73 Horowitz and Horowitz, "Firms in a Declining Market," 129–53; Brouwer, "The European Beer Industry," 157–82; Scherer, "The Determinants of Industrial Plant Sizes in Six Nations," 135–45; Weiss, "Optimal Plant Size and the Extent of the Sub-optimal Capacity," 126–34.

74 Van Der Hallen, "Concentration in the Belgium Brewing Industry and the Breakthrough of Lager in the Interwar Years"; Peles, "Economies of Scale in Advertising Beer and Cigarettes," 32–7; Ackoff and Emshoff, "Advertising Research at Anheuser-Busch Inc.," 1–15; Tremblay, "Strategic Groups and the Demand for Beer," 183–98.

75 McGahan, "The Emergence of the National Brewing Oligopoly: Competition in the American Market, 1933–1958," 229–84; Greer, "The Causes of Concentration in the U.S. Brewing Industry," 100; Sutton, *Sunk Costs and Market Structure*, 287–95. Tremblay and Tremblay, *The U.S. Brewing Industry*, 41–66.

76 George, "The Growth of Television and the Decline of Local Beer," 213–27.

77 Jones, "The New Zealand Brewing Industry," 257–60; Merrett, "Stability and Change in the Australian Brewing Industry," 237–43.

78 Gourvish, "Economics of Brewing," 260; Boje and Johansen, "The Danish Brewing Industry after 1880," 59–74.

79 Millns, "The British Brewing Industry," 154.

80 Ibid.

81 Lopes, *Global Brands*.

82 Joyner, *Shared Traditions*, 1. For more on microhistory as a methodology, see Ginzburg, Carlo, John Tedeschi, and Anne C. Tedeschi, "Microhistory."

83 Heron, *Booze*, 87.

84 Jones, "Working-Class Culture and Working-Class Politics in London," 460–508.

85 Denison, *The Barley and the Stream*; Molson, *The Molsons*; Woods, *The Molson Saga, 1763–1983*; Hunter, *Molson*; Antoniou, *Back to Beer and Hockey*.

86 Landes, *Dynasties*, xix.

87 Dyer and Sicilia, *Labors of a Modern Hercules*, xxi.

Chapter One

1 Robert Kell to John Labatt (14 January 1848), Box LATXT0038, *Labatt Collection*, University of Western Ontario Archives (hereafter *Labatt Collection*).

2 Wilson, "The Enterprises of Robert Hamilton"; McCalla, "The Loyalist Economy of Upper Canada, 1784–1806," 279–304; McCalla, "An Introduction to the Nineteenth Century Business World," 13–23; Forster, "Finding the Right Size," 150–73.

3 McCalla, *Planting the Province*, 141–61.

4 Katz, *The People of Hamilton*, 176–208; Baskerville, "Donald Bethune's Steamship Business," 135–49; McCalla, *The Upper Canada Trade*.

5 McCalla, "Nineteenth Century Business World," 16.

6 Mark, "Entrepreneurship and the Theory of the Firm," 344.

7 Kirkwood, "Is a Lack of Self-Confidence Hindering Women Entrepreneurs?" 118–33.

8 Bliss, *Northern Enterprise*.

9 Ibid., 8.

10 Ross and Smith, *Canada's Entrepreneurs*.

11 Tucker, "Labatt's," 2.

12 Ibid., 2–3.

13 Ibid.

14 Bielenberg and Solar, "The Irish Cotton Industry from the Industrial Revolution to Partition," 1–28.

15 Bielenberg, "The Irish Brewing Industry and the Rise of Guinness, 1790–1914," 91.

16 Toynbee, *The Industrial Revolution*.

17 Landes, *The Unbound Prometheus*, 41–123.

18 Cronin and O'Callaghan, *A History of Ireland*, 108–9.

19 Dickens, *Sketches by Boz*, 54.

20 Tucker, "Labatt's," 3–4.

21 Brandon and Brooke, *Bankside*, chapters 6, 12, and 13.

22 Bennett, *Ale, Beer, and Brewsters in England,* chapter 2.

23 Ibid.

24 Brown, "Whitbread Brewery," 841–2.

25 Wilson, "The Changing Taste for Beer in Victorian Britain," 79.

26 Gourvish and Wilson, *The British Brewing Industry 1830–1980*, 79.

27 Mathias, *The Brewing Industry in England, 1700–1830*.

28 Quoted in Ackroyd, *London*, 356.

29 Ibid., 356.

30 Toone, *A Chronological Record of the Remarkable Public Events*, 655.

31 Tucker, "Labatt's," 4.

32 Ibid., 5.

33 Ibid.

34 Ibid., 6.

35 Duffy, *Bankruptcy and Insolvency in London during the Industrial Revolution* and Finn, *The Character of Credit*.

36 White, *Mansions of Misery*.

37 Tucker, 6–7.

38 Ibid.

39 Stuart, *The Emigrant's Guide to Upper Canada*.

40 Cattermole, *The Advantages of Emigration to Canada*, iii.

41 Radcliff, *Authentic Letters from Upper Canada*.

42 Akenson, *The Irish in Ontario*.

43 Elliott, *Irish Migrants in the Canadas*, 232–4.

44 Geoffrey Bilson, "Cholera and Public Health in Canada," 352–5.

45 Tucker, "Labatt's," 14.

46 Ibid., 10–11.

47 Goodspeed, *History of the County of Middlesex*, 208.

48 Armstrong, *The Forest City*, 31–61.

49 Miller, *A Century of Western Ontario*, 28–9.

50 Bellamy, "Brewers, Barkeepers, Redcoats and Rebels: Beer and the Rebellions of 1837–1838," 89–91.

51 Tucker, "Labatt's," 17–18.

52 Henderson, "A Study of the British Garrison in London, Canada West, 1838–1869."

53 Denison, *The Barley and the Stream*, 26–48, and McCreath, *The Life and Times of Alexander Keith*, 23–32.

54 Anonymous, "London – Farming in Canada West," *The Canadian Agriculturalist and Journal of the Transaction of the Board of Agriculture*, 7, no. 3 (March 1855), 68.

55 Ashurst, "Hops and Their Use in Brewing," 31–59. See also Unger, *Beer in the Middle Ages and the Renaissance*, 53–106.

56 Haughton, "Teetotalism Advantageous to Farmers," *Canadian Temperance Advocate*, 11, no. 9 (1 May 1845), 142.

57 One of the major changes in the history of brewing occurred in the fourteenth

century when beer began to replace ale, by which the former was reinforced, made more durable, and given a deeper flavour by the introduction of hops. (See Unger, *Beer in the Middle Ages and the Renaissance,* 53–106.)

58 Ashurst, "Hops and Their Use in Brewing," 32–4.

59 Phillips, *On Tap,* 22.

60 John Carling, "Pioneers of Middlesex," 22.

61 Moodie, *Roughing It in the Bush, or Forest Life in Canada,* 339.

62 Phillips, *On Tap,* 57–8.

63 Tucker, "Labatt's," 23–4.

64 C.O. Ermatinger, "The Talbot Regime," Box LATXT0039, *Labatt Collection.*

65 Bellamy, "'Rich by Nature, Poor by Policy'?" 48–70.

66 C.O. Ermatinger, "The Talbot Regime," Box LATXT0039, *Labatt Collection.*

67 Tucker, "Labatt's," 17–18.

68 Goodspeed, *History of the County of Middlesex,* 152–8.

69 Mathias, *The Brewing Industry in England, 1700–1830,* 252–338.

70 McCreath, *The Life and Times of Alexander Keith,* 33.

71 Molson, *The Molsons,* 223; Denison, *The Barley and the Stream,* 190.

72 *London Times,* 28 May 1847, 3.

73 John Labatt to Eliza Labatt (30 March 1847), Box LATXT0038, *Labatt Collection.*

74 Tucker, "Labatt's," 19.

75 Ibid., 20.

76 Ibid., 21.

77 Ibid.

78 John Labatt to Eliza Labatt (30 March 1847), Box LATXT0038, *Labatt Collection.*

79 Ibid.

80 Ibid.

81 Ibid.

82 Tucker, "Labatt's," 24.

83 Quoted in Tucker, "Labatt's," 24.

84 John Labatt to Eliza Labatt (16 April 1847), Box LATXT0038, *Labatt Collection.*

85 Tucker, "Labatt's," 24.

86 Robert Kell to John Labatt (14 January 1848), Box LATXT0038, *Labatt Collection.*

87 Tucker, "Labatt's," 24–5.

88 Ibid., 24–6.

89 Ibid., 24.

90 McCalla, "An Introduction to the Nineteenth Century Business World," 13–23.

91 Tucker, "Labatt's," 25.

92 Maria Kell to John Labatt (11 October 1849), Box LATXT0038, *Labatt Collection*.

93 Goodspeed, *History of the County of Middlesex*, 209.

94 Anonymous, "London," *Anglo-American Magazine*, vol. II (March, 1853).

95 *Canadian Free Press*, 27 March 1849.

96 Heron, *Booze*, 17–50.

97 Gywn, *John A.*, 265.

98 Roberts, *In Mixed Company*.

99 Bonnycastle, *Canada and the Canadians in 1846*, 124.

100 Phillips, *On Tap*, 58.

101 Ibid., 64.

102 *London Gazette*, 28 October 1837.

103 *London Times*, 6 June 1845.

104 *Anglo-American Magazine*, vol. II (March 1853).

105 Ibid.

106 Noel, *Canada Dry*, 135.

107 Ibid., 137.

108 McCarty, *Distilled in Maine*, 48–53.

109 Robert Kell to John Labatt (7 July 1854), Box LATXT0038, *Labatt Collection*.

110 Ibid.

111 Ibid.

112 Tucker, "Labatt's," 42–3.

Chapter Two

1 Chandler, "The Organization of Manufacturing and Transportation," 206.

2 Keefer, *The Philosophy of Railroads*, 9.

3 den Otter, *The Philosophy of Railways*.

4 McCalla, *Planting the Province*, 203.

5 Gilmour, *Spatial Evolution of Manufacturing*, 153–68.

6 Tucker, "Labatt's," 34.

7 Armstrong, "John Kinder Labatt," *Dictionary of Canadian Biography*, vol. 9, 436–7.

8 Henderson, "A Study of the British Garrison in London," 18–32.

9 Anonymous, "John K. Labatt and the London Brewery, 1847–1853," Box LATXT0118, *Labatt Collection*.

10 Stacey, *Canada and the British Army*, 35.

11 Anonymous, "John K. Labatt and the London Brewery, 1847–1853," Box
    LATXT0118, *Labatt Collection.*

12 Careless, *Toronto to 1918,* 200.

13 Ibid., 43–109.

14 *Globe,* 5 February 1853.

15 Gilmour, *Spatial Evolution of* Manufacturing, 155.

16 In 1853, Toronto had eleven breweries, while Hamilton had four in operation.
    See Richard Sweet, "The Dictionary of Canadian Brewers," 73–5, 103–11.

17 Timperlake, *Illustrated Toronto,* 267.

18 Power, "Eugene O'Keefe," 796–7.

19 Bowering, *The Art and Mystery of Brewing in Ontario,* 95–7.

20 Royal Commission on the Liquor Traffic, *Minutes of Evidence, Ontario,* vol. 4,
    729.

21 Tucker, "Labatt's," 36–7.

22 *London Free Press,* 28 December 1858.

23 Gourvish and Wilson, *The British Brewing Industry,* 151–68.

24 Phillips, *On Tap,* 67 and 147.

25 John Labatt to Eliza Labatt (1 August 1863), Box LATXT0038, *Labatt Collection.*

26 *London Prototype* (1865).

27 Anderson, *One Hundred Years of Brewing,* 616. This circular process directly
    contributed to the drop in the number of breweries during the thirty years 1862
    to 1892, from 182 to 122, respectively.

28 *London Free Press,* 29 October 1866.

29 Armstrong, "John Kinder Labatt," 436–7. His estate consisted of the brewery,
    the ground on which it was built, a large brick house located on the brewery
    grounds, an insurance policy for five hundred pounds sterling, and ten shares
    in the Huron and Erie Saving and Loan Company.

30 *London Free Press,* 29 October 1866.

31 John Kinder Labatt, "Last Will and Testament" (25 April 1864), Box 94-335A,
    Labatt Collection.

32 Ibid.

33 Landes, *Dynasties.*

34 Tucker, "Labatt's," 49.

35 Ibid., 50.

36 Wilson, "Changing Tastes in Victorian Britain," 99.

37 The partnership came to an end when Ephraim died, in 1867, at the age of thirty.

38 Oliver, "Brewmaster," 170–1.

39 *London Prototype* (1865).

40 Wilson, "Changing Tastes in Victorian Britain," 93–104.

41 Gourvish and Wilson, *The British Brewing Industry,* 90–8.

42 Sigsworth, "Science and the Brewing Industry, 1850–1900," 544.

43 Gourvish and Wilson, *The British Brewing Industry*, 88.

44 Sigsworth, "Science and the Brewing Industry, 1850–1900," 543.

45 John Labatt quoted in Tucker, "Labatt's," 85.

46 Ibid.

47 Phillips, *On Tap*, 37.

48 Ibid., 68.

49 Ibid.

50 Tucker, "Labatt's," 66–7.

51 Ibid., 57.

52 Anderson, *One Hundred Years of Brewing*, 618.

53 Tucker, "Labatt's," 62.

54 The principal amount of the first mortgage was $22,000 payable in irregular amounts over a six-year period, beginning in 1873. After making the last payment in 1879, John Labatt signed another mortgage with his mother for $21,640 payable over five years in equal annual amounts.

55 Luckhurst, *The Story of Exhibitions*, 10–12.

56 Winder, "A Trans-national Machine on the World Stage," 356–9.

57 Ibid., 352–76.

58 Greenhalgh, *Ephemeral Vistas*; Rydell, *World of Fairs*; Heaman, *The Inglorious Arts of Peace: Exhibitions in Canadian Society During the Nineteenth Century*; Walden, *Becoming Modern in Toronto*.

59 Centennial Board of Finance, *Visitor's Guide to the Centennial Exhibition and Philadelphia*, 10.

60 Gross and Snyder, *Philadelphia's 1876 Centennial Exhibition*, 8.

61 Centennial Board of Finance, *Visitor's Guide*, 15.

62 Ingram, *The Centennial Exposition*, 248–50.

63 Ibid., 629.

64 Ibid., 248–50.

65 *On Tap*, 100–1.

66 Timperlake, *Illustrated Toronto*, 270.

67 *Report of the Canadian Commission at the International Exhibition of Philadelphia, 1876*, 37.

68 United States Centennial Commission, *International Exhibition, 1876*, 293.

69 Ibid.

70 Ibid., 501.

71 *Globe*, 30 December 1876, 7.

72 Ibid., 27 February 1877, 7.

73 Ibid., 19 April 1877, 3.

74 Phillips, *On Tap*, 139.

75 Ibid.

76 *Montreal Herald*, 1 January 1890, 6.

77 Phillips, *On Tap*, 136–41.

Chapter Three

1 Canada, Royal Commission on the Liquor Traffic, *Minutes of Evidence*, vol. 4, part 1 (1895), 366.

2 Sulkunen, *History of the Finnish Temperance Movement*; Carter, *The English Temperance Movement*; Barrows and Room (eds.), *Drinking: Behavior and Belief in Modern History*; Tyrrell, *Sobering Up*; Sinclair, *Era of Excess*; Krout, *The Origins of Prohibition*.

3 Noel, *Canada Dry*; Barron, "The American Origins of the Temperance Movement in Ontario, 1828–1850"; Barry, "'Shades of Vice ... and Moral Glory'"; Chapman, "The Mid-Nineteenth-Century Temperance Movement in New Brunswick and Maine"; Dick, "From Temperance to Prohibition in 19th Century Nova Scotia."

4 Heron, *Booze*, 79–128.

5 Spence, *Prohibition in Canada*, 4–15.

6 Kerr, *Organized for Prohibition*; Greenway, *Drink and British Politics since 1830*; Rumbarger, *Profits, Power and Prohibition, Alcohol Reform and the Industrializing of America, 1800–1930*; Quinn, *Father Mathew's Crusade*.

7 Ibid., 116–17.

8 Canada, Royal Commission on the Liquor Traffic, *Minutes of Evidence*, 4, part 1 (1895), 732.

9 Ibid., 365–67.

10 Kingston *Chronicle* (15 September 1821).

11 George Wallis, "Coffee versus Beer," Halifax *Abstainer*, 1, no. 8 (15 May 1857), 117.

12 Heron, *Booze*, 82.

13 *Globe*, 18 March 1882.

14 Bellamy, "The Canadian Brewing Industry's Response to Prohibition," 2–17.

15 Heron, *Booze*, 112–28.

16 A reproduction of Bengough's cartoon can be found in Carman Cumming, *Sketches from a Young Country*, 220.

17 Canada. Parliament. House of Commons, *Canada Temperance Act, 1878*, 16.

18 Ibid.

19 Ibid.

20 F.W. Raymond to John Labatt (19 June 1885), Letter Book, vol. I, 47, *Labatt Collection*.

21 Waite, "The Political Ideas of John A. Macdonald," 51–68.

22 Neill, *A History of Canadian Economic Thought*, 72–91.

23 MacLean, *The Complete Tariff Hand-Book, Shewing Canadian Customs Tariff with the Various Changes Made during the Last Thirty Years*, 36.

24 In 1867 the federal government of John A. Macdonald rescinded the gallonage duty on malt liquor and placed a tax of one cent per pound of malt manufactured in the country. The rate imposed was intended to be equivalent to the duty previously collected on beer. In 1877, the Liberal government of Alexander Mackenzie raised the duty on manufactured malt to two cents per pound, only to reduce it two years later to one cent per pound before raising it again to two cents per pound in 1891. See Anderson, *One Hundred Years of Brewing*, 618.

25 MacLean, *The Complete Tariff Hand-Book*, 36.

26 Raymond to John Labatt (5 June 1885), Letter Book, vol. I, 41, *Labatt Collection*.

27 Spence, *The Facts of the Case*, 156–8.

28 Canada, Royal Commission on the Liquor Traffic, *Minutes of Evidence*, vol. 4, part 1 (1895), 734.

29 Ibid., 366.

30 Denison, *The Barley and the Stream*, 263.

31 Careless, *Toronto to 1918*, table iv, 200.

32 *Halifax Herald*, 28 June 1880; Testimony of Robert R. Bell before the Royal Commission on the Liquor Traffic, House of Commons, *Sessional Paper*, No. 21 1894, 584–9.

33 Canada, Royal Commission on the Liquor Traffic, vol. 2, 280.

34 *Montreal Witness*, 4 April 1881.

35 DeLottinville, "Joe Beef of Montreal," 9–40. Heron, *Booze*, 105–21.

36 Spence, *The Facts of the Case*, 19.

37 Anonymous, *Montreal by Gaslight*, 104–5.

38 Provencher, "Charles McKiernan," *Dictionary of Canadian Biography* (online). www.biographi.ca/en/bio/mckiernan_charles_11E.html (accessed 6 February 2019).

39 Spence, *The Facts of the* Case, 20.

40 Canada, Royal Commission on the Liquor Traffic, *Report*, 18.

41 Denison, *The Barley and the Stream*, 233.

42 For production figures see ibid. For an extended discussion of Molson's "primary business ventures during the period 1850–1890 — i.e., banking and distilling," see Hunter, *Molson*, 385–434.

43 Ibid., 186.

44 "Memorandum," Box LATXT039, file "Production – Quantity in Barrels/Bottles per Week/Month/Year," *Labatt Collection*.

45 John Labatt to P. Beaudry (30 December 1885), Letter Book, vol. 1, 237, *Labatt Collection*.

46 Ibid.

47 Canada, Royal Commission on the Liquor Traffic, *Minutes of Evidence*, vol. 4, part 1 (1895), 366.

48 Ibid.

49 Ibid.

50 "Articles of Agreement" (1 February 1884), Box LATXT0039, *Labatt Collection*.

51 John Labatt to Walter Thayer (19 September 1889), Letter Book, vol. I, 123, *Labatt Collection*.

52 F.W. Raymond to John Labatt (14 August 1891), Letter Book, vol. II, 71, *Labatt Collection*.

53 F.W. Raymond to John Labatt (13 September 1894), Letter Book, vol. II, 179, *Labatt Collection*.

54 F.W. Raymond to John Labatt (4 August 1893), Letter Book, vol. I, 114, *Labatt Collection*.

55 "Memorandum" (12 October 1893), Letter Book, vol. II, 142, *Labatt Collection*. During the same period, Labatt was shipping 41,250 gallons of ale in quart and pint bottles to Hamilton. See Letter Book, vol. I, 178, *Labatt Collection*.

56 Phillips, *On Tap*, 131–4.

57 Canada, Royal Commission on the Liquor Traffic, *Report*, 22

58 Sweet, "The Dictionary of Canadian Breweries," 45–52.

59 Bliss, *Northern Enterprise*, 292.

60 Beer consumption was lowest in Eastern Canada in Canada's tiniest province,

Prince Edward Island. In 1878, Islanders consumed 52,704 gallons (2,108 barrels) of beer, which meant that each person was consuming, on average, roughly half a gallon of malt liquor. By 1889, total consumption had declined on the island to 31,198 gallons (1,247 barrels), or .286 gallons per person.[60] Whereas yearly per capita beer consumption declined in PEI, it remained relatively stable at approximately 1 gallon per person in the two remaining East-Coast provinces, Nova Scotia and New Brunswick. Despite the falling off of consumption in the Maritimes during the Scott Act period, Labatt continued to supply these markets, sending shipments of ale, stout, and malt to the east coast on a weekly basis. Canada, Royal Commission on the Liquor Traffic, *Report*, 17–18.

61 Canada, Royal Commission on the Liquor Traffic, *Report*, 24.

62 Bellamy, "'Rich by Nature, Poor by Policy'?" 48–70.

63 Evans, "The Vancouver Island Brewing Industry," 18–56.

64 Ibid., 57–65.

65 Ibid., 37.

66 *British Colonist*, 7 January 1886, 1; *British Colonist*, 17 February 1886, 2.

67 Labatt's freight costs were ninety-nine cents per 100 pounds to Victoria and eighty-seven cents to Winnipeg.

68 John Labatt to Walter Thayer (19 September 1889), Letter Book, vol. I, 123, *Labatt Collection*.

69 Anderson, *One Hundred Years of Brewing*, 619.

70 Wilson and Gourvish, *The Dynamics of the International Brewing Industry since 1800*, 116.

71 Ibid., 31.

72 Kribs, *Report of Louis P. Kribs in Connection with the Investigation Held by the Canadian Royal Commission on the Liquor Traffic*, 11.

73 Ontario, *Bureau of Industries* (Toronto, Grip Printing and Publishing Co., 1884), 112

74 Gilmour, *Spatial Evolution of Manufacturing*, 154.

75 Ibid., 158.

76 Anonymous, "The Great Fire and Subsequent Growth, 1874–1900," Box LATXT01118, *Labatt Collection*.

77 Gilmour, *Spatial Evolution of Manufacturing*, 158.

78 Ibid.

79 Canada, Royal Commission on the Liquor Traffic, *Minutes of Evidence*, vol. 4, part 1 (1895), 359.

80 For an excellent history of the Royal Bank expansion during this period, see McDowall, *Quick to the Frontier*.

81 Ibid., 366.

82 Denison, *The Barley and the Stream*, 55, 190, 231, and 281.

83 Bottle cleaning also significantly improved during this period. In 1884, the Goulding bottle-washing machine was introduced. But while the big American brewers were quick to embrace this new technology, Labatt continued to have his bottles washed by hand until after the turn of the century. Innovation often came more slowly to Canadian brewing than it did among U.S. brewers. Canadian brewers were also slow to embrace the crown cap, which was invented in 1892. The smaller Canadian market and the prolonged depression of the late nineteenth century worked against economies of scale.

84 Canada, Royal Commission on the Liquor Traffic, *Minutes of Evidence*, vol. 4, part 1 (1895), 366.

85 Ibid.

86 Ibid.

87 Ibid., 731.

Chapter Four

1 Armstrong and Nelles, *Southern Exposure*; McDowall, *The Light*.

2 McDowall, *Quick to the Frontier: Canada's Royal Bank*.

3 Chandler, *Scale and Scope*, 117, 122, 171–5, 213–17, 446–52.

4 McCreath, *The Life and Times of Alexander Keith*; Brenton Haliburton, *What's Brewing*; Phillips, *On Tap*; Sneath, *Brewed in Canada*; Hagelund, *House of Suds*; Hunter, *Molson*.

5 Rudy, "Sleeman's," 39–41; Denison, *The Barley and the Stream*, 57–61, 83, 92–5, 123, 159–60, 176–9, 188–90, 208, 214, 265–75, 282, 326, 334; Brent, *Lager Heads*, 137–48, 173–86.

6 Klassen, "Entrepreneurship in the Canadian West," 313–33.

7 Phillips, *On Tap*, 152–3.

8 R.D. Millar to John Labatt (3 September 1883), Box LATXT0038, *Labatt Collection*.

9 Bliss, *A Living Profit*, 33–54.

10 Ibid., 54; Cruickshank, "Taking the Bitter with the Sweet," 367–94.

11 F.W. Raymond to John Labatt (18 July 1891), *Letter Book*, vol. 2, 55–6, *Labatt Collection*.

12 Labatt had wanted the prices fixed at thirty-four cents a gallon, $1.10 per dozen quarts, and seventy-five cents for a dozen pints of ale. See F.W. Raymond to John Labatt (21 July 1891), *Letter Book*, vol. 2, 59, *Labatt Collection*.

13 F.W. Raymond to John Labatt (21 July 1891), *Letter Book*, vol. II, 61, *Labatt Collection*.

14 F.W. Raymond to John Labatt (21 July 1891), *Letter Book*, vol. II, 57–63, *Labatt Collection*.

15 "Sample of Cut Prices" (24 April 1894), *Letter Book*, vol. II, 159, *Labatt Collection*.

16 C.P. Mulvany and G.M. Adamp, *History of Toronto and County of York, Ontario*, vol. I, 379; "Sample of Cut Prices" (24 Apr. 1894), *Letter Book*, vol. II, 159, *Labatt Collection*.

17 John Labatt to James Lotridge (2 June 1894), *Letter Book*, vol. I, 211–13, *Labatt Collection*.

18 John Labatt to Eugene O'Keefe (4 May 1894), *Letter Book*, vol. I, 208–9, *Labatt Collection*.

19 *Canadian Grocer*, 10 July 1891; *Canadian Grocer*, 4 December 1896.

20 Bliss, *A Living Profit*, 33–54.

21 John Labatt to J.W.G. Whitney (27 February 1895), Letter Book, vol. II, 224–7, *Labatt Collection*.

22 John Labatt to Walter Thayer (19 September 1889, Letter Book, vol. I, 123–9, *Labatt Collection*.

23 Cochran, *The Pabst Brewing Company*, 180; United Brewers' Foundation, *The Brewing Industry in the United States*, 55–6.

24 Canada, Royal Commission on the Liquor Traffic, *Report*, 16.

25 John Labatt to Mr Rogers (11 March 1893), Letter Book, vol. I, 188, *Labatt Collection*.

26 John Labatt to Mr Rogers (25 February 1893), Letter Book, vol. I, 183, *Labatt Collection*.

27 Anonymous, *Mixed Drinks, The Saloon Keeper's Journal*, 2 (January 1890), 1.

28 John Labatt to Mr Rogers (25 February 1893) Letter Book, vol. I, 183, *Labatt Collection*.

29 Tucker, "Labatt's," 87–109.

30 United States, *The Tariff of 1883 and 1890 on Imports into the United States*, 28.

31 John Labatt to Walter Thayer (19 September 1889), Letter Book, vol. I, 123–9, *Labatt Collection*.

32 Ibid.

33 Ibid.

34 Ibid.

35 John Labatt to Rogers (11 March 1893), Letter Book, vol. I, 188, *Labatt Collection*.

36 Kerr, "The American Brewing Industry, 1865–1920," 176–93.

37 Stack, "Local and Regional Breweries in America's Brewing Industry, 1865 to 1920," 435–63.

38 Baron, *Brewed in America*, 257–64.

39 Ibid.

40 Cochran, *Pabst*, 72.

41 Skilnik, *Beer*, 1–4.

42 Ibid., 41.

43 Ibid., 61.

44 Armstrong and Nelles, *Southern Exposure*, 43–61.

45 Skilnik, *Beer*, 55–66.

46 Englemann, "O Whiskey!" 84–9.

47 *Western Brewer* (March–May 1892).

48 Kerr, "The American Brewing Industry, 1865–1920," 184.

49 Skilnik, *Beer*, 61–2.

50 Pierce, *A History of Chicago*, 151.

51 Ibid.

52 John Labatt to Jeffery Hale (5 May 1908), Letter Book, vol. II, 776, *Labatt Collection*.

53 Heron, *Booze*, 98–9.

54 John Labatt to Mr Rogers (13 October 1892), Letter Book, vol. II, 165–71, *Labatt Collection*.

55 John Labatt to Mr Rogers (25 February 1893), Letter Book, vol. I, 183, *Labatt Collection*.

56 Ogle, *Ambitious Brew*, 100.

57 John Labatt to Mr Rogers (11 March 1893), Letter Book, vol. I, 188–91, *Labatt Collection*.

58 John Labatt to Mr Rogers (31 October 1892), Letter Book, vol. I, 165–71, *Labatt Collection*.

59 F.W. Raymond to John Labatt (2 October 1893), Letter Book, vol. II, 39, *Labatt Collection*.

60 John Labatt to H.G. Beresford (21 December 1904), Letter Book, vol. I, 466, *Labatt Collection*.

61 Tucker, "Labatt's," 117–19.

62 Kerr, "The American Brewing Industry, 1865–1920," 176.

63 Gourvish and Wilson, *The British Brewing Industry, 1830–1980*, 169–75.

64 The extent of the Canadian shift toward lager was manifest at the Royal Com-
    mission on the Liquor Traffic in 1894. When asked about the nature of the do-
    mestic beer market, Eugene O'Keefe told the commissioners that there "was
    already a trend towards the consumption of lager beer." The statistical evidence
    supported his statement. In 1865, the total quantity of lager beer brewed in
    Toronto was 4,625 wine gallons, according to excise returns. By 1893, there were
    four lager breweries in Toronto producing 1.2 million wine gallons (48,000 bar-
    rels), which O'Keefe reported was an increase in lager consumption "out of all
    proportion to the increase of population." (See his testimony before the *Royal
    Commission on the Liquor Traffic, Minutes of Evidence*, vol. 4, part 1, 1895, 730.)

65 John Labatt to John Annan, 15 December 1898, Letter Book, vol. I, 313–17, *Labatt
    Collection*.

66 Ucbasaran et al. "The Nature of Entrepreneurial Experience," 541–55.

67 John Labatt to Mr Rogers (13 October 1892), Letter Book, vol. II, 165–71, *Labatt
    Collection*.

68 John Labatt to John Annan (22 February 1899), Letter Book, vol. I, 324–5, *Labatt
    Collection*; John Labatt to Hugh Fox (8 January 1897), Letter Book, vol. I, 261–2,
    Labatt Collection; John Labatt to John Annan (15 December 1898), Letter Book,
    vol. I, 313–7, *Labatt Collection*.

69 Landes, *Dynasties*, especially chapter 1.

70 Tucker, "Labatt's," 113.

71 John Labatt to J.W. Moffat (11 August 1908), Letter Book, vol. II, 787, *Labatt
    Collection*.

72 Ibid.

73 Ibid.

74 John Labatt (5 January 1910), Letter Book, vol. II, 859–61, *Labatt Collection*.

75 Ibid.

76 Tucker, "Labatt's," 125.

77 Ibid., 124.

78 Chandler, "The Emergence of Managerial Capitalism," 473.

79 Tucker, "Labatt's," 125.

80 Ibid.

81 McLeod and St John, *Ontario Beer*, chapter 4.

82 Tucker, "Labatt's," 126.

Chapter Five

1 Borden quoted in Brown and Cook, *Canada*, 212.
2 Shortt, "The Economic Effect of War upon Canada," 65–74.
3 Ibid.
4 Robert Colin Scatcherd to John Labatt Scatcherd (10 August 1914), "Letters of Lieut. John Labatt Scatcherd, 1914–1918," *Labatt Collection*.
5 Gourvish and Wilson, *The British Brewing Industry*, 291.
6 *London Free Press*, 28 April 1915, 14.
7 Tucker, "Labatt's," 127–9.
8 Will of John Labatt, 3 July 1911.
9 Tucker, "Labatt's," 127–9.
10 Ibid.
11 Ibid.
12 Lopes, *Global Brands*, 80–5.
13 Tucker, "Labatt's," 151.
14 Ibid.
15 Ibid.
16 Labatt, *A Different Road*, 5.
17 Ibid.
18 Rudy, *The Freedom to Smoke*, 132–41.
19 Tucker, "Labatt's," 152.
20 Ibid.
21 Ibid., 153.
22 Bliss, "The Methodist Church and World War I," 213–33.
23 Cook, "Wet Canteens and Worrying Mothers," 318.
24 Morton, *When Your Number's Up*, 181–206, 227–52.
25 Cook, "Wet Canteens and Worrying Mothers," 311–30.
26 Quoted in Cook, "Wet Canteens and Worrying Mothers," 319; Fetherstonhaugh, *The 13th Battalion Royal Highlanders of Canada*, 22.
27 Anonymous, "Alderson Announces End of Teetotal Rule for Canteens," *Mail and Empire*, 21 October 1914.
28 English, *The Decline of Politics, 1901–20*.
29 Robert Borden to George Perley (16 June 1915), Library and Archives Canada, RG 25, vol. 263, file P-3-99.
30 Ibid.
31 Cook, "'More a Medicine than a Beverage,'" 6–22.

32 Gourvish and Wilson, *The British Brewing Industry*, 317–35.

33 Weston and Lee, "Lloyd George's Beer" (1915).

34 Merrett, "Stability and Change in the Australian Brewing Industry, 1920–94," 230–3.

35 *Minutes*, 3 September 1915.

36 Ibid.

37 Dominion Brewers' Association, *Facts on The Brewing Industry in Canada*, 69.

38 Urquhart and Buckley, *Historical Statistics of Canada*, 359.

39 *Minutes*, 15 January 1916.

40 John Labatt to W.S. Rome (11 January 1941), Box LATXT0039, *Labatt Collection*.

41 Ibid.

42 Blum, *Brewed in Detroit*, 172.

43 Ibid.

44 Noel, *Canada Dry*; Heron, *Booze*, 53–77, 113–28, 174–85; Cook, *Through Sunshine and Shadow*; Spence, *Prohibition in Canada*; Dick, "From Temperance to Prohibition in 19th Century Nova Scotia," 530–52; Forbes, "Prohibition and the Social Gospel in Nova Scotia," 62–86; Lockwood, "Temperance in Upper Canada as Ethnic Subterfuge," 43–69; O'Neill, "The Temperance Movement, Prohibition and Scarcity in Ontario, 1900–1916"; Sturgis, "Beer under Pressure," 83–100.

45 *Toronto Daily Star*, 5 April 1915, 4.

46 Quoted in Heron's *Booze*, 178.

47 *Christian Guardian*, 18 November 1914.

48 Ibid., 22 September 1915.

49 *Pioneer*, 22 June 1917.

50 Thompson, *The Harvests of War*, 102.

51 Heron, *Booze*, 176.

52 Quoted in Bliss, *A Canadian Millionaire*, 2.

53 Ibid., 3–10.

54 *Toronto Daily Star*, 5 April 1915, 4.

55 Tennyson, "Sir William Hearst and the Ontario Temperance Act," 241.

56 Heron, *Booze*, 180.

57 Leacock, "The Tyranny of Prohibition," 65.

58 Heron, *Booze*, 24–5.

59 *Toronto Daily Star*, 7 April 1916, 1.

60 *Toronto Star*, 24 March 1916, 8.

61 *The Times*, 7 September 1916.

62 See Crapster, "'Our Trade, Our Politics,'" and Fahey, "Brewers, Publicans and Working Class Drinkers."

63 Mathias, "The Brewing Industry, Temperance and Politics," 97–114; Valverde and O'Malley, "Pleasure, Freedom and Drugs," 28–31.

64 Lefebvre, "Prohibition and the Smuggling of Intoxicating Liquors between the Two Saults," 34.

65 *Minutes*, 12 August 1916.

66 *Montreal Gazette*, 22 February 1911.

67 "Beer Is Necessary for Munitions Workers," *Montreal Gazette*, 2 July 1917.

68 See "National Breweries Ltd, Campaigns, 1915–1925," Library and Archives Canada, MG 28 III 57, vol. 404, *Molson Papers*.

69 Heron, *Booze*, 270.

70 John Labatt Ltd, "Financial Statement 1917," Box LATXT 73, *Labatt Collection*.

71 *Toronto Star*, 10 August 1916, 5.

72 Ibid.

73 Ibid., 23 May 1917.

74 *Minutes*, 27 May 1916.

75 Ibid.

76 *Minutes*, 27 April 1916.

77 Klassen, "Entrepreneurship in the Canadian West," 331.

78 *Globe*, 18 October 1916, 9.

79 *Minutes*, 28 October 1916.

80 *Minutes*, 12 August 1916.

81 *Globe*, 7 October 1919, 8.

82 *Minutes*, 23 May 1917.

83 *Minutes* of the Sixth Annual General Meeting of the Shareholders of John Labatt's Limited, 23 May 1917.

84 Ibid.

85 Rudy, "Sleeman's," 44.

Chapter Six

1 *Canadian Annual Review*, 1920, 612.

2 Auditor's *Report* (30 September 1920).

3 *Minutes*, 28 November 1921.

4 *Minutes*, 3 September 1921.

5 Tremblay and Tremblay, *The U.S. Brewing Industry*, 94–100.
6 See Plavchan, *A History of Anheuser-Busch*; Cochran, *The Pabst Brewing Company*; Ronnenberg, "The American Brewing Industry since 1920," 193–5.
7 *Toronto Star*, 17 October 1919, 5.
8 Tom Mallet, "Company History," Box LATXT122, *Labatt Collection*.
9 Ibid.
10 *Minutes*, 24 February 1919.
11 Ibid.
12 Library and Archives Canada, RG150, Accession 1992-93/166, Box 5270-62.
13 *Globe*, 11 October 1919, 10.
14 *Minutes*, 22 March 1919.
15 Ronnenberg, "The American Brewing Industry since 1920," 193–5.
16 Behr, *Prohibition*, 78–9.
17 Shane and Venkataraman, "The Promise of Entrepreneurship as a Field of Research," 217–26; Kirzner, "Entrepreneurial Discovery and the Competitive Market Process," 60–85: Gaglio and Katz, "The Psychological Basis of Opportunity Identification," 96–111.
18 *Toronto Star Weekly*, 5 June 1920.
19 Cole, *The Whiskey King*, 131.
20 Ibid., 174.
21 Okrent, *Last Call*, 122.
22 Heron, *Booze*, 258.
23 Ibid.
24 Taylor, "The Whiskey Kings," 189.
25 Cole, *The Whiskey King*, 167.
26 Ibid., 164–5.
27 Moore, *Bootleggers and Borderlands*, 103–17.
28 Hume Cronyn to John S. Labatt (6 June 1922), Box LATXT0048, *Labatt Collection*.
29 "Sales of Temperance Beer versus Strong Beer, 1920–1926," *Minutes*, 6 January 1926, 197.
30 "Interviews, 1980–1985," File 0604, *Albert Tucker Papers*.
31 Ibid.
32 *Toronto Star*, 7 April 1927, 4.
33 Ibid.
34 Cole, *The Whiskey King*, 3.

35 Heron, *Booze*, 250.

36 *Minutes*, 18 October 1924; *Minutes*, 11 April 1925.

37 *Labatt Papers*, File Orange 039h. The annual rent for all of these buildings came to just over $3,000.

38 Tom Mallet, "Company History," Box LATXT122, *Labatt Collection*.

39 Canada. Royal Commission on Customs and Excise (1928), *Minutes of Evidence*, 564–6.

40 *London Free Press*, 10 July 1922, 10.

41 *Globe*, 10 July 1922, 3; *Globe*, 14 July 1922, 3.

42 *Minutes*, 24 November 1922.

43 *Minutes*, 12 February 1922; *Minutes*, 20 March 1922; *Minutes*, 24 November 1922; *Minutes*, 2 October 1923.

44 Tom Mallet, "Company History," Box LATXT122, *Labatt Collection*.

45 Ibid.

46 *Toronto Star*, 7 April 1927, 4; *London Free Press*, 7 April 1927, 8.

47 Cole, *The Whiskey King*, 139.

48 *Globe and Mail*, 8 April 1927, 4.

49 Tom Mallet, "Company History," Box LATXT122, *Labatt Collection*.

50 Heron, *Booze*, 240–6.

51 Tom Mallet, "Company History," Box LATXT122, *Labatt Collection*.

52 *Globe*, 7 April 1927, 4.

53 Guccione, "Baron of the Bootleggers," *Financial Post*, June 1981, 13–18.

54 *Toronto Star*, 7 April 1927, 4.

55 *London Free Press*, 7 April 1927, 8.

56 *Globe*, 1 April 1927, 1–2.

57 Canada, Royal Commission on Customs and Excise, *Interim Reports* (Nos. 1 to 10), 68–70.

58 Carlsruhe Brewery (1879–1929), Formosa Springs Brewery (1876–1922, 1927–1972), Kekabeka Falls Brewery (1906–1960), Grant's Springs Brewery (1853–1932), Hamilton Brewing Association (1903–1930), Labatt (1847–present), Brading Brewing Co. (1865–1948); The Capital Brewing Co. (1899–1944), Northern Breweries (1907–2007), Cosgrove Brewery Co. (1863–1945), O'Keefe Brewery Co. (1863–1967), Kormann Brewing Co. (1888–1931), Walkerville Brewery (1890–1944), Kuntz Brewery (1840–1930), British America Brewing Co. (1885–1930).

59 Bygrave and Hoffer, "Theorizing about entrepreneurship," 14.

60 Hall, *In the Company of Heroes*, 3.

Chapter Seven

1 E.P. Taylor to J.A. Paul (25 July 1938), *P.A.O. Regina vs Canadian Breweries Limited*, 318–19 and 459.
2 Marchand, *Creating the Corporate Soul*.
3 Anbinder, "Selling the World," 483–507; Lewis, *The Public Image of Henry Ford*, 330–46; Tedlow, "The National Association of Manufacturers and Public Relations during the New Deal," 25–45; Fones-Wolf, "Creating a Favorable Business Climate," 221–55.
4 Bird, *"Better Living."*
5 Urquhart and Buckley, *Historical Statistics of Canada*, 471.
6 Ibid., 463.
7 Gourvish and Wilson, *The British Brewing Industry*, 341–3; Yenne, *Guinness*, chapter 11.
8 Guccione, "Baron of Bootleggers," 17.
9 Dominion Brewers' Association, *Facts on the Brewing Industry in Canada*, 37.
10 *Financial Post*, 31 July 1930, 17.
11 Canada. Dominion Bureau of Statistics Census of Industry, *Report on the Brewing Industry in Canada 1933*, 4.
12 Ibid., 4.
13 Clarkson, Gordon, Dilworth, Guilfoyle, and Nash, *John Labatt, Balance Sheet* (1929 and 1933).
14 Tucker, "Labatt's," 178.
15 Tom Mallet, "Company History," Box LATXT122, *Labatt Collection*.
16 *Minutes*, 19 September 1932.
17 Armstrong, *The Forest City*, 185.
18 *Financial Post*, 27 March 1930, 1; *Financial Post*, 17 April 1930, 26; *Financial Post*, 22 May 1930, 11; *Financial Post*, 20 November 1930, 30; *Financial* Post, 23 January 1932, 11.
19 *Financial Post*, 20 March 1930.
20 Ibid., 14 August 1930, 11.
21 Ibid., 23 October 1930, 1.
22 Schumpeter, *Capitalism, Socialism, and Democracy*, 83.
23 Coutts, *Brew North*, 81.
24 Heron, *Booze*, 303.
25 *Financial Post*, 13 March 1930, 5; *Financial Post*, 27 March 1930, 1; *Financial Post*,

17 April 1930, 26; *Financial Post*, 22 May 1930, 1; *Financial Post*, 21 August 1930, 1; *Financial Post*, 16 October 1930, 1.

26 Jones, "Competition in the Canadian Brewing Industry," 53.

27 Ibid., 65.

28 Petricca, "Edward Plunket Taylor's Entrepreneurial Visions of Expansion," 113.

29 Jones, "Competition in the Canadian Brewing Industry," 51–65.

30 *Financial Post*, 18 July 1931, 10.

31 Jones, "Competition in the Canadian Brewing Industry," 51–65.

32 Saywell, '*Just Call Me Mitch*,' 120; *Financial Post*, 2 July 1932.

33 *Minutes*, 24 June 1932.

34 Taylor, "The Whiskey Kings," 190–1.

35 Jacobson, "Navigating the Boundaries of Respectability and Desire," 122–46.

36 John Labatt Limited, *Regional Sales Meeting Report* (1945), Box LATXT161, *Labatt Collection*.

37 Boyns and Edwards, "Cost and Management Accounting in Early Victorian Britain: A Chandleresque Analysis?" 19–46; Boyns and Edwards, "The Construction of Cost Accounting Systems in Britain to 1900," 1–29; McDowall, *The Sum of the Satisfactions*, 33.

38 Arnold, "'A Paradise for Profiteers'?" 61–81.

39 Loft, "Towards a Critical Understanding of Accounting," 137–69.

40 Matthews, "The Business Doctors: Accountants in British Management from the Nineteenth Century to the Present Day," 72–103. Matthews, "The Influence of the Accountant on British Business Performance from the Late Nineteenth Century to the Present Day," 329–51; Matthews, Anderson, and Edwards, "The Rise of the Professional Accountant in British Management," 407–29.

41 Hiebl, Carmen, and Franco, "An Analysis of the Role of a Chief Accountant at Guinness, c. 1920–1940," 145–65.

42 John Labatt Ltd, "The Spearhead, Bulletin #10" (February 1938), 1–2, *Labatt Collection*.

43 Tucker, "Labatt's," 203–8.

44 MacKenzie, *The Clarkson Gordon Story*, 30–8.

45 Tucker, "Labatt's," 203–8.

46 Hugh Mackenzie, "Address Delivered to the Canadian Chamber of Commerce" (29 October 1943), *Labatt Collection*.

47 Ibid.

48 Ibid.

49 *Minutes*, 4 March 1931. From this date forward, Mackenzie rather than Burke attended the meetings of the board of directors.

50 Berton, *The Great Depression, 1929–1939*, 148.

51 *Minutes*, 19 September 1932.

52 Malleck, *Try to Control Yourself*, 54–66.

53 Glassford, "Hepburn, Mitchell Frederick."

54 Malleck, *Try to Control Yourself*, 17–21, 35–40.

55 Saywell, '*Just Call Me Mitch*,' 49.

56 Ibid., 121.

57 Ibid., 45–6.

58 Ibid., 47.

59 Ibid.

60 Hepburn quoted in Abella, *On Strike*, 88.

61 Saywell, '*Just Call Me Mitch*,' 121.

62 *London Free Press*, 2 November 1933, 4.

63 *Globe*, 4 April 1933.

64 Saywell, '*Just Call Me Mitch*,' 143.

65 Ibid., 143.

66 Tucker, "Labatt's," 210.

67 *London Free Press*, 20 June 1934, 10.

68 Tucker, "Labatt's," 236.

69 Ibid., 237.

70 Ibid.

71 Ibid., 210, 236–8.

72 Campbell, *Sit Down and Drink Your Beer*.

73 Malleck, *Try to Control Yourself*, 69–77.

74 *London Free Press*, 25 July 1934, 10.

75 *Minutes*, 14 September 1934.

76 Frank Crowe, "The Kidnapping of John Labatt," 24–6. Box LATXT0189, *Labatt Collection*.

77 Goldenberg, *Snatched*, 21.

78 Tucker, "Labatt's," 182.

79 Ibid., 193.

80 Goldenberg, *Snatched*, 21.

81 Michael McCardell to Hugh Labatt (14 August 1934), Box A08-053-1010, *Labatt Collection*.

82 Tucker, "Labatt's," 184–5.

83 *Globe*, 15 August 1934, 1.

84 *London Free Press*, 14 August 1934.

85 *Globe*, 15 August 1934, 1.

86 *Toronto Star*, 15 August 1934, 1.

87 Ibid.

88 *London Free Press*, 15 August 1934.

89 WLMK *Diary*, 9 September 1934.

90 Goldenberg, *Snatched*, 47.

91 Frances Biddulph to John S. Labatt (18 August 34), Box A08-053-1010, *Labatt Collection*.

92 *Financial Post*, 1 September 1934, 1.

93 "Comparison of the Sales Made by this Company with the Total Sales Made by All Breweries in the Province of Ontario," Box LATXT0036, *Labatt Collection*.

94 *Minutes*, 14 September 1934.

95 Jones, "Competition in the Canadian Brewing Industry," table 4.

96 *Lethbridge Herald*, 10 September 1935, 2.

97 *Minutes*, 19 December 1935.

98 Ibid.

99 *Minutes*, 17 June 1935.

100 Tucker, "Labatt's," 235.

101 Ibid., 236.

102 Heron, "The Boys and Their Booze," 411–52.

103 *Minutes*, 19 November 1935.

104 Jessup, "Bushwhackers in the Gallery," 130–54. Jessup, "The Group of Seven and the Tourist Landscape in Western Canada, or The More Things Change …," 144–79.

105 Evenden, "The Northern Vision of Harold Adams Innis," 162–86.

106 McKay, *The Quest of the Folk*.

107 Wall, *The Nurture of Nature*; MacEachern, *Natural Selections*.

108 Tucker, "Labatt's," 249–53.

109 *Bus and Truck Transportation* (July 1936), *Exide News* (Feb 1940).

110 *Toronto Star*, 26 December 1936, 1–2, 19; *London Free Press*, 26 December 1936, 2; *Globe and Mail*, 26 December 1936, 1.

111 Ibid.

112 *Toronto Star*, 26 December 1936, 1.

113 Ibid., 2.

114 Dominion Brewers' Association, *Facts on the Brewing Industry in Canada*, 37.

115 Ibid., 38.

116 Ibid.

117 H.S. Pritchard to Hugh Labatt (22 December 1936), Box LATXT28, *Labatt Collection.*

118 Hugh Labatt to H.S. Pritchard (15 September 1936), Box LATXT28, *Labatt Collection.*

119 H.S. Pritchard to the Editor of *Maclean's* magazine (21 December 1936), Box LATXT28, *Labatt Collection.*

120 John Cartwright to Hugh Labatt (30 December 1936), Box LATXT28, *Labatt Collection.*

121 Hugh Labatt to Colonel R.H. Greer (6 January 1937), Box LATXT28, *Labatt Collection.*

122 Hunt, *Whiskey and Ice,* chapter 15.

123 Hugh Labatt to Colonel R.H. Greer (6 January 1937), Box LATXT28, *Labatt Collection.*

124 "Prohibition Is the Opposite of True Temperance," Box LAGR0054, *Labatt Collection.*

125 "Let's Teach Temperance," Box LAGR0054, *Labatt Collection.*

126 "What Is the Object of Government Control," Box LAGR0054, *Labatt Collection.*

127 "Propaganda That Defeats Itself," Box LAGR0054, *Labatt Collection.*

128 "A Dialogue on Moderation," Box LAGR0054, *Labatt Collection.*

129 Ibid.

130 J. Walter Thompson Co. Ltd, "Readership Survey of Brewers' Campaign" (Toronto, 1938), Box LATXT28, *Labatt Collection.*

131 Malleck, *Try to Control Yourself,* 12.

132 John Labatt's Ltd *Consumer Survey* (1940), Box LATXT195, *Labatt Collection.*

133 Gilbert E. Jackson, "Present Position of the Brewing Industry: Text of Memorandum" (January 1941), 6, Box 002, *Gilbert E. Jackson Papers.*

134 *Minutes,* 16 November 1935.

Chapter Eight

1 Matthew H. Halton, "They Drank Canadian Beer at Solum," Box LATXT28, *Labatt Collection.*

2 Jackall and Hirota, *Image Makers,* 7.

3 "Memorandum Re: Brewers Public Relations" (no date), Box LATXT28, *Labatt Collection.*

4 Ibid.

5 John Labatt Ltd, *Report of the Management Committee to the Chairman of the Board of Directors* (November 1940), 1.

6 "Minutes of a Meeting Held at O'Keefe House" (26 February 1941), Box LATXT76, *Labatt Collection*.

7 L.C. Bonnycastle, "Memorandum on the Brewers' Industrial Foundation" (15 February 1941), Box LATXT28, *Labatt Collection*.

8 Ibid.

9 Ibid.

10 Ibid.

11 Hugh Mackenzie to Frank Mathers (24 February 1941), Box LATXT28, *Labatt Collection*.

12 Ibid.

13 Tedlow, "The National Association of Manufacturers and Public Relations during the New Deal," 25–45; Marchand, "The Corporation Nobody Knew," 825–75; Marchand, *Creating the Corporate Soul*; Nye, *Image Worlds*; Johnston, *Selling Themselves*; Griffith, "The Selling of America," 388–412.

14 Stole, *Advertising at War*; Cynthia Lee Henthorn, *From Submarines to Suburbs*; Workman, "Manufacturing Power," 279–317.

15 Fones-Wolf, "Creating a Favorable Business Climate: Corporations and Radio Broadcasting, 1934 to 1954," 221–55.

16 Marchand, *Creating the Corporate Soul*, 288–91.

17 G.F. Mills to J.C. Ryan (3 August 1941), Box LATXT28, *Labatt Collection*.

18 "The Necessity of Maintaining a Brewers' Public Relations Programme to Ensure the Continued Life of the Industry" (8 February 1941), Box LATXT76, *Labatt Collection*.

19 Malleck, *Try to Control Yourself*.

20 Brewers Association of Canada, *Brewing in Canada*, 123.

21 Lord & Thomas to the Ontario Brewing Industry (20 March 1941), Box LATXT28, *Labatt Collection*.

22 Heron, *Booze*, 231, 284–93, and "The Boys and Their Booze," 411–52.

23 Jackall and Hirota, *Image Makers*, 138.

24 "Lord & Thomas Contact Report" (18 September 1941), Box LATXT76, *Labatt Collection*.

25 Lord & Thomas to John Labatt (March 1941), Box LATXT28, *Labatt Collection*.

26 "Memorandum Re. The Necessity of the Promotional Public Relations Programme for the Brewing Industry," Box LATXT76, *Labatt Collection*.

27 Sotiron, *From Politics to Profits*, especially 52–69.

28 Lord & Thomas to the Ontario Brewing Industry (March 1941), Box LATXT28, *Labatt Collection*.

29 Ibid.

30 L.C. Bonneycastle to Hugh Mackenzie (24 October 1941), Box LATXT76, *Labatt Collection*.

31 A.F. Blake to L.C. Bonneycastle (28 August 1941), Box LATXT76, *Labatt Collection*.

32 Ibid.

33 Ibid.

34 Henry Janes to Hugh Mackenzie (24 June 1941), Box LATXT76, *Labatt Collection*.

35 Frank Mills to Hugh Mackenzie (24 June 1941), Box LATXT76, *Labatt Collection*.

36 Ibid.

37 Two days after Canada formally entered the conflict, the malt tax was increased by two-thirds, to ten cents a pound. In 1941, it was raised again to twelve cents and then, in 1942, to sixteen cents a pound. At the same time as the federal tax was increased on malt, the gallonage tax on beer was increased by 13 per cent. But the wartime taxes did not end there. Labatt also had to pay federal and provincial sales taxes, licensing fees, municipal taxes, income taxes, gasoline and motor vehicle taxes, and often, excess profit taxes. According to the Dominion Bureau of Statistics, by 1942, wartime duties and taxes represented approximately 70 per cent of the total cost of brewing materials and almost 40 per cent of the cost of the gross selling value at the brewery. (See Dominion Brewers' Association, *Facts on the Brewing Industry in Canada*, 67.)

38 Ibid.

39 "Field Work Report" (31 January 1942), Box LATXT76, *Labatt Collection*.

40 "Propaganda Releases" (2 April 1942), Box LATXT76, *Labatt* Collection.

41 Tucker, 277.

42 Quoted in Gault MacGowan, *The Canadian Veteran*, 30 April 1943, 7.

43 In a speech at Bangor on 28 February 1915, Lloyd George stated: "We are fighting Germany, Austria and Drink; and as far as I can see the greatest of these three deadly foes is Drink." See *The Times*, 1 March 1915, 8.

44 Ibid.

45 Ibid.

46 *Toronto Daily Star*, 3 July 1942, 11.

47 *Newmarket Era*, 5 December 1940, 1.

48 L.C. Bonnycastle to J.A. Cowan (8 June 1942), Box LATXT76, *Labatt Collection.*

49 "Memorandum of the Meeting of the Plan Board of the Ontario Brewers Industry Public Relations Committee" (17 September 1941), Box LATXT76, *Labatt Collec*tion.

50 See for example, "Beer Shipments," *Windsor Daily Star,* 10 November 1942; "Canada Is Not Providing Ships to Carry *Beer," Galt Daily Reporter,* 12 November 1942; "Beer for the Troops," *Ingersoll Daily Sentinel,* 24 November 1942.

51 Canada, House of Commons, *Debates,* 8 June 1942, 3149.

52 *Toronto Star,* 3 July 1942, 11.

53 *Mackenzie King Diaries,* 26 February 2013, 143; ibid., 14 March 1944, 246.

54 Quoted in MacGowan, *The Canadian Veteran,* 30 April 1943, 7.

55 Dominion Brewers' Association, *Facts on the Brewing Industry,* 37.

56 Ibid.

57 *Mackenzie King Diaries,* 10 December 1942, 1.

58 Ibid., 14 September 1942, 2.

59 Ibid.

60 "Public Relations Efforts on Behalf of the Brewing Industry of Ontario, Nov. 15th to Dec. 17th, 1942," Box LATXT76, *Labatt Collection.*

61 Ibid.

62 *Mackenzie King Diary,* 10 December 1942, 2.

63 Ibid., 19 November 1942, 2.

64 Malleck, *Try to Control Yourself,* 227.

65 William Lyon Mackenzie King, *Canada and the War.*

66 Pett, "Nutrition as a National Problem," 21–9.

67 McCann, "Canada's Faulty Diet Is Adolf Hitler's Ally," 8.

68 Glover, *Brewing for Victory,* 7–17.

69 Ibid., 13.

70 Cochran, *The Pabst Brewing Company,* 394–6.

71 "Draft of Suggested Letter to Prof. McHenry *et al."* Box LATXT76, *Labatt Collection.*

72 "Report on Public Relations Brewing Industry Ontario: Response from the Nutrition Campaign" (29 April 1943), Box LATXT76, *Labatt Collection.*

73 Brewing Industry of Ontario, *Nutrition for Victory.*

74 Anonymous, "Report on Public Relations Brewing Industry Ontario: Response from the Nutrition Campaign," Box LATXT76, *Labatt Collection.*

75 Ibid.

76 "Curb on Beer Held Unjust – War Veterans, Labor Protest at Kitchener," *Globe and Mail*, 8 March 1943, 10.

77 L.M. Heard to Rt. Hon. Mackenzie King (3 March 1943), Box LATXT76, *Labatt Collection*.

78 Ibid.

79 *Globe and Mail*, 11 February 1943, 4.

80 James Cook to Hugh Labatt (1 February 1943), Box LATXT76, *Labatt Collection*.

81 Hugh Labatt to James Cowan (3 February 1943), Box LATXT76, *Labatt Collection*.

82 Ibid.

83 *Globe and Mail*, 17 December 1943, 4; *Globe and Mail*, 10 March 1943, 4.

84 *Maclean's*, 15 April 1943, 57.

85 "Newspaper Clipping Analysis" (10 June 1943), LATXT76, *Labatt Collection*.

86 Jackall and Hirota, *Image Makers*, 36–46.

87 "Press Publicity, Month of February 1944," Box LATXT76, *Labatt Collection*.

88 *Globe and Mail*, 14 March 1944, 1.

89 *Toronto Star*, 1 April 1944, 18

90 Canadian Institute of Public Opinion, "Public Opinion News Service Release," 16 March 1946, 424.

91 Anonymous, "New Trends in the Dry Campaign" (15 February 1948), Box LATXT0028, *Labatt Collection*.

92 Dominion Brewers' Association, *Facts on the Brewing Industry in Canada*, 31.

93 Ibid., 38.

94 Ibid.

95 John Labatt Ltd, *Balance Sheets*, 1939–1945, Box LATXT74, *Labatt Collection*.

Chapter Nine

1 J.H. Moore, "The Outlook for the Brewing Industry," Box A08-053-1077, *Labatt Collection*.

2 The northern Ontario market was protected by a Wartime Prices and Trade Board order that prohibited brewers south of the 46th parallel from selling their products in the north. See Ontario, Department of Provincial Secretary and Citizenship, *Report of the Inquiry into the Brewing Industry of Northern Ontario* (1972): 2–3.

3 Jones, "The New Zealand Brewing Industry, 1840–1995," 247–65; Merrett,

"Stability and Change in the Australian Brewing Industry, 1930–94," 229–48; Millns, "The British Brewing Industry, 1945–95," 142–59; Gourvish, "Economics of Brewing, Theory and Practice," 253–61.

4 Gourvish, "Economics of Brewing," 256.

5 Tom and Wright, "Corporate Governance, Strategy and Structure in British Business History," 91–124.

6 Bryce and Bellamy, *Canada and the Cost of World War II*, 71; Granatstein, *The Ottawa Men*, chapter 6; Owram, *The Government Generation*, chapters 10 and 11.

7 W.L. Gordon to Major-General S.C. Mewburn (23 June 1944), Box LATXT23, *Labatt Collection*.

8 M. Denison, *The Barley and the Stream*, 363–5.

9 W.L. Gordon to Major-General S.C. Mewburn (23 June 1944), Box LATXT23, *Labatt Collection*.

10 Tucker, "Labatt's," 285.

11 W.L. Gordon to Major-General S.C. Mewburn (23 June 1944), Box LATXT23, *Labatt Collection*.

12 Ibid.

13 Hugh Mackenzie to John Labatt (2 June 1944), Box LATXT23, *Labatt Collection*.

14 Hugh Mackenzie, "Company Structure and Objectives of Management" (April 1949), Box LATXT0118, *Labatt Collection*.

15 Ibid.

16 Tucker, "Labatt's," 286.

17 W.L. Gordon to Major-General S.C. Mewburn (23 June 1944), Box LATXT23, *Labatt Collection*.

18 *Minutes*, 7 June 1945, 149.

19 John Labatt Limited, *Annual Report* (15 December 1945), 2.

20 Tucker, "Labatt's," 288.

21 At the time, the board was made up of John Labatt, Hugh Labatt, S.C. Mewburn, R.H. Cronyn, and W.H.R. Jarvis.

22 Tucker, "Labatt's," 288.

23 Roseman, "The Canadian Brewing Industry," 159.

24 Brewers Association of Canada, *Brewing in Canada*, 118–19.

25 Shea, *Vision in Action*, 57–64.

26 Sneath, *Brewed in Canada*, 169.

27 *Globe and Mail*, 17 November 1953, 22.

28 Cochran, *The Pabst Brewing Company*, 72–8; McGahan, "The Emergence of the National Brewing Oligopoly," 237–43.

29 E.P. Taylor (26 October 1942) quoted in Sneath, *Brewed in Canada*, 169.

30 Stack, "Local and Regional Breweries in America's Brewing Industry, 1865 to 1920," 435–63.

31 Ibid.

32 E.P. Taylor quoted in Tucker, "Labatt's," 309.

33 See Bliss, "Another Anti-Trust Tradition," 180.

34 *Globe and Mail*, 10 February 1960.

35 Anonymous, "Bigness Isn't Necessarily Badness," *Financial Post*, 13 February 1960.

36 Ibid.

37 Hugh Labatt, "Remarks, Labatt Annual Meeting (18 December 1953), Box LATXT001, *Labatt Collection*.

38 *Minutes*, 1 November 1951, 1.

39 John Labatt Ltd, *Annual Report* (30 September 1949), 11.

40 Hugh Mackenzie to the Board of Directors (2 September 1947), Box A08-053-1077, *Labatt Collection*.

41 Tucker, "Labatt's," 311.

42 *Minutes*, 31 August 1951.

43 Roseman, "The Canadian Brewing Industry," 204.

44 *Minutes*, 24 March 1952.

45 *Minutes*, 23 June 1954. The Montreal plant was to be about one-third of the size of the London plant, which at the time had a capacity of 680,000 barrels.

46 *Minutes*, 27 April 1953.

47 *Minutes*, 23 June 1954.

48 Jones, "Competition in the Canadian Beer Industry," 72.

49 E.P. Taylor (26 October 1942) quoted in Sneath, *Brewed in Canada*, 169.

50 Roseman, "The Canadian Brewing Industry," 229.

51 Ibid., 230.

52 *Minutes*, 20 July 1953.

53 *Minutes*, 17 February 1953.

54 Tucker, "Labatt's," 320.

55 Armstrong, *The Forest City*, 148.

56 *Minutes*, 1 September 1953.

57 Ibid.

58 Jake Moore, "Speech to the Staff" (10 May 1967), Box A08-053-1126, file "Management Philosophy," *Labatt Collection*.

59 John Labatt Ltd, *Minutes*, vol. 9 (5 March 1956), 15.

60 Brewers Association of Canada, *Brewing in Canada*, 127.

61 *Minutes*, 11 December 1957, 73.

62 Ibid.

63 Tucker, "Labatt's," 328.

64 Ibid.

65 *Minutes*, 25 November 1957.

66 *Minutes*, 26 August 1957, 61.

67 John Labatt Limited, *Directors' Meeting Report* (25 November 1957), 13–14.

68 *Minutes*, 11 December 1957, 73.

69 *Minutes*, 26 August 1957, 61.

70 *Minutes*, 20 June 1958.

71 *Globe and Mail*, 12 May 1958.

72 Jake Moore, "Know Your Company" (29 October 1962), 5.

73 For the brewers' influence on provincial liquor authorities, see Jones, "Mergers and Competition," 557–9. For a discussion of "regulatory capture" see: Stigler, "The Theory of Economic Regulation," 3–21.

74 Jones, "Competition in the Canadian Brewing Industry," 142.

75 Jake Moore, "The Outlook for the Brewing Industry," Box A08-053-1077, file "Histories of John Labatt Limited," *Labatt Collection*.

76 Ibid., 148 and 150.

77 Warsh and Marquis, "Gender, Spirits, and Beer," 204–8. Heron, *Booze*, 331–2.

78 Jones, "Competition in the Canadian Brewing Industry," 146–55; Heron, *Booze*, 317–18.

79 *Globe and Mail*, 11 September 1963, 1.

80 Jones, "Competition in the Canadian Brewing Industry," 148.

81 "Remarks on Main Areas of Marketing Opportunity" (17 October 1962), Box A08-53-1022, file "Directors' Meetings," *Labatt Collection*.

82 Tucker, "Labatt's," 305.

83 Anonymous, *Trades and Labour Journal* (1950s), Box A08-053-1252, *Labatt Collection*.

84 Smith, "Product Differentiation and Market Segmentation as Alternative Marketing Strategies," 3–8.

85 Quelch and Jocz, "Milestones in Marketing," 838.

86 Warsh and Marquis, "Gender, Spirits, and Beer," 212.

87 Gardner and Levy, "The Product and the Brand," 33–9.

88 Brewers Association of Canada, *Brewing in Canada*, 97.

89 Ibid., 25.

90 Jones, "Competition in the Canadian Brewing Industry," 208.

91 *Financial Post*, 10 October 1964, 33.

92 *Regina vs. Canadian Breweries Ltd*, 5004.

Chapter Ten

1 Chandler, *Scale and Scope*, 117, 122, 171–5, 213–17, 446–52.

2 Kindleberger, *American Business Abroad*, 6.

3 Galbraith, *The New Industrial State*.

4 Rotstein, *The Precarious Homestead*; Lexer, *Canada Ltd*; Gordon, *Troubled Canada*; Grant, *Lament for a Nation*; Pope, *The Elephant and the Mouse*; Creighton, *Takeover*; Lumsden, *Close the 49th Parallel etc.*

5 Levitt, *Silent Surrender: The Multinational Corporation in Canada*.

6 Servan-Schreiber, *Le défi américain*.

7 Dennison and MacDonagh, *Guinness 1886–1939*, 229–82.

8 *Chicago Tribune*, 11 June 1964, 8.

9 J.H. Moore, "Know Your Company" (29 October 1962), Box LATXT0039, *Labatt Collection*.

10 W.F. Read, "Production" (19 March 1963), Box LATXT0039, *Labatt Collection*.

11 In 1955, Jake Moore had placed restrictions on the level of the company's debt. The company had pledged that its earnings would always be at least five times the annual interest requirements, that it would not borrow more than half the value of its consolidated assets plus borrowings, and that it would not pay out dividends to its common shareholders when working capital (i.e., net current assets) was more than 30 per cent of its debt.

12 Since acquiring the company in 1958, Labatt had increased its holding in Lucky Lager and had changed the name of the California subsidiary back to the original General Brewing Corporation in order to protect the Canadian version of the Lucky Lager brand in British Columbia.

13 J.H. Moore "Address to the Security Analysts Association of Montreal" (14 December 1961), Box LATXT0039, *Labatt Collection*.

14 Ibid.

15 California Department of Public Health, *California Review and Treatment Digest*, 31, and Brewers Association of Canada, *Brewing in Canada*, 119.

16 J.H. Moore, "Know Your Company" (29 October 1962), LATXT0039, *Labatt Collection*.

17 Tucker, "Labatt's," 344.

18 J.H. Moore, "Address to the Security Analysts Association of Montreal" (14 December 1961), LATXT0039, *Labatt Collection*.

19 Lopez, *Global Brands*, 81–2.

20 McGahan, "The Emergence of the National Brewing Oligopoly," 271–3, 279.

21 *Milwaukee Journal*, 13 November 1976, 2.

22 *Fortune Magazine*, October 1964, 106; *Milwaukee Journal*, 13 November 1976, 1–2.

23 Ogle, *Ambitious Brew*, 248.

24 Ibid., 249.

25 The 7,843,253 barrels of beer produced by Schlitz in 1963 was almost four times the amount manufactured by Labatt that year.

26 *Milwaukee Journal*, 8 January 1964, 21.

27 *Chicago Tribune*, 11 June 1964, 8.

28 Phillips, "Carling Breweries," 135–6.

29 John Labatt Limited, "Ten Year Review" (November 1970), 2.

30 Brewers Association of Canada, *Brewing in Canada*, 25.

31 John Labatt Ltd, "Director's Meeting" (10 June 1964), 1, 4, 17–18. At Molson, net profits in 1964 were up 3.6 per cent from the previous year to $8,397,000 on sales of $125 million. Canadian breweries had net profits of $3 million on sales of $91.1 million, while Labatt had net profits of $5.6 million on sales of $97.2 million.

32 In 1963, imported beer amounted to just 15,192 barrels, or less than .15 per cent of all beer sold. See Brewers Association of Canada, *Brewing in Canada*, 96.

33 Wilkins, *Multinational Enterprise*, 379. Understanding when and why direct investment has taken place has preoccupied historians and economists like Wilkins for decades. According to economist Peter Grey, firms sometimes expand abroad for defensive reasons, either to forestall competition in a new market or to obtain a secure source of supply of some raw material vital to the domestic operation and the parent company (See Grey, *The Economics of Business Investment Abroad*, 8). At other times — as was the case with American industrial expansion into Canada after 1870 — firms invested in distant production facilities to avoid taxes and other discriminatory legislation that would raise the cost of finished goods shipped across national borders. In such cases, direct investment occurs because of the greater cost-effectiveness and profitability resulting from what economists term "country-specific advantages."

34 Labatt, *A Different Road*, 72–6.

35 Tucker, "Labatt's," 348.

36 *Minutes*, 7 February 1964.

37 Labatt, *A Different Road*, 75.

38 Tucker, "Labatt's," 348.

39 Canada, *House of Commons Debates*, 20 February 1964, 41.

40 Gordon, *Troubled Canada*, 90.

41 See, for example, Rotstein, *The Precarious Homestead*.

42 Azzi, *Walter Gordon and the Rise of Canadian Nationalism*, 92.

43 Ibid.

44 Ibid., 95–109.

45 Ibid., 111.

46 Ibid., 134.

47 Canada, *House of Commons Debates*, 19 February 1964, 11.

48 Canada, *House of Commons Debates*, 26th Parliament, 2nd Session, vol.1, 50.

49 Labatt, *A Different Road*, 76.

50 Tucker, "Labatt's," 349.

51 Ibid.

52 *London Free Press* and *Toronto Globe*, 4–7 February 1964; *Financial Post*, 8 and 15 February 1964.

53 Tucker, "Labatt's," 349.

54 Labatt, *A Different Road*, 75.

55 Tucker "Labatt's," 346.

56 *Minutes*, 3 February 1964, 22.

57 *Minutes*, 6 February 1964, 23.

58 Tucker, "Labatt's," 349–50.

59 *Minutes*, 6 February 1964, 24.

60 Tucker, "Labatt's," 350.

61 *Minutes*, 3–6 February 1964, 21–5.

62 Tucker, "Labatt's," 351.

63 Galbraith, *The New Industrial State*, chapter 16.

64 Leonard Sloane, "Problems Are Brewing in the Beer Industry," *New York Times*, 14 December 1966.

65 McGahan, "The Emergence of the National Brew Oligopoly," 279–83.

66 Tucker, "Labatt's," 353.

67 Ibid.

68 *Minutes*, 26 March 1965.

69 *Minutes*, 21 October 1963.

70 Some firms, like Schlitz, were spending two and a half times as much as General Brewing on advertising in California. See *Minutes*, 16 October 1964, 68.

71 *Minutes*, 26 March 1965.

72 Tucker, "Labatt's," 354.

73 Ibid., 355.

74 *Minutes*, 31 March 1964, 39.

75 Ibid.

76 Tucker, "Labatt's," 356.

77 *Minutes*, 16 October 1964.

78 Quoted in Tucker, "Labatt's," 356.

79 *Minutes*, 10 December 1965; Tucker, "Labatt's," 365.

80 Tucker, "Labatt's," 357.

81 *Milwaukee Sentinel*, 8 November 1966, 4.

82 Ferguson, *High Financier,* especially chapter 1.

83 *Globe and Mail*, 11 April 1967, B1.

84 Tucker, "Labatt's," 358.

85 *Globe and Mail*, 16 June 1967, 1.

86 Tucker, "Labatt's," 359.

87 Ibid.

88 "Statement for Press Conference by J.H. Moore" (23 February 1967), Box A08-053-1085, *Labatt Collection.*

89 Ibid.

Chapter Eleven

1 For more on economies of scale in advertising, see Peles, "Economies of Scale in Advertising," 32–7.

2 Penfold, *The Donut,* 176. For an analysis of some of the regional and international hurdles faced by early twentieth-century "universal" branding efforts, see Strasser, *Satisfaction Guaranteed,* 139–44.

3 Iacovetta, *Gatekeepers,* 1–19.

4 Peter Widdrington to D.G. McGill and N.E. Hardy (30 June 1965), Box A08-053-603, *Labatt Collection.*

5 Heron, *Booze,* 305–6.

6 Opp, "Branding 'the Bay/la Baie,'" 223–56; Carstairs, "Roots Nationalism," 235–55; Wagman, "Peace, Order, and Good Banking," 538–68; Rutherford, *The New Icons*; Penfold, "'Eddie Shack Was No Tim Horton,'" 48–66.

7 "An Awareness and Attitude Study of Alberta Breweries and Brands, vol. 2 – Analysis and Summary," Box A08-053-594, *Labatt Collection.*

8   "A Review of Labatt's Position in the Saskatchewan Market" (August 1977), Box A08-057-566, *Labatt Collection*.

9   Anonymous, "Report of a March Research Project – Summer 1960," Box A08-053-603, *Labatt Collection*.

10 Brewers Association of Canada, *Brewing in Canada*, 38.

11 Heron, *Booze*, 269–71, and Marquis, "A Reluctant Concession to Modernity," 44.

12 In 1962, total beer consumption in all the provinces and territories excluding Ontario and Quebec totalled 36.4 million litres. Brewer's Association of Canada, *Brewing in Canada*, Appendix III.

13 P.J. Henderson to B.G. Elliot (29 October 1964), Box A08-053-603, *Labatt Collection*.

14 Anonymous, "Report of a March Research Project – Summer 1960," Box A08-053-603, *Labatt Collection*.

15 P.J. Henderson to N.E. Hardy (31 December 1964), Box A08-053-603, *Labatt Collection*.

16 P.J. Henderson to B.G. Elliot (29 October 1964), Box A08-053-603, *Labatt Collection*.

17 P.J. Henderson to N.E. Hardy (31 December 1964), Box A08-053-603, *Labatt Collection*.

18 P.J. Henderson, "Working Document – Ontario Lager Study" (28 October 1964), Box A08-053-603, *Labatt Collection*.

19 "Highlights of Research of Significance of Alberta Marketing," Box A08-053-595, *Labatt Collection*.

20 John Compton, "Quality Control" (19 February 1963), Box LATXT0039, *Labatt Collection*.

21 "An Awareness and Attitude Study of Alberta Breweries and Brands," Box A08-053-595, *Labatt Collection*, 42.

22 "Ontario Lager Inquiry" (5 November 1964), Box A08-053-603, *Labatt Collection*.

23 "Notes on a Meeting Held in Toronto" (5 July 1965), Box A08-053-603, *Labatt Collection*.

24 Ibid.

25 "Research Objectives – Ontario Lager Problems – June/67," Box A08-053-603, *Labatt Collection*.

26 Iacovetta, *Gatekeepers*, 203–32.

27 "Pilsener Survey – Windsor-Welland – December 1964," Box A08-053-603, *Labatt Collection*, 2; "Pilsener Survey – Toronto – March 1965," Box A08-053-603, *Labatt Collection*, 4.

28 C.A. Stock, "What Research to Date Tells Us about Pilsner," Box A08-053-603, *Labatt Collection.*

29 "Generalized Summary of Consumer Research on New Pilsener Label" (9 May 1961), Box A08-053-1252, *Labatt Collection.*

30 For more on the difference between cocktail lounges and beer parlours, see Heron, *Booze,* 322–32.

31 Warsh and Marquis, "Gender, Spirits and Beer," 213–15.

32 *Toronto Courier,* 4 January 1962.

33 Pilsener Survey – Toronto – March 1965," Box A08-053-603, *Labatt Collection,* 40–1.

34 Ibid.

35 Beverland, "The 'Real Thing'": 251–258.

36 Pilsener Survey – Toronto – March 1965," Box A08-053-603, *Labatt Collection,* 40–1.

37 "B.W. Crow, Letter of April 7, re 'Blue' and Colour in General," Box A08-053-603, *Labatt Collection.*

38 R.C. Dill to C.A. Stock and P.J. Henderson (23 April 1970), Box A08-053-603, *Labatt Collection.*

39 "Recommendation for a Brand Name" (18 April 1963), Box A08-053-603, *Labatt Collection.*

40 Ibid.

41 Ibid.

42 Ibid.

43 T.O. Cadham to P.J. Henderson (14 December 1966), Box A08-053-603, *Labatt Collection.*

44 P.J. Henderson to T.O. Cadham (16 December 1966), Box A08-053-603, *Labatt Collection.*

45 J.R. Robertson to J.W. Howell (9 November 1964), Box A08-053-603, *Labatt Collection.*

46 At the Hudson's Bay Company, for example, the tension between regional managers and modernist corporate elites was clearly evident in the early 1960s, since traditionally the individual stores controlled their advertising copy for local newspapers. See Opp, "Branding 'the Bay/la Baie.'" For a discussion of this trend in America, see Jackall and Hirota, *The Image Makers;* Frank, *The Conquest of Cool;* and Warlaumont, *Advertising in the 60s.* On the British scene, see Fletcher, *Powers of Persuasion.*

47 J.R. Robertson to J.W. Howell (9 November 1964), Box A08-053-603, *Labatt Collection.*

48 Ibid.

49 N.E. Hardy to P.J. Henderson (1 June 1967), Box A08-053-603, *Labatt Collection*.

50 "Notes on a Meeting Held in Toronto" (5 July 1965), Box A08-053-603, *Labatt Collection*.

51 M.D. Hurst, "Pros/Cons Labatt Labatt Blue (?) Brand Designation Committee Meeting" (11 June 1970), Box A08-053-603, *Labatt Collection*.

52 N.E. Hardy to P.J. Henderson (1 June 1967), Box A08-053-603, *Labatt Collection*.

53 T.C. Fleming to P.J. Henderson (26 February 1969), Box A08-053-603, *Labatt Collection*.

54 Brand Designation Committee, "A Working Paper – Problem Definition" (March 1970), Box A08-053-603, *Labatt Collection*.

55 Ibid.

56 Tucker, "Labatt's," 394.

57 *Wall Street Journal*, 23 February 1967, 1.

58 "Ontario Lager Benchmark Analysis" (29 November 1971), Box A08-053-602, *Labatt Collection*, table 47.

59 Brand Designation Committee, "Minutes of Meeting Held on 24 July 1970," Box A08-053-603, *Labatt Collection*.

60 Ibid. In Quebec, Labatt Blue's share of the packaged lager market increased from 14 per cent in 1965 to 52.81 per cent in 1973.

61 "Ontario Lager Benchmark Analysis" (29 November 1971), Box A08-053-602, *Labatt Collection*, 2.

62 John Labatt Limited, "Marketing Priorities F81 and Beyond," Box A08-053-598, *Labatt Collection*.

63 John Labatt Limited, "Director's Report" (11 June 1976), Box AFC101-30, *Labatt Collection*.

64 C.A. Stock to E.G. Bradley (31 January 1977), *Labatt Collection*, Box A08-053-590,

65 Gazette, 20 December 1977, 4.

66 Ogle, *Ambitious Brew*, 283.

67 Tremblay and Tremblay, *The U.S. Brewing* Industry, 143–4.

68 Gazette, 20 December 1977, 4.

69 *Globe and Mail*, 20 December 1977, B1.

70 *Globe and Mail*, 2 January 1978.

71 *Globe and Mail*, 30 May 1979, 3.

72 C.A. Stock to M.D. Hurst (18 May 1978), Box A08-053-710, *Labatt Collection*.

73 Kwechansky Marketing Research, "Report for Labatt's Ontario Breweries Ltd:

Special Lite" (1 October 1980), Box A08-053-656, *Labatt Collection*; "Segmentation '78: Specialty Brand Segments – The Western Provinces" (November 1979), Box A08-053-592, *Labatt Collection*.

74 Kwechansky Marketing Research, "Report for Labatt's Ontario Breweries Ltd: Special Lite" (1 October 1980), Box A08-053-656, *Labatt Collection*.

75 Ogle, *Ambitious Brew*, 321.

76 Brent, *Lager Heads*, 63–4.

77 Ibid., 63.

78 Don McDougall to S. Keohane (14 November 1980), Box A10-039-085, *Labatt Collection*.

79 Hagelund, *House of Suds*.

80 Brent, *Lager Heads*, 69.

81 "Possible Questions/Answers vis-à-vis CBC *Journal* interview with S.M. Oland on Tuesday, May 4, 1982," Box A08-053-384, *Labatt Collection*.

82 Ibid.

83 Brent, *Lager Heads*, 70.

84 Ibid.

85 L.S. Leung to W.R. Cairns et al. (21 September 1983), Box A08-053-318, *Labatt Collection*.

86 Ibid.

87 Shea, *The Untold Story of Canada's 350-Year-Old Brewing Industry*, 260–1.

88 P.J. Henderson, "Labatt's Eight Beer Marketing Laws" (5 February 1963), Box A08-053-112, *Labatt Collection*.

89 *Globe and Mail*, 23 September 1961, 2

90 P.J. Henderson, "Labatt's Eight Beer Marketing Laws" (5 February 1963), Box A08-053-112, *Labatt Collection*.

91 *Globe and Mail*, 8 September 1984, B2.

92 In 1985, Carling only commanded 25 per cent of the Canadian beer market compared with about 40 per cent for Labatt and 32 per cent for Molson.

93 Appleton, *Brewing Revolution*, 51.

94 Ibid., 50.

95 Ibid., 81. There were fifty-four microbreweries founded between 1984 and 1990.

96 J.R. McLeod to R.A. Binnendyk (15 June 1984), Box A08-053-337, *Labatt Collection*.

97 R.A. Binnendyk to J.R. McLeod (9 July 1984), Box A08-053-337, *Labatt Collection*.

98 Ibid.

Chapter Twelve

1   Chandler, *Scale and Scope*, 617–21; Dyas and Thanheiser, *Emerging European Enterprise*, 50–63; Sobel, *The Age of Giant Corporations*, chapters 8 and 9; Ansoff, "Strategies for Diversification," 113–24; Penrose, *The Theory of the Growth of the Firm*, 111–12.

2   Drucker, *The Practice of Management*.

3   Prahalad and Hamel, "The Core Competence of the Corporation," 79–91; Robbins and. Wiersema, "A Resource-Based Approach to the Multi-business Firm," 277–99; Snow and Hrebiniak, "Strategy, Distinctive Competence, and Organizational Performance," 317–36.

4   Rumelt, *Strategy, Structure*, 53–5; Chandler, *Scale and Scope*, 622.

5   Lubatkin and Chatterjee, "Extending Modern Portfolio Theory into the Domain of Corporate Diversification" 109; Amit and Wernerfelt, "Why Do Firms Reduce Business Risk?" 520–34.

6   Edwards, "Conglomerate Bigness as a Source of Power," 331–52; Seth, "Value Creation in Acquisitions," 99–115.

7   Lewellen, "A Pure Financial Rationale for the Conglomerate Merger," 521–37.

8   Teece, "Economies of Scope and the Scope of Enterprise," 223–47.

9   Szeless, Wiersema, and Müller-Stewens, "Portfolio Interrelationships and Financial Performance in the Context of European Firms," 146–63; Penrose, *The Theory of the Growth of the Firm*.

10 Lopes, *Global Brands*, 107–28.

11 Sandberg, "The Creation of Big Business in the Swedish Brewing Industry during the Aftermath of the Second World War," 43–59.

12 Lopes, *Global Brands*, 111.

13 Editors of *Fortune* magazine, *The Conglomerate Commotion*.

14 Jake Moore, "Address Given to the Toronto Society of Financial Analysts" (12 April 1967), Box A08-053-1085, *Labatt Collection*.

15 John Labatt Limited, "Submission to the Royal Commission on Corporate Concentration," 12.

16 Hurst, Gregory, and Gussman, *Alcoholic Beverage Taxation and Control Policies*, 70.

17 John Labatt Limited, "Submission to the Royal Commission on Corporate Concentration," 12.

18 *Minutes*, 8 December 1972.

19 *The Labatt News,* March 1957, 2.

20 *Minutes,* 15 June 1973, 229.

21 Ibid.

22 *Minutes,* 7 December 1973.

23 John Labatt Limited, "Submission to the Royal Commission on Corporate Concentration," 4.

24 Ibid., 366.

25 Tucker, "Labatt's," 263–6.

26 John Labatt Limited, "Submission to the Royal Commission on Corporate Concentration," 14

27 Tucker, "Labatt's," 368.

28 Jake Moore "Speech to Montreal Financial Analysts" (5 March 1969), Box A08-053-1126, *Labatt Collection*

29 *Minutes,* 15 January 1968, 193.

30 In 1967, Ogilvie produced 25 per cent of Canada's flour and had gross sales of $136.5 million. See Tucker, "Labatt's," 369.

31 *Montreal Gazette,* 21 October 1967, 12.

32 Rohmer, *Ultimatum,* and Purdy, *The New Romans.*

33 Lumsden, *Close the 49th parallel etc.*

34 *Globe and Mail,* 14 June 1969, B2.

35 Brent, *Lager Heads,* 139–40.

36 Ibid.

37 Peter Widdrington, "Speech to Head Office Brewing Group," Box A08-053-1126, *Labatt Collection.*

38 "Summary of Analysis of Toronto-Hamilton Lager Study" (October 1966), Box A08-053-603, file "Pilsner Problem – Renaming Blue," *Labatt Collection.*

39 J.A. Bruce to B.J. Hartford (30 October 1970), Box A10-039-095, *Labatt Collection.*

40 "Sports/Beer Relationships" (no date), Box A08-053-821, *Labatt Collection.*

41 *Minutes,* 15 March 1968, 207.

42 In 1976, Labatt's share of the beer market in Hamilton, Windsor, and Toronto was between 32 and 34 per cent. See Peter Widdrington, "Speech to the Young Professional Organization" (July 1986), Box A10-039-210, *Labatt Collection.*

43 "Labatt Involvement in Baseball for Toronto," Box AFC-101-30/3, *Labatt Collection.*

44 Ibid.

45 Tucker, "Labatt's," 396.

46 Ibid., 397.

47 "Labatt Involvement in Baseball for Toronto," Box AFC-101-30/3, *Labatt Collection*.

48 Ibid.

49 Ibid.

50 Tucker, "Labatt's," 398.

51 *Minutes*, 8 January 1976.

52 Tucker, "Labatt's," 399.

53 Heron, *Booze*, 333.

54 *Globe and Mail*, 10 April 1982, S3.

55 Ibid., 15 September 1977, 7.

56 Ibid., 23 March 1977, 5.

57 Ibid., 19 March 1977, 4.

58 Ibid., 27 July 1977, 5.

59 Kwechansky Marketing Research, "Labatt Brewing Company's Moderation Advertising" (November 1986), Box A08-053-791, *Labatt Collection*.

60 Tucker, "Labatt's," 405.

61 *Globe and Mail*, 6 October 1973, B5; *Globe and Mail*, 28 May 1976, B1; *Globe and Mail*, 28 May 1977, B14.

62 Tucker, "Labatt's," 410.

63 Ibid. 410–11.

64 Ibid.

65 Ibid., 412.

66 Ibid., 413.

67 *Minutes*, 16 February 1979.

68 *Minutes*, 12 April 1979.

69 Ibid.

70 *Globe and Mail*, 4 May 1979, 7.

71 Ibid., 26 June 1979, B10.

72 Ibid.

73 Hayes and Abernathy, "Managing Our Way," 69–77.

74 "P.T. Widdrington Speech to the Head Office Brewing Group" (January 1980), Box A10-039-085, *Labatt Collection*.

75 *Globe and Mail*, 10 January 1986, B2.

76 Warren Berger, "Labatt's Southern Strategy," *Food and Beverage Marketing* (January 1988), 25.

77 Ibid.

78 Tucker, "Labatt's," 430.

79 *London Free Press*, 1 September 1990.

80 Ibid.

81 Prahalad and Hamel, "The Core Competence of the Corporation," 79–91.

82 Tucker, "Labatt's," 430.

Chapter Thirteen

1 Between 1945 and 1970, Canadian corporations such as Inco, Brascan, Noranda, Cominco, Alcan, MacMillan Bloedel, and Massey-Ferguson made substantial investments abroad. See Campbell, *Global Mission*; MacKay, *Empire of Wood*, 245–75; Neufeld, *A Global Corporation*, 290–302.

2 Watson, *Golden Arches East*, 15.

3 Ritzer, *The McDonaldization of Society*.

4 Chandler, *Scale and Scope*, 117, 122, 171–5, 213–17, 446–52.

5 Ibid.

6 Lopes, *Global Brands*, especially 23–42.

7 *Fortune*, 5 January 1987.

8 Ibid.

9 Conference Board of Canada, "The Canadian Brewing Industry: An Assessment of the Impacts of Liberalized Interprovincial Trade in Canada," June 1990, 7.

10 Kathryn Collins, "The Canadian Brewing Industry" (Midland Walwyn Research, February 1991), 11.

11 Ibid.

12 Doern and Tomlin, *The Free Trade Story*, 78–9.

13 This was set out in the FTA Article 1204, which read: "With respect to measures related to the internal sale and distribution of beer and malt containing beverages, Chapter Five [which incorporates the GATT rules on national treatment] shall not apply."

14 The concentration was substantially less than in related industries. In the soft drinks sector, for instance, the top four players shared 80 per cent of the world market.

15 Gregory, Hurst, and Gussman, *Alcoholic Beverage Taxation and Control Policies*, 50.

16 Boje and Johansen, "The Danish Brewing Industry after 1880," 70–2.

17 Lopes, *Global Brands*, 242–3.

18 Gioffre, "Growth Opportunities that Exist for Canada's Brewing Industry," 5–7.

19 In 1970, the volume of wine sales in Canada represented 4.65 per cent of total sales volume of alcoholic beverages, while in 1982, the volume of wine sales represented 8.9 per cent. In 1970, beer sales represented 88.9 per cent of total sales volume of alcoholic beverages, while in 1982, the volume of beer sales represented 83.2 per cent. See Gioffre, "Growth Opportunities That Exist for Canada's Brewing Industry," 6.

20 Binge drinking is episodic drinking, defined as anything over five drinks in one evening or sitting. For the rising rates on binge drinking during the 1980s, see Rod Mickleburg, "Student Drinking, Drug Abuse on Rise, ARF Says," *Globe and Mail*, 20 November 1991, A7.

21 Ibid., 276.

22 Bliss, *Northern Enterprise*, 547.

23 McDowall, *Quick to the Frontier*.

24 Peters and Waterman, *In Search of Excellence*.

25 Sherbrooke Associates, "Management Report for John Labatt Limited" (14 July 1989), Box A08-053-574, *Labatt Collection*, 43–4.

26 Ibid.

27 Ibid.

28 Ibid.

29 Ibid.

30 Peters and Waterman, *In Search of Excellence*.

31 Markides, "Back to Basics," 12–25.

32 "Management Brief," *The Economist*, 28 October 1989, 78.

33 Brent, *Lager Heads*, 147, 151–3, 155–6.

34 *Financial Post*, 9 February 1991, 5.

35 *National Post*, 13 December 2008.

36 *London Free Press*, 7 September 1989.

37 *Globe and Mail*, 13 May 1989, B3.

38 Ibid., 14 May 1991, B1.

39 Ibid.

40 Ibid., 13 May 1989, B3.

41 Sidney Oland, "The Year-End Review of John Labatt Limited Annual General Meeting" (10 September 1992), Box A01-039-348, *Labatt Collection*.

42 Brent, *Lager Heads*, 153.

43 Colli, "The Italian Brewing Industry," 55.

44 Gregory, Hurst, and Gussman, *Alcoholic Beverage Taxation and Control Policies*, 222–3.

45 Colli, "The Italian Brewing Industry," 55.

46 Ibid.

47 *Globe and Mail*, 2 June 1989, B8.

48 Ibid.

49 *Globe and Mail*, 1 April 1991, B3.

50 Brent, *Lager Heads*, 153.

51 *Globe and Mail*, 1 April 1991, B3.

52 Ibid., 2 June 1989, B8.

53 Ibid.

54 Brent, *Lager Heads*, 153.

55 "Notes for Remarks by George S. Taylor to Wood Gundy" (13 April 1994), Box A10-039-440, *Labatt Collection*.

56 *Globe and Mail*, 2 June 1989, B8.

57 Ibid., 12 January 1990, B1.

58 Ibid., 22 November 1990, B24.

59 Brent, *Lager Heads*, 154.

60 Ibid., 153.

61 *Globe and Mail*, 17 November 1992, B4.

62 R.J. Clark to Sid Oland (26 March 1991), Box A10-039-088, *Labatt Collection*.

63 For an excellent history of the pub, see Jennings, *The Local*.

64 Bower and Cox, "How Scottish & Newcastle Became the U.K.'s Largest Brewer," 59–61.

65 R.J. Clark to S.M. Oland (26 March 1991), Box A10-039-088, *Labatt Collection*.

66 *Minutes*, 10 December 1992.

67 Brent, *Lager Heads*, 155.

68 Sid Oland, "Year-End Review John Labatt Limited Annual General Meeting" (10 September 1992), Box A10-039-088, *Labatt Collection*.

69 *Globe and Mail*, 17 November 1992, B4.

70 Ibid., 11 November 1992, B1.

71 Ibid., 12 September 1992, B1.

72 *Maclean's*, 22 February 1993, 18–22.

73 Brent, *Lager Heads*, 155.

74 Alexander, *Brewed in Japan*, 12–13.

75 Byran Harrell, "Kirin Brewery Company," 516–17.

76 Lopes, *Global Brands*, 123.

77 Brent, *Lager Heads*, 153–6.

78 Ibid., 156.

79 *Globe and Mail*, 13 February 1993, A1.

80 *Maclean's*, 22 February 1993, 22.

81 *Globe and Mail*, 30 April 1993, B5.

82 Ibid., 13 February 1993, B1.

83 Ibid., 1 May 1993, A1 and A6.

84 *Minutes*, 9 September 1993.

85 Brent, *Lager Heads*, 124–30.

86 In 1993, Blue was still the best-selling beer in Canada with 16 per cent of the market.

87 *Globe and Mail*, 22 June 1990, B5.

88 Ibid., 11 October 1991, B8.

89 Ibid., 31 March 1992, B2.

90 Ibid.

91 Ibid., 29 May 1992, B3.

92 Ibid., 26 March 1993, A1 and A2.

93 Ibid.

94 Ibid., 1 May 1993, A1 and A6.

95 Ibid., 10 September 1991, B2.

96 Ibid., 5 June 1991, B1 and B6.

97 Ibid., 9 June 1994, B6.

98 Ibid., 1 May 1993, A6.

99 Beverland, "The 'Real Thing,'" 251–8; Peñaloza, "The Commodification of the American West," 82–109; Grayson and Martinec, "Consumer Perceptions of Iconicity and Indexicality and Their Influence on Assessments of Authentic Market Offerings," 296–312; Beverland, Lindgreen, and Vink, "Projecting Authenticity through Advertising," 5–15; O'Neill, Houtman, and Aupers, "Advertising Real Beer," 5–15.

100 *Minutes*, 9 September 1993.

101 Ibid.

102 *Globe and Mail*, 27 August 1993, B3.

103 *Minutes*, 9 December 1993.

104 Paul Kix, "How David Fincher, Sharon Stone and a Bunch of Scheming Canadians Conspired to Create Ice Beer," www.thrillist.com/drink/nation/the-insane-improbable-unbelievable-history-of-ice-beer (accessed 8 February 2019).

105 Hampson, "Ice Beer," 475.

106 Kix, "How David Fincher, Sharon Stone and a Bunch of Scheming Canadians Conspired to Create Ice Beer."

107 Brent, *Lager Heads*, 117.

108 *Globe and Mail*, 9 June 1994, B6.

109 George Taylor, "Remarks to Wood Gundy" (13 April 1994), Box A10-039-348, *Labatt Collection*.

110 Brewers Association of Canada, *Alcoholic Beverage Taxation and Control Policies*, 276.

111 "Project Argo, Meeting Report" (3 May 1994), Box A10-039-143, *Labatt Collection*.

112 Bellamy, "John Labatt Blows In and Out of the Windy City," 30–53.

113 "Project Argo, Meeting Report" (3 May 1994), Box A10-039-143, *Labatt Collection*.

114 Mora-Torres, *The Making of the Mexican Border*, 236–54.

115 Ibid, 239.

116 Ibid, 236.

117 John Labatt, "A Winning North American Brewing Partnership" (6 July 1994), Box A10-039-107, *Labatt Collection*.

118 "Project Argo, Meeting Report" (3 May 1994), Box A10-039-143, *Labatt Collection*.

119 *Globe and Mail*, 7 July 1994, B1.

120 "Mexico: Don't Panic over the Peso," *New York Times*, 29 December 1994.

121 George S. Taylor to the Members of the Board of Directors (29 June 1994), Box A10-039-143, *Labatt Collection*.

122 Ibid.

123 Mariana Strauss, "Labatt Caught in Peso Plunge," *Globe and Mail*, 10 March 1995, B1.

124 Ibid.

125 "The Adventurous Life of the Belgians," *The Economist*, 10 June 1995, 56.

126 Ibid, B2.

127 *Globe and Mail*, 25 February 1995, B3.

128 Brent, *Lager Heads*, 166.

129 Newman, *Titans*, 226–8.

130 Brent, *Lager Heads*, 166.

131 Newman, *Titans*, 232–3.

132 George Taylor, "Interoffice Memorandum" (26 May 1995), Box A08-053-991, *Labatt Collection*.

133 Ibid.

134 Sluyterman and Bouwens, "From Colonial Empires to Developing Countries and on to Emerging Economies," 103–18.

135 Yenne, *Guinness*.

136 Lopes, *Global Brands,* 1–66, 129–79; Duguid, "Developing the Brand," 405–41;
     Merrett and Whitwell, "The Empire Strikes Back," 162–90; Wilson, "Selling Beer
     in Victorian Britain," 103–25; Johansen, "Marketing and Competition in Danish
     Brewing," 126–38; Weir, "Managing Decline," 139–62.

137 Barwise and Robertson, "Brand Portfolios," 277–85.

138 Schumacher, "The Global Beer Industry 2001 Review," 7–9.

139 Stack, "Interbrew," 315–16.

140 Brooks, "InBev," 480–1.

141 *Maclean's,* 19 June 1995, 44–5.

142 Newman, *Titans,* 232–3.

143 John Labatt Limited, 1994 *Annual Report,* 38. Higher interest expense and a
     higher effective rate of income tax resulted in net earnings of $155 million.

144 "The Adventurous Life of the Belgians," *The Economist,* 10 June 1995, 56.

145 *Wall Street Journal,* 7 June 1995.

146 *Maclean's,* 19 June 1995.

Conclusion

1   Scranton and Fridenson, *Reimagining Business History,* 108–13.

2   Ibid., 108.

3   Fridenson, "Business Failure and the Agenda of Business History," 572.

4   Ibid., 567 and 572.

5   Colli, *The History of Family Business;* James, *Family Capitalism;* Lorandini,
    "Looking beyond the Buddenbrooks Syndrome," 1005–19.

6   Brewers Association of Canada, "Perspectives on Canada-United States Free
    Trade"(Ottawa, May 1985), 1.

7   Rodrik, *The Globalization Paradox.*

8   Cormack, "'True Stories' of Canada," 369–84; Opp, "Branding 'the Bay/la Baie,'"
    223–56.

9   Penfold, "'Eddie Shack Was No Tim Horton,'" 48–66.

10 *Toronto Star,* 4 December 1983, A3.

11 Ibid.

12 For more on "forever young" brands, see Lopes, *Global Brands,* 165 and 187.

13 Lopes, *Global Brands,* 242–3; United Nations, Economic Commission for
    Latin America and the Caribbean, *Foreign Investment in Latin America and
    the Caribbean,* 127–9; Gammelgaard and Dörrenbächer, *The Global Brewery
    Industry,* 278–80.

14 However, some argue that it is the licensor that is often disadvantaged by the licensing agreements because the product characteristics are not always preserved under such agreements and the "import identity" of the brand is denigrated. (See Tremblay and Tremblay, *The U.S. Brewing Industry*, 109.)

15 Boke and Johansen, "The Danish Brewing Industry after 1880," 70–2.

16 The first mega merger came in 2004 when Interbrew acquired AmBev, which was Brazil's largest brewery and the maker of such brands as Brahma and Antarctica. The takeover created InBev and gave the company a global platform to build on Interbrew's strength in Europe, Asia, and North America, and AmBev's strong position in Latin America. Four years later, InBev made a $46.4 billion unsolicited takeover bid for the maker of the "King of Beers," Anheuser-Busch. The move was in response to SABMiller's acquisition of the Dutch brewer Grolsch in 2007, which had catapulted the company ahead of InBev to the top spot in the global beer market (by volume). At the same time, mergers in the American brewing industry were putting pressure on Anheuser-Busch, which, like other big domestic brewers, was losing business to purveyors of wine, liquor, and craft brews. Still, the storied Busch family behind the "King of Beers" was not eager to sell to the Belgians. But fortunately for InBev, the Busch family could do little to prevent a takeover because the Buschs by then owned less than 4 per cent of the iconic company's shares and did not have the ability to block the deal with super-voting powers. The acquisition launched the Belgian-based brewer back into the top spot in the world of brewing. The mega mergers continued thereafter. In October 2016, AB InBev announced the successful completion of its amalgamation with SABMiller. The third-largest merger in human history was valued at US$123 billion and gave AB InBev a larger presence in developing markets like China, South America, and Africa. In 2017, AB InBev was the third-largest beverage and food company in the world, just ahead of Coca Cola and just behind Pepsi Co. The age of the global brewery had truly arrived.

17 Landes, Mokyr, and Baumol, *The Invention of Enterprise*; Landes, *The Unbound Prometheus*; Landes, "French Entrepreneurship and Industrial Growth in the Nineteenth Century," 45–61.

18 Aitken, "Defensive Capitalism," 183–221; Fossum, *Oil, the States and Federalism*; Laux and Molot, *State Capitalism*; Mullington, "The Federal Government as Entrepreneur"; Bellamy, *Profiting the Crown*.

19 Rudy, "Sleeman's," 39–41; Denison, *The Barley and the Stream*, 57–61, 83, 92–5, 123, 159–60, 176–9, 188–90, 208, 214, 265–75, 282, 326, 334; Brent, *Lager Heads*, 137–48, 173–86.

20 *John Labatt Annual Report* (1987), 9–11.

21 Lopes, *Global Brands*, 115.

22 Owen, *The Rise and Fall of Great Companies*, 6.

Bibliography

Archival Collections

Albert Tucker Papers, York University (Toronto, Ontario)
Borden Papers, Library and Archives Canada (Ottawa, Ontario)
Calgary Brewing and Malting Company Papers, Glenbow Archives (Calgary, Alberta)
Gilbert E. Jackson Papers, University of Toronto (Toronto, Ontario)
Labatt Collection, Western University Archives (London, Ontario)
Molson Papers, Library and Archives Canada (Ottawa, Ontario)

Newspapers and Magazines

Acton Free Press
Anglo-American Magazine
British Colonist
Canadian Annual Review
Canadian Free Press
Canadian Temperance Advocate
Chinook Advance
Christian Guardian
Colonial Patriot
Globe (Toronto)
Globe and Mail
Halifax Herald

Kingston Chronicle
London Free Press
London Gazette
London Prototype
London Times
Maclean's
Mail and Empire
Monetary Times
Montreal Gazette
Montreal Witness
National Post
Pioneer
The Saloon Keeper's Journal
The Times (London, England)
Toronto Daily News
Toronto Star
Toronto Telegram
University Magazine
Vancouver World
Winnipeg Commercial

Published Sources

Aaker, David. *Building Strong Brands*. London: Simon & Schuster, 2010.

Abella, Irving. *On Strike: Six Key Labour Struggles in Canada 1919–1949*. Toronto: Lorimer, 1974.

Ackoff, Russell, and James Emshoff. "Advertising Research at Anheuser-Busch Inc. (1968–74)." *Sloan Management Review* 16, no. 2 (1975): 1–15.

Ackroyd, Peter. *London: The Biography*. London: Vintage, 2000.

Aitken, Hugh. "Defensive Capitalism: The State and Economic Growth in Canada." In *Approaches to Canadian Economic History*, edited by William T. Easterbrook and Mel H. Watkins, 183–221. Montreal and Kingston: McGill-Queen's University Press, 1984.

Akenson, Donald. *The Irish in Ontario: A Study in Rural History*. Montreal and Kingston: McGill-Queen's University Press, 1988.

Alexander, Jeffrey. *Brewed in Japan: The Evolution of the Japanese Beer Industry*. Vancouver: UBC Press, 2013.

Amit, Raphael, and Birger Wernerfelt. "Why Do Firms Reduce Business Risk?" *Academy of Management Journal* 33 (1988): 520–34.

Anbinder, Jacob. "Selling the World: Public Relations and the Global Expansion of General Motors, 1922–1940." *Business History Review* 92, no. 3 (2018): 483–507.

Anderson, James. *One Hundred Years of Brewing: A Complete History of the Progress Made in the Art, Science and Industry of Brewing in the World, particularly during the Nineteenth Century*. New York: H.S. Rich, 1903.

Anonymous. "John Labatt," Canadian *Who's Who*. Toronto: Musson Book Company Ltd, 1910.

Ansoff, H. Igor. "Strategies for Diversification." *Harvard Business Review* 35, no. 5 (1957): 113–24.

Antoniou, Helen. *Back to Beer and Hockey: The Story of Eric Molson*. Montreal and Kingston: McGill-Queen's University Press, 2018.

Appleton, Frank. *Brewing Revolution: Pioneering the Craft Beer Movement*. Madeira Park, BC: Harbour Publishing Co. Ltd, 2016.

Armstrong, Christopher, and H. Viv Nelles. *Southern Exposure: Canadian Promoters in Latin America and the Caribbean*. Toronto: University of Toronto Press, 1988.

Armstrong, Frederick. *The Forest City: An Illustrated History of London, Canada*. Windsor: Windsor Publishing Ltd, 1986.

– "John Kinder Labatt." *Dictionary of Canadian Biography* 9: 436–7.

Arnesen, Eric. *Encyclopedia of U.S. Labor and Working-class History*. New York: Routledge, 2007.

Arnold, Anthony. "'A Paradise for Profiteers'? The Importance and Treatment of Profits during the First World War." *Accounting History Review* 24 (2014): 61–81.

Ashurst, P.R. "Hops and Their Use in Brewing." In *Modern Brewing Technology*, edited by Walter P. Findlay, 31–59. London: Macmillan Press, 1971.

Azzi, Stephen. *Walter Gordon and the Rise of Canadian Nationalism*. Montreal and Kingston: McGill-Queen's University Press, 1999.

Badgely, Kerry. *Ringing in the Common Love of Good: The United Farmers of Ontario, 1914–1926*. Montreal and Kingston: McGill-Queen's University Press, 2000.

Bain, Joe. *Industrial Organization*. New York: Wiley, 1968.

Balasubramanyan, M.N., and M.A. Salisu. "Brands and the Alcoholic Drinks Industry." In *Adding Value: Brands and Marketing in Food and Drink*, edited by Geoffrey Jones and Nicholas J. Morgan, 59–75. London: Routledge, 1994.

Baldwin, Harold. *Holding the Line*. Chicago: A.C. McClung, 1918.

Baldwin, William. *Antitrust and the Changing Corporation*. Durham, NC: Duke University Press, 1961.

Baron, Stanley. *Brewed in America: A History of Beer & Ale in the United States*. Boston: Little, Brown and Co., 1963.

Barron, F.L. "The American Origins of the Temperance Movement in Ontario, 1828–1850." *Canadian Review of American Studies* 11, no. 2 (Fall 1980): 131–50.

Barrows, Susanna, and Robin Room, eds. *Drinking: Behavior and Belief in Modern History*. Berkley: University of California Press, 1991.

Barry, Sandra. "'Shades of Vice ... and Moral Glory': The Temperance Movement in Nova Scotia, 1828–1848." MA thesis: University of New Brunswick, 1986.

Barwise, Patrick, and Thomas Robertson. "Brand Portfolios." *European Management Journal* 10, no. 1 (1992): 277–85.

Baskerville, Peter. "Donald Bethune's Steamship Business: A Study of Upper Canadian Commercial and Financial Enterprise." *Ontario History* 67, no. 3 (1975): 135–49.

Behr, Edward. *Prohibition: Thirteen Years That Changed America*. Boston, MA: Little, Brown and Co., 1996.

Belasco, Warren, and Philip Scranton. *Food Nations: Selling Taste in Consumer Societies*. New York: Routledge, 2002.

Belisle, Donica. *Retail Nation: Department Stores and the Making of Modern Canada*. Vancouver: UBC Press, 2011.

Bellamy, Matthew. "Brewers, Barkeeps, Redcoats and Rebels: Beer and the Rebellions of 1837–1838." *Taps: The Beer Magazine* (2011): 89–91.

– "The Canadian Brewing Industry's Response to Prohibition, 1874–1920." *Brewery History* 132 (2009): 2–17.

– "I Was Canadian: The Globalization of the Canadian Brewing Industry." In *Smart Globalization: The Canadian Business and Economic Experience*, edited by Andrew Smith and Dimitry Anastakis, 206–30. Toronto: University of Toronto Press, 2014.

– "John Labatt Blows In and Out of the Windy City: A Case Study in Entrepreneurship and Business Failure, 1889–1896." *Canadian Historical Review* 95, no. 1 (March 2014): 30–53.

– "The Making of Labatt 'Blue': The Quest for a National Lager Brand, 1959–1971." *Business History* (September, 2017): DOI: 10.1080/00076791.2017.1310195.

– "'More Money than Since or Before': How John Labatt's Brewery Prospered during the Canada Temperance Act Period, 1878–1889." *Brewery History* 152 (2013): 20–32.

– *Profiting the Crown: Canada's Polymer Corporation, 1942–1990*. Montreal and Kingston: McGill-Queen's University Press, 2005.

– "'Rich by Nature, Poor by Policy'? The Premature Birth and Quick Death of Commercial Brewing in Canada, 1667–1675." *Brewery History* 137 (2010): 48–70.

– "'To Ensure the Continued Life of the Industry:' The Public Relations Campaign of the Ontario Brewers during WWII." *Histoire sociale/Social History* 48, no. 97 (November 2015): 403–23.

Bennett, Judith M. *Ale, Beer, and Brewsters in England: Women's Work in a Changing World, 1300–1600*. Oxford: Oxford University Press, 1996.

Bernstein, Barton. "America in War and Peace: The Test of Liberalism." In *Towards a New Past: Dissenting Essays in American History*, edited by Barton Bernstein, 289–312. New York: Pantheon Books, 1968.

Berton, Pierre. *The Great Depression, 1929–1939*. Toronto: Anchor Canada, 2001.

Beverland, Michael. "The 'Real Thing': Branding Authenticity in the Luxury Wine Trade." *Journal of Business Research* 59, no. 2 (February 2006): 251–8.

Beverland, Michael, Adam Lindgreen, and Michiel W. Vink. "Projecting Authenticity through Advertising: Consumer Judgments of Advertisers' Claims." *Journal of Advertising* 37, no. 1 (Spring 2008): 5–15.

Bielenberg, Andy. "The Irish Brewing Industry and the Rise of Guinness, 1790–1914." In *The Dynamics of the International Brewing Industry since 1800*, edited by R.G. Wilson and T.R. Gourvish, 105–22. London and New York: Routledge, 1998.

Bielenberg, Andy, and Peter Solar. "The Irish Cotton Industry from the Industrial Revolution to Partition." *Irish Economic and Social History* 34, no. 1 (2007): 1–28.

Bilkey, Warren, and Erik Nes. "Country-of-Origin Effects on Products Evaluations." *Journal of International Business Studies* 13, no. 1 (1982): 89–99.

Bilson, Geoffrey. "Cholera and Public Health in Canada." *Canadian Journal of Public Health/Revue canadienne de santé publique* 75, no. 5 (September/October 1984): 352–5.

Blair, Paul. *Economic Concentration: Structure, Behavior and Public Policy*. New York: Harcourt Brace Jovanovich, 1972.

Bliss, Michael. "Another Anti-Trust Tradition: Canadian Anti-Combines Policy, 1889–1910." *Business History Review* 47, no. 2 (Summer 1973), 180.

– *A Canadian Millionaire: The Life and Times of Sir Joseph Flavelle, Bart. 1859–1939*. Toronto: Macmillan, 1978.

– *A Living Profit: Studies in the Social History of Canadian Business, 1883–1911*. Toronto: McClelland and Stewart, 1974.

– "The Methodist Church and World War I," *Canadian Historical Review* 49, no. 3, (September 1968): 213–33.

– *Northern Enterprise: Five Centuries of Canadian Business*. Toronto: McClelland and Stewart, 1987.

Blocker, Jack, David M. Fahey, and Ian R. Tyrrell, eds. *Alcohol and Temperance in Modern History: A Global Encyclopedia*. Oxford: ABC Clio, 2003.

Blum, John Morton. *The Roosevelt Republican*. Cambridge, MA: Harvard University Press, 1977.

Boje, Per, and Hans Chr. Johansen. "The Danish Brewing Industry after 1880: Entrepreneurs, Market Structure and Technology." In *The Dynamics of International Brewing Industry since 1800*, edited by Richard Wilson and Terence Gourvish, 59–74. London and New York: Routledge, 1998.

Bolotin, Norm, and Christine Laing. *The World's Columbian Exposition: The Chicago World's Fair of 1893*. Chicago: University of Illinois Press, 2002.

Bonnycastle, Richard. *Canada and the Canadians in 1846*. London: Henry Colburn Publisher, 1846.

Boothman, Barry. "High Finance/Low Strategy: Corporate Collapse in the Canadian Pulp and Paper Industry, 1919–1932." *Business History Review* 74 (Winter 2000): 611–56.

Borg, Erik, and Karl Gratzer. "Theories of Brands and Entrepreneurship: Conceptualizing Brand Strategies." *Annual International Conference on Business Strategy & Organizational Behaviour* (2013): 58–64.

Bower, Julie, and Howard Cox. "How Scottish & Newcastle Became the U.K.'s Largest Brewer: A Case of Regulatory Capture?" *Business History Review* 86 (Spring 2012): 59–61.

Bowering, Ian. *The Art and Mystery of Brewing in Ontario*. Toronto: General Store Publishing House, 1988.

Boyns, Trevor, and John R. Edwards. "The Construction of Cost Accounting Systems in Britain to 1900: The Case of the Coal, Iron and Steel Industries." *Business History* 39 (1997): 1–29.

– "Cost and Management Accounting in Early Victorian Britain: A Chandleresque Analysis?" *Management Accounting Research* 8 (1997): 19–46.

Brandon, David, and Alan Brooke. *Bankside: London's Original District of Sin*. Gloucestershire: Amberley Publishing, 2011.

Brent, Paul. *Lager Heads: Labatt, Molson and the People Who Created Canada's Beer Wars*. Toronto: HarperCollins, 2004.

Brewers Association of Canada. *Alcoholic Beverage Taxation and Control Policies*. Ottawa: Brewers Association of Canada, 1982.

– *Brewing in Canada*. Ottawa: Ronalds-Federated Limited, 1965.

Brewing Industry of Ontario. *Nutrition for Victory: Eat to Work to Win*. Toronto: Brewing Industry of Ontario, 1943.

Brooks, Jay. "InBev." In *The Oxford Companion to Beer*, edited by Garrett Oliver, 480–1. Oxford: Oxford University Press, 2012.

Brouwer, M.T. "The European Beer Industry: Concentration and Competition." In *The Structure of European Industry*, edited by H.W. de Jong, 157–82. Dordrecht: Kluwer Academic Publishers, 1988.

Brown, Craig, and Ramsey Cook. *Canada: A Nation Transformed*. Toronto: McClelland and Stewart, 1974.

Brown, Pete. "Whitbread Brewery." In *The Oxford Companion to Beer*, edited by Garrett Oliver, 841–2. Oxford: Oxford University Press, 2012.

Brown, Stephen, Robert Kozinets, and John F. Sherry Jr. "Teaching Old Brands New Tricks: Retro Branding and the Revival of Brand Meaning." *Journal of Marketing* 67 (July 2003): 19–33.

Bryce, R.B., and Matthew J. Bellamy. *Canada and the Cost of World War II: The International Operations of Canada's Department of Finance*. Montreal and Kingston: McGill-Queen's University Press, 2005.

Campbell, Duncan. *Global Mission: The Story of Alcan*. Toronto: Ontario Publishing Company, 1985.

Campbell, Robert. *Sit Down and Drink Your Beer: Regulating Vancouver's Beer Parlours, 1925–1954*. Toronto: University of Toronto Press, 2001.

Canada. Department of Trade and Commerce. Dominion Bureau of Statistics Census of Industry. *Report on the Brewing Industry in Canada 1933*. Ottawa: 1934.

– Royal Commission on the Liquor Traffic, *Minutes of Evidence, Ontario*, vols. 1–5. Ottawa: S.E. Dawson, 1894–5.

– Royal Commission on the Liquor Traffic, *Report*.

Careless, James. *Toronto to 1918: An Illustrated History*. Toronto: James Lorimer and Company, 1984.

Carstairs, Catherine. "Roots Nationalism: Branding English Canada Cool in the 1980s and 1990s." *Histoire sociale/Social History* 39, no. 77 (2006): 235–55.

Carter, Henry. *The English Temperance Movement: A Study in Objectives*. London: Epworth, 1933.

Cartwright, Richard. *Reminiscences*. Toronto: William Briggs, 1912.

Casson, Mark. "Brands: Economic Ideology and Consumer Society." In *Adding Value: Brands and Marketing in Food and Drink*, edited by Geoffrey Jones and Nicholas Morgan, 41–58. London: Routledge, 1994.

– "The Economics of the Family Firm." *Scandinavian Economic History Review*, 47 (1999): 10–23.

– *The Entrepreneur: An Economic Theory*. Cheltenham, U.K.: Edward Elgar Publishing Limited, 2004.

– "Entrepreneurship and the Theory of the Firm." *Journal of Economic Behavior & Organization* 58 (2005): 327–58.

Cattermole, William. *The Advantages of Emigration to* Canada. London: Longman, 1831.

Chandler, Alfred. "The Development of Modern Management Structure in the US and UK." In *The Essential Alfred Chandler: Essays Towards a Historical Theory of Big Business*, edited by Thomas K. McCraw, 356–381. Boston: Harvard Business School Press, 1988.

– "The Emergence of Managerial Capitalism." *Business History Review* 58, no. 4 (Winter 1984): 473–503.

– "The Organization of Manufacturing and Transportation." In *The Essential Alfred Chandler: Essays Towards a Historical Theory of Big Business*, edited by Thomas K. McCraw, 202–24. Boston: Harvard Business School Press, 1988.

– *Scale and Scope: The Dynamics of Industrial Capitalism*. Cambridge, MA: Harvard University Press, 1990.

– *The Visible Hand: The Managerial Revolution: In American Business*. Cambridge, MA: Harvard University Press, 1977.

Chapman, J.K. "The Mid-Nineteenth-Century Temperance Movement in New Brunswick and Maine." *Canadian Historical Review* 25, no. 1 (March 1954): 43–60.

Chematony, Leslie, and Francesca Riley. "Defining a 'Brand': Beyond the Literature with Experts' Interpretations." *Journal of Marketing Management* 14, no. 5 (1998): 417–43.

– "Modelling the Components of the Brand." *European Journal of Marketing* 32, no. 11/12 (1998): 1077–90.

Church, Roy, and Christine Clark. "Origins of Competitive Advantage in the Marketing of Branded Package Consumer Goods: Coleman's and Reckitt's in Early Victorian Britain." *Journal of Industrial History* 3, no. 2 (2000): 621–45.

Clark, Samuel, Linda Grayson, and Paul Grayson, eds. *Prophecy and Protest: Social Movements in Twentieth Century Canada*. Toronto: Gage, 1975.

Clement, Wallace. *The Canadian Corporate Elite: An Analysis of Economic Power*. Toronto: McClelland and Stewart, 1975.

Cochran, Thomas. *The American Business System: A Historical Perspective, 1900–1955*. Cambridge, MA: Harvard University Press, 1960.

– *The Pabst Brewing Company: History of an American Business*. Westport, CT: Greenwood Press, 1975.

Cole, Trevor. *The Whiskey King*. Toronto: HarperCollins, 2017.

Colli, Andrea. *The History of Family Business, 1850–2000*. Cambridge, U.K.: Cambridge University Press, 2002.

– "The Italian Brewing Industry c. 1815–1990." In *The Dynamics of the International Brewing Industry since 1800*, edited by Richard G. Wilson and Terence Gourvish, 32–58. London and New York: Routledge, 1998.

Cook, Sharon. "*Through Sunshine and Shadow*": *The Women's Christian Temperance Union, Evangelicalism, and Reform in Ontario, 1874–1930*. Montreal and Kingston: McGill-Queen's University Press, 1995.

Cook, Tim. *At the Sharp End: Canadians Fighting the Great War, 1914–1916*. Toronto: Viking, 2007.

– "'More a Medicine than a Beverage': 'Demon Rum' and the Canadian Trench Soldier of the First World War." *Canadian Military History* 9/1 (Winter 2000): 6–22.

– "Wet Canteens and Worrying Mothers: Alcohol, Soldiers and Temperance Groups in the Great War." *Histoire sociale/Social History* 35, no. 70 (November, 2002): 311–30.

Cormack, Patricia. "'True Stories' of Canada: Tim Hortons and the Branding of National Identity." *Cultural Sociology* 2, no. 3 (November 2008): 369–84.

Coutts, Ian. *Brew North: How Canadians Made Beer and Beer Made Canada*. Toronto: Greystone Books, 2010.

Crapster, Basil. "'Our Trade, Our Politics': A Study of the Political Activity of the British Liquor Industry, 1868–1910." PhD dissertation: Harvard University, 1949.

Cronin, Mike, and Liam O'Callaghan. *A History of Ireland*. London: Palgrave, 2001.

Cruickshank, Ken. "Taking the Bitter with the Sweet: Sugar Refiners and the Canadian Regulatory State, 1904–20." *Canadian Historical Review* 74, no. 3 (1993): 367–94.

Cumming, Carman. *Sketches from a Young Country: The Images of Grip Magazine*. Toronto: University of Toronto Press, 1997.

Daniel, Todd. *Navies and Shipbuilding Industries: The Sustained Symbiosis*. Westport, CT: Praeger, 1996.

de Brisay, Richard. "Canada Turns against Prohibition." *Nation* 120 (April 1925): 462–3.

Deconinck, Koen, and Johan Swinnen. "Tied Houses: Why They Are So Common and Why Brewers Charge High Prices for Their Beer." In *Brewing, Beer and Pubs: A Global Perspective*, edited by Ignazio Cabras, David Higgins, and David Preece, 231–6. London: Palgrave Macmillan, 2016.

DeLottinville, Peter. "Joe Beef of Montreal: Working Class Culture and the Tavern, 1869–1889." *Labour/Le Travailleur* 8/9 (Autumn/Spring 1981/1982): 9–40.

Denison, Merrill. *The Barley and the Stream: The Molson Story.* Toronto: McClelland & Stewart, 1955.

Dennison, S.R., and Oliver MacDonagh. *Guinness 1886–1939: From Incorporation to the Second World War.* Cork, Ireland: Cork University Press, 1998.

den Otter, Andy A. *The Philosophy of Railways: The Transcontinental Idea in British North America.* Toronto: University of Toronto Press, 1997.

Dick, E.J. "From Temperance to Prohibition in 19th Century Nova Scotia." *Dalhousie Review* 61, no. 3 (Autumn 1981): 530–52.

Dickens, Charles. *Sketches by Boz.* Philadelphia: Pennsylvania State University Press, 2000.

Doern, G.B., and B.W. Tomlin. *Faith and Fear: The Free Trade Story.* Toronto: Stoddart, 1991.

Dominion Brewers' Association. *Facts on the Brewing Industry in Canada.* Montreal: Federated Press, 1948.

Doyle, Peter. "Building Successful Brands: The Strategic Options." *Journal of Marketing Management* 5, no. 11 (1989): 77–95.

Drucker, Peter. *The Practice of Management.* New York: Harper and Row, 1954.

Duffy, Ian. *Bankruptcy and Insolvency in London during the Industrial Revolution.* New York and London: Garland, 1985.

Duguid, Paul. "Developing the Brand: The Case of Alcohol, 1800–1880." *Enterprise & Society* 4, no. 3 (2003): 405–41.

Dunning, John. *International Production and the Multinational Enterprise.* London: Allen & Unwin, 1981.

– "Trade, Location of Economic Activity and the MNE: A Search for an Eclectic Approach." In *The International Allocation of Economic Activity*, edited by Per-Ove Hesselborn, Bertil Ohlin, and Magnus Per Wijkman, 395–418. London: MacMillan, 1977.

Dyas, Gareth, and Heinz Thanheiser. *The Emerging European Enterprise Strategy and Structure in French and German Industry.* London: Palgrave Macmillan, 1976.

Easterbrook, William, and Mel Watkins, eds. *Approaches to Canadian Economic History.* Toronto: McClelland and Stewart, 1967.

Editors of *Fortune* magazine. *The Conglomerate Commotion.* New York: Viking Press, 1970.

Edwards, Corwin. "Conglomerate Bigness as a Source of Power." In *Business Concentration and Price Policy*, edited by Universities-National Bureau Committee for Economic Research, 331–52. Princeton, NJ: Princeton University Press, 1955.

Elliott, Bruce. *Irish Migrants in Canadas: A New Approach.* Montreal and Kingston: McGill-Queen's University Press, 1988.

Englemann, Larry. "O Whiskey! The History of Prohibition in Michigan." PhD dissertation: University of Chicago, 1975.

English, John. *The Decline of Politics: The Conservatives and the Party System, 1901–20.* Toronto: University of Toronto Press, 1977.

Esteve-Pérez, Silviano. "Consolidation by Merger: the U.K. Beer Market." *Small Business Economics* 39, no. 1 (July 2012): 207–29.

Evans, Gregory. "The Vancouver Island Brewing Industry: 1858–1917." MA thesis: University of Victoria, 1991.

Evenden, Matthew. "The Northern Vision of Harold Adams Innis." *Journal of Canadian Studies* 34, no. 3 (Fall 1999): 162–86.

Fahey, David. "Brewers, Publicans and Working-Class Drinkers: Pressure Group Politics in Late Victorian and Edwardian England." *Histoire sociale/Social History* 13, no. 25 (May 1980): 85–103.

Ferguson, Niall. *High Financier: The Lives and Times of Siegmund Warburg.* New York: Penguin Press, 2010.

Fernández, Eva. "Unsuccessful Responses to Quality Uncertainty: Brands in Spain's Sherry Industry, 1920–1990." *Business History* 52, no. 1 (2010): 100–19.

Findlay, Walter, ed. *Modern Brewing Technology.* London: Macmillan Press, 1971.

Finkel, Alvin. *Social Policy and Practice in Canada: A History.* Waterloo: Wilfrid Laurier University Press, 2006.

Finn, Margot. *The Character of Credit: Personal Debt in English Culture, 1740–1914.* Cambridge: Cambridge University Press, 2003.

Fletcher, Winston. *Powers of Persuasion: The Inside Story of British Advertising: 1951–2000.* Oxford: Oxford University Press, 2008.

Fones-Wolf, Elizabeth. "Creating a Favourable Business Climate: Corporations and Radio Broadcasting, 1934 to 1954." *Business History Review* 73 (Summer 1999): 221–55.

Forbes, Ernest. "Prohibition and the Social Gospel in Nova Scotia." In *Prophecy and Protest: Social Movements in Twentieth Century Canada*, edited by Samuel Clark, Linda Grayson, and Paul Grayson, 62–86. Toronto: Gage, 1975.

Forster, Ben. *A Conjunction of Interest, Business, Politics and Tariffs, 1825–1879.* Toronto: Toronto University Press, 1986.

– "Finding the Right Size: Markets and Competition in Mid- and Late-Nineteenth Century Ontario." In *Patterns of the Past: Interpreting Ontario's History*, edited by Roger Hall et al., 150–73. Toronto: Dundurn, 1998.

Fossum, John. *Oil, the States and Federalism: The Rise and Demise of Petro-Canada as a State Impulse.* Toronto: University of Toronto Press, 1997.

Frank, Thomas. *The Conquest of Cool: Business Culture, Counterculture and the Rise of Hip Consumerism*. Chicago: University of Chicago Press, 1997.

Frederick, Elkin. *Rebels and Colleagues: Advertising and Social Change in French Canada*. Montreal and Kingston: McGill-Queen's University Press, 1973.

Fridenson, Patrick. "Business Failure and the Agenda of Business History." *Enterprise & Society* 5 (December 2004): 562–82.

Frith, Kirk, and Gerard McElwee. "An Emergent Entrepreneur?: A Story of a Drug Dealer in a Restricted Entrepreneurial Environment." *Society and Business Review* 2, no. 3 (2007): 270–86.

Gaglio, Connie Marie, and Jerome A. Katz. "The Psychological Basis of Opportunity Identification: Entrepreneurial Alertness." *Small Business Economics* 16 (2001): 96–111.

Galbraith, John K. *The New Industrial State*. Princeton, NJ: Princeton University Press, 1967.

Gammelgaard, Jens, and Christoph Dörrenbächer, eds. *The Global Brewery Industry: Markets, Strategies and Rivalries*. Cheltenham, U.K.: Edward Elgar Publishing, 2013.

Gardner, Burleigh, and Sidney Levy. "The Product and the Brand." *Harvard Business Review* 33, no. 2 (March–April 1955): 33–9.

George, Lisa. "The Growth of Television and the Decline of Local Beer." In *The Economics of Beer*, edited by Johan Swinnen, 213–27. Oxford: Oxford University Press, 2011.

Gilmour, James. *Spatial Evolution of Manufacturing: Southern Ontario, 1851–1891*. Toronto: University of Toronto Press, 1972.

Gimeno, Javier, Timothy Folta, Arnold Cooper, and Carolyn Woo. "Survival of the Fittest? Entrepreneurial Human Capital and the Persistence of Underperforming Firms." *Administrative Science Quarterly* 42 (1997): 750–83.

Ginzburg, Carlo, John Tedeschi, and Anne C. Tedeschi. "Microhistory: Two or Three Things That I Know about It." *Critical Inquiry* 20, no. 1 (1993): 10–35.

Gioffre, Saverio. "Growth Opportunities That Exist for Canada's Brewing Industry: A Market Study." MA thesis: Ryerson Polytechnical Institute, Toronto, 1984.

Glassford, Larry. "Hepburn, Mitchell Frederick." In *Dictionary of Canadian Biography* 18. Toronto and Quebec City: University of Toronto Press and Université Laval Press, 2003.

– *Reaction and Reform: The Politics of the Conservative Party under R. B. Bennett, 1927–1938*. Toronto: University of Toronto Press, 1992.

Goldenberg, Susan. *Snatched: The Peculiar Kidnapping of the Beer Tycoon John Labatt*. Toronto: Dundurn, 2004.

Goodspeed, C.L. *History of the County of Middlesex*. Toronto: Goodspeed, 1889.

Gourvish, Terence R. "Economics of Brewing, Theory and Practice: Concentration and Technological Change in the USA, UK and West Germany since 1945." *Business and Economic History* 23, no. 1 (Fall 1994): 253–61.

Gourvish, Terence R., and Richard Wilson. *The British Brewing Industry 1830–1980*. Cambridge: Cambridge University Press, 1994.

– *The Dynamics of the International Brewing Industry since 1800*. London: Routledge, 1998.

Graham, Otis L. *From Roosevelt to Roosevelt: American Politics and Diplomacy, 1901–1941*. New York: Appleton-Century-Crofts, Inc., 1971.

Granatstein, Jack. *Canada's War: The Politics of the Mackenzie King Government 1939–1945*. Oxford: University Press, 1975.

– *The Ottawa Men: The Civil Service Mandarins, 1935–1957*. Toronto: Oxford University Press, 1982.

Grant, George. *Lament for a Nation: The Defeat of Canadian Nationalism*. Toronto: Macmillan, 1965.

Gray, Horace, and Walter Adams. *Monopoly in America: The Government as Promoter*. New York: The Macmillan Company, 1955.

Grayson, Kent, and Radan Martinec. "Consumer Perceptions of Iconicity and Indexicality and Their Influence on Assessments of Authentic Market Offerings." *Journal of Consumer Research* 31 (September 2004): 296–312.

Greber, David. *Rising to Power: Paul Desmarais & Power Corporation*. Toronto: Methuen, 1987.

Greenhalgh, Paul. *Ephemeral Vistas: The Expositions Universelles, Great Exhibitions and World's Fairs 1851–1939*. Manchester: Manchester University Press, 1991.

Greenway, John. *Drink and British Politics since 1830: A Study in Policy-Making*. New York: Palgrave Macmillan, 2003.

Greer, D.F. "The Causes of Concentration in the U.S. Brewing Industry." *Quarterly Review of Economics and Business* 21, no. 4 (Winter 1981): 87–106.

Griffith, Robert. "The Selling of America: The Advertising Council and American Politics, 1942–1960." *Business History Review* 57 (Autumn 1983): 388–412.

Gross, Linda, and Theresa Snyder. *Philadelphia's 1876 Centennial Exhibition*. Charleston, SC: Arcadia Publishing Library Editions, 2005.

Guccione, Liz. "Baron of Bootleggers." *Financial Post Magazine* (June 1981): 17–18.

Guy, Kolleen. *When Champagne Became French: Wine and the Making of a National Identity*. Baltimore, MD: John Hopkins University Press, Baltimore, 2002.

Gywn, Richard. *John A.: The Man That Made Us: The Life and Times of John A. Macdonald*. Toronto: Random House, 2007.

Hagelund, William. *House of Suds: A History of Beer Brewing in Western Canada*. Surrey, BC: Hancock House Publishers, 2003.

Haliburton, G. Brenton. *What's Brewing: Oland, 1867–1971*. Tantallon, Nova Scotia: Four East Publications, 1994.

Hall, David. *In the Company of Heroes: An Insider's Guide to Entrepreneurs at Work*. London: Kogan Page, 1999.

Hallowell, Gerald. "Prohibition in Ontario, 1919–1923." MA thesis: Carleton University, 1966.

Hamelin, Marcel, ed. *The Political Ideas of the Prime Ministers*. Ottawa: University of Ottawa Press, 1969.

Hammerschmidt, Hildegard. "Images of Canadian Advertising." *Journal of Canadian Studies* 18, no. 4 (1984): 154–71.

Hampson, Tim. "Ice Beer." In *The Oxford Companion to Beer*, edited by Garnett Oliver, 475. Oxford: Oxford University Press, 2012.

Hannah, Leslie. *The Rise of the Corporate Economy*. London: Methuen, 1976.

– "Scale and Scope: Towards a European Visible Hand?" *Business History Review* 33, no. 1 (April 1990): 297–310.

Hansen, John. *Gaining Access: Congress and the Farm Lobby, 1919–1981*. Chicago: University of Chicago Press, 1991.

Harrell, Byran. "Kirin Brewery Company." In *The Oxford Companion to Beer*, edited by Garnett Oliver, 516–17. Oxford: Oxford University Press, 2012.

Hawkins, K.H. *A History of Bass Charrington*. Oxford: Oxford University Press, 1978.

Hayes, Robert, and William Abernathy. "Managing Our Way to Economic Decline." *Harvard Business Review* (July–August 1980): 67–77.

Heaman, Elsbeth. *The Inglorious Arts of Peace: Exhibitions in Canadian Society during the Nineteenth Century*. Toronto: University of Toronto Press, 1999.

Henderson, James. "A Study of the British Garrison in London, Canada West (Later Ontario), 1838–1869." MA thesis: University of Windsor, 1967.

Henthorn, Cynthia Lee. *From Submarines to Suburbs: Selling a Better America, 1939–1959*. Athens: Ohio University Press, 2006.

Heron, Craig. *Booze: A Distilled History*. Toronto: Between the Lines Press, 2003.

– "The Boys and Their Booze: Masculinities and Public Drinking in Working-class Hamilton, 1890–1949." *Canadian Historical Review* 86, no. 3 (2005): 411–52.

Hiebl, Martin, Martin Quinn, and Carmen Martínez Franco. "An Analysis of the Role of a Chief Accountant at Guinness, c. 1920–1940." *Accounting History Review* 25 (2015): 145–65.

Higgins, David, and Mads Mordhorst. "Bringing Home the 'Danish' Bacon: Food

Chains, National Branding and Danish Supremacy over the British Bacon Market, c. 1900–1938." *Enterprise & Society* 16, no. 1 (2015): 141–85.

Higgins, David, and Shraddha Verma. "The Business of Protection: Bass & Co. and Trade Mark Defence, c. 1870–1914." *Accounting, Business & Financial History* 19, no. 1 (2009): 1–19.

Horowitz, Ira, and Ann Horowitz, "Firms in a Declining Market: The Brewing Case." *The Journal of Industrial Economics* 13, no. 2 (1965): 129–53.

Hunt, Claude. *Whiskey and Ice: The Saga of Ben Kerr, Canada's Most Daring Rumrunner*. Toronto: Dundurn, 1996.

Hunter, Douglas. *Molson: The Birth of a Business Enterprise*. Toronto: Penguin, 2001.

Hurst, Wendy, Ed Gregory, and Thomas Gussman. *Alcoholic Beverage Taxation and Control Policies*. Ottawa: Brewers Association of Canada, 1997.

Iacovetta, Franca. *Gatekeepers, Gatekeepers: Reshaping Immigrant Lives in Cold War Canada*. Toronto: Between the Lines Press, 2006.

Ingram, J.S. *The Centennial Exposition, Described and Illustrated: Being a Concise and Graphic Description of This Grand Enterprise, Commemorative of the First Centenary of American Independence*. Philadelphia: Hubbard Bros, 1876.

Jackall, Robert, and Janice Hirota. *The Image Makers: Advertising, Public Relations, and the Ethos of Advocacy*. Chicago: University of Chicago Press, 2000.

Jacobson, Lisa. "Navigating the Boundaries of Respectability and Desire: Seagram's Advertising and the Meanings of Moderation after Repeal." *History of Alcohol and Drugs* 26, no. 2 (Summer 2012): 122–46.

James, Harold. *Family Capitalism: Wendels, Haniels, Falcks, and the Continental European Model*. Cambridge, MA: The Belknap Press of Harvard University Press, 2006.

Jennings, Paul. *The Local: A History of the English Pub*. Stroud, U.K.: Tempus, 2007.

Jessup, Lynda. "Bushwhackers in the Gallery: Antimodernism and the Group of Seven." In *Anti-modernism and the Artistic Experience: Policing the Boundaries of Modernity*, edited by Lynda Jessup, 130–54. Toronto: University of Toronto Press, 2001.

– "The Group of Seven and the Tourist Landscape in Western Canada, or The More Things Change ..." *Journal of Canadian Studies* 37, no. 1 (Spring 2002): 144–79.

Johansen, Hans Chr. "Marketing and Competition in Danish Brewing." In *Adding Value: Brands and Marketing in Food and Drink*, edited by Geoffrey Jones and Nicholas Morgan, 126–38. London: Routledge, 1994.

Johnson, Yvonne, ed. *Feminist Frontiers: Women Who Shaped the Midwest*. Kirkville, MO: Truman State University Press, 2010.

Johnston, Russel. *Selling Themselves: The Emergence of Canadian Advertising*. Toronto: University of Toronto Press, 2001.

Jones, Geoffrey. "Brands and Marketing." In *Adding Value: Brands and Marketing in Food and Drink*, edited by Geoffrey Jones and Nicholas Morgan, 1–12. London: Routledge, 1994.

– *Renewing Unilever: Transformation and Tradition*. Oxford: Oxford University Press, 2005.

Jones, Geoffrey, and Nicholas J. Morgan. *Adding Value: Brands and Marketing in Food and Drink*. London: Routledge, 1994.

Jones, J.C.H. "Competition in the Canadian Brewing Industry." PhD dissertation: Queen's University, 1966.

– Mergers and Competition: The Brewing Case." *Canadian Journal of Economics and Political Science* 33, no. 4 (November 1967): 551–68.

Jones, S.R.H. "The New Zealand Brewing Industry, 1840–1995." In *The Dynamics of the International Brewing Industry since 1800*, edited by Richard Wilson and Terence Gourvish, 247–65. London and New York: Routledge, 1998.

Joyner, Charles. *Shared Traditions: Southern History and Folk Culture*. Urbana: University of Illinois, 1999.

Kaplan, Abraham. *Big Enterprise in a Competitive System*. Washington, DC: The Brookings Institute, 1954.

Karlsson, Gunnar. *The History of Iceland*. Minneapolis: University of Minnesota Press, 2000.

Kasson, John. *Houdini, Tarzan, and the Perfect Man: The White Male Body and the Challenge of Modernity in America*. New York: Hill and Wang, 2001.

Katz, Michael. *The People of Hamilton, Canada West: Family and Class in a Mid-Nineteenth-Century City*. Cambridge, MA: Harvard University Press, 1975.

Katz, Solomon, and Fritz Maytag. "Brewing an Ancient Beer." *Expedition* 44, no. 4 (1991): 24–33.

Kay, Neil. *Patterns of Corporate Evolution*. Oxford: Oxford University Press, 1997.

Kealey, Greg, and Brian Palmer. *Dreaming of What Might Be: The Knights of Labor in Ontario, 1880–1900*. Cambridge, U.K.: Cambridge University Press, 1882.

Keefer, Thomas. *The Philosophy of Railroads*. Montreal: Armour and Ramsay, 1850.

Kemp, Peter. *The British Sailor: A Social History of the Lower Deck*. London: J.M. Dent and Sons, 1970.

Kerr, Austin. "The American Brewing Industry, 1865–1920." In *The Dynamics of the International Brewing Industry since 1800*, edited by Richard Wilson and Terence Gourvish, 176–92. London and New York: Routledge, 1998.

– *Organized for Prohibition: A New History of the Anti-saloon League*. New Haven, CT: Yale University Press, 1985.

Kindleberger, Charles. *American Business Abroad: Six Lecture on Direct Investment.* New Haven, CT: Yale University Press, 1969.

King, William Lyon Mackenzie. *Canada and the War: Temperance and a Total War Effort.* Ottawa: Edmond Cloutier, 1942.

King, Stephen. *Developing New Brands.* Bath, U.K.: John Wiley and Sons, 1973.

Kirzner, Israel. "Entrepreneurial Discovery and the Competitive Market Process: An Austrian Approach." *Journal of Economic Literature* 35 (1997): 60–85.

– *Perception, Opportunity, and Profit.* Chicago: University of Chicago Press, 1979.

Klassen, Henry. "Entrepreneurship in the Canadian West: The Enterprises of A.E. Cross, 1886–1920." *The Western Historical Quarterly* 22 (August 1991): 313–33.

Knowles, Valeria. *From Telegrapher to Titan: The Life of William C. Van Horne.* Toronto: Dundurn Press, 2004.

Kohern, Nancy. *Brand New: How Entrepreneurs Earned Consumers from Wedgewood to Dell.* Boston: Harvard University Press, 2001.

Kribs, Louis. *Report of Louis P. Kribs in Connection with the Investigation Held by the Canadian Royal Commission on the Liquor Traffic.* Ottawa: Nobel Press, 1895.

Krout, John A. *The Origins of Prohibition.* New York: Russell and Russel, 1967.

Labatt, Arthur. *A Different Road: A Memoir.* Toronto: BPS Books, 2012.

Lampman, A. "To a Millionaire." In *The Poems of Archibald Lampman*, edited by Duncan Campbell. Toronto: George N. Morang Co., 1900.

Landes, David. *Dynasties: Fortunes and Misfortunes of the World's Great Family Businesses.* New York: Viking, 2006.

– "French Entrepreneurship and Industrial Growth in the Nineteenth Century." *Journal of Economic History* 9 (1949): 45–61.

– *The Unbound Prometheus: Technological Change and Industrial Development in Western Europe from 1750 to the Present.* New York: Cambridge University Press, 1969.

Landes, David, Joel Mokyr, and William Baumol. *The Invention of Enterprise: Entrepreneurship from Ancient Mesopotamia to Modern Times.* Princeton, NJ: Princeton University Press, 2010.

Landström, Hans, and Franz Lohrke. *Historical Foundations of Entrepreneurship Research.* Cheltenham: Edward Elgar Publishing, 2010.

Larsen, Karen. *History of Norway.* Princeton, NJ: Princeton University Press, 1948.

Laux, Jeanne, and Maureen Molot. *State Capitalism: Public Enterprise in Canada.* Ithaca, NY: Cornell University Press, 1988.

Leacock, Stephen. *Elements of Political Science.* New York: Hough Mifflin, 1906.

– "How to Make a Million Dollars." In *A Treasury of Stephen Leacock.* Toronto: Key Porter Books, 2002.

– "Wet or Dry." *Observer* 39 (April 1919).

Lefebvre, Andrew. "Prohibition and the Smuggling of Intoxicating Liquors between the Two Saults." *The Northern Mariner* 11, no. 3 (July 2001).

Levitt, Kari. *Silent Surrender: The Multinational Corporation in Canada*. Montreal and Kingston: McGill-Queen's University Press, 1970.

Lewellen, Wilbur. "A Pure Financial Rationale for the Conglomerate Merger." *Journal of Finance* 26 (1971): 521–37.

Lewis, David. *The Public Image of Henry Ford: An American Fold Hero and His Company*. Detroit: Wayne State University Press, 1976.

Lexer, Robert. *Canada Ltd: The Political Economy of Dependency*. Toronto: McClelland and Stewart, 1971.

Lockwood, Glenn J. "Temperance in Upper Canada as Ethnic Subterfuge." In *Drink in Canada: Historical Essays*, edited by Cheryl Warsh Krasnick, 43–69. Montreal and Kingston: McGill-Queen's University Press, 1993.

Loft, Anne. "Towards a Critical Understanding of Accounting: The Case of Cost Accounting in the UK, 1914–1925." *Accounting, Organizations and Society* 11 (1986): 137–69.

Lonier, Terri. "Alchemy in Eden: Entrepreneurialism, Branding, and Food Marketing in the United States, 1880–1920." *Enterprise & Society* 11, no. 4 (2010): 695–708.

Lopes, Teresa Da Silva. "Brands and the Evolution of Multinationals in the Alcoholic Beverages." *Business History* 44 (July 2002): 1–30.

– *Global Brands: The Evolution of Multinationals in the Alcoholic Beverages*. Cambridge, MA: Cambridge University Press, 2007.

Lorandini, Cinzia. "Looking Beyond the Buddenbrooks Syndrome: The Salvadori Firm of Trento, 1660s–1880s." *Business History* 57 (2015): 1005–19.

Lubatkin, Michael, and Sayan Chatterjee. "Extending Modern Portfolio Theory into the Domain of Corporate Diversification: Does It Apply?" *Academy of Management Journal* 37 (1994): 109–36.

Lumsden, Ian, ed. *Close the 49th Parallel etc.: The Americanization of Canada*. Toronto: University of Toronto Press, 1970.

MacEachern, Alan. *Natural Selections: National Parks in Atlantic Canada, 1935–1977*. Montreal and Kingston: McGill-Queen's University Press, 2001.

MacKay, Donald. *Empire of Wood: The MacMillan Bloedel Story*. Vancouver: Douglas & McIntyre, 1982.

MacKenzie, David. *The Clarkson Gordon Story*. Toronto: University of Toronto Press, 1989.

MacLean, John. *The Complete Tariff Hand-Book, Shewing Canadian Customs Tariff with the Various Changes Made during the Last Thirty Years*. Toronto: Hunter, Rose and Co., 1879.

Malleck, Dan. *Try to Control Yourself: The Regulation of Public Drinking in Post-Prohibition Ontario, 1927–1944*. Vancouver: UBC Press, 2012.

Marchand, Roland. "The Corporation Nobody Knew: Bruce Barton, Alfred Sloan, and the Founding of the General Motors Family." *Business History Review* 65 (Winter 1991): 825–75.

– *Creating the Corporate Soul: The Rise of Public Relations and Corporate Imagery in American Big Business*. Berkeley: University of California Press, 1998.

Marchildon, Greg. *Profits and Politics: Beaverbrook and the Gilded Age of Canadian Finance*. Toronto: University of Toronto Press, 1996.

– "Promotion, Finance and Mergers in Canadian Manufacturing, 1885–1918." PhD dissertation: University of London, 1990.

Markides, Constantinos. "Back to Basics: Reversing Corporate Diversification." *Multinational Business* 4 (1991): 12–25.

Martel, Marcel. *Canada the Good: A Short History of Vice since 1500*. Waterloo: Wilfrid Laurier University Press, 2014.

Martin, Ged. "John A. MacDonald and the Bottle." *Journal of Canadian Studies/Revue d'études canadiennes* 40, no. 3 (2006): 162–85.

Marquis, Greg. "'A Reluctant Concession to Modernity': Alcohol and Modernization in the Maritimes, 1945–1980." *Acadiensis* 32, no. 2 (Spring 2013): 31–59.

Mathias, Peter. *The Brewing Industry in England, 1700–1830*. New York: Cambridge University Press, 1959.

– "The Brewing Industry, Temperance and Politics." *Historical Journal* 1 (1958): 97–114.

Matthews, Derek. "The Business Doctors: Accountants in British Management from the Nineteenth Century to the Present Day." *Business History* 40 (1998): 72–103.

– "The Influence of the Accountant on British Business Performance from the Late Nineteenth Century to the Present Day." *Abacus* 37 (2001): 329–51.

Matthews, Derek, M. Anderson, and J.R. Edwards. "The Rise of the Professional Accountant in British Management." *The Economic History Review* 50 (1997): 407–29.

McCalla, Douglas. "An Introduction to the Nineteenth Century Business World." In *Essays in Canadian Business History,* edited by Tom Traves, 13–23. Toronto: McClelland and Stewart, 1984.

– "The Loyalist Economy of Upper Canada, 1784–1806." *Histoire sociale/Social History* 16 (November 1983): 279–304.

– *Planting the Province: The Economic History of Upper Canada, 1784–1870*. Toronto: University of Toronto Press, 1993.

McCann, Hiram. "Canada's Faulty Diet Is Adolf Hitler's Ally." *Saturday Night*, 14 (June 1941): 8–9.

McCarty, Kate. *Distilled in Maine: A History of Libations, Temperance & Craft Spirits*. Charleston, SC: The History Press, 2015.

McCreath, Peter. *The Life and Times of Alexander Keith*. Tantallon, Nova Scotia: Four East Publications, 2001.

McDonald, Donna. *Lord Strathcona: A Biography of Donald Alexander Smith*. Toronto: Dundurn Press, 1996.

McDowall, Duncan. *The Light: Brazilian Traction, Light and Power Company Limited*. Toronto: University of Toronto Press, 1988.

– *Quick to the Frontier: Canada's Royal Bank*. Toronto: McClelland and Stewart, 1993.

– *Steel at the Sault: Francis H. Clergue, Sir James Dunn, and the Algoma Steel Corporation, 1901–1956*. Toronto: Toronto University Press, 1984.

– *The Sum of the Satisfactions: Canada in the Age of National Accounting*. Montreal and Kingston: McGill-Queen's University Press, 2008.

McGahan, Anita. "The Emergence of the National Brewing Oligopoly: Competition in the American Market, 1933–1958." *Business History Review* 65, no. 2 (Summer, 1991): 229–84.

McKay, Ian. *The Quest of the Folk: Antimodernism and Cultural Selection in Twentieth-Century Nova Scotia*. Montreal and Kingston, McGill-Queen's University Press, 1994.

McLeod, Alan, and Jordan St John. *Ontario Beer: The Heady History of Beer from the Great Lakes to Hudson Bay*. Charleston, SC: The History Press, 2014.

McQueen, Rod. *The Eatons: The Rise and Fall of Canada's Royal Family*. Toronto: Stoddart, 1998.

Mellahi, Kamel, and Adrian Wilkinson. "Managing and Coping with Organizational Failure: Introduction to the Special Issue." *Group and Organizational Management* 35, no. 5 (2010): 531–41.

Mercer, John. "A Mark of Distinction: Branding and Trade Mark Law in the UK from the 1860s." *Business History* 52, no. 1 (2010): 17–42.

Merrett, David. "Stability and Change in the Australian Brewing Industry, 1920–94." In *The Dynamics of the International Brewing Industry since 1800*, edited by Richard Wilson and Terence Gourvish, 229–48. London and New York: Routledge, 1998.

Merrett, David, and Greg Whitwell. "The Empire Strikes Back: Marketing Australian Beer and Wine in the United Kingdom." In *Adding Value: Brands and Marketing in Food and Drink*, edited by Geoffrey Jones and Nicholas Morgan, 162–90. London: Routledge, 1994.

Miller, Karen. "Air Power Is Peace Power: The Aircraft Industry's Campaign for Public and Political Support, 1943–1949." *Business History Review* 70, no. 3 (Autumn, 1996): 297–327.

Miller, Orlo. *A Century of Western Ontario.* Toronto: Greenwood Press, 1949.

Millns, Tony. "The British Brewing Industry, 1945–95." In *The Dynamics of the International Brewing Industry since 1800,* edited by Richard Wilson and Terence Gourvish, 142–59. London and New York: Routledge, 1998.

Mittelman, Amy. *Brewing Battles: A History of American Beer.* New York: Algora Publishing, 2008.

Molson, Karen. *The Molsons: Their Lives and Times, 1780–2000.* Willowdale: Firefly Books, 2001.

Moodie, Susanna. *Roughing It in the Bush, or, Forest Life in Canada.* London: R. Bentley, 1852.

Moore, Stephen. *Bootleggers and Borderlands: The Paradox of Prohibition on the Canada-U.S. Borderland.* Lincoln: University of Nebraska Press, 2014.

Mora-Torres, Juan. *The Making of the Mexican Border: The State, Capitalism, and Society in Nuevo León, 1848–1910.* Austin, TX: University of Texas Press, 2001.

Morton, Desmond. *When Your Number's Up: The Canadian Soldier in the First World War.* Toronto: Random House, 1993.

Mullington, Hugh. "The Federal Government as Entrepreneur: The Canadian Experience." MA thesis: Carleton University, 1969.

Murton, James. "'The Normandy of the New World': Canada Steamship Lines, Anti-modernism, and the Selling of Old Quebec." In *Settling and Unsettling Memories: Essays in Canadian Public History,* edited by Nicole Neatby and Peter Hodgins, 419–53. Toronto: University of Toronto Press, 2012.

Myers, Gustavus. *History of Canadian Wealth.* New York: Lorimer, 1914.

Neatby, Nicole, and Peter Hodgins, eds. *Settling and Unsettling Memories: Essays in Canadian Public History.* Toronto: University of Toronto Press, 2012.

Neill, Robin. *A History of Canadian Economic Thought.* London: Routledge, 1991.

Nelles, H. Viv. *The Politics of Development: Forests, Mines and Hydro-Electric Power in Ontario, 1849–1941.* Toronto: Macmillan, 1974.

Neufeld, E.P. *A Global Corporation: A History of the International Development of Massey-Ferguson Limited.* Toronto: University of Toronto Press, 1969.

Newman, Peter. *Titans: How the New Canadian Establishment Seized Power.* Toronto: Viking, 1998.

Nodoushani, Omid, and Patricia Nodoushani. "Second Thoughts on the Entrepreneurial Myth." *International Journal of Entrepreneurship and Innovation* 1, no. 1 (2000): 7–13.

Noel, Jan. *Canada Dry: Temperance Crusades before Confederation*. Toronto: University of Toronto Press, 1995.

Nolan, Brian. *King's War: Mackenzie King and the Politics of War 1939–1945*. Toronto: Random House, 1988.

Nye, David. *Image Worlds: Corporate Identities at General Electric*. Cambridge, MA: The MIT Press, 1985.

Ogle, Maureen. *Ambitious Brew: The Story of American Beer*. London: Harcourt, 2006.

Okrent, Daniel. *Last Call: The Rise and Fall of Prohibition*. New York: Scribner, 2010.

Oliver, G. "Brewmaster." In *The Oxford Companion to Beer*, edited by Garrett Oliver, 170–1. Oxford: Oxford University Press, 2012.

Oliver, Garrett, ed. *The Oxford Companion to Beer*. Oxford: Oxford University Press, 2012.

Oliver, Peter. *Howard Ferguson: Ontario Tory*. Toronto: University of Toronto Press, 1977.

O'Neill, Carly, Dick Houtman, and Stef Aupers. "Advertising Real Beer: Authenticity Claims beyond Truth and Falsity." *European Journal of Cultural Studies* 17, no. 5 (October 2014): 5–15.

O'Neill, R.D. "The Temperance Movement, Prohibition and Scarcity in Ontario, 1900–1916." DEd thesis: University of Toronto, 1984.

Opp, James. "Branding 'the Bay/la Baie': Corporate Identity, the Hudson's Bay Company, and the Burden of History in the 1960s." *Canadian Historical Review* 96, no. 2 (June 2015): 223–56.

Owen, Colin. *The Greatest Brewery in the World: A History of Bass, Ratcliff & Gretton*. Chesterfield: Derbyshire Record Society, 1992.

Owen, Geoffrey. *The Rise and Fall of Great Companies: Courtaulds and the Reshaping of Man-Made Fibres*. Oxford: Oxford University Press, 2010.

Owram, Doug. *The Government Generation, Canadian Intellectuals and the State, 1900–1945*. Toronto: University of Toronto Press, 1986.

Pashley, Nicholas. *Cheers! An Intemperate History of Beer in Canada*. Toronto: Collins, 2009.

Pasteur, Louis. *Études sur le vin, ses maladies, causes qui les provoquent, procédés nouveaus pour le conserver et pour le viellir*. Paris: imprimerie imperiale, 1866.

– *Studies on Fermentation: The Diseases of Beer, Their Causes, and the Means of Preventing Them*, trans. F. Faulkner and D.C. Robb. London: Macmillan & Co., 1879.

Peles, Yoram. "Economies of Scale in Advertising Beer and Cigarettes." *The Journal of Business* 44, no. 1 (January 1971): 32–7.

Peñaloza, Lisa. "The Commodification of the American West: Marketers' Production of Cultural Meanings at the Trade Show." *Journal of Marketing* 64, no. 4 (October 2000): 82–109.

Penfold, Steve. *The Donut: A Canadian History*. Toronto: University of Toronto Press, 2008.

– "'Eddie Shack Was No Tim Horton': Donuts and the Folklore of Mass Culture in Canada." In *Food Nations: Selling Taste in Consumer Societies*, edited by William Belasco and Phillip Scranton, 48–66. New York: Routledge, 2002.

Penrose, Edith. *The Theory of the Growth of the Firm*. Oxford: Oxford University Press, 1959/1995.

Perry, Harvey. *Taxes, Tariff and Subsidies: A History of Canadian Fiscal Development*. Toronto: University of Toronto Press, 1955.

Peters, Thomas, and Robert Waterman. *In Search of Excellence: Lessons from America's Best-Run Companies*. New York: Harper Collins, 1982.

Petricca, Michael Loreto. "Edward Plunket Taylor's Entrepreneurial Visions of Expansion: The Interrelated Development of Canadian Breweries and Argus Corporation, 1930–1975." MA thesis: University of Western Ontario, 2001.

Pett, L.B. "Nutrition as a National Problem," *Canadian Welfare* 18 (April 1942): 21–9.

Phillips, Glen. "Carling Breweries." In *Alcohol and Temperance in Modern History: A Global Encyclopedia*, edited by Jock Blocker, David Fahey, and Ian Tyrrell, 135–6. Oxford: ABC-CLIO, 2003.

– *On Tap: The Odyssey of Beer and Brewing in Victorian London-Middlesex*. Sarnia: Cheshire Cat Press, 2000.

Phoenix, Claire. "The World's Top 100 Food & Beverage Companies: Globalization, Innovation and a New Way of Grocery Shopping." *Food Engineering* 89, no. 9 (September 2017).

Pierce, Louise. *A History of Chicago, Volume III: The Rise of a Modern City*. Chicago: University of Chicago Press, 1957.

Pitts, Gordon. *In the Blood: Battles to Succeed in Canada's Family Businesses*. Toronto: Doubleday Canada, 2000.

Plavchan, Roland. "A History of Anheuser-Busch, 1852–1933." PhD dissertation: St Louis University, 1969.

Pope, William, *The Elephant and the Mouse*. Toronto: Macmillan, 1971.

Power, Michael. "Eugene O'Keefe." *Dictionary of Canadian Biography* 14, 796–7.

Prahalad, C.K., and Gary Hamel. "The Core Competence of the Corporation." *Harvard Business Review* 68 (May–June 1990): 79–91.

Prang, Margret. *N.W. Rowell: Ontario Nationalist*. Toronto: University of Toronto Press, 1975.

Purdy, Al. *The New Romans: Candid Canadian Opinions of the U.S.* Edmonton: Hurtig, 1968.

Quelch, John, and Katherine E. Jocz. "Milestones in Marketing." *Business History Review* 82 (Winter 2008): 827–38.

Quinn, John. *Father Mathew's Crusade: Temperance in Nineteenth-Century Ireland and Irish America.* Amherst: University of Massachusetts Press, 2002.

Ray, Arthur. *The Canadian Fur Trade in the Industrial Age.* Toronto: University of Toronto Press, 1990.

Reichardt, Otto. "Industrial Concentration and World War II: A Note on the Aircraft Industry." *Business History Review* 49, no. 4 (Winter 1975): 498–503.

Ritzer, George. *The McDonaldization of Society: An Investigation into the Changing Character of Contemporary Social Life.* Los Angeles: Pine Forge Press, 1993.

Robbins, J., and M.F. Wiersema. "A Resource-Based Approach to the Multi-business Firm: Empirical Analysis of Portfolio Interrelationships and Corporate Financial Responsibility." *Strategic Management Journal* 16 (1990): 277–99.

Roberts, Julia. *In Mixed Company: Taverns and Public Life in Upper Canada.* Vancouver: UBC Press, 2009.

Rodrik, Dani. *The Globalization Paradox: Why Global Markets, States, and Democracy Can't Coexist.* New York: Norton, 2011.

Rohmer, Richard. *E.P. Taylor: The Biography of Edward Plunket Taylor.* Toronto: McClelland and Stewart, 1978.

– *Ultimatum.* Toronto: Clark Irwin, 1973.

Rose, Clifford. *Four Years with the Demon Rum.* Fredericton, NB: Acadiensis Press, 1980.

Roseman, Frank. "The Canadian Brewing Industry: The Effect of Mergers and Provincial Regulation on Economic Conduct and Performance." PhD dissertation: Northwestern University, 1968.

Ross, Andrew, and Andrew Smith. *Canada's Entrepreneurs: From the Fur Trade to the 1929 Stock Market Crash.* Toronto: University of Toronto Press, 2011.

Rotstein, Abraham. *The Precarious Homestead: Essays on Economics, Technology and Nationalism.* Toronto: New Press, 1973.

Rudy, Jarrett. *The Freedom to Smoke: Tobacco Consumption and Identity.* Montreal and Kingston: McGill-Queen's University Press, 2005.

– "Sleeman's: Small Business in the Ontario Brewing Industry, 1847–1916." MA thesis: University of Ottawa, 1994.

Rumbarger, John. *Profits, Power and Prohibition, Alcohol Reform and the Industrializing of America, 1800–1930.* Albany: State of New York Press, 1989.

Rutherford, Paul. *The New Icons: The Art of Television Advertising*. Toronto: University of Toronto Press, 1994.

Rydell, Robert. *World of Fairs: The Century of Progress Expositions*. Chicago: Chicago University Press, 1993.

Saiz, Patricio, and P. Fernandez Perez. "Catalonian Trademarks and the Development of Marketing Knowledge in Spain, 1850–1946." *Business History Review* 86 (Summer 2012): 239–60.

Sandberg, Peter. "The Creation of Big Business in the Swedish Brewing Industry during the Aftermath of the Second World War." *Scandinavian Economic History Review* 58, no. 1 (March 2010): 43–59.

Sawler, Harvey. *Last Canadian Beer: The Moosehead Story*. Halifax: Nimbus Publishing, 2008.

Saywell, John T. *'Just Call Me Mitch': The Life of Mitchell F. Hepburn*. Toronto: University of Toronto Press, 1991.

Scherer, Frederic. "The Determinants of Industrial Plant Sizes in Six Nations." *The Review of Economics and Statistics* 55, no. 2 (1973): 135–45.

Schrad, Mark. *Vodka Politics: Alcohol, Autocracy, and the Secret History of the Russian State*. Oxford, U.K.: Oxford University Press, 2014.

Schulter, Herman. *The Brewing Industry and the Brewery Worker's Movement in America*. Cincinnati: International Union of United Brewery Workmen of America, 1910.

Schumacher, H. "The Global Beer Industry 2001 Review: Toto, We Are Not in Kansas Anymore." *Modern Beverage Age* 36, no. 5 (2002): 7–9.

Schumpeter, Joseph. *Capitalism, Socialism, and Democracy*. New York: Harper & Bros, 1942.

– *The Theory of Economic Development: An Inquiry into Profits, Capital, Credit, Interest and the Business Cycle*. Cambridge, MA: Harvard University Press, 1934.

Scott, Francis R. "W.L.M.K." In *The Eye of the Needle: Satires, Sorties, Sundries*. Montreal: Contact Press, 1957.

Servan-Schreiber, Jean-Jacques. *le défi américain*. Paris: Denoël, 1967.

Seth, Anju. "Value Creation in Acquisitions: A Re-examination of Performance Issues." *Strategic Management Journal* 11 (1990): 99–115.

Shane, Scott, and Sankaran Venkataraman. "The Promise of Entrepreneurship as a Field of Research." *Academy of Management Review* 25, no. 1 (2000): 217–26.

Shea, Albert. *Vision in Action: The Story of Canadian Breweries Limited from 1930 to 1955*. Toronto: Canadian Breweries, 1955.

Shortt, Adam. "The Economic Effect of War upon Canada." *Transactions of the Royal Society of Canada* 10 (May 1916): 65–74.

Sigsworth, E.M. "Science and the Brewing Industry, 1850–1900." *Economic History Review* 17, no. 3 (1965): 536–50.

Sinclair, Andrew. *Era of Excess: A Social History of the Prohibition Movement.* New York: Harper and Row, 1964.

Skilnik, Bob. *Beer: A History of Brewing in Chicago.* Fort Lee, NJ: Barricade Books, 2006.

Sluyterman, Katie, and Bram Bouwens. "From Colonial Empires to Developing Countries and on to Emerging Economies: The International Expansion of the Dutch Brewery Heineken, 1930–2010." *Management & Organizational* History 10, no. 2 (2015): 103–18.

Smith, Andrew, and Dimitry Anastankis. *Smart Globalization: The Canadian Business and Economic History Experience.* Toronto: University of Toronto Press, 2014.

Smith, Goldwin. *Progress of Revolution: A Letter to a Labour Friend.* Toronto: W.T. and Co., 1906.

Smith, Wendell. "Product Differentiation and Market Segmentation as Alternative Marketing Strategies." *Journal of Marketing* 21 (July 1956): 3–8.

Sneath, Allen Winn. *Brewed in Canada: The Untold Story of Canada's 350-Year-Old Brewing Industry.* Toronto: Dundurn Group, 2001.

Snow, Charles, and Lawrence Hrebiniak. "Strategy, Distinctive Competence, and Organizational Performance." *Administrative Science Quarterly* 25 (1980): 317–36.

Sobel, Robert. *The Age of Giant Corporations: Microeconomic History of American Business, 1914–1992.* London: Greenwood Press, 1973.

Sotiron, Minko. *From Politics to Profits: The Commercialization of Canadian Newspapers, 1890–1920.* Montreal and Kingston: McGill-Queen's University Press, 1997.

Spence, Francis. *The Facts of the Case: A Summary of the Most Important Evidence and Arguments Presented in the Report of the Royal Commission on the Liquor Traffic.* Ottawa: Queen's Printer, 1895.

Spence, Ruth. *Prohibition in Canada.* Toronto: Ontario Branch of the Dominion Alliance, 1919.

Stacey, Charles. *Canada and the British Army, 1846–1871.* Toronto: University of Toronto Press, 1963.

Stack, Martin. "Interbrew." In *Alcohol and Temperance in Modern History: A Global Encyclopedia*, edited by Jock Blocker, David Fahey, and Ian Tyrrell, 315–16. Oxford: ABC-CLIO, 2003.

– "Local and Regional Breweries in America's Brewing Industry, 1865 to 1920." *Business History Review* 74 (Autumn, 2000): 435–63.

Stamper, Anita, and Jill Condra. *Clothing through American History: The Civil War through the Gilded Age 1861–1899*. Oxford: ABC-CLIO, 2011.

Stedman Jones, Gareth. "Working-Class Culture and Working-Class Politics in London, 1870–1900; Notes on the Remaking of a Working Class." *Journal of Social History* 7, no. 4 (Summer 1974): 460–508.

Stevens, G.R. *The History of Canadian National Railways*. New York, NY: Macmillan 1973.

Stigler, George. "The Theory of Economic Regulation." *Bell Journal of Economics and Management Science* 2 (Spring 1971): 3–21.

Stole, Inger. *Advertising at War: Business, Consumers, and Government in the 1940s*. Urbana and Chicago: University of Illinois Press, 2012.

St-Pierre, Majella. *Alphonse Desjardins, Entrepreneur*. Montreal and Charlesbourg, QC: Divers, 2001.

Strasser, Susan. *Satisfaction Guaranteed: The Making of the American Mass Market*. Washington, DC: Smithsonian Institution Press, 1989.

Struthers, James. *No Fault of Their Own: Unemployment and the Canadian Welfare State, 1914–1941*. Toronto: University of Toronto Press, 1983.

Stuart, Charles. *The Emigrant's Guide to Upper Canada; or, Sketches of the Present State of that Province, Collected from a Residence therein during the Years 1817, 1818, 1819, Interspersed with Reflections*. London: Longman, 1820.

Sturgis, James. "Beer under Pressure: The Origins of Prohibition in Canada." *Bulletin of Canadian Studies* 8, no. 1 (Spring 1984): 83–100.

Sulkunen, Irma. *History of the Finnish Temperance Movement: Temperance as a Civic Religion*. Lewiston, NY: Edwin Mellen Press, 1991.

Surtees, Lawrence. *Pa Bell: A. Jean de Grandpre & the Meteoric Rise of Bell Canada Enterprises*. Toronto: Random House of Canada, 1992.

Sutton, John. *Sunk Costs and Market Structure: Price Competition, Advertising, and the Evolution of Concentration*. Cambridge, MA: MIT Press, 1991.

Szeless, Georg, Margarethe Wiersema, and Günter Müller-Stewens. "Portfolio Interrelationships and Financial Performance in the Context of European Firms." *European Management Journal* 21 (2003): 146–63.

Taylor, Graham. "The Whiskey Kings: The International Expansion of the Seagram Company, 1933–1995." In *Smart Globalization: The Canadian Business and Economic History Experience*, edited by Andrew Smith and Dimitry Anastankis, 184–205. Toronto: University of Toronto Press, 2014.

Tedlow, Richard. "The National Association of Manufacturers and Public Relations during the New Deal." *Business History Review* 50 (Spring 1976): 25–45.

Teece, David. "Economies of Scope and the Scope of Enterprise." *Journal of Economic Behavior and Organization* 1 (1980): 223–47.

Tennyson, Brian. "Sir William Hearst and the Ontario Temperance Act." *Ontario History* 55 (1963): 233–45.

Thompson, John. *The Harvests of War: The Prairie West, 1914–1918*. Toronto: Oxford University Press, 1997.

Timperlake, J. *Illustrated Toronto: Past and Present*. Toronto: Peter Gross, 1877.

Tom, Steve, and Mike Wright. "Corporate Governance, Strategy and Structure in British Business History, 1950–2000." *Business History* 44 (July 2002): 91–124.

Toynbee, Arnold. *The Industrial Revolution*. Boston: Beacon Press, 1966.

Tremblay, Victor. "Strategic Groups and the Demand for Beer." *Journal of Industrial Economics* 34, no. 2 (1985): 183–98.

Tremblay, Victor, and Carol Horton Tremblay. *The U.S. Brewing Industry: Data and Economic Analysis*. Cambridge, MA: MIT Press, 2005.

Tucker, Albert. "Labatt's: A History – From Immigrant Family to Canadian Corporation." Unpublished manuscript in author's possession, 1980.

Tyrrell, Ian. *Sobering Up: From Temperance to Prohibition in Antebellum America, 1800–1860*. Westport, CT: Greenwood Press, 1979.

Ucbasaran, Deniz, Paul Westhead, Mike Wright, and Manuel Flores. "The Nature of Entrepreneurial Experience, Business Failure and Comparative Optimism." *Journal of Business Venturing* 25 (2010): 541–55.

Unger, Richard. *Beer in the Middle Ages and the Renaissance*. Philadelphia: University of Pennsylvania Press, 2004.

United Brewers' Foundation. *The Brewing Industry in the United States: The Brewers' Almanac*. New York: United Brewers' Foundation, 1944.

United Nations: Economic Commission for Latin America and the Caribbean. *Foreign Investment in Latin America and the Caribbean*. Santiago, Chile: United Nations, 2005.

Universities-National Bureau Committee for Economic Research, ed. *Business Concentration and Price Policy*. New Jersey: Princeton University Press, 1955.

Urquhart, Malcolm, and Kenneth Buckley. *Historical Statistics of Canada*. Toronto: Macmillan, 1965.

Valverde, Marianna. *The Age of Light, Soap and Water: Moral Reform in English Canada, 1885–1925*. Toronto: McClelland and Stewart, 1991.

Valverde, Marianna, and Pat O'Malley. "Pleasure, Freedom and Drugs: The Uses of 'Pleasure' in Liberal Governance of Drug and Alcohol Consumption." *Sociology* 38, no. 1. (2004): 25–42.

Van Den Eeckhout, Patricia Scholliers, and Peter Scholliers. "The Proliferation of Brands: The Case of Food in Belgium, 1890–1940." *Enterprise & Society* 13, no. 1 (2012): 53–84.

Van Der Hallen, Peter. "Concentration in the Belgium Brewing Industry and the Breakthrough of Lager in the Interwar Years." Discussion paper, Katholieke Universiteit Leuven, 2007.

Wagman, Ira. "Peace, Order, and Good Banking: Packaging History and Memory in Canadian Commercial Advertising." In *Settling and Unsettling Memories: Essays in Canadian Public History*, edited by Nicole Neatby, and Peter Hodgins, 538–68. Toronto: University of Toronto Press, 2012.

Waite, Peter. "The Political Ideas of John A. Macdonald." In *The Political Ideas of the Prime Ministers*, edited by Marcel Hamelin, 51–68. Ottawa: Editions de l'Université d'Ottawa, 1968.

Walden, Keith. *Becoming Modern in Toronto: The Industrial Exhibition and the Shaping of Late Victorian Culture*. Toronto: University of Toronto Press, 1997.

Wall, Shannon. *The Nurture of Nature: Childhood, Antimodernism, and Ontario Summer Camps, 1920–1955*. Vancouver: UBC Press, 2009.

Warlaumont, Hazel. *Advertising in the 60s: Turncoats, Traditionalists, and Waste Makers in America's Turbulent Decade*. Westport, CT: Praeger, 2001.

Warsh, Cheryl, and Greg Marquis. "Gender, Spirits, and Beer: Representing Female and Male Bodies in Canadian Alcohol Ads, 1930s–1970s." In *Contesting Bodies and Nation in Canadian History*, edited by Patrizia Gentile and Jane Nicholas, 203–25. Toronto: University of Toronto Press, 2013.

Waterhouse, Benjamin. *Lobbying America: The Politics of Business from Nixon to NAFTA*. Princeton, NJ: Princeton University Press, 2014.

Watson, James. *Golden Arches East: McDonald's in East Asia*. Stanford: Stanford University Press, 2006.

Weir, Ronald. "Managing Decline: Brands and Marketing in Two Mergers, 'The Big Amalgamation' 1925 and Guinness-DCL 1986." In *Adding Value: Brands and Marketing in Food and Drink*, edited by Geoffrey Jones and Nicholas Morgan, 139–62. London and New York: Routledge, 2015.

Weiss, Leonard. "Optimal Plant Size and the Extent of the Sub-optimal Capacity." In *Essays in Industrial Organization in Honor of Joe S. Bain*, edited by Robert T. Masson and P.D. Qualls, 126–34. Cambridge, MA: Ballinger Publishing Co., 1976.

Weldon, J.C. "Consolidations in Canadian Industry, 1900–1948." In *Restrictive Trade Practices in Canada: Selective Readings*, edited by Lawrence Skeoch, 228–79. Toronto: McClelland and Stewart, 1966.

Wilkins, Mira. "The Neglected Intangible Asset: The Influence of the Trademark on the Rise of the Modern Corporation." *Business History* 34, no. 1 (1992): 66–99.

Wilson, Bruce. "The Enterprises of Robert Hamilton: A Study of Wealth and Influence in Early Upper Canada: 1776–1812." PhD dissertation: University of Toronto, 1978.

Wilson, Richard. "The Changing Taste for Beer in Victorian Britain." In *The Dynamics of the International Brewing Industry since 1800*, edited Richard Wilson and Terence Gourvish, 93–104. London and New York: Routledge, 1998.

Wilson, Richard, and Terence Gourvish, eds. *The Dynamics of the International Brewing Industry since 1800*. London and New York: Routledge, 1998.

Winder, Gordon. "A Trans-national Machine on the World Stage: Representing McCormick's Reaper through World's Fairs, 1851–1902." *Journal of Historical Geography* 33, no. 2 (2007): 352–76.

Woods, Shirley. *The Molson Saga, 1763–1983*. Toronto: Doubleday Canada, 1983.

Workman, Andrew. "Manufacturing Power: The Organization Revival of the National Association of Manufacturers, 1941–1945." *Business History Review* 72 (Summer 1998): 279–317.

Yenne, Bill. *Guinness: The 250-Year Quest for the Perfect Pint*. Hoboken, NJ: John Wiley & Sons Inc., 2007.

Zangger, Andreas. "Chops and Trademarks: Asian Trading Ports and Textile Branding, 1840–1920." *Enterprise & Society* 15, no. 4 (2015): 759–90.

Index